D1565949

# The Final Solution and
# the German Foreign Office

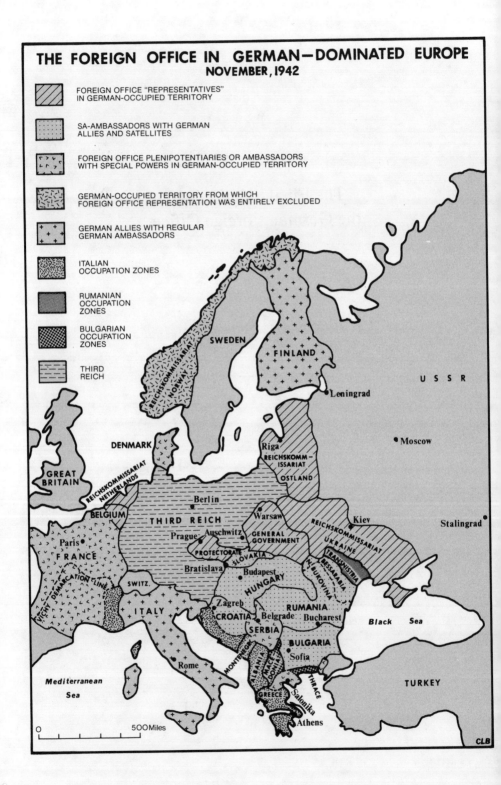

# THE FOREIGN OFFICE IN GERMAN—DOMINATED EUROPE
## NOVEMBER, 1942

FOREIGN OFFICE "REPRESENTATIVES" IN GERMAN-OCCUPIED TERRITORY

SA-AMBASSADORS WITH GERMAN ALLIES AND SATELLITES

FOREIGN OFFICE PLENIPOTENTIARIES OR AMBASSADORS WITH SPECIAL POWERS IN GERMAN-OCCUPIED TERRITORY

GERMAN-OCCUPIED TERRITORY FROM WHICH FOREIGN OFFICE REPRESENTATION WAS ENTIRELY EXCLUDED

GERMAN ALLIES WITH REGULAR GERMAN AMBASSADORS

ITALIAN OCCUPATION ZONES

RUMANIAN OCCUPATION ZONES

BULGARIAN OCCUPATION ZONES

THIRD REICH

USSR

SWEDEN

FINLAND

Leningrad

Moscow

DENMARK

Riga
REICHSKOMM-
ISSARIAT
OSTLAND

REICHSKOMMISSARIAT
NORWAY

GREAT BRITAIN

REICHSKOMMISSARIAT NETHERLANDS

BELGIUM

Berlin

THIRD REICH

Warsaw

GENERAL GOVERNMENT

Kiev

REICHSKOMMISSARIAT UKRAINE

Stalingrad

Paris
FRANCE

Prague
Auschwitz
PROTECTORATE
SLOVAKIA

Bratislava

Budapest

HUNGARY

TRANSNISTRIA
BESSARABIA
N.BUKOVINA

VICHY DEMARCATION LINE

SWITZ.

ITALY

Zagreb
CROATIA

Belgrade

Bucharest

RUMANIA

SERBIA

Black    Sea

MONTENEGRO

ALBANIA

MACEDONIA

BULGARIA

Sofia

Rome

THRACE

Salonika

GREECE

Athens

TURKEY

Mediterranean
Sea

0        500 Miles

CLB

# THE FINAL SOLUTION AND THE GERMAN FOREIGN OFFICE

A Study of Referat D III of
Abteilung Deutschland 1940-43

*by*

*Christopher R. Browning*

HOLMES & MEIER PUBLISHERS, INC.
New York                    London

First published in the United States of America 1978 by
Holmes & Meier Publishers, Inc.
30 Irving Place
New York, N.Y. 10003

Great Britain:
Holmes & Meier Publishers, Ltd.
Hillview House
1, Hallswelle Parade, Finchley Road
London NW11 ODL

**Library of Congress Cataloging in Publication Data**

Browning, Christopher R.
   The final solution and the German Foreign Office.

Bibliography: p.
   Includes index.
    1. Holocaust, Jewish (1940–1943)   2. Germany.
Auswärtiges Amt. I. Title.
D810.J4B77      940.53'15'03924     78-8996
ISBN 0-8419-0403-0

# Contents

# Acknowledgments

This book could not have been written without the help of many people. The staffs of the Berlin Document Center, the *Institut für Zeitgeschichte,* and the Nürnberg *Staatsarchiv* assisted my research at their respective institutions. Dr. Robert M. W. Kempner was kind enough to grant me a most helpful interview. *Erster Staatsanwalt* Richter of the *Landgericht* Frankfurt granted me permission to read the Hahn judgment. At the *Landgericht* Bamberg *Vorsitzender Richter* Dr. Maas provided me with my personal copy of the second Rademacher judgment and *Erster Staatsanwalt* Dr. Klarmann lent me copies of several other important judgments. Professor Karl Dietrich Bracher of the University of Bonn supported my efforts to gain access to the entire records of the Rademacher trials. *Erster Staatsanwalt* Horn of the *Landgericht* Nürnberg-Fürth not only granted me permission to study these records but provided me with a private office for the entire month that I worked there and, along with his colleagues, made my stay a most congenial one. The gracious hospitality of Anne and Michael Britt also greatly facilitated my study in Nürnberg.

The bulk of my research was carried out at the Political Archives of the German Foreign Office, where Dr. Weinandy and the entire staff were most helpful. Frau Eva Magka deserves special mention for her endless patience in assisting me through the mysteries of German handwriting. A generous grant from the *Deutscher Akademischer Austausch Dienst* made possible a year of study in the Federal Republic of Germany, and Franz Eschbach of the DAAD was especially helpful in securing for me a second grant to return to Germany for a month after I received permission to study the Rademacher court records.

Professors George Mosse and Theodore Hamerow of the University of Wisconsin, Yehuda Bauer of the Hebrew University of Jerusalem, and Raul Hilberg of the University of Vermont all read the manuscript at some stage of its development; it has been immeasurably improved by their suggestions and constructive criticism. For the errors that remain, I am solely responsible. I owe a special debt of gratitude to Professor Robert Koehl of the University of Wisconsin, my dissertation supervisor, who gave readily of his time and experience throughout my graduate studies, which culminated in the initial version of this book.

The editors of the *Journal of Contemporary History* and *Yad Vashem Studies* kindly granted permission to include portions of my articles which appeared in their journals.

Finally, I am especially grateful to my wife, Jennifer, who provided support in too many ways to enumerate.

Tacoma, Washington
February, 1978

*In memory of my father*
*Robert W. Browning*

# 1. The Evolution of the German Jewish Policy

German Jewish policy was not the result of a conspiratorial plot hatched in Hitler's mind following Germany's defeat in World War I and then carried out with single-minded purpose and patient cunning through the instrumentation of a monolithic dictatorship. It evolved from a conjuncture of several factors of which Hitler's anti-Semitism was only one. To deny the existence of a long-standing Hitlerian blueprint for the extermination of the Jews does not deny the centrality of anti-Semitism in Hitler's Social Darwinian ideology nor its importance for the evolution of German Jewish policy. The Jew as universal scapegoat provided consistency in Hitler's *Weltanschauung* by forming the connecting link between all that he opposed and attacked: the parasitic Jewish capitalists and department store owners and the communistic Jewish labor agitators; the Jewish-dominated plutocratic democracies of the West and Jewish-Bolshevik Russia. The monstrous irrationality at the center of his thought provided a superficial rationality to the diverse and contradictory allegations that he made. It lent plausibility to what otherwise would not have hung together.[1]

If anti-Semitism was the ideological keystone of Hitler's *Weltanschauung,* it also served an important function in holding his movement together. The economic and social grievances of the lower middle class and Party radicals, pandered to in Nazi propaganda before 1933 but ignored by Nazi policy thereafter, were deflected or channeled into anti-Semitism. Under Hitler the modernization of German society continued, for one does not rearm by restoring an economy of artisans, peasants, and shopkeepers. Those hostile to the modernization process, a major element of the Nazi constituency, were compensated in part with a verbal exaltation of racial superiority. As George Mosse has written: "The German revolution became the anti-Jewish revolution"—a safe revolution which did not threaten property or traditional class relationships.[2]

Thus anti-Semitism was not just one of Hitler's obsessions but a special one. It was impossible within the framework of the Nazi Party to deny or even to question the existence of a Jewish problem. No one could proclaim that "the Emperor wore no clothes," that the Jewish problem existed only as a figment of Hitler's imagination having no basis in reality. Anyone in a position of authority had to start from the premise that the Jewish problem existed as Hitler envisaged it. It was the explanation of all other problems and was thus the ultimate problem. Hitler's anti-Semitism created an ideological imperative; the ultimate problem required an escalating search for an ultimate or final solution.

What was the link between ideology and political action? What was the mechanism by which Jewish policy was formed? Nazi Germany was not a monolithic state in which everything was decided at the top and carried out through a chain of absolute obedience running downward to the lowest echelons. Rather, the Nazi system was composed of factions centered around the Nazi chieftains, who were in perpetual competition to outperform one another. Like a feudal monarch, Hitler stood above his squabbling vassals. He alloted "fiefs" to build up the domains of his competing vassals as they demonstrated their ability to accomplish the tasks most appreciated by the Führer.[3] The Third Reich was therefore in a state of permanent internal war.

Jewish policy did not stand above this perpetual power struggle. On the contrary, between 1933 and 1939 it was often at the center of it. Because Hitler was the supreme arbiter over his vassals, none of them could afford to ignore or challenge his personal obsessions. Hitler did not have to develop a blueprint or time schedule for solving the Jewish question and then demand absolute obedience from his reluctant subordinates in carrying it out. He merely had to proclaim the continuing existence of the Jewish problem to have his vassals vying with one another to help solve it. Given the dynamics of the Nazi political system, "final solutions" inevitably became the only ones worthy of submission to the Führer, and it was not surprising that the most final of all solutions, extermination, eventually prevailed.

This evolutionary process was not rapid, however, for the conjuncture of ideological and political factors did not insure a deliberate and systematic approach to Jewish policy. On the contrary, Nazi Jewish policy between 1933 and 1939 followed a "twisted road."[4] The existence of the Jewish problem could never be questioned or disavowed, but neither could the formulation of Jewish policy escape the political and economic realities of the time. In the early phase of the Nazi dictatorship, Hitler's wooing of his conservative allies, his cautious sensitivity to foreign opinion, and the charade of the "legal revolution" all conflicted with the frustrated ambitions and revolutionary energies of the SA and Party rank and file. The political necessity of lowering unemployment and the goal of economic recovery as a precondition for rearmament were incompatible with any frontal attack upon the alleged Jewish domination of the economy. Hitler as arbiter had to balance these conflicting pressures.

Throughout March 1933 there had been much pressure from the Party radicals to deal with the Jewish question, which culminated in the boycott of Jewish businesses in early April. The opposition of Hindenburg and the conservatives within Hitler's coalition, the fragile state of the German economy, fierce reaction abroad, and the indifference of large sections of the German populace all made the boycott less than a success.[5] It was hastily cancelled after one day. However, it did prepare the way for the relatively smooth acceptance of Jewish legislation restricting the participation of "non-Aryans" in the civil service, schools, and legal and medical professions, as the orderly and respectable way to deal with the Jewish question. As schemes to purge the civil service, end the naturalization of *Ostjuden,* and prohibit changing of names to disguise Jewish identity were already being devised during von Papen's regime before the Nazis came to power, the legislative approach struck a responsive chord among Hitler's conservative partners and in the German bureaucracy.[6]

In July 1933 Hitler announced the end of the National Revolution and sought to prevent unruly Party elements from disturbing German economic life.[7] Nevertheless, under the leadership of Ernst Röhm, the SA increased its pressure for a Second Revolution. While this pressure focused primarily upon the privileged position of Hitler's conservative allies in the military, bureaucracy, and economy, the Jews were not immune. When Hitler was prodded by Röhm's rivals to eliminate the SA leadership in the Blood Purge of June 1934, however, the effect upon surviving Party radicals was sufficiently intimidating to produce a relatively prolonged respite in Jewish affairs.

Party pressure for a more active anti-Jewish policy resumed in 1935, inspired in part by the notorious *Gauleiter* of Nürnberg, Julius Streicher. Hjalmar Schacht, the non-Nazi financial expert who was both minister of economics and president of the *Reichsbank,* successfully defended the immunity of the economic sphere against the intrusion of Party radicals by emphasizing the delicate state of the German economy and the overriding concern for rearmament. Hitler did not publicly side with Schacht and disavow Streicher but must have given his minister of economics the necessary support privately.[8] Once again, however, anti-Jewish legislation compensated the frustrated Party radicals. The Nürnberg Laws of September 1935, prohibiting marriage or extramarital relations between Jews and Aryans and the hiring of young German women as maids in Jewish households, seemed particularly designed to gratify the sexually obsessed anti-Semitism of the Streicher gang.

Just as the 1933 assault upon the Jews was followed by a lull in 1934, due to Hitler's problems with the Second Revolution, so the 1935 agitation and legislation were followed by a drop in activity the next year, this time owing to the 1936 Olympic Games held in Berlin. Clearly Hitler was capable of restraining his own anti-Semitism as well as that of his most rabid followers when it was politically expedient. Behind the scenes, however, the formation of Jewish policy was becoming increasingly complicated. Until 1936 a three-way struggle had taken place among Party radicals advocating the pogrom-approach, the bureaucrats of the Interior Ministry following the orderly path of discriminatory legislation, and Schacht's economic experts demanding at least temporary immunity for the economy from all Jewish measures. On rare occasions Hitler intervened, usually to restrain the radicals and sanction another legislative attack as compensation, but for the most part he offered little direct guidance.[9] In the years following the Nürnberg Laws, however, two new elements entered the competition over Jewish policy: Herman Göring's multifarious empire and Heinrich Himmler's SS.

In 1936 Hermann Göring was appointed head of the Four Year Plan, charged with preparing the economy for war. Schacht's persistent warnings about the dangerously rapid pace of German rearmament brought about his dismissal as economics minister in the fall of 1937. As Schacht's successor, Walter Funk, was subservient to Göring, control of the German economy was in new hands. Moreover, the economy was on much firmer ground now, and large businesses were anxious to expand for the first time since the depression, especially at the expense of their Jewish competition. The time was "ripe" for a major assault on the economic position of the Jews in Germany.[10] In April 1938, Göring decreed the registration of all Jewish property as the initial step in eliminating the Jews from the economic life of Germany.

The pace and procedure for this action were still matters of contention, however. Minister of the Interior Wilhelm Frick advocated compulsory aryanization with the transferred property going to Germany's middle class. This was a direct appeal to Party radicals, probably motivated by Frick's desire to recover ground lost to Göring and Funk. Schacht, still president of the *Reichsbank,* and Schwerin von Krosigk, the finance minister, advocated the continuation of voluntary aryanization.[11] The latter policy would have left out the capital-poor middle class and hardly suited the pace of aryanization desired by the radicals. Göring favored a middle course which speeded the pace of aryanization but benefitted the state, not the middle class, and which did not damage the German economy.[12]

In the SS the Jewish section within the Security Service (*Sicherheitsdienst* or SD) of Himmler's deputy, Reinhard Heydrich, opposed the "wild actions" of the Party radicals and advocated systematic and total emigration as the solution to the Jewish problem.[13] The SD Jewish experts were especially interested in emigration to Palestine, even though the Nazis feared that a drastic increase in the Jewish population enhanced the chances for the founding of an independent Jewish state there. These men called for "the centralization of the entire work on the Jewish question in the hands of the SD and Gestapo."[14]

In fact, the SD remained on the periphery of Jewish policy until 1938, while Jewish emigration struggled against seemingly insuperable obstacles. In the midst of the world depression, foreign countries were reluctant to accept unemployable immigrants who would become public charges. Nor were the German Jews the only ones competing to fill miniscule immigration quotas; a rising tide of anti-Semitism in much of eastern Europe meant that many other European Jews were putting intense pressure on the limited immigration opportunities. Within Germany the currency restrictions and "flight tax" prevented emigrants from taking more than a fraction of their property with them. Moreover, a deep attachment to what had been their country for many generations made it exceedingly difficult for all but the young and adventure-some to tear up their roots and accept the risks of starting a new life abroad.[15]

Following the *Anschluss* of March 1938 the SD expert on Zionism, Adolf Eichmann, was sent to Austria to organize Jewish emigration. He created an assembly-line technique to cut red-tape and utilized the property of wealthy Jews to subsidize the emigration of poor Jews. Moreover, the terror apparatus was freely used to prod the hesitant. In fact, Eichmann's methods could be more accurately characterized as expulsion than emigration, but he did establish a rate of departure far exceeding that which had prevailed in Germany between 1933 and 1937. Eichmann's personal triumph repre-sented a major breakthrough for the SS in shaping German Jewish policy.

By the summer of 1938 that policy was a mass of contradictions, as rival factions attempted to force through their own programs with no central coordination or direction. Göring and others were trying to eliminate the Jews from the economy, but could not agree how. The SS had accelerated emigration through Eichmann's expulsion measures in Austria, but the resulting flood of refugees only increased the reluctance of foreign countries to receive them. And the more thorough and systematic Göring's aryanization measures threatened to become, the greater would be the reluctance abroad to permit the immigration of the increasingly impoverished German Jews. Aryanization and emigration worked at cross-purposes. But this was not all. Alongside these attempts to solve the Jewish problem systematically was the growing unrest of the Party radicals, the Streicher gang, the SA, and Göring's and Himmler's major rival, Joseph Goebbels. They were all frustrated by the slow pace of legislative and bureaucratic persecution and fearful that they were being excluded from any voice in Jewish affairs.

The death of the German diplomat Ernst vom Rath at the hands of a Jewish assassin, Herschel Grynszpan, on November 9, 1938, offered Goebbels the chance to take "revolutionary" action against the Jews and to give the Party radicals their "day in the streets." With Hitler's approval he launched the *Kristallnacht* pogrom, in the course of which Jewish synagogues went up in flames and Jewish businesses were vandalized throughout Germany. Göring and Himmler, taken by surprise and resentful of Goebbels' initiative, seized upon the incredible publicity and property damage to attempt Goebbels' ouster.[16] Hitler did not abandon Goebbels, but he did finally centralize authority for Jewish affairs under Göring, as the latter emphatically an-nounced to an interministerial conference held November 12, 1938.

The Göring-Himmler-Heydrich alliance, which had destroyed Röhm and the SA leadership in 1934 and had ousted the two top army commanders in the spring of 1938, thus succeeded in finally eliminating the influence of Party radicals in Jewish affairs. The bureaucratic approach had triumphed over the pogrom. Not surprisingly, however, the new triumvirate of Jewish affairs made no attempt to decide between their conflicting policies of aryanization and emigration and instead proceeded to accelerate both.

This non-decision in fact meant the success of aryanization and the failure of emigration. Very quickly the German Jews were stripped of their remaining property. At the same time Göring authorized Schacht to negotiate with representatives of the Evian Conference, an international meeting assembled to resolve the Jewish refugee problem. In January 1939 the Germans finally agreed to permit the transfer abroad of a portion of Jewish property through the purchase of German exports, a method used since 1933 in cooperation with the Zionists to encourage emigration to Palestine. However, the executive committee of the Evian Conference could find neither areas of settlement for the Jewish emigrants nor financial sources outside of Germany to pay the immediate costs of resettlement. Thus the so-called Schacht-Rublee plan for the organized emigration of German Jews was never put into effect.[17] Göring therefore turned elsewhere.

At the post-*Kristallnacht* conference of November 12, 1938, Heydrich had boasted of the success of Eichmann's methods in Austria. In January 1939 Göring finally authorized Heydrich to create a Reich Central Office for Jewish Emigration in Germany, analogous to Eichmann's organization in Vienna, to prepare all measures for increased Jewish emigration.[18] However, even expulsion measures could not cope with the ever rising walls against Jewish immigration abroad. With aryanization complete, Göring had no further interest in the trapped and impoverished Jewish community. In July 1939 the Reich Union of Jews was established as the sole Jewish organization in Germany, subordinate to Heydrich. Now not only all matters pertaining to emigration but also total control of the German Jewish community had been delivered into the hands of the SS. It had failed to solve the Jewish problem but it had succeeded in ending the six-year competence struggle for the direction of Jewish policy.[19]

For six years the conjuncture of ideological and political factors had been operative without producing the fatal acceleration in Jewish policy toward systematic extermination which occurred after 1939. In that year the SS consolidated its supremacy over Jewish affairs and Germany went to war. It was the interaction of these two additional factors that had such a drastic effect. The war completely upset the SS policy of Jewish emigration pursued up to that time. First, the outbreak of hostilities closed down many frontiers, leaving open only the most tenuous of emigration routes. Every successive spread of hostilities aggravated the situation. Second, every military conquest increased the number of Jews under German domination. The military successes also led to a growing list of German allies, especially in southeast Europe, which had large Jewish populations. Europe had been turned into a German sphere of influence with millions of Jews trapped inside. The old solution of emigration collapsed and the problem mushroomed simultaneously. A new final solution had to be found, but this time the SS could react quickly and freely in Jewish affairs with little interference from others.

The outbreak of the war altered the situation in another way as well. All extraneous factors which had previously exerted a braking effect on Jewish policy were now irrelevant. Considerations of public opinion abroad, expediency in foreign policy, and economic calculations no longer weighed on the scales of decision-making. Moreover, unlike the churches, army, civil service, or industry, the Jews had no defenders among the conservative elements of German society which had become collaborators and allies of the Nazis. These conservative-nationalists could scarcely conceive of opposing government policies while their country was at war, even when these policies threatened what they cherished most. Even less, then, could they take a stand on the Jewish question. They had supported and defended anti-Jewish measures in the beginning. When the extremity of the anti-Jewish measures began to surpass that with which they felt comfortable, they were too compromised and morally crippled to offer effective opposition. It was difficult to defend their own vested interests; they were not about to take risks for the Jews, whom they themselves had done so much to harm already. Thus after the outbreak of the war there were no serious countervailing forces requiring compromise on the Jewish question. Jewish policy could therefore evolve rapidly and almost without friction to the extreme.

Under these circumstances the SS embraced in rapid succession two further versions of a final solution to the Jewish question—the Lublin Reservation and the Madagascar Plan.[20] The first surfaced in the fall of 1939, following the lightning conquest of Poland. A vicious circle had become apparent; the addition of the Jewish population of the newly incorporated territories (annexed from Poland) on top of those of Austria and the Bohemian Protectorate demonstrated that every step forward in military and foreign affairs constituted a step backwards in reaching the promised solution to the Jewish question—a *judenrein* Germany through emigration. The number of Jews on German territory was increasing, not diminishing. To break this vicious circle Heydrich announced on September 21, 1939, the Führer's decision to clear the newly incorporated territories of Jews as soon as possible. As a preliminary step to the "final goal" (*Endziel*), first the Jews of the incorporated territories and then those in western Poland were to be concentrated in cities along rail lines. The "final goal" at this time meant deporting Jews to a reservation in the area of Lublin, not extermination, for Heydrich explicitly exempted the eastern part of the General Government from the measures of concentration undertaken elsewhere.[21]

Following Heydrich's directive, many proposals were made and projects undertaken for deporting Jews and Poles from the incorporated territories and western Poland, as well as from the Protectorate and Austria. The first transports from the latter areas left for Eichmann's "retraining camp" at Nisko near Lublin in mid-October, and more massive transports from the former areas began in December, uprooting 200,000 people within two months.[22]

In February and March of 1940, the Jewish communities of Stettin and Schneidemühl were also deported, the first time Jews of German citizenship were included. This, however, was not the prelude to major deportations from old German territory but the last gasp of the reservation plan. Hans Frank of the General Government became fearful of the impact upon his unprepared bailiwick of this deluge of Jews. He enlisted the help of a sympathetic Göring who ordered the deportations stopped in late March 1940. This rare example of Göring's interference in SS handling of the Jewish question spelled the end of the reservation scheme.[23]

The conquest of Holland, Belgium, and France in May and June 1940 once again increased the number of Jews within the German sphere but offered the possibility of yet another solution—the annexation of the French colony of Madagascar to be used as an island super-ghetto for the Jews of Europe.[24] It proved even more ephemeral than the Lublin Reservation, for victory over Great Britain and consequent control of the seas was the obvious prerequisite for its realization. When Hitler decided in the fall of 1940 to attack Russia before defeating Great Britain, the Madagascar Plan had to be shelved.

The decision to attack Russia not only meant the indefinite postponement of the Madagascar Plan but also raised the old dilemma. The anticipated conquest of Russia would bring additional millions of Jews under German control. Sometime between the fall of 1940 and the spring of 1941, however, Hitler made the fatal decision that conquest of Russia would not further aggravate a final solution to the Jewish question. Instead the Russian Jews would be systematically exterminated as they fell into German hands. This decision was a quantum jump in German Jewish policy. The previous final solutions to the Jewish question all meant physical removal; henceforth the Final Solution meant physical destruction. Once begun the killing process could not be reversed, only extended.

As part of the preparations for the attack on Russia, Heydrich organized *Einsatzgruppen* (action squads) to carry out "special tasks" arising from the final confrontation between two opposing political systems. The extermination of Russian Jewry was one such task. Following the outbreak of hostilities and in close cooperation with the German army, the *Einsatzgruppen* carried out massacres by firing squad in the areas behind the fast-advancing German lines.[25]

The vicious circle was broken; more conquests no longer meant more Jews. But the existence of millions of Jews within German-dominated Europe was still a problem which the Nazis were committed to solve. The killing process begun in Russia now beckoned. By the summer of 1941 Hitler had decided to exterminate the European Jews as well. On July 31, 1941, Göring authorized Heydrich to prepare a "total solution" (*Gesamtlösung*) of the Jewish question in those territories of Europe under German influence and to coordinate the participation of those organizations whose competency was touched.[26]

However, the *Einsatzgruppen* method of extermination was proving scarcely adequate even to deal with the Russian Jews. The heavy psychological burden upon the killers, the impossibility of keeping the massacres secret, and above all the staggering number of victims to be dealt with rendered this method unsuitable for wider use, particularly in areas outside the war zone. Therefore the Nazis had to devise a new killing process. Three programs already in operation—the concentration camp system, the euthanasia program, and large-scale ventures in forced emigration and population resettlement—were merged together to solve this technical problem. The European Jews would be uprooted and deported to camps in eastern Germany and Poland which were specially equipped with the gassing facilities developed by the euthanasia experts over the previous two years.[27] In terms of productivity, secrecy, and psychological cost to the killers, the factories of death, processing their victims on an assembly-line basis, rendered the old *Einsatzgruppen* method as obsolete as a cottage industry.

The death factories, like any sophisticated institution of modern society, required an extensive support system to keep them operating. Above all the supply of raw materials, the endless flow of victims, had to be assured. The Jews of Germany and Poland were already at hand, awaiting transportation; the Jews of the rest of Europe had yet to be procured. It was in regard to these problems that Göring had enjoined Heydrich to coordinate the participation of the pertinent agencies of the German government whose help was needed. In mid-October the first deportation trains had left Germany, and in December the first massacres of German Jews had taken place in Riga and the first gassings had been carried out in the death camp at Chelmno. The necessary coordination could wait no longer.

On January 20, 1942, in a villa outside Berlin overlooking the Wannsee, the state secretaries of the German ministries and representatives from the civil administrations of the occupied territories of the east were assembled by Heydrich and informed in veiled but nonetheless unmistakeable language of the fate decreed by Hitler for the European Jews. Heydrich made it clear to the state secretaries that he expected their cooperation, and no one disappointed him. The ministries of the Third Reich, involved by varying degrees in Jewish policy until 1939 but then largely shunted aside by a jealous SS guarding its newly won prerogatives, became once again entangled. The SS bureaucrats could not do it alone, so the considerable energies of the ministerial bureaucracy were now harnessed to the Final Solution as well.

In addition to the ideological and political factors behind the evolution of German Jewish policy and the radicalizing and accelerating impact of the war, the bureaucratic element must also be taken into consideration. Since the appearance of Raul Hilberg's classic study, *The Destruction of the European Jews,* in 1961, the concept of the Final Solution as a bureaucratic and administrative process has not been seriously challenged. Nonetheless, like any important historical work, Hilberg's book raised new questions and stimulated further research. For example, while admitting that the German bureaucracy had "no master plan, no basic blueprint," Hilberg held that "the German administration knew what it was doing. . . . With uncanny pathfinding ability, the German bureaucracy found the shortest road to the final goal."[28] Recent studies show, however, that the German bureaucracy travelled a "twisted road to Auschwitz," not the shortest road.[29]

Other questions about the German bureaucracy also emerge. Speaking of the ministries, army, industry, and party, Hilberg states: "The cooperation of these hierarchies was, in fact, so complete that we may truly speak of their fushion into a machinery of destruction."[30] How, when, and to what degree did such a fusion take place? Though Hilberg often speaks as if the bureaucracy were a monolithic entity, he concedes that "upon close examination the machinery of destruction turns out to have been a loose organization of part-timers."[31] What sorts of people were these part-time Jewish experts? What motivated them?

Hilberg himself notes: "One of our difficult problems is to understand how the German bureaucracy started its work, how its very first moves were made." In that he assumes "that the administrative apparatus was ready to act, that it did not have to be told what to do," his answers are more poetic than historical. With conquered Europe at his feet, "the bureaucrat beckoned to his Faustian fate" and "had to attempt the ultimate." Or: "The German bureaucracy was so sensitive a mechanism that in the right climate it began to function almost by itself." Finally, the German bureaucracy was compared to a ball subject to inertia. "In 1933 the missing push was applied, and the ball started to roll."[32]

But if one can no longer speak of a linear progression from 1933 to 1942, can one speak of a single start? Did not very different factors determine the early participation of various elements of this "very decentralized apparatus" in the 1930s and the subsequent reinvolvement of some of them at the time of the Final Solution? What was the decision-making process which led organizations largely excluded from Jewish affairs since 1939 to become entangled in the killing process?

This case study of the Jewish experts and the Jewish policy of the German Foreign Office between 1940 and 1943 attempts to throw additional light upon the workings of the Final Solution by answering these questions for at least one cog in the machinery of destruction.

## 2. The Background: *Referat Deutschland,* Jewish Policy, and the German Foreign Office, 1933–40

The German Foreign Office played only a minor role in the formulation of Jewish policy before 1940. Jewish affairs were considered to be an internal matter, and the Foreign Office restricted itself to those facets of the Jewish question which touched upon foreign relations. Moreover, in a competition dominated by Göring, the SS, the Interior Ministry, the Economics Ministry, and the Party radicals allied with Goebbels, the inept leadership of Foreign Ministers Konstantin von Neurath before 1938 and Joachim von Ribbentrop thereafter often limited the effectiveness of the Foreign Office even when Jewish policy and foreign policy were intertwined. Nonetheless, the attitude displayed by its officials towards the Jewish question in this period is significant for understanding its role later.

Like their colleagues throughout the German bureaucracy, the conservative-nationalist officials of the Foreign Office did not look favorably upon the anti-Semitic "excesses" of the Party radicals. They feared that the Jewish question would be exploited by others to isolate Germany and damage its international position, and Neurath supported Hindenburg in urging the cancellation of the boycott of Jewish businesses in early April 1933.[1] On the other hand, they found the legislative approach to the Jewish question more congenial. Anxious to restore the situation of 1918, they had little sympathy for the Jews that were the victims of this "restoration." Neurath, State Secretary Bernhard von Bülow, and the divisional heads of the Foreign Office were determined to defend Germany's reputation and honor against unjustified attacks from abroad and unwarranted intervention in internal affairs caused by the new government's "legitimate" legal restrictions on the role of Jews in the life of Germany.

One major instrument to achieve this goal was *Referat Deutschland,* established on March 20, 1933, under State Secretary Bülow's cousin, Vicco von Bülow-Schwante, as the liaison office between the Wilhelmstrasse and the Party.[2] As Jewish affairs were among the most important Nazi activities affecting Germany's foreign relations, it was not unnatural that from the very beginning they were a major concern of the new *Referat.* On March 23, even before the boycott and first racial legislation, Bernhard von Bülow sent cousin Vicco a "confidential" handwritten letter which revealed his own unsympathetic view toward the Jews and his desire to defend the regime's measures against them.

> For the directors and myself, eventually also for the missions [abroad], it would be good as support for conversations with diplomats and foreigners to assemble some material that elucidates the causes of the anti-Semitic movement in Germany. Perhaps the Nazis, otherwise the internal authorities, can deliver *sub rosa* numbers and dates.
>
> I have always pointed out to diplomats the strong influx of eastern Jews, as well as their naturalization in mass by the socialist Prussian government. Numbers pertaining to it must be available. Furthermore I have stated, that for example the entire city administration and city hospital [staffs] were swamped with Jews. I believe that that is correct and can also be proven. Furthermore perhaps a strong percentage of Jews in the Communist caucus of the last Reichstag can be discovered. Certainly there are also blatant examples for the advance of Jews in law, universities, schools, etc., since 1918.[3]

Clearly, whatever Bülow's reservations about the danger of Hitler's foreign policy, he was even less disturbed by the rise of anti-Semitism in Germany than he was by the demise of Weimar democracy.[4]

On the basis of the state secretary's handwritten instructions, *Referat Deutschland* began its activities in Jewish affairs as the Foreign Office apologist and propagandist for the "anti-Semitic movement in Germany." Bülow-Schwante saw Goebbels personally to procure material on the Jewish question which he submitted with a covering memorandum on April 19, 1933. Bülow-Schwante argued that the present situation in Germany was primarily a reaction against developments which had taken place since 1918, during which time the Social Democrats had abetted massive immigration of eastern Jews and conceded to Jews an influence on public life out of all proportion to their percentage of the population. Having stated a thesis agreeable to most conservative Germans, he then moved on to endorse, in the crudest terms, the Nazi theory of the Communist-Jewish world conspiracy. He wrote that the Jewish quarters of the major cities served as the "opulent breeding pens" (*üppigsten Brutstätten*) of communists who worked together with the rich Jews of the Kurfürstendamm, the so-called "refined communists or salon Bolsheviks" (*Edelkommunisten oder Salon-Bolschewisten*). Thus the battle against Jewish advances in German life was merely the logical consequence of the struggle against Marxism and Communism.[5]

Bülow felt that the quality of the material provided by Goebbels was "quite poor" (*recht dürftig*). He made many corrections in cousing Vicco's draft and added some statistics, alleging that over half the lawyers in Berlin were Jews as were over half the doctors in the Berlin hospitals. Despite Bülow's revisions, however, the crassest parts were left intact. Both Bülow and Neurath then approved the memorandum for distribution to all Foreign Office missions abroad to be used to increase understanding of German Jewish policy.[6] Thus within three months of the *Machtergreifung* and on their own initiative, the highest echelons of the Foreign Office approved the official dissemination throughout the world of the crudest kind of anti-Semitic propaganda in order to preserve Germany's honor and reputation.

Bülow-Schwante, an ex-calvary captain, owed his position in the Foreign Office to family connections and had never passed the required exams. In May 1933 he was joined by an assistant, Legation Secretary Dr. Emil Schumburg, a career official since 1926, who henceforth specialized in Jewish and police matters.[7] The work of the university trained Schumburg was more sophisticated and attuned to use by Germany's diplomats abroad. The future Foreign Office circulars on the Jewish question emphasized the discipline of the "German Revolution." Measures against the Jews had been kept within legal boundaries; the Jews had not been delivered to their ruin but permitted complete freedom of economic activity. However, the final position of the Jews in Germany could not be determined as long as the campaign of lies and boycott of German goods continued.[8]

Given the initial anti-Semitism of the old guard of the Foreign Office, as manifested by Bülow, it is not surprising that under the impact of the boycott of German exports and the barrage of foreign criticism which Nazi treatment of the Jews had provoked, the Wilhelmstrasse became habituated to the Nazi premise that the Jews of the world were Germany's enemies.[9] It was not just *Referat Deutschland* but the entire Foreign Office that defended and justified German Jewish policy. No retreat could be envisaged in response to these Jewish protests against Germany, for this the Wilhelmstrasse officials felt would be an abject surrender to Germany's enemies. The Nazis could be assured of Foreign Office defense of its Jewish policy merely by draping it with the flag of patriotism.

The officials of *Referat Deutschland* articulated this hardening attitude. In September 1934 the German embassy in London received word that the leaders of the boycott movement in Great Britain were willing to come to Berlin to negotiate an agreement on the basis of lifting the boycott in return for the assurance that, aside from existing legislation, German Jews would be left undisturbed. Bülow-Schwante wrote to Bülow that in the opinion of *Referat Deutschland* any negotiations or agreements with any Jewish organizations or representatives were excluded for all time. Germany must always act from strength, not weakness, and any concessions in the Jewish question under economic or political pressure would not pacify the Jews but merely undermine Germany's ideological position. "The worse the economic situation is, therefore, the less shall a compromise be thought of in the Jewish question." This advice so perfectly fit the mood of the Wilhelmstrasse that Neurath sent out Bülow-Schwante's memorandum *verbatim* to all missions abroad.[10]

The Foreign Office knew what it was against in Jewish affairs—unruly excesses providing material for anti-German propaganda on the one hand and any retreat in the face of foreign protest on the other. But it did not know what it was for. There was no positive Jewish policy with a clearly articulated goal, only negative obstructionism. As a result the various bureaus within the Foreign Office often engaged in the same type of tug-of-war over Jewish policy as was taking place on a wider scale throughout the Nazi regime. Neither Neurath nor his successor Ribbentrop imposed clear-cut priorities on the Foreign Office any more than Hitler did upon the government and Party. Thus even with facets of the Jewish question inseparable from considerations of foreign policy, such as emigration and the treatment of Jewish property, the German Foreign Office had relatively little effect upon policy making.

Since 1933 the Nazi regime had facilitated the emigration of German Jews to Palestine by permitting these emigrants, through the Haavara Agreement with Zionists in Palestine, to recover some of their money blocked in Germany through the resale of German exports to that country.[11] Initially *Referat Deutschland* supported the Haavara Agreement and cooperation with Zionists on Jewish emigration to Palestine as entirely compatible with the goal of eliminating Jewry from Germany.[12] However, growing Jewish-Arab tensions in Palestine caused Britain to study the whole question of her Palestine mandate. The advent of the Peel Commission in 1936 and the possibility of a partition of Palestine between Arabs and Jews, leading to the creation of an independent Jewish state, led to a reversal of opinion within *Referat Deutschland.* Schumburg and Bülow-Schwante argued that the Haavara Agreement should be discontinued. Increased Jewish emigration from Germany must not be achieved through administrative measures involving a sacrifice of foreign exchange, but through increasing "emigration pressure" (*Auswanderungsdrang*) by means of internal measures, such as special taxes on the Jews, which "would automatically result in the departure of the Jews on their own initiative." Furthermore, Jewish emigration should be "fragmented," not concentrated in Palestine where it enhanced the possibility of an independent Jewish state.[13]

The Economic Division of the Foreign Office opposed *Referat Deutschland,* arguing that from the economic point of view Jewish emigration to Palestine was preferable to a fragmentation among many countries, where the emigrants would reinforce the boycott of German exports.[14] This split within the Foreign Office over the primacy of political or economic considerations in evaluating the Haavara Agreement paralleled a wider split in the German government, where the Ministry of Economics staunchly defended its continuation against a host of critics. Hitler delayed making a decision until Great Britain postponed indefinitely any plan for the partition of Palestine in January, 1938. With the danger of an independent Jewish state no longer imminent, Hitler finally ordered that Jewish emigration would continue to be stimulated by every possible means.[15]

Though the Foreign Office boasted abroad about the relatively unrestricted economic activities of the Jews in Germany, it contributed little to the continuation of this policy at home. In 1935 Hjalmar Schacht, minister of economics and director of the *Reichsbank,* fought off the renewed attacks of Julius Streicher and the Party radicals upon Jewish economic activities, winning Hitler's support at least temporarily through arguments that the fragile state of the German economy and the overriding need for rearmament did not permit the intrusion of the anti-Jewish campaign into his jurisdiction at that time.[16]

Schacht's success owed nothing to Foreign Office support. Its position at the interministerial conference of August 20, 1935, summoned by Schacht to discuss the problem was extremely equivocal. Schumburg's preparatory memorandum for Bülow emphasized that internal measures against the Jews could not be postponed or weakened under foreign pressure. From a strictly politial—not economic—viewpoint, *Referat Deutschland* did not think it desirable to moderate German Jewish policy. However, in maintaining fully the Jewish policies of the NSDAP, the most inconspicuous methods ought to be chosen, so as not to deliver material into the hands of the anti-German agitation abroad.[17] Bülow's contribution to the conference reflected this general confusion. On the one hand, he stated that excesses against the Jews were a burden for German foreign policy. In view of the coming Olympics and the expected influx of foreigners, incidents like the Kurfürstendamm riots were simply intolerable. On the other hand, Bülow opposed the publication of Minister of the Interior Frick's order aimed at ending such excesses, because it would be interpreted by world Jewry as a victory for the boycott movement.[18]

In February 1938 Joachim von Ribbentrop replaced Neurath as Foreign Minister, and Vicco von Bülow-Schwante was named ambassador to Belgium. Dr. Walter Hinrichs, a rather elderly career official, became the new head of *Referat Deutschland* until September 1939. At that point, Dr. Emil Schumburg finally assumed official leadership, though he had been the driving spirit behind much of the activity of *Referat Deutschland* long before.[19] *Referat Deutschland* not only underwent a change of leadership, but also lost part of its functions. At the end of 1938, its role as liaison to the NSDAP was given to the newly created *Referat Partei* under a protégé of Ribbentrop named Martin Luther. The truncated *Referat Deutschland* was left jurisdiction over Jewish affairs and liaison to the SS and police.[20]

The year 1938 witnessed rapid and dramatic change in Jewish policy, culminating in the triumph of Göring and Himmler over their rivals, the elimination of Jews from the economic life of Germany, and the attempt to accelerate Jewish emigration. Göring opened the offensive against Jewish economic activity with the April decree that every Jew with property in Germany had to register his property (both in Germany and abroad) and that this property could be used in accordance with the interests of the German economy.[21] As no exception was made in the proposed law for Jews of foreign citizenship, the Foreign Office was asked for its position.

Hitherto the Foreign Office had insisted that all foreign Jews residing in Germany were subject to German Jewish legislation. Foreign protests were answered that no violation of treaty rights existed, for the foreign Jews were accorded the same rights as German Jews. However, this applied only to questions of civil rights. As late as 1937 the Foreign Office had requested that the property of foreign Jews be exempted from discriminatory treatment.[22]

Initially *Referat Deutschland* now took the viewpoint that even in property matters foreign Jews should be fully subjected to Göring's new legislation. The volume of foreign protest, however, caused Schumburg to have second thoughts, and he advised Bülow's successor, State Secretary Ernst von Weizsäcker, that the internal results of the present policy would stand in no proper relation to the foreign political disadvantages.[23] Weizsäcker approached the Economics Ministry with Foreign Office reservations, and Göring did grant two modifications. Only foreign Jews residing in Germany, but not those residing abroad, would have to register their German property; concerning the use of this property, the treaty rights of foreigners would be taken into consideration.[24] Thus in the face of the first major attack on Jewish property, the Wilhelmstrasse did not attempt to preserve a blanket exemption for foreign Jewish property in Germany. The application of all future laws affecting Jewish property would now be subject to individual examination in the light of treaty rights and political expediency. The Foreign Office found this complicated procedure preferable to any general exemption of foreign Jews, which would lead to the false conclusion abroad that Germany gave into foreign pressure.[25]

In early October 1938 the Polish government, which had already passed a law providing for the possibility of deprivation of citizenship of Poles who had been out of the country for five years, ordered that as of October 30, only passports stamped by a consul were valid for reentry into Poland. Fearful that large numbers of Polish Jews would be trapped in Germany after the October 30th deadline, and unable to extract any assurances from Poland that this fear was not fully justified, Ribbentrop requested Heydrich and the Gestapo to begin expelling the Polish Jews on October 28. Poland closed its borders and threatened in turn to expel German citizens from Poland. A "cease-fire" was agreed upon, and the fate of the deported Jews formed the subject of lengthy negoiations between the Foreign Office and Poland, eventually leading to a compromise settlement.[26] The lower echelon work in these negotiations was done by the Legal Division, which had jurisdiction over questions of foreign residents, passports, and expulsions, not *Referat Deutschland.*

An offshoot of the affair was the murder of the German diplomat Ernst vom Rath in Paris by Herschel Grynszpan, whose family was among the deported Polish Jews. Thereupon Goebbels triggered the *Kristallnacht* riots. In the aftermath Hitler finally centralized Jewish affairs under Göring, who ordered the acceleration of both aryanization and emigration. As cases involving the property of foreign Jews had to be examined individually, the speed-up in aryanization required considerable paperwork in the Foreign Office but no new policy decision. However, Göring's desire to intensify Jewish emigration "by every means" forced the Foreign Office to reconsider its previous position. Emigration measures could not be divorced from foreign policy considerations, and the Foreign Office had the opportunity to play a role. This opportunity was lost, however, by the ineptitude and stubborness of the Foreign Office leadership.

In the summer of 1938, Ribbentrop had rejected any cooperation with the international conference meeting in Evian, France, to discuss the problem of Jewish refugees, a problem made critical by Eichmann's systematic program of forced emigration of Austrian Jews following the *Anschluss.* Without German assurance that Jewish emigration would be pursued in an orderly fashion and that emigrants would be permitted to take out sufficient property to make a new start abroad, no agreement could be reached by the participating countries on their willingness to accept Jewish refugees. The conference adjourned after setting up an executive committee under the American lawyer, George Rublee, with the double task of persuading the Germans to adopt agreeable procedures of emigration and other countries to accept the refugees.[27]

In the fall of 1938, Great Britain, France, and the United States made repeated requests to the Foreign Office that a representative of the executive committee be permitted to come to Berlin to discuss the question of Jewish emigration, but Ribbentrop instructed that such a visit was out of the question and such requests should not be answered.[28] He was strongly supported by State Secretary Weizsäcker, who claimed that since the Evian Conference had not found any other countries willing to accept Jewish refugees, they now wanted to come to Germany and, with the discovery that it could grant Jewish emigrants no foreign exchange, shift the blame for failure to that country.[29] The old guard at the Foreign Office still viewed foreign interest in the Jewish question as outside interference in Germany's internal affairs and an attempt to besmirch Germany's prestige.

Only Schumburg appeared to realize the inadequacy of Foreign Office policy on Jewish emigration. In late October, shortly before *Kristallnacht,* he wrote that the increasing elimination of Jews from the German economy meant that Jewish immigration constituted an increasingly heavy burden on the receiving countries and had led to countermeasures to prevent it. In turn German authorities had increasingly resorted to illegal deportations over unguarded borders—the "green frontier." But it was clear that the emigration of Jews from Germany would soon be stuck and "thus required a timely, boldly prepared, and definitive solution." If the foreign minister's policy of non-cooperation with the Evian Conference continued, a basic decision was required over the form that Jewish emigration should take.[30]

Despite Schumburg's urging, the Foreign Office by itself proved incapable of moving beyond a policy of simple obstruction on the question of Jewish emigration. In the wake of *Kristallnacht* and the decision to accelerate Jewish emigration, the initiative to negotiate with Rublee came from elsewhere. When one of Göring's men, Hans Fischböck, suggested tieing Jewish emigration with German exports, analogous to the Haavara Agreement, Ribbentrop agreed only to informal, nonbiding contacts outside of Germany and planned an elaborate cloak and dagger rendezvous in a Brussels hotel between Fischböck and Rublee's deputy, Robert Pell. Meanwhile, Hjalmar Schacht won Hitler's permission for his own trip to London to discuss the financing of Jewish emigration. The Brussels rendezvous was cancelled, leaving Ribbentrop totally out of the picture.[31]

Schacht not only held discussions in London with Rublee and others, but upon his return to Berlin planted a news article on December 19, 1938, which foresaw further meetings between the executive committee and competent German authorities.[32] Ribbentrop was furious and had Weizsäcker telephone Schacht to "take him to task" (zur Rede stellen) concerning the article (which disavowed the foreign minister's policy) and the discussions in London (which impinged upon foreign affairs). Since negotiations with the Evian Conference had been rejected by the Foreign Office for the past six months, Weizsäcker demanded to know if Schacht had an order to carry out such discussions. Schacht replied that he had explicit authorization from both Göring and Hitler; that he had first to report back to Hitler before he could discuss the matter with Ribbentrop; and that he had not had time to inform Ribbentrop of his trip to London before his departure even if he had considered it within the competency of the Foreign Office. On January 4, 1939, Schacht informed Weizsäcker that two days earlier he had met with Hitler, who had authorized him to continue his discussions and even to invite Rublee to Berlin.[33]

As long as Schacht had the backing of both Hitler and Göring, Ribbentrop and Weizsäcker realized the futility of further outright obstruction. They attempted instead to cripple Schacht's negotiations from within. Ribbentrop therefore declared his agreement to the continuation of these negotiations and even assigned a liaison man, Ernst Eisenlohr, to follow their course. But Ribbentrop instructed Eisenlohr that the signing of any agreement with Rublee was not to be considered, and that any promise to Rublee over the treatment of Jews within Germany, a major concern to the executive committee, could not take place.[34]

The Schacht-Rublee negotiations continued until Schacht was suddenly relieved as head of the Reichsbank on January 20, 1939. This was unrelated to the Rublee negotiations, for Göring immediately appointed his own deputy for the Four Year Plan, Helmuth Wohlthat, to continue them.[35] Wohlthat quickly confirmed the Schacht-Rublee plan. It provided for the emigration of 150,000 Jewish wage earners between the ages of 15 and 45 over a three-year period and in accordance with the laws of the receiving countries. After they were established, they would be followed by their 250,000 dependents. Some 200,000 Jews who were too old and infirm to emigrate would be permitted to live in peace in Germany. The emigrating Jews would be permitted to take their personal effects and professional tools with them. Of the rest of their property, 25 percent would be put into a trust fund transferable by the Haavara method of purchasing German exports with it. The other 75 percent of Jewish property would support the Jews waiting to emigrate as well as those unfit for emigration who would remain in Germany.[36] Having reached agreement with Germany, the executive committee of the Evian Conference still had to locate areas of settlement for the Jewish emigrants and financial sources outside of Germany to pay the immediate costs of resettlement.[37] It could find neither and the Schacht-Rublee plan for the organized emigration of German Jews was never put into effect.

When Göring ordered the furthering of Jewish emigration by every means, he not unnaturally pursued possibilities other than the Schacht-Rublee talks. On January 24, 1939, he authorized Reinhard Heydrich to create a Reich Central Office for Jewish Emigration in Germany, an enlarged version of Eichmann's organization in Vienna. As part of the Reich Central Office, Heydrich established a committee made up of representatives of the various ministries involved in Jewish affairs, and Hinrichs pleaded with Ribbentrop to name a member of *Referat Deutschland* to represent the Foreign Office. To strengthen his case he forwarded to Ribbentrop the latest circular from *Referat Deutschland*, "The Jewish Question as a factor in German foreign policy in the year 1938," written by Schumburg on January 25, 1939.[38]

In this circular Schumburg stated that the final goal of German Jewish policy was the emigration of all Jews from the Reich. The Jewish desire to emigrate could best be furthered by measures preventing them from earning a living in Germany. The Evian Conference could answer neither the question of how organized emigration could be financed nor where the emigrants were to go. Other countries, like Poland, were anxious only to get rid of their own Jews. Thus Germany by herself had to find the ways, means, and destination of Jewish emigration. Palestine could not absorb a massive influx of German Jews, nor was the formation of a Jewish state in Palestine in Germany's interest. Germany was interested instead in a dispersal of Jewry, which would evoke a wave of anti-Semitism throughout the world and form the best propaganda for German Jewish policy. Hinrich's plea and Schumburg's circular were sufficiently persuasive, and Ribbentrop agreed to a member of *Referat Deutschland* as permanent Foreign Office representative on Heydrich's committee. Hinrichs then nominated Schumburg.[39]

This victory of *Referat Deutschland* within the Foreign Office was in fact a hollow one. Heydrich had accomplished a rapid ascendency in Jewish affairs, soon to culminate in control over not only emigration but also the Jewish community in Germany. He was not about to share out his newly won powers with the interministerial committee of the Reich Central Office for Jewish Emigration. Emigration matters were in fact handled within Heydrich's Gestapo, and despite his position on the interministerial commitee Schumburg was without influence. When shiploads of Jews from Germany, without entry visas of any sort, sailed from port to port trying to unload their unwelcome cargoes, the volume of foreign protest forced *Referat Deutschland* to ask the Gestapo to stop such "wild transports."[40] This request had no perceptible effect.

After the war broke out Schumburg and the Foreign Office were progressively excluded even from information on SS Jewish policy, especially the design for a Jewish reservation near Lublin as an alternative to faltering emigration. When the first transports of Jews left from Austria and the Protectorate in mid-October, rumors of the reservation spread rapidly. Following inquiries from the Rumanian embassy, Schumburg first consulted Göring's man, Wohlthat, who knew nothing, and then the Gestapo, which admitted only that territory in Poland east of Cracow had been inspected in order to concentrate 1.5 million Polish Jews but denied that any deportation of Jews from the Old Reich was being considered. On the contrary, Jewish emigration, mostly via Italy, was still being pursued.[41] Shortly thereafter, a German News Bureau report stated that 2,000 Jews from Vienna were on their way to a "resettlement area" (*Siedlungsraum*) near Lublin. When Schumburg inquired again, the Gestapo confirmed the truth of the report but refused to give any details over the construction of the Jewish reservation.[42] *Referat Deutschland* also received reports that the Rome press treated the Lublin reservation as fact and that the London *Daily Herald* told of the deportation of Polish Jews from Germany.[43] Thus while the Gestapo would share only minimal information with Schumburg, he and the Foreign Office were well aware that the creation of a Jewish reservation near Lublin was underway.

As Jews (and Poles) were being deported from the incorporated territories to the General Government, the SS also had plans for bringing back to the Reich ethnic Germans settled in eastern Europe. On January 30, 1940, Heydrich announced that the apartments of 1,000 Jews living in Stettin were needed for this program, and these Jews would thus be deported to the General Government.[44] This deportation, involving Jews of German citizenship for the first time, caused a sensation. Foreign radio and press reports gave graphic descriptions of the cruelty and hardships of the deportation, and one Swiss correspondent claimed that preparations were being carried out for similar deportations throughout northern Germany. An anonymous letter to the Foreign Office, the first of a series over the next year and one-half devoted to the Jewish question, also protested the deportation.[45]

Weizsäcker asked *Referat Deutschland* to inquire whether the Stettin deportation was in fact the beginning of general measures of this sort throughout the Reich. Both Walter Schellenberg and Heinrich Müller in the Reich Security Main Office (*Reichssicherheitshauptamt* or RSHA, Heydrich's new conglomeration of police and intelligence agencies) claimed that the Stettin affair was an individual action to make room for returning Baltic Germans, not a prelude to wider measures of the same sort. Schumburg requested that deportation measures be carried out "in a noiseless and cautious way" in order not to excite attention abroad.[46]

Despite the assurances of the RSHA, however, the Foreign Office received reports in mid-March of the deportation to Lublin of 160 German Jews from Schneidemühl. Like the Stettin Jews before them, of which 250 of 1200 had already died, the Jews of Schneidemühl were thrown off the train near Lublin and forced to make a fourteen hour march in bitter cold weather to villages which had no lodging or food for them. When Schumburg again inquired of the RSHA, Eichmann (recently promoted to head the Gestapo section on Evacuations and Jews within the RSHA) told him that the Schneidemühl Jews had already been brought back from Poland but not to Schneidemühl itself, where their apartments were needed by others.[47]

Disturbed by the continuing rumors about impending large-scale deportations from Germany, Schumburg and Wohlthat prepared a plan whereby the Foreign Office would request Himmler to refrain "if possible" from Jewish evacuations and in turn would pass on to foreign diplomats the recent RSHA assurance that the Stettin and Schneidemühl actions were emergency measures, not a prelude to a general deportation of German Jewry.[48] Before this was done, however, they learned that due to complaints of Hans Frank, the head of the General Government, that no reception possibilities existed at the moment, Göring had forbade further deportations there.[49] Göring's prohibition ended not only the sporadic deportations from the Old Reich but also much larger deportations from the incorporated territories, Austria, and the Protectorate. Plans for the Lublin reservation were gradually abandoned. Both the rise and fall of the reservation scheme were entirely outside the pale of Foreign Office influence.

The end of the Lublin reservation plan preceded the demise of *Referat Deutschland* by only one month. On May 7, 1940, Ribbentrop created a new division in the Foreign Office, *Abteilung Deutschland* (Division Germany), under his protégé Martin Luther, which absorbed the jurisdiction of *Referat Deutschland* over Jewish affairs and liaison to the SS and police. Schumburg was reassigned, and a new generation of Foreign Office Jewish experts in the new Jewish desk, *Referat D III*, took his place.

*Referat Deutschland's* involvement in Jewish affairs had spanned seven years but had never been of great importance. In the first place the Foreign Office itself did not play a major role in shaping Jewish policy. It was primarily an internal matter, and even when foreign policy was involved, the indolent Neurath and incompetent Ribbentrop could not hold their own in a competition ultimately won by Göring, Himmler, and Heydrich. Secondly, within the Foreign Office the supremacy of *Referat Deutschland* was by no means an accomplished fact. When Jewish affairs involved economics, as in the Haavara Agreement, the Economic Division effectively maintained its position against the opposition of *Referat Deutschland.* When Jewish affairs involved legal technicalities, as was the case during the expulsion of the Polish Jews, they were handled by the Legal Division. Thus *Referat Deutschland* was only one among many bureaus which shaped Foreign Office *Judenpolitik,* and the Foreign Office in turn played only a minimal role in shaping German *Judenpolitik.*

*Referat Deutschland* was important not so much for what it did as for what it revealed about the attitude toward the Jewish question within the Foreign Office. In the beginning, the old guard at the Wilhelmstrasse showed little concern for the fate of German Jews and considerable sympathy for legal, orderly anti-Jewish measures. In this they were not distinguished from the bulk of the conservative German bureaucracy. Foreign criticism of German Jewish policy and the boycott of German goods organized by Jews abroad soon made defense of this policy not only a matter of sympathy but an act of patriotism. Thus any retreat or amelioration in Jewish policy, or for that matter even any negotiation on the subject, was out of the question. It would indicate a weakness in German will and vulnerability to foreign pressure, diminishing German prestige. Created by the old guard as an instrument to defend German Jewish policy, *Referat Deutschland* was symbolic of this early complicity of the Foreign Office.

The attitude of the Foreign Office in 1940 in fact mattered little. The SS had successfully excluded it, along with many other institutions in Germany, from any effective role in Jewish affairs. This situation did not last, however. When Ribbentrop's tough political infighter, Martin Luther, took Foreign Office Jewish policy under his wing, he accomplished a decisive reversal. The Foreign Office not only regained its lost position in Jewish affairs but greatly enhanced its influence in this regard, making a signficant contribution to the last phase of German Jewish policy—the Final Solution. The old guard, already compromised by their eager defense of Jewish policy in the thirties, were in no position to resist or hinder this development. Clinging to their posts, allegedly "to prevent worse," they would passively acquiesce to Foreign Office participation in the mass murder of the Jews.

# 3. The Personnel

After the dissolution of *Referat Deutschland* in May 1940, *Referat* D III of *Abteilung Deutschland* handled Jewish affairs within the German Foreign Office. The work of the new Foreign Office Jewish desk, or *Judenreferat,* was intimately connected to the institutional power of *Abteilung Deutschland* and the ambition and energy of its creator, *Unterstaatssekretär* Martin Luther. The attitudes and calculations of this man, Ribbentrop's Grey Eminence, determined the political environment within which the Jewish experts of D III operated.

## Martin Luther and *Abteilung Deutschland*

Martin Franz Julius Luther was born December 16, 1895, in Berlin.[1] Abandoning his unfinished *Gymnasium* studies to join the German army in August 1914, he served in railway units throughout the war. He then went into business, engaging in such various activities as exporting, hauling, and furniture removal and supply. Despite bankruptcy in his initial venture, he was a propertied man by the 1930s.[2]

Luther joined the NSDAP and SA on March 1, 1932, and became active in local government and party affairs in the Berlin district of Dahlem. While collecting contributions for the Nazi relief organization, he made the acquaintance of the Ribbentrops and was commissioned to redecorate their Dahlem villa. When Ribbentrop went to London as ambassador in the fall of 1936, Luther accompanied him, allegedly at the suggestion of Frau Ribbentrop, to supervise the remodeling of the interior of the German embassy. Throughout his career Luther was to utilize the tactic of ingratiating himself with the Ribbentrops by satisfying Frau Ribbentrop's appetite for luxury.

Luther's ties to the Ribbentrops soon extended beyond that of interior decorator. In August 1936, three months before Ribbentrop's departure for London, Luther entered Bureau Ribbentrop, a Nazi Party agency for advising

Hitler on foreign policy. In November he was commissioned to create a new Party Liaison Office (*Parteiverbindungsstelle*) within the Bureau to handle relations with other Party organizations, a matter of some importance to Ribbentrop because he was not counted as an *Altkämpfer* by the other Nazi chieftains. Just as Luther made himself indispensable to the Ribbentrop household in the many errands continually necessary to elevate their standard of living, Luther also made himself the bulwark of the future foreign minister's defense against Party rivals.

In constructing the Party Liaison Office, Luther demonstrated the phenomenal talent for organization that would become a trademark of his career. In contrast to Ribbentrop's rather lax methods of recruitment, Luther worked systematically. He visited the various *Gauleiter* and leaders of the Party organizations asking them to nominate suitable young Party members to act as liaisons to Bureau Ribbentrop. Luther then selected the best of the nominees, assuring himself of relatively frictionless lines of communication to the Party organizations and simultaneously surrounding himself with a group of very young, active, and loyal men—a *junge Garde*.

Consumed by ambition and uninhibited in his methods of political infighting, by mid-1937 Luther had secured an autonomous position for his Liaison Office within Bureau Ribbentrop.[3] Then misfortune struck. Luther's liaison to the SS, Lothar Kühne, made a very unflattering report to the SD on Bureau Ribbentrop, which infuriated the ambassador. Luther was abruptly dismissed and his organization disbanded. While Luther inspired loathing and hatred among his rivals, paradoxically he always retained the intense loyalty of his subordinates. Headed by Walter Büttner, Luther's men plotted to restore their leader, drumming up support on Luther's behalf from Martin Mutschmann, *Gauleiter* of Saxony, and the Reich Student Leader, Dr. Scheel. Probably more decisive was the backing of Werner Lorenz, head of the Ethnic German Liaison Office (*Volksdeutsche Mittelstelle* or *VoMi*) and Ribbentrop's permanent deputy in Bureau Ribbentrop. Early in 1938 Ribbentrop relented and agreed to reinstate Luther, though the new Party Advisory Office (*Parteiberatungsstelle*), also known as Bureau Luther, was more modest than its predecessor, with Luther's staff reduced from 12 to four.[4]

Luther's reinstatement coincided with Ribbentrop's promotion to foreign minister. Back in good graces, Luther had as his major concern securing his own entry into the Foreign Office. Serious obstacles stood in his way. Ribbentrop was not transferring many Bureau personnel into the Foreign Office, which moved Luther to complain that the foreign minister was surrounding himself with "Father Christmases" (*Weihnachtsmänner*). More importantly, Luther had been indicted for embezzlement of Party funds and could not be taken into state service while the threat of Party expulsion hung over him.

This did not deter Luther, who was desperate not to be abandoned along with the rest of Bureau Ribbentrop. He deluged the foreign minister with examples of how various Party agencies were playing off the Foreign Office and Bureau Ribbentrop against one another and even carrying on foreign contacts and negotiations behind Ribbentrop's back. To insure uniform handling of Party organizations' affairs touching upon foreign policy, Luther suggested that *Referat Deutschland,* the Foreign Office bureau which handled both the Jewish question and Party affairs, be divided in two. He further proposed, however immodestly, that he then be named head of the Foreign Office *Referat* for Party affairs, thus creating a personal union between it and the Party Advisory Office of Bureau Ribbentrop, which he would continue to run as well.[5]

Ribbentrop reacted favorably enough to intervene with Martin Bormann concerning Luther's pending embezzlement trial. Bormann in turn wrote the Supreme Party Court that he wanted the matter settled speedily. As part of an amnesty issued following the conclusion of the Munich Agreement, charges against Luther were dropped.[6] In November Luther entered the Foreign Office as head of the new *Referat Partei,* though not with quite the jurisdiction for which he had hoped. While losing its Party liaison functions, *Referat Deutschland* continued to act as liaison to the half-Party, half-state SS and Police conglomerate of Himmler and Heydrich. It also retained, of course, its jurisdiction in Jewish affairs, the one area which Luther had not contested.[7]

The period from the fall of 1938, when Luther first entered the Foreign Office, to the spring of 1940 was the most uneventful stretch of his political career. He continued to defend Ribbentrop against the attacks of Party rivals, to monitor jealously the foreign contacts of Party and now also state organizations, and to supervise the procurement, construction, and decoration of a growing list of Ribbentrop properties. But this did not satisfy his burning ambition. Very sensitive about his status in the Foreign Office (where the professionals despised the "former furniture remover" as much as they did Ribbentrop, the "champagne salesman"), Luther felt that the diverse activities which he controlled entitled him to the rank of division (*Abteilung*) chief, rather than head of a mere *Referat.*[8]

Luther made his bid in a meeting with Ribbentrop on April 16, 1940. He proposed to the foreign minister that a new Division Germany (*Abteilung Deutschland*) be formed within the Foreign Office under Luther's leadership. In addition to the activities which Luther already managed—Party liaison, foreign contacts of Party and state organizations, and special construction (a euphemism for managing Ribbentrop's properties)—it would encompass several new areas. *Referat Deutschland,* Luther's victim in 1938, was to be dissolved and its jurisdiction divided into two sections, one for liaison to the *Reichsführer*-SS and Police and the second primarily for Jewish affairs. Luther also asked for control over the Foreign Office's technical apparatus for the printing and distributing of all Foreign Office publications. Ribbentrop initialed his agreement.[9]

*Abteilung Deutschland,* officially created May 7, 1940, was organized as follows:

Referat Partei: Liaison to all Party organizations, with the exceptions of German citizens abroad (responsibility of the *Auslandsorganisation*) and the SS and Police.

Referat DII: Affairs of the Reichsführer-SS, Reich Security Main Office, international police cooperation, free masonry.

Referat DIII: Jewish question, racial policy, German refugees, national movements abroad.

Referat D IV: Production and distribution of printed material.

Referat D V: Travel abroad by important German personalities.

Referat D VI: Special construction.

In July the Geographical Service was added as Referat D VII and charged with supplying information and maps to various branches of the government.[10] These seven sections formed the foundation upon which Luther was to construct his own personal empire within the Foreign Office.

Luther's expansionist designs were greatly facilitated when Ribbentrop named him as head of a *Sonderreferat Organisation,* responsible directly to the foreign minister, with the task of proposing reorganization schemes for the Foreign Office. This commission gave Luther license to interfere in all of the divisions and led him, in view of his name, to style himself the "Reformer" of the Foreign Office. His reforms amounted to a stunning campaign of bureaucratic imperialism.[11]

Luther became responsible for the entire propaganda of the Foreign Office, as *Sonderreferat Organization* added to its functions the "coordination" of the relevant activities of the German Information Agency, the Foreign Office radio-monitoring service, the Information and Cultural Divisions, and Luther's own *Referat* D IV. The Cultural Division was left a shattered remnant, with some of its sections scattered as patronage to Luther's allies in the Information Division and others annexed directly to Abteilung Deutschland (*Referat* D VIII and IX for the political and economic affairs respectively of German minorities abroad). The latter was accomplished in the face of the open opposition of *Unterstaatssekretär* Ernst Woermann of the Political Division, who coveted ethnic German affairs for himself. Three other sections were also added to *Abteilung Deutschland:* D X for handling problems relating to foreign workers in Germany, D XI for the international affairs of veterans' organizations, and D XII for church questions. Luther also helped engineer the appointment of three prominent SA-men to ambassadorial posts in southeast Europe.[12]

*Abteilung Deutschland* was a sprawling, variegated organization, which had cohesion because of the energetic leadership and personnel policy of Martin Luther. From the earliest days of his career, Luther was very careful about recruitment, personally interviewing all prospective employees before making the final decision on their suitability as colleagues.[13] The staff that Luther gathered around himself was a group of able and educated young men, most of them Party members before the seizure of power, who had been active at the *Gau*-level of the Party organization. Typical was Luther's deputy, Walter Büttner, who was born in 1908, joined the Party and SA in 1929, worked on the staff of the *Gauleiter* of Saxony, earned his engineering degree in 1936, and transferred from the SA to SS in 1938.[14]

Luther's staff became a potent weapon because of his ability to instill therein loyalty and esprit de corps. While the older officials of the Foreign Office languished in deteriorating morale under Ribbentrop and felt nothing but hatred and disgust for his protégé, Luther, Luther's men worked for their leader efficiently and loyally. In comparison to the old men, they saw Luther as an unconventional, hard-headed "type of modern manager" who knew how to create a good working climate and how to get things done.[15]

It was more than just his organizational talent and efficiency that won Luther this valuable loyalty, however. He never ceased to work for the advancement and promotion of those he recruited, quite aware of what the prospects of rapid promotion did for men's morale.[16] But Luther also cared for "his" men. When they were particularly hard hit by military call-ups following the failure of the first Russian campaign, he carried on a voluminous correspondence with those in the field and operated as a central clearing house for information, keeping everyone informed about the others. He also made special efforts through the Rome embassy to secure special treatment for two of his men wounded in North Africa.[17]

What sort of man was Luther? His enemies, of which there were many, vied with each other for purple adjectives to describe him. To Ulrich von Hassell, he was "uncouth, presumptuous, false and probably corrupt." To Peter Kleist, he was "unscrupulous" and a "gravedigger." Adolf Steengracht labeled his methods "atrocious and abominable." Weizsäcker called him a "reptile." And Himmler allegedly described him as "a common, unpleasant sort of fellow—slimy and uncouth."[18]

Those who were not outright enemies were only slightly more charitable. Walter Schellenberg found him "energetic, very quick to grasp a point, and not ungifted as an organizer" but "quite unfit to be a government official" and "governed solely by the calculations of the businessman." He was aggressive, cold, ruthless, "capable of saying and doing anything . . . a dangerous figure such as only a totalitarian system could produce."[19] Rudolf Rahn described him as "doubtless a capable organizer, of great will power and work stamina, monstrously robust and fully unscrupulous in his choice of means. . . . He was concerned exclusively with the conquest of internal power, and in this he demonstrated an incontestable cleverness."[20]

But men are rarely so one-sided and simple as these witnesses portray Luther. Much about him was paradoxical. All testify to his energy, but this did not derive from physical strength. His health was mediocre at best. His eyes were poor, requiring thick corrective lenses, and permanently swollen because of a sinus infection.[21] He was frequently ill and had to work at home. In August 1942, he suffered a severe attack of angina, presaging the heart condition that killed him within three years.[22] Luther's energy, then, was not physical; it was based on a burning ambition that drove him forward despite his chronic sinus trouble, his weak heart, and other bouts of illness.

Luther could be abrasive and contentious with his rivals. Yet he won the loyalty of those who worked for him. He was sincerely concerned for the welfare of his men, especially when they were at the front. But if an employee betrayed him, he was vengeful. When the caretaker of the apartment building that Luther owned tried to quit without giving proper notice to take a better job with the Foreign Office caring for the confiscated Polish embassy, Luther made sure the man was blacklisted from any Foreign Office employment.[23]

Despite his growing power and continual promotion (from mere *Legationsrat* in November 1938 to *Unterstaatssekretär* in July 1941), Luther felt insecure vis-à-vis the old professionals of the Foreign Office and was very sensitive to personal snubs. When State Secretary Weizsäcker ended a general conference by asking the division chiefs to stay behind, and for "Herr Luther also to remain," Luther was furious. He demanded once again that his position in the Foreign Office be clarified for all times. Weizsäcker apologetically agreed.[24] When Ernst Bohle, head of the *Auslandsorganisation* (the Nazi Party agency for Germans living abroad), ostentatiously refused to greet Luther at an official dinner for a visiting Spanish dignitary, Luther complained directly to Ribbentrop.[25]

In his pursuit of power, Luther was guided by no higher aim or mission. He never articulated any guiding principles, any future goal to be strived for. Power was used simply to gain more power. To be sure, he played the part of a good National Socialist and made his workers wear their party insignia.[26] But he was not a doctrinaire racist like Heinrich Himmler, dreaming fantasies of a future Aryan heaven-on-earth. Nor was he an *Altkämpfer* like Goebbels, wallowing in nostalgia and ready to stick by Hitler to the end. Luther served the hard-core Nazis and helped to provide the expertise that made their horrible dreams possible. But he was not one of them. Primarily, Luther was an amoral technician of power, and it is not difficult to imagine his putting himself at the service of any regime which offered scope to his ambition. Certainly the Nazi environment offered greater chance of success for the methods which suited Luther's temperament, but here again Luther's affinity to Nazism was based on means, not ends.

Gerald Reitlinger claims that Luther "made anti-Semitism his life's work."[27] This is an absurd statement. When Luther entered the Foreign Office in 1938, he requested Ribbentrop to give him jurisdiction over Party affairs and explicitly suggested that Jewish affairs be left with *Referat Deutschland*—a very strange course of action for a man supposedly devoting his life to the anti-Semitic cause. When Jewish affairs finally came under his jurisdiction in 1940, they were but one of two dozen activities carried on by Luther simultaneously and could hardly constitute "his life's work." Luther was anti-Semitic, no doubt, but this emotion was not the driving force behind his career. If he carried out anti-Jewish measures efficiently and ruthlessly, this was no different from the manner in which he carried out any policy whose effective and ruthless execution would help him ascend the hierarchy of power. Political ambition, not anti-Semitism, was the fuel of Luther's meteoric career.

## The Jewish Experts of D III

The personnel of Referat D III contrasted sharply with the typical members of *Abteilung Deutschland.* For the most part, Luther surrounded himself with young men who had joined the Nazi party in their student days before 1933 and were Party activists before entering the foreign service. The men of D III, on the other hand, were intent upon a civil service career and entered the Party as "bandwagon" Nazis between March and May 1933, when it became clear that this was the most opportune way to further their ambitions. Thus a great irony emerged. It was the lifetime Party activists who formed the core of Luther's empire, but it was the nazified civil servants who carried out the most horrendous of all Nazi policies.

The head of the Jewish *Referat* throughout the entire existence of *Abteilung Deutschland* was Franz Rademacher. He was born on February 20, 1906, in the town of Neustrelitz in Mecklenburg. The son of a locomotive engineer, Rademacher wanted to join the navy. But his father insisted on an education, and Rademacher attended the humanistic *Gymnasium* in Rostock, working his own way from the age of sixteen.[28] On his Foreign Office records Rademacher claims to have joined the Ehrhardt Brigade in December 1923, when he would have been a seventeen-year-old *Gymnasium* student in Rostock. This is seriously open to question, since on the same form Rademacher lied about his date of Party membership, which he listed as the summer of 1932. In fact, this was when he joined the SA; he did not become a Party member until March 1, 1933. As he never repeated the claim of membership in the Ehrhardt Brigade, this episode must be regarded as an invention of Rademacher's imagination to enhance his credentials.[29]

Rademacher passed the *Abitur* in 1924 and went on to study law at the Universities of Munich and Rostock. He passed his first *Staatsprüfung* in 1928 and became a law clerk in the Mecklenburg court system in preparation for his second *Staatsprüfung,* which he passed in April 1932. He thereupon became an assistant judge.[30]

In the spring of 1934, Rademacher quit the SA. "Drillmarching every Sunday was not my style," he explained in one version.[31] Another time he claimed that he had always wanted to enter the foreign service, but it had been made clear to him by the SA that he would retain a "special obligation" to Röhm. Allegedly feeling himself too good to be an informant, he quit. His brigade commander, a sports comrade, secured him an honorable discharge.[32] Whether he sensed already in the spring of 1934, that the SA was no longer the best bet for an ambitious careerist, he did not say. In any case, he obviously did not feel at home among the radicals of the SA.

To fulfill his goal of entering the foreign service, he had already transferred from the judicial system to the internal administration in Mecklenburg in November 1933. Attending the NSDAP civil service school at Bad Tölz, a necessity to achieve promotion to the rank of *Regierungsrat,* Rademacher gave his required talk on foreign policy. This led to an invitation to enter the

Foreign Office as legation secretary in December 1937.[33] The humble son of a locomotive engineer had already come a long way through a combination of hard work and opportunistic politics.

His first job in the Foreign Office was in the Cultural Division, where he specialized in affairs concerning university professors. In 1938 he was assigned to the German embassy in Montevideo as chargé d'affaires, a post he held until April 1940.[34] His recall from Montevideo was at his own request. Officers from the scuttled pocket battleship *Graf Spee,* interned in Montevideo since the fall of 1939, were frequently entertained by embassy personnel, and Rademacher's wife had an affair with one of them. Rademacher threatened to have it come to a duel unless he and his family were returned to Germany.[35] By his own account Rademacher tried to join the navy in fulfillment of his boyhood dream, but he was not released from the Foreign Office.[36] Instead, Rademacher was assigned to head D III, the *Judenreferat* of the newly formed *Abteilung Deutschland.*

Rademacher had had no special experience in Jewish affairs that qualified him for this post, but he was obviously well versed in the proper racial rhetoric and brandished his anti-Semitism effectively. After meeting Rademacher for the first time in early June 1940, Paul Wurm, the foreign editor of Julius Streicher's *Der Stürmer* as well as founder of the Anti-Jewish League, wrote him: "I am glad to have made your acquaintance and I know to value you as a really good authority on the Jewish question and old fighter."[37] This was no mean compliment, coming from one of the obscenely anti-Semitic Streicher gang. Despite this accolade from Wurm, Rademacher was not satisfied with his expertise in Jewish affairs. In the true spirit of the self-made man, he frequently wrote to Anti-Semitic Action in Goebbels' Propaganda Ministry, Euler's Reich Institut for the New German History, the German Information Agency, and to the *Stürmer's* publishing house for books on the Jewish question. By the summer of 1941, over half of Rademacher's library was composed of such books.[38]

Upon his return to Berlin, Rademacher had to find a place to live. Through Albert Speer's office, where Luther had good contacts, the search was successful. "I have succeeded in receiving the *sub rosa* assurance that a Jewish apartment will be evacuated for me through special measures," he wrote.[39] Residing in his "Jewish" apartment, surrounded by his library of books on the Jewish question, Rademacher quickly established himself as the Jewish expert in the Foreign Office.

Staffing the *Judenreferat* proved to be a continual problem for Rademacher. Due to military call-ups, as well as the distinct dislike of some for working on Jewish affairs, D III experienced a rapid turnover of personnel. Occasionally Rademacher tried to recruit a SS-man to his staff, as when he wrote in early 1941, "I would welcome it, if . . . one of the newly employed SS-men were transferred to me."[40] He also tried to require proficiency in Nazi racial ideology. "D III must attach great importance to receiving a co-worker, who guarantees that he works scientifically completely accurately in the sense of the racial policy pursued by the Racial Political Office."[41] But in the end it was neither SS-membership nor ideological reliability that determined the staff of D III. Instead it was the time-honored system of personal connections that played the biggest role.

Rademacher's first assistant, Gerhard Todenhöfer, was much more typical of *Abteilung Deutschland* in general than D III, for he came into D III as a Party activist, not a nazified civil servant. He had been recruited by Luther's deputy, Walter Büttner, a student friend of his, not by Rademacher.[42] Todenhöfer served in D III from August 1940 to July 1941, but was occupied primarily with D III's responsibilities for national movements abroad, such as the Flemish, Walloons, Ukrainians, Arrow Cross in Hungary and Iron Guard in Rumania. It was Rademacher who handled the Jewish affairs of D III in this period.

Todenhöfer moved on to other positions in *Abteilung Deutschland* (liaison-man to the Propaganda Ministry and SA), and to replace him Rademacher arranged for the assignment to D III of Dr. Herbert Müller, an old acquaintance from his days in the Mecklenburg civil service. Müller was born in Schwerin in Mecklenburg in 1910. Like Rademacher, he had been a student of law. He had belonged to the *Stahlhelm* in Rostock in 1931 and 1932, but after the *Machtergreifung* he quickly joined the Nazi Party on May 1, 1933. He had passed his first *Staatsprüfung* in 1932, and as a law clerk became acquainted with Rademacher, who helped train him. He became a doctor of law in 1934, spent a year abroad as a student at the University of Kansas, and passed his second *Staatsprüfung* in 1936. He then worked three years in the Reich Economics Ministry.[43]

Müller entered the Foreign Office in 1939. After a short stint in the Economics Division, he served in the German embassy in Teheran from December 1939 to October 1941, when diplomatic relations with Iran were broken. He was immediately reassigned to the German embassy in Sofia, Bulgaria, but could not take up his post there due to a case of amoebic dysentery. At this point Rademacher intervened and arranged his assignment to D III. Müller worked there from November 11, 1941, until April 1, 1942, when he was drafted into the army.[44]

Rademacher once again tried to recruit an SS man as his deputy. Heydrich nominated a *Hauptsturmführer* Girke, who had been in the Gestapo and had a good knowledge of the Jewish question. Rademacher interviewed Girke and found him ideologically strong, but other problems arose. Heinrich Müller of the Gestapo wanted Girke to remain subordinate to the SD while temporarily assigned to Foreign Office duty, but the Foreign Office only wanted someone completely taken into its service. If this happened, however, Girke would lose his military deferment and be drafted. Thus this final attempt to employ an SS man also failed.[45]

In the months following Müller's departure in 1942, Rademacher got by with makeshift help. First Luther assigned another doctor of law, Kurt Weege, to help out in March and April. Weege had been invited into the Foreign Office on a probationary basis after an audience with Ribbentrop in 1939. Scheduled to enter the army in the late spring of 1942, Weege was suddenly dismissed from his Foreign Office position in February. An old Party member (a member of the Hitler Youth in 1929), Weege petitioned Luther to find him another position in the Foreign Office until he entered the army.[46] Luther arranged for him to work in D III. Weege was followed briefly by *Vizekonsul* Weiler of the German consulate in Lulea, Sweden, who was temporarily in Berlin until recalled to his post in June 1942.[47]

The shortage of Foreign Office personnel due to military call-ups was temporarily ended in the late spring of 1942, when nearly all the German embassies in North and South America were closed down and the diplomats returned to Berlin. From this group of returnees, Rademacher selected an acquaintance from his days in Uruguay, Dr. Karl Otto Klingenfuss. Klingenfuss was born in Mannheim in 1901, the son of a railway official. After *Volksschule* he had spent three years as an apprentice in the Mannheim city administration and then attended the Wertheim am Rhein *Gymnasium*, where he passed his *Abitur* in 1921.[48] He attended the University of Heidelberg and received his doctorate in history and public law in 1925. He received a three-year postdoctoral stipend to study nationality rights and cultural autonomy and then worked at the German *Auslandsinstitut* in Stuttgart. He joined the NSDAP on May 1, 1933, and served one year as *Blockleiter* in Stuttgart. In 1934 he left the *Auslandsinstitut* and joined Ernst Bohle's *Auslandsorganisation*, where he worked as head of the Cultural Office until 1937.[49]

Klingenfuss had unsuccessfully been trying to enter the foreign service since 1930. In January 1938, due to the intervention of Bohle, Klingenfuss was finally taken into the Foreign Office. He worked first in the Cultural Division and then in January 1939 was sent to the German embassy in Buenos Aires, across the estuary of the River Platte from Rademacher in Montevideo.[50] While legation secretary in the Buenos Aires embassy, Klingenfuss was simultaneously the head of the *Auslandsorganisation* for all of Argentina, the highest position that any member of D III ever achieved in a Party organization.[51] When Rademacher left the Montevideo embassy in April 1940, Klingenfuss took his place there until April 1942, when he too returned to Germany.[52] Rademacher thereupon requested his services in D III, where Klingenfuss worked from July to December, 1942.

Rademacher's last deputy in D III was Fritz-Gebhardt von Hahn. He was born in 1911 in Shanghai, the son of the German *Vizekonsul* there.[53] He was reared by his paternal grandmother in Darmstadt, because his father was always travelling and his mother was confined to a sanatorium. He then rejoined his father and attended *Gymnasium* in Berlin and Rotterdam, passing the *Abitur* in 1929. Like all his predecessors in D III, he went on to study law at the university level at Munich, Giessen, and Leipzig, and passed his first *Staatsprüfung* in 1933. In April of the same year he joined the Nazi Party and also entered the *Marine*-SA the following fall.

Hahn spent his training period in the legal office of the *Auslandsorganisation* and passed the second *Staatsprüfung* in 1937. He then worked on the personal staff of Ernst Bohle, while preparing to follow his father's career in the foreign service. While studying for the preliminary language exams, he wrote Bohle a "strictly confidential" report that the Foreign Office was using the preliminary language exams not only to test language ability but also to weed out politically undesirable candidates, whose rejections could not be otherwise safely justified. Hahn suggested that someone from the staff of the Führer's deputy should sit on the examination commission to make sure that candidates with the proper Nazi *Weltanschauung* were not discriminated against.

Despite his fears of discrimination, Hahn was taken into the Foreign Office in March 1937. But he maintained his ties with Bohle and frequently went riding with Bohle's wife. In 1938 he attended the same NSDAP school for civil servants at Bad Tölz as Rademacher and Müller before him. At least one official there detected the political chameleon in Hahn.

Von Hahn welcomes the national-socialist state and has at his disposal a very good knowledge of the foundations of the national-socialist world view. . . . However at particular points his very strongly critical attitude is expressed again and again. He understands also how to transmit ideological thoughts clearly and convincingly to others, but in so doing arouses the impression that it happens not always out of loyalty to the idea but out of clever calculations.

Hahn was assigned to the German consulate in Geneva, Switzerland, in June 1938. The head of the consulate, Dr. Krauel, was not a Nazi and was skeptical about receiving a known protégé of Bohle. But the adaptable Hahn soon impressed everyone there with his moderation. He even had a quarrel with Reich Student Leader Scheel over the provocative behavior of German students in Geneva, in particular vis-à-vis German emigrants there.

A member of the Naval Reserve since 1934, Hahn went on active duty in the navy in February 1940, and worked as a translator when the Germans moved into Holland. In late June 1940, he was wounded by a German sentry when he refused to halt despite a challenge. Hahn's upper right arm was severely fractured. He was still not fully recuperated in the summer of 1941, over a year later. But anxious not to lose the chance to build up seniority, he received permission to work in the Foreign Office when he was not undergoing medical treatment. At first he was assigned duties as an adjutant in the Economic Division, where once again no one found him a radical Nazi or anti-Semite. But the long hours of the adjutant's job were too much for his health. He asked for reassignment and was sent to D III. Hahn worked in D III for less than four weeks (December 12, 1941 to January 5, 1942) before he had to return to the hospital, and again on a half-day basis for a few weeks in the summer. After his final release from the hospital in December 1942, but with his arm still in a sling, he was given four weeks' sick leave from the navy to recuperate further. Instead he voluntarily reported to D III for the third time. He succeeded in getting his leave extended and continued to work in the *Judenreferat* until May 1943, before returning to the navy.

Thus the Jewish experts of the Foreign Office—Rademacher, Müller, Klingenfuss, and Hahn (Todenhöfer played no major role in Jewish affairs and need not be considered further)—had much in common. They were all students of law intent upon a career in the civil service. They all opportunistically joined the NSDAP between March and May 1933, as part of the wave of "bandwagon" Nazis that deluged the Party as soon as it came to power. All but Müller had entered the foreign service under Neurath, not Ribbentrop, and two—Klingenfuss and Hahn—were protégés of Ernst Bohle, a hatred rival of Martin Luther. Yet they ended up under Martin Luther, in the division of the Foreign Office most densely staffed with Party activists, working on the most radical of all Nazi policies.

Though Rademacher attempted occasionally to recruit an SS man, not a single member of D III was in fact ever a member of the SS. Though Rademacher paid lip service to proficiency in racial ideology, none had a previous record of radical anti-Semitism or expertise on the Jewish question (though Rademacher and Hahn developed rather quickly in this direction once given the chance). Their assignments to D III occurred more through a conjuncture of fortuitous events and past acquaintances than on ideological or political grounds. The men of D III—Rademacher, Müller, Klingenfuss, and Hahn—were in fact only four very career-minded but unremarkable bureaucrats.

# 4. Cooperation and Competition with the SS from the Invasion of France to the Invasion of Russia (May 1940–June 1941)

*Referat Deutschland* had been symbolic of the Wilhelmstrasse's willingness to wrap the defense of Nazi Jewish policy in the flag of German patriotism. On the level of policy making, however, the impact of the Foreign Office Jewish desk had been slight. When Luther and Rademacher took over Foreign Office Jewish affairs in May 1940, the new *Judenreferat*, D III, immediately surpassed its successor in importance. The most spectacular manifestation of this new role was Rademacher's involvement in the Madagascar Plan.

### The Madagascar Plan

The idea of resettling European Jewry in a colony on another continent was not new, and no single potential area of resettlement attracted as much attention as did the French colony off the coast of Africa, the island of Madagascar.[1] Mentioned by such Nazi luminaries as Streicher, Göring, Rosenberg, and Ribbentrop (as well as by the fellow traveller Schacht) between 1938 and 1940, it was an idea that had wide currency at the time. But a concrete plan for the forced deportation of European Jewry to Madagascar, under the direction of a victorious Germany, had not yet emerged. This was Franz Rademacher's first contribution to German Jewish policy.

On June 3, 1940, less than a month into his new job, Rademacher prepared a lengthy memorandum for Luther, "Thoughts on the activities and tasks of *Referat* D III."[2]

After the short glimpse that I have been able to take into the work of the *Referat* in these days, it appears to me essentially as the occupation with 1,000 individual decisions over—I might say—the fate of individual Jews (denaturalization, compensation to Jews of foreign citizenship—on account of damages in connection with the murder of Rath, emigration of individual Jews); in addition participation in basic questions, such as internal legislation on the Jewish question, decrees of similar regulations in the Protectorate, in the General Government, etc.

For the accomplishment of this work the apparatus runs frictionlessly, the best evidence for the enormous labor that the *Referat* and its director have expended up until now, which certainly was not simple with the many, different, internal authorities that had to be brought under one hat, and with the significance that these individual questions had in the pre-war period, especially in view of the atrocity propaganda of the western pseudo-democracies over the persecution of the Jews in Germany.

Through the war itself and the final showdown thereby precipitated with the western empires and the supranational powers ruling there, the foreign political significance of the individual questions to be decided in each case in Jewish affairs has receded. In my opinion therefore, the question in Jewish affairs is to be decided in accordance with German war aims. One question must be clarified, whereto with the Jews? Conceivable war aims in this regard could be:
a) all Jews out of Europe.
b) separation between East and West Jews; the East Jews, which supply the regenerative and Talmudic recruits for the militant Jewish intelligentsia, stay, for example, in the district of Lublin as a pledge in German hands, so that the American Jews remain paralyzed in their fight against Germany. The West Jews on the other hand are removed from Europe, to Madagascar for example.
c) in this connection the question of a Jewish national home in Palestine (danger of a second Rome!).
For the clarification of these questions, no technical preliminary studies have been possible in Ref. D III up till now.

As preparatory work I am thinking of taking up intimate discussions with interested internal party, state, and scientific agencies. Discovery of possible plans at hand there, bringing these plans into line with the wishes of the foreign minister, compilation of technical data (estimated number of Jews to be transplanted, the necessary money and materials, how much money and how many ships shall France provide for this purpose, how many shall England provide? Ascertainment of the evacuation deadline that can be imposed upon both countries in the peace treaty, etc.).

In my opinion Ref. D III is called upon to develop these questions. The work must commence immediately, so that the Division [*Abteilung Deutschland*] does not get the worst of it vis-à-vis the Political Division in the peace negotiations that eventually arise; because the danger exists, that with the Political Division an inherently imperialistic way of thinking will prevail, and that insuring *Gross-Deutschland* in the peace treaty insofar as possible against supra-national powers can be easily overlooked.

The present war has a double face: one is imperialistic—the securing of political, military and economic space necessary for Germany as a world power, one supra-national—liberation of the world from the chains of Jewry and free masonry—.

Rademacher then proceeded to request Luther to ascertain what basic war aim in the Jewish question the foreign minister wanted to carry through, and also to reinforce the personnel of D III so that he would be free to undertake the necessary negotiations with other agencies.

This memorandum revealed much about Rademacher. Though *Referat* D III had jurisdiction over other matters, especially the treatment of national movements abroad, Rademacher mentioned no other task but the Jewish question which clearly fascinated him. He wished to impress his new boss as a man who eschewed the humdrum daily routine; he wanted to tackle big problems, cutting red tape through interdepartmental negotiations. As a new recruit to the most nazified division of the Foreign Office, he freely displayed his facility with Nazi jargon ("supra-national powers" and "chains of Jewry and free masonry"). Already he had realized that the best way to enlist Luther's support was to raise the specter of rivalry in the form of the Political Division. A short synopsis of this memorandum, purged of such references, was circulated for administrative purposes.[3] Finally, though Rademacher was thinking in terms of big solutions, such as the expulsion of all Jews from Europe or Jewish reservations in Lublin and Madagascar, he had not yet received any instructions in this regard from above. The initiative for Foreign Office participation in a real solution to the Jewish question, not just paperwork on the periphery, was his, but Rademacher wanted some directional nod from Luther and Ribbentrop; he had no definite plans as yet, other than the clear desire to make a positive impression on his new boss.

Where did Rademacher get his ideas? The Gestapo had never given the Foreign Office the full story of its plans for a Lublin reservation. But *Referat Deutschland* had sufficient press clippings and correspondence in its files for Rademacher to realize very quickly that this was one of the most fashionable solutions being weighed at the time. No such recent file existed in the case of Madagascar, however. And as chargé d'affaires in Montevideo for the previous two years, it is most unlikely that Rademacher had either been able or sufficiently interested to pick up the scattered references to Madgascar made by prominent Nazi leaders. Rademacher's stimulus in this case came from a publication from the 1920s of the Dutch anti-Semite, H. H. Beamish, which advocated shipping all the Jews to Madagascar. Rademacher claimed to have found it in the files of *Referat Deutschland.*[4]

Rademacher's inclination toward Madagascar as a Jewish reservation was quickly reinforced when he met Paul Wurm, the foreign editor of *Der Stürmer,* on June 4, 1940, the day after his initial memorandum. The meeting took place at Rademacher's invitation. While they obviously discussed a number of aspects of the Jewish question, Madagascar must have received more than a passing mention. Two days later Wurm wrote to thank Rade-macker for the invitation. He enclosed an article that he had written the year before, which, in typical *Stürmer*-style, proposed Madagascar as a home for 15 million Jewish "bloodsuckers." Wurm inquired if the time had come for its publication. Rademacher replied on June 12. He apologized for the late answer, but he had been trying to clear up a number of basic questions "that we recently touched upon in our conversation." However, the situation was still not clear, and therefore he requested Wurm to abstain from publication for the moment.[5]

If the situation was still unclear on June 12, it did not remain so for long. Luther presented to Ribbentrop Rademacher's proposal that D III be charged with preparing a solution to the Jewish question within the framework of the peace treaty. Ribbentrop agreed.[6] Of the various options Rademacher listed, the Lublin reservation had already been tried and found wanting in the spring of 1940. But the idea of deporting all the Jews out of Europe, and to a Madagascar reservation in particular, was well received, especially in view of Germany's victory over France, which owned the island, and the seemingly imminent victory over Great Britain, which controlled the sea. Both Ribben-trop and Hitler mentioned the plan to use Madagascar for a Jewish reser-vation to Ciano and Mussolini respectively in their talks in Munich on June 17–18 over the future of the French empire.[7]

The exact date on which Rademacher was authorized to begin work on the Madagascar Plan cannot be determined. In any case, the well-informed Heydrich quickly learned either of Ribbentrop's remarks to Ciano or of Rademacher's preliminary work and wrote the foreign minister on June 24.[8] Heydrich noted that he had been in charge of Jewish emigration since January 1939, and claimed that since then 200,000 Jews had left Reich territory. But with the recent German victories, there were now 3.25 million Jews in the territories under German control. Emigration could not possibly cope with this number. "Thus a territorial final solution becomes necessary." In the case that anything of this sort was being planned in the Foreign Office, its participation was requested in a forthcoming conference on the final solution of the Jewish question. Thus Heydrich's letter was not the origin of the Madagascar Plan, though it has been suggested that he had toyed with the idea as early as 1938.[9] Rather it was Heydrich's move to insure that he was not excluded from a project emerging independently within the Foreign Office that impinged upon his competency for Jewish emigration.

Heydrich had his way, and Rademacher was instructed to prepare his plan in agreement with the agencies of the *Reichsführer*-SS.[10] The above-men-tioned meeting was not held, but Rademacher contacted officials in the Ministry of the Interior as well as in various Party agencies, all of whom approved Rademacher's initial plan which emerged in early July. "The imminent victory gives Germany the possibility and, according to my opinion, also the obligation to solve the Jewish question in Europe," wrote Rade-macher. "The desirable solution is: All Jews out of Europe."[11] Therefore, in the peace treaty France would cede the island of Madagascar to Germany as a mandate. Strategic points would be used as military bases; the rest of the island would be placed under a police governor directly subordinate to the *Reichsführer*-SS. "The Madagascar solution means, as seen from the German point of view, the creation of a great ghetto. Only the Security Police has the necessary experience in this area."[12] The Jews would be held financially responsible for the real estate given them on Madagascar, and their entire European property would be transferred to a special bank, which would then buy land and the supplies necessary for the reconstruction of the island. Should their European property not suffice for this, the bank would grant them credit!

Incredibly, Rademacher felt that this plan for the total dispossession of European Jewry and its forced deportation to an island super-ghetto under SS control could be used to enhance Germany's image abroad. There would be no colonial administration in addition to the police governor; this would constitute a "superfluous overlap of authorities," and the treatment of European Jewry as a colonial people would cause an uproar among American Jews. Rather than a colonial administration, the Jews would have autonomy within their own territory, with their own mayors, police, postal adminsitration, etc.

> Propagandistically one can exploit the generosity that Germany shows in bestowing cultural, economic, administrative, and legal autonomy on the Jews, and thereby emphasize that our German sense of responsibility toward the world forbids our immediately granting an independent state to a race that has had no national independence for thousands of years; for that it must still stand the test of history.[13]

Bolstered by the approval of the other authorities for his initial outline of the Madagascar Plan, Rademacher plunged into the "scientific" aspects of the problem and began collecting statistical data. A new acquisition to his rapidly growing anti-Semitic library was Zander's *Die Verbreitung der Juden in der Welt*. Rademacher sent Zander's statistics for each European country to the respective German embassy, with the request to check the figures and send any pertinent literature that could be procured. Rademacher was particularly interested to know how many Jews were in each country, in what economic areas they were of decisive importance, and the estimated total capital they possessed.[14] Most responses were perfunctory.

Rademacher also called upon his new friend, Paul Wurm, for statistics. Wurm estimated that there were slightly under 10 million unbaptized Jews, as well as three to four million half-Jews. The latter would probably not be considered for deportation, "because otherwise they would provide a blood-refresher (*Blutauffrischung*) for the Jewish people. Sterilization of the half-breeds can solve this problem."[15]

The most detailed statistics that Rademacher received were from Dr. Burgdörfer, well-known demographer and president of the Bavarian State Office of Statistics. He calculated 9.8 million Jews in Europe, of which exactly

half, 4.9 million, were under Russian control. Thus only the other 4.9 million
need be considered for resettlement. But he suggested adding 1.6 million Jews
from other parts of the world, excluding only the United States in addition to
Russia, reaching a total of 6.5 million. Even if this number were added to the
3.8 million present inhabitants of Madagascar, it created a population density
of only 16 per qkm., about the average for the earth's surface and only one-
tenth of Germany's population density. Without the slightest concern for the
realities of Madagascar, Dr. Burgdörfer and Rademacher concluded that this
number could preserve itself within the natural capacity of the island.[16] Dr.
Schumacher of the Freiburg Mining Academy assured Rademacher that, aside
from graphite, there were no mineral deposits of significance on Madagascar.[17]
In *Meyer's Lexicon* Rademacher found that the hot and humid coastal climate
of Madagascar was "very unhealthy for Europeans" but that the highlands
were cooler and more wholesome.[18]

In addition to the statistical aspects, Rademacher also became intrigued by
the economic side of the Madagascar Plan. Thus he found time to draw up and
submit to Helmut Wohlthat of Göring's Four Year Plan a memorandum on the
foundation of an intra-European bank for the utilization of Jewish property.
The main idea was to replace Jewish economic influence in Europe with that of
Germany in one blow, without disrupting the economy of any country through
shutting down Jewish businesses. Jewish capital in Europe would be administered in trusteeship through the new bank and gradually liquidated to pay for
the cost of the transportation and land in Madagascar. The bank would likewise
administer in trusteeship the land and buildings on Madagascar and gradually
transfer them to the Jews. Jewish property in Germany would be seized by the
SS, which already possessed the proper experience, and turned over to the bank.
The treaties reached with other European countries to settle the Jewish
question would provide for similar organizations outside of Germany to carry
out this function. The bank would then pay cash to the SS for carrying out the
transportation of Jews to Madagascar. The bank would also act as an economic
intermediary between the Jewish reservation in Madagascar and the outside
world, as no direct economic contact between the Jews and others would be
permitted.[19]

Rademacher was not the only one deeply involved in the Madagascar Plan.
Within Heydrich's RSHA (Reich Security Main Office or *Reichssicherheitshauptamt*), the Jewish experts of the Gestapo, Adolf Eichmann and
Theodor Dannecker, were working hard to solidify the threatened control of
the SS over Jewish emigration. Rademacher's plan assigned major functions to
the SS, particularly in the areas of seizing Jewish property, organizing
transportation, and supervising the security of the super-ghetto. But Heydrich's experts were outlining their own version of the Madagascar Plan which
did not recognize the existence or participation of any other authorities.

On August 15, 1940, Theo Dannecker delivered a summary of the SS plan
to Rademacher. It was a neatly printed brochure, complete with table of
contents and maps, entitled: *Reichssicherheitshauptamt: Madagaskar
Projekt.*[20] This plan provided for the deportation of four million Jews from

Europe, but did not include those of Spain, Portugal, Hungary, Rumania, Bulgaria, Greece, Italy and Yugoslavia in its calculations. (RSHA figures for the Jewish population of Poland and Germany were much higher than the professional Burgdörfer's.) Nor did it mention resettlement of non-European Jews. The practical men of the SS were concerned solely with the Jews actually under their control. The RSHA plan contained no nonsense about demonstrating Germany's generosity to the world by granting Jewish autonomy. Internally, the mandate would be a *Polizei-Staat* (police state). Jewish organizations would indeed be created, but their sole function was to enforce SS orders as quickly as possible. Most importantly, the plan emphasized that the total direction of the project would be under Reinhard Heydrich, who had been named special deputy for Jewish emigration by Göring in January 1939. He would control every aspect of the project from transportation and security measures to financing. Participation of the Foreign Office was only indirectly implied by references to certain necessary stipulations in the peace treaty.

As early as August 2, 1940, Luther had informed Rademacher that the foreign minister had agreed in principle to the preparations for the expulsion of European Jews, but had reiterated that planning must proceed in close agreement with the SS.[21] In mid-August, Rademacher received confirmation that not only Ribbentrop but also Hitler was continuing to support plans for the expulsion of the European Jews. Luther passed on to Rademacher a report from Otto Abetz, the German ambassador in Paris, over the latter's discussions with the Führer in Paris in early August. According to Abetz, Hitler intended to evacuate all Jews from Europe once the war was over.[22] With this reinforcement, even the lack of reciprocity on the part of the SS did not dampen Rademacher's enthusiasm.

At the end of August, Rademacher prepared a progress report for Luther on D III's Madagascar Plan.[23] Despite Rademacher's assurances that he was maintaining closest contact with the RSHA, his latest report bore even less similarity to the RSHA plan than before. While the latter was a one-man show, Rademacher's was a multi-star production. The Foreign Office would be in charge of conducting negotiations for the peace treaty with the defeated enemies as well as for special treaties with other European countries to regulate the Jewish question. The SS was still in charge of collecting the Jews in Europe and administering the island ghetto. But the colleciton, administration, and utilization of Jewish property, the founding of an intra-European bank, and the financing of the resettlement were in the hands of Wohlthat of the Four Year Plan. Propaganda preparation internally was under the Propaganda Ministry's Dr. Eberhard Taubert and his *Antisemitische Aktion*. Propaganda preparation abroad was in the hands of the Information Division of the Foreign Office. Transportation of the Jews from Europe to Madagascar, in Rademacher's view, would best be transferred from the SS to Viktor Brack on Philippe Bouhler's staff in the Führer Chancellery. According to Rademacher's information, Brack had received a special commission from the Führer for transportation organization, and it would be wiser to utilize an existing, experienced organization than to create a new one. Rademacher felt that it was time to summon the various participating agencies to a conference at the Foreign Office in order to put together a preparatory commission, which would visit Madagascar for one or two months and carry out an on-the-spot investigation. The Foreign Office role as host for this conference reflected Rademacher's view of himself as coordinator of the Madagascar Plan.

There was no response to this last proposal of Rademacher's. No Foreign Office conference was held and no preparatory commission appointed. Further work upon the Madagascar Plan within the Foreign Office ceased. Moreover, Rademacher's counterpart in the Gestapo, Adolf Eichmann, had no more success in obtaining final approval from his boss, Heydrich, than Rademacher had with Ribbentrop. As late as December 1940, Eichmann told the Jewish expert in the Interior Ministry, Bernhard Lösener, that the Madagascar Plan was still awaiting Heydrich's signature.[24]

The Madagascar Plan was born and died of military circumstances. The defeat of France and seemingly imminent victory over Great Britain promised the necessary preconditions for a massive overseas expulsion of European Jewry. The failure to defeat Great Britain made its realization impossible, and the decision to attack Russia opened the way to a new kind of final solution that was no longer territorial.

Though the Madagascar Plan was stillborn, the episode is not uninstructive. It clearly points up the new position occupied by D III in shaping Jewish policy within the Foreign Office. With Luther's power and access to Ribbentrop, Jewish policy would now be determined within his own division, not by the old guard surrounding Weizsäcker. The plan likewise demonstrates the naive, dilettantish and pseudoscientific nature of Rademacher's anti-Semitism. He drew conclusions from population statistics that were meaningless in the context of Madagascar's terrain and climate. He churned out memoranda in the fervid conviction that paper solutions overcame physical realities. And through it all he warmed himself with the thought that Germany's "generosity" would be demonstrated to the world. Most significant, however, was the Foreign Office acceptance of the principle that a final solution to the European Jewish question was an obligation incumbent upon victorious Germany. When an equally fantastic, though unfortunately more realizable, version of the Final Solution finally emerged, the Foreign Office would not shirk this responsibility.

Finally, the planning surrounding the Madagascar project points up the incipient tensions involved in dealing with the SS on Jewish affairs. To Rademacher, interdepartmental cooperation seemed natural and desirable. To the SS, however, cooperation meant surrendering some of the almost total control they had established in Jewish affairs. Cooperation was thus viewed by them as competition. Since the Madagascar Plan was never put into effect, the differences between Rademacher's and Eichmann's versions of the plan were not resolved. Rademacher did not represent a real threat to SS control, and his willing cooperation could in fact facilitate their work in Jewish affairs. But the SS was reluctant to concede any jurisdiction to the Foreign Office as the price for this cooperation. This uncertainty in the SS attitude toward Rademacher marked the work of D III throughout its first year.

## Emigration and Expulsion

Rademacher's planning for the massive expulsion of European Jewry to Madagascar was the most spectacular of his activities during the first year of his work in *Referat* D III, but the day-to-day work which he had belittled as "the occupation with 1,000 individual decisions over . . . the fate of individual Jews" also continued. One such activity concerned Jewish emigration.

The outbreak of the war severely hampered but did not alter in principle the German policy of furthering Jewish emigration. The Foreign Office urged only that Jewish intellectuals and specialists, who could aid the enemy's propaganda and economy, should be denied emigration approval.[23] The major emigration route, worked out by negotiations among Britain, Italy, the German Foreign Office, and the Gestapo in October 1939, was from Germany through Trieste to Palestine. But in May 1940, obviously contemplating entry into the war against Britain and not wanting German Jews stranded in Trieste when the sea route to Palestine was cut off, Italy refused to issue further transit visas.[26]

Thus Rademacher began his work in D III when the last major route for Jewish emigration closed. Only the tenuous overland routes through eastern Europe and the Soviet Union remained. Rademacher and Eichmann worked together harmoniously to maximize the use of the Soviet route to the Far East. On his side, Rademacher centralized and simplified procedures within the Foreign Office. As almost all emigration was Jewish emigration, Rademacher successfully insisted that D III, not the Far Eastern *Referat* of the Political Division, was competent. Instead of issuing a certificate of nonobjection (*Unbedenklichkeitsbescheinigung*) to each aspiring emigrant who would then seek transit visas from the Berlin embassies of the Soviet Union, Manchuko, and Japan, Rademacher sent lists of the Jewish applicants to the foreign embassies with the recommendation to grant transit visas, once the applicants had been screened to eliminate the politically undesirable emigration of university professors, engineers, and economic specialists.[27] For his part Eichmann likewise centralized the handling of all emigration applications in his own bureau in the Reich Security Main Office (RSHA), where all the necessary papers were filled out and required only a Foreign Office stamp and signature.[28] Thus Eichmann and Rademacher cooperated to create an assembly-line procedure to cut bureaucratic delays and maximize the use of the overland route to the Far East, a route used by several thousand Jews before the German attack on Russia in June 1941.

In his desire to keep open the increasingly threatened emigration routes exclusively for German Jews, Eichmann consistently enlisted Foreign Office support to block the movement of other Jewish emigrants, whether they were ex-German Jews stranded in other European countries or simply foreign Jews wishing to leave Europe.[29] This policy was finally systemized by the RSHA circular of May 20, 1941, signed by Walter Schellenberg in Heydrich's absence, which explicitly prohibited Jewish emigration from Belgium and occupied France, in order not to diminish the already insufficient emigration possibilities for German Jews through Lisbon.[30]

In much of the correspondence between the RSHA and D III concerning Jewish emigration, requests for emigration were rejected "in view of the doubtless imminent final solution of the Jewish question." (*im Hinblick auf die zweifellos kommende Endlösung der Judenfrage*) This stock formulation first appeared in September 1940,[31] and was increasingly used in the spring of 1941. This correspondence, however, only rejected the emigration of Jews from non-German territory and often stated explicitly that Jewish emigration from Germany itself was still the goal of German *Judenpolitik*. The final solution at this time did not yet mean the physical extermination of European Jewry, but rather the immediate creation of a *judenfrei* Germany with the expulsion of Jews from the rest of Europe reserved until after the war.[32]

In matters of Jewish emigration, Rademacher's office played a secondary role to Eichmann's. Rademacher took the initiative in a few cases, such as streamlining Foreign Office procedures for facilitating emigration to the Far East, but most questions that reached Rademacher were simply forwarded to Eichmann for decision. Likewise Rademacher always sought to enlist Foreign Office support for Eichmann's policies. Despite Rademacher's constant cooperation in routine emigration matters, however, Eichmann did not seek his aid or give him prior notice in more drastic measures of expulsion. In these cases, the RSHA acted entirely on its own, despite the inevitable repercussions in the field of foreign policy.

On October 23, 1940, the French delegation to the German Armistice Commission at Wiesbaden delivered a note, complaining that seven trains carrying over 6,000 German citizens had crossed into unoccupied France that morning. The French border guards had no prior warning about the trains and had permitted them to pass in the mistaken belief that they contained Frenchmen expelled from areas of eastern Europe now occupied by Germany. The French government wanted to know what further travel plans the German government had for these expelled German citizens.[33]

This information was forwarded on October 29 to *Abteilung Deutschland*. Luther must have immediately contacted the RSHA for further information, for on the same day he received a personal letter originating from Eichmann's office and signed by Heydrich. Heydrich stated that the Führer had ordered the deportation of all Jews from Baden and Pfalz, and that a total of 6,504 had been sent into unoccupied France without previous notification of the French authorities. The operation had been carried out without friction or incident and was scarcely noticed by the local population.[34] The attempt of Gerhard Todenhöfer, Rademacher's deputy, to find out from the RSHA why the operation had been carried out without informing the French government was unsuccessful. A full report and the request of the German delegation to the Armistice Commission for instructions were forwarded to Ribbentrop. Ribbentrop's initial response was to treat the matter dilatorily.[35]

An anonymous writer informed the Foreign Office of the more gruesome details omitted from the official correspondence, as in fact had occurred once already in the spring of 1940 after the deportation of German Jews from Stettin to Poland. The anonymous report was sent to Friedrich Gaus, who was head of the Legal Division and whose wife was one-quarter Jewish. Gaus forwarded it to Luther, who sent it on through D III to the Gestapo after reading it. The report told how Jews except those in mixed marriage were evacuated, regardless of age, including even a 97-year old woman. Old people's homes were emptied, with many carried to the trains on stretchers. The deportees were given between one-half and two hours to prepare for departure, and at least eleven used the opportunity to commit suicide. The survivors were interned in a French concentration camp in the Pyrenees, without sufficient rations, and would probably be sent to Madagascar by the French government as soon as the sea ways were open. Luther's only reaction was to scribble "very interesting!" by the mention of Madagascar.[36]

Rademacher relayed Ribbentrop's initial instructions to stall the matter at the Armistice Commission.[37] But the French delegation returned to the question every day, and the German delegation under General Stülpnagel became exasperated at receiving no further instructions from the Foreign Office.[38] In response to these pleas for further instructions, Rademacher prepared a draft instruction for Luther, along with a supporting memorandum. In his view the affair could no longer be treated with silence from the German side. He therefore suggested that the question be handled not in Wiesbaden through the Armistice Commission but in Paris privately by the German ambassador, Otto Abetz. The French must stop insisting on Germany's taking the 6,000 Jews back. Instead they should collect them in camps and deport them overseas when the opportunity arose. Germany had no further interest in their fate, and insofar as individual Jews were capable of work, the French could induct them into construction labor.[39] Rademacher's suggestion was not put into effect, however, as further instructions from the foreign minister's staff finally arrived the following day, November 22. Ribbentrop merely reiterated his earlier decision that the matter be handled dilatorily and emphasized that the return of the expellees to Germany was excluded under any conditions.[40]

On November 30, 1940, the Foreign Office was alerted that the French delegation to the Armistice Commission had complained that yet another train, this one carrying some 280 Luxemburg Jews, had attempted to cross the demarcation line into unoccupied France. This time, however, the French authorities had not been caught by surprise, and the train was turned back. The Foreign Office did not get the full story until the Army High Command (OKH) forwarded a report from the military administration in Bordeaux more than a month later. The Luxemburg Jews desired to emigrate to America through Portugal, a desire supported by the RSHA. As was the case with Italy before May 1940, the German Foreign Office had negotiated an agreement that Jews could emigrate through Portugal, but the Germans had to take them back if embarkation in Lisbon was not possible. In this case the train of Luxemburg Jews reached Portugal on November 14 and was sent back from Portugal on November 19. The train returned to Bayonne, where the commander of the SS-*Sonderkommando,* a man named Hagen, declared he had exclusive control over the further treatment of the Luxemburg Jews. Hagen sent the train toward unoccupied France on November 26, but it was turned back by French authorities. The Jews were now stuck in Bayonne, and the military administration had declared their continued presence an intolerable threat to security. Hagen had told the army that negotiations were under way with Portugal to take the Jews back once again but were not yet concluded. The army thus requested assistance from the Foreign Office to remove the Jews as soon as possible.[41]

In early December 1940, Rademacher had contacted SS-*Hauptscharführer* (staff sergeant) Hartmann on Eichmann's staff about the Luxemburg Jews. Hartmann had gone so far as to admit that the Security Policy stationed in Luxemburg had blundered. The RSHA was in constant telephone contact with the Luxemburg Security Police, and the problem would have to be straightened out from there.[42] Deluged by telegrams from the Armistice Commission and the army, including a report that yet another 38 Luxemburg Jews had been infiltrated into unoccupied France with German assistance, Rademacher repeatedly sought further explanations from the RSHA.[43] After nearly three months of disdainful silence, the RSHA replied on February 28, 1941, that most of the Jews in Bayonne were gone and the departure of the rest could be reckoned with in a short time. After two further inquiries the RSHA replied cryptically at the end of March that the affair of the Luxemburg Jews in Bayonne was settled. There were no more Luxemburg Jews there to cross the demarcation line.[44]

The OKH confirmed that all the Luxemburg Jews in Bayonne were gone. Hagen's SS-*Sonderkommando* in Bordeaux had simply sneaked them over the Spanish border and the demarcation line in small groups until the entire trainload was dispersed.[45] Wearied by the constant French complaints, the Foreign Office representative to the Armistice Commission asked D III to find out if further deportations could be expected. Eichmann's office did not reply until July 7, 1941, but then stated that the deportations of Jews from Luxemburg, Baden, and Pfalz had been "special individual measures" (*besondere Einzelmassnahmen*). These *Aktionen* were concluded, and no further deportations to unoccupied France would be carried out.[46]

Over the six-month period from October 1940 through March 1941, the RSHA was expelling Jews into unoccupied France. These expulsions were carried out in secret, not only from the French but also from the other agencies of the German government.[47] Nonetheless, the Foreign Office remained relatively well informed, particularly through reports from the Armistice Commission and the military administration in Bordeaux. Moreover, as the bureau in charge of watching over the repercussions of German *Judenpolitik* abroad, D III continually received clippings from the foreign press. Rademacher was thus aware of the hunger and privation in the internment camps in southern France, where the Jews from Baden and Pfalz had been sent.[48] D III's sources of information extended into other areas as well. The Foreign Office liaison man to the General Government reported the expulsion of 50,000 Jews from Cracow.[49] And when deportations from Vienna to Poland were undertaken in early 1941, D III learned of it from press clippings and once again from an anonymous letter writer, presumably the same one that had given such graphic details over the Stettin and Baden-Pfalz deportations in 1940.[50] While the RSHA did not give prior information to the Foreign Office about its various expulsion measures, whether into France or elsewhere, these measures did not remain secret.

In routine measures of emigration, the RSHA sought Foreign Office help, but in the more drastic measures of expulsion, it apparently felt that Foreign Office participation would be more of a hindrance. As a result, the expulsion program was short-lived. The first massive expulsion of Jews from Baden and Pfalz was successful only because it took the French by surprise. Thereafter the French were prepared to turn back Jewish transports at the demarcation line. Without an agreement negotiated by the Foreign Office and backed by the power of the German army, the SS was in no position to force the French to accept further transports. On its own, the RSHA could still carry out piecemeal infiltration of Jews into unoccupied France, but this rid them of only a very small number of Jews for a disproportionately large effort. No wonder that by the summer of 1941, the RSHA was willing to state that no further expulsions would be attempted. They were now beginning to think in terms of deportations in the opposite direction. In these deportations, however, they would no longer act alone. The Jewish experts of the Foreign Office would be drawn into the operation.

### Jewish Legislation

The Foreign Office had little to say about the formulation of legislation concerning German Jews. It could offer an opinion whether the expected internal political benefits were in reasonable proportion to possible external disadvantages, such as propaganda exploitation by enemy states.[51] But these observations were seldom decisive. On the other hand, the extension of German influence into other parts of Europe by virtue of German military success offered the opportunity, in certain cases, for the Foreign Office to play a more decisive role in shaping Jewish legislation beyond German borders. The Foreign Office was virtually never consulted about internal measures in Poland and Norway. It might have had much greater room for maneuver in Germany's satellite, Slovakia, as well as in the newly occupied western territories (Belgium, the Netherlands, and France). These opportunities were not effectively utilized, however.

*Slovakia.*    In March 1939, Hitler had successfully encouraged the Slovaks to secede from Czechoslovakia as part of his campaign to destroy that state. As a result Slovakia was rewarded with the quasi-independent status of a satellite, while the Czech lands were directly ruled as the Protectorate of Bohemia and Moravia. The Germans initially hoped that Slovakia would be a showcase of the benefits of cooperation with the Third Reich to the other countries of southeastern Europe. However, the victories in the west enabled Germany to place less value upon the external appearance of independence in Slovakia, where a movement for greater autonomy, led by Ferdinand Durcansky (minister of both interior and foreign affairs) was gaining the upper hand over the chief German collaborators, Prime Minister Vojtech Tuka and Sano Mach. In June 1940, Foreign Office troubleshooter Manfred von Killinger was dispatched to Bratislava, where he recommended the ouster of Durcansky, the elevation of the pro-German Hlinka Guard faction, and the establishment of German advisers to control the Slovak government. After Hitler met with the Slovak leadership in Salzburg in late July, Durcansky was replaced by Mach as minister of the interior, Tuka took over the Foreign Ministry, and Killinger was named ambassador to Slovakia, charged by Ribbentrop with setting up the system of German advisers.[52] Killinger wanted the advisers installed in the embassy, not in the Slovak government. They were to be directly subordinate to him and paid by the Foreign Office. Among the first advisers he requested was one for the Jewish question.[53]

If Killinger had dreams of himself as a Slovak "Protector," he was soon disillusioned, for the adviser system did not develop as he had envisaged. The various advisers were paid by the sponsoring German agencies, not by the Foreign Office. In October 1940, Heydrich insisted to Luther that the SS-advisers in Slovakia be subordinate to the police adviser, Dr. Hahn, not directly to the ambassador. In particular, this included the adviser for the Jewish question, because, as Heydrich explained to Luther, all Jewish questions were being handled in the RSHA.[54] Dieter Wisliceny, a close friend of Adolf Eichmann, was chosen for the position, which further enhanced direct communication between the Jewish adviser and the RSHA. Wisliceny and the other advisers took their orders from their superiors in Berlin; the Foreign Office served only as postman.[55] Thus Germany exerted a strong influence on the shaping of Jewish legislation in Slovakia, but it was exercised through Dieter Wisliceny and the RSHA, not through the Foreign Office Jewish experts in *Abteilung Deutschland.*

Though Ribbentrop and Killinger had created the adviser system, it did not work to their benefit. The more the Foreign Office facilitated German encroachment upon the sovereignty of satellites like Slovakia, the more other internal German agencies could work directly with collaborators in these satellites, and the less important became the role of the Foreign Office. In Slovakia in particular, the German embassy became so insignificant that Martin Bormann suggested replacing it with a *Generalresident* to act as a counterweight to SS hegemony there.[56]

*France.* Defeated France had been divided into occupied and unoccupied zones by the armistice agreement of June 1940. A German military administration governed the former zone, while the new French government resided at Vichy in the latter. The Foreign Office maintained its presence in France through the Paris embassy under Otto Abetz. Upon explicit orders of the Führer, he was responsible for the treatment of all political questions in both the occupied and unoccupied zones, though he was to consult with the military administration when his political tasks touched military interests.[57] Abetz, an early member of Bureau Ribbentrop, was not one of the *Altkämpfer,* whom he allegedly characterized as "scoundrels, Balkan-types, racial sub-humans." Though an honorary SS-officer, he was no favorite of Himmler's, who wrote Ribbentrop, "In contrast to you, I do not look upon Abetz as a good but as a bad and dangerous man."[58] In Abetz, the Foreign Office appeared to have a man who could hold his own.

Indeed, it was Abetz, not the SS, who took the initiative in attacking the Jewish question in France. In late August 1940, he requested Foreign Office agreement to the immediate implementation of Jewish legislation to serve as a foundation for the later removal of the Jews from France. No Jews were to be permitted to return over the demarcation line from unoccupied to occupied France. All Jews in the occupied territory were to be subjected to compulsory registration. All Jewish businesses in occupied France were to be marked. Trustees were to be appointed for all Jewish businesses whose owners had fled. Abetz felt these measures should be carried out by the French authorities and later extended to unoccupied France.[59]

Luther and Rademacher did not grant Abetz the immediate consent he had requested. Instead they consulted both Himmler's and Göring's staffs.[60] Rademacher and *Reichsoberbankinspector* Hoppe of the Four-Year Plan discussed Abetz's proposals and agreed that they were not advisable. The reasoning behind this decision was not given.[61] After waiting one month, Luther finally received Heydrich's opinion. He had no objection to the proposed measures, nor to their being carried out through the French authorities. But it was "indispensable" that the German Security Police in France, with their extensive experience in Jewish affairs, be utilized. The activities could be carried out by the French police, but should be controlled by the Security Police, with whom the French police were in close touch.[62]

Rademacher drafted a very cautious response for Luther to send to Abetz, which gave Abetz discretion but no encouragement. It said that the expediency of the measures against the Jews in occupied France could not be judged from Berlin. It was important that the psychological preparation for such measures be ready, in order not to achieve quite the opposite of the desired effect. Above all the measures should be carried out by the Vichy government, which would carry the responsibility in case of failure. No mention was made of Heydrich's insistence upon an expanded role for the Security Police in these measures.[63]

In fact Abetz and the military administration in France had not waited for Luther's reply of September 28. The day before it was sent off, the chief of the military administration, obviously with Abetz's consent, issued the proposed measures, which made no exception in the case of foreign citizenship. The field commanders, however, were secretly instructed to exempt American Jews. Rudolf Schleier, Abetz's deputy, requested the position of the Foreign Office on the measures that had been taken, and instructions for the treatment of foreign Jews.[64] Caught by surprise, Luther belatedly relayed Heydrich's demand for the extensive participation of the Security Police.[65]

In Slovakia, Killinger had requested an adviser for the Jewish question. In France, Abetz had taken the initiative in proposing Jewish legislation. Yet the Foreign Office did not utilize these opportunities to gain a decisive role in formulating Jewish legislation in the expanding sphere of German influence. Luther offered no resistance to Heydrich when he made the Jewish adviser in Slovakia a means for bypassing the Foreign Office and exercising direct RSHA influence upon Slovak Jewish measures. Likewise Luther reacted very hesitantly to Abetz's initiatives in France, with the result that the dominant role in shaping Jewish legislation fell to the military administration and Security Police. It is less surprising that Rademacher did not exert himself. He looked down upon local legislative matters as mundane, in comparison to his plans for the Madagascar Project. But this passivity on Luther's part, given his sensitivity to questions of jurisdiction and competence, is surprising. Perhaps he was still so absorbed in laying the foundations of his empire within the Foreign Office that he was left no time or energy for contesting outside his agency.

*The Homefront.* Indeed, it was only against rivals within the Foreign Office that Luther had any success in exerting control over Jewish policy at this time. After the Jewish measures in France were announced, a number of countries indicated their displeasure. Ribbentrop thereupon reversed the decision of the military administration to grant American Jews special treatment, declaring that it would be an error to reject the claims of friendly nations like Spain and Hungary on the one hand and show weakness vis-à-vis the American claims on the other.[66] The military was alarmed and wrote directly to Weizsäcker, warning of the effects it might have on German property in America. Weizsäcker, more passive than usual, simply asked *Abteilung Deutschland* to draft a reply affirming the personal decision of the foreign minister.[67]

In Germany itself a very unsystematic arrangement had evolved for the treatment of foreign Jews, because each case was decided individually. In some matters all foreign Jews had been exempted, but as various European countries adopted anti-Semitic legislation of their own or were defeated by Germany, their Jews were no longer granted special treatment. In other matters, only the Jews of certain politically sensitive countries were exempted. Thus, on the basis of Ribbentrop's decision against favored treatment for American Jews in France, Rademacher proposed to simplify the whole system of foreign exemptions in Germany by treating all Jews alike, regardless of nationality.[68]

Rademacher circulated his proposal through the Foreign Office, where the American *Referent* Freytag and the heads of the Political and Economic Divisions, Woermann and Wiehl, all protested the inclusion of American Jews.[69] Rademacher was unmoved from his hardline, but Luther overruled him and formulated a compromise proposal to submit to the foreign minister. On the basis of Ribbentrop's earlier decision that it was not suitable to reject the claims of friendly countries while giving special treatment to American Jews and in response to the passage of Lend-Lease, the Foreign Office would raise no objection to the wholesale cancellation of special treatment for foreign Jews in Germany, but with one exception. In the question of the property of foreign Jews, the Foreign Office must continue to insist upon a case-by-case examination to check whether reprisals against German property abroad was to be feared.[70] Luther's compromise was accepted by Ribbentrop and became official Foreign Office policy in June 1941.[71]

As the old guard had previously decided the delicate question of the application of Jewish legislation to foreign Jews, Luther's success in this matter indicated a shift in power over Jewish policy within the Foreign Office in his favor. Rademacher's centralization of all Foreign Office activities relating to Jewish emigration within D III as well as his authorization to prepare the Madagascar Plan were likewise part of this trend. Concerning Foreign Office relations to other German agencies regarding the Jewish question, however, Luther and Rademacher were not so successful. Rademacher's Madagascar Plan was practically brushed aside by the RSHA. Heydrich's outfit also undertook expulsions into unoccupied France, a matter clearly within the prerogative of the Foreign Office, without any prior consultation with it. Opportunities to influence Jewish policy in Slovakia and occupied France were allowed to slip by. In short, the first year of Luther's and Rademacher's involvement in Jewish affairs was not very significant outside the confines of the Foreign Office.

# 5. Launching the Final Solution: From the Invasion of Russia Through the Wannsee Conference (June 1941–March 1942)

### First Exposure

The *Einsatzgruppen* operations which commenced with the invasion of Russia in June 1941 represented a fatal turning point in German Jewish policy. Systematic killing was being tried for the first time as a final solution to the Jewish question. The Foreign Office was not officially informed of the *Einsatzgruppen* campaign either prior to or immediately following the invasion of Russia. As earlier, however, the Foreign Office was in a position to gather unofficial information. In this case, the first signs of a drastic change in German Jewish policy emanated from the embassy in Rumania, the Foreign Office "window" on the eastern front.

The German ambassador in Rumania was Manfred von Killinger, a leading SA-man who had narrowly escaped execution at the hands of the SS during the Röhm affair in 1934. He had been transferred from Slovakia to Rumania in early 1941. Killinger was viewed by many of his own staff as quite incompetent, but his relations with the SS were understandably even worse. In particular the Jewish adviser assigned to the Bucharest embassy, SS-*Hauptsturmführer* Gustav Richter, frequently tried to make difficulties for him.[1] In early August 1941, without warning or explanation, Reinhard Heydrich ordered the recall of Richter (as well as the Jewish adviser in Bratislava, Dieter Wisliceny). Under pressure from the Rumanian government, Killinger was put in the awkward position of requesting via Luther the reinstatement of the insubordinate Richter.[2] Though it may have galled him, Luther composed an obsequious letter to be sent "immediately by motorcycle driver" to Heydrich. Having consulted neither Ribbentrop nor Weizsäcker, Luther declared that the Foreign Office gave its "warmest support" to the requests of Killinger and Hans Ludin, the new ambassador to Slovakia, to have the Jewish advisers remain at their posts.[3]

Heydrich's reply indicated that Wisliceny's reinstatement merely awaited the outcome of negotiations between the Foreign Office and the SS on the question of police liaison officers (*Polizeiverbindungsführer*) to be assigned to the embassies of pro-German countries. Wisliceny was thus nothing more than a pawn in these negotiations.[4] On the other hand, Heydrich specifically opposed the return of a Jewish adviser to Rumania because the Rumanian government showed no unified attitude toward the Jewish problem. "The actions of the Rumanians in the newly occupied territories repeatedly displayed a strong friendliness to the Jews" (*starke Judenfreundlichkeit*). In fact, reports concerning Rumanian anti-Jewish activities that Heydrich was receiving did not characterize them as pro-Jewish but as haphazard and unsystematic. Thus Heydrich not only wanted to strengthen Richter's hand vis-à-vis Killinger, but hoped also to force the Rumanians to adopt more systematic, German-like measures to vindicate themselves of the accusation of pro-Jewish behavior.[5]

In sharp contrast to Heydrich's charge of Rumanian *Judenfreundlichkeit* was the picture portrayed by reports from the Bucharest embassy at this time. Chief of State Ion Antonescu's call-up of 60,000 Jews for road construction in Bessarabia had caused havoc in the economy, due to the lack of suitable substitutes for these Jews, and also threatened German windfalls from ayranization because Jewish sellers were no longer around to turn over their impounded goods to German purchasers. Thus Killinger had prevailed upon Deputy Premier Mihai Antonescu to retract the measure and proceed with the elimination of Jews from the economy only slowly and systematically.[6]

If Rumanian economic measures against the Jews were too radical for German interests, Rumanian opposition to an influx of Jews from the east into their territory was also not lacking in zeal. In August 1941, Ion Antonescu repeatedly complained that the German army was dumping Jews across the Dniester River into Bessarabia, "which contradicts the guidelines for the treatment of the eastern Jews which the Führer had given him [Antonescu] in Munich." It also contradicted an agreement reached with the German adviser to the Rumanian Interior Ministry, SS-*Brigadeführer* Pflaumer, to free Rumania of alien and communist elements.[7] The 11th Army countered that it was the Rumanians who had driven Jews eastward over the Dniester, and therefore *Einsatzgruppe* D had merely been instructed to drive them back again.[8] The issue was resolved on August 31, 1941, when German and Rumanian military authorities signed the Tighina Agreement. It turned over administration of Transnistria (the territory between the Dniester and Bug Rivers) to Rumania, but prohibited any deportation of Jews from there over the Bug River into the German-occupied Ukraine at that time. The Jews of Transnistria were to be collected in concentration camps and set to work until deportation to the east was possible after the end of operations.[9] Under this agreement, therefore, the whole area between the Dniester and Bug Rivers was opened to the Rumanians as a dumping ground for their Jews, an opportunity they did not long neglect.

In addition to these incidents, Killinger cited other facts to counter Heydrich's accusation of Rumanian *Judenfreundlichkeit.* "The Jews were exposed to unheard-of persecution (*unerhörter Verfolgung*) on the Rumanian border," he noted. Among other things, 4,000 Jews had been killed in Jassy. Moreover, the Rumanians had accepted Richter's draft legislation and requested his return. Killinger suggested that the Foreign Office should seek a Jewish adviser from somewhere else than the SS in order to avoid further unpleasantness from Heydrich.[10] However, Luther ignored this advice and twice more urged Heydrich to relent. Finally, both Wisliceny and Richter returned to their posts.[11]

Thus by early September Luther and Rademacher had still received no official information on German Jewish policy in the eastern territories. But they knew that many Jews had been shot in Rumania, and they had been told that Antonescu, in cooperation with the two German advisers from the SS, Richter and Pflaumer, was planning to deport the surviving Jews and other "alien elements" to Transnistria. From Killinger's account they knew that the Jews in this border area were suffering "unheard-of persecution." Yet they also knew that Heydrich professed to feel that these Rumanian actions displayed strong *Judenfreundlichkeit.* If Rumanian behavior was "friendly," the SS policy toward the Jews could only be worse.

Hints and rumors over the new *Judenpolitik* were not restricted to the hard-core Nazis of *Abteilung Deutschland.* Weizsäcker was informed of the *Einsatzgruppen* atrocities "at a rather early time" by Admiral Canaris, head of military intelligence.[12] Thus he could not have been too surprised at the contents of a suggestion forwarded to him by Ernst Bohle of the *Auslandsorganisation* from a subordinate of his named Hübner, dated September 5, 1941. Hübner was upset by the mistreatment that Germans were suffering in North and South America, caused "of course" by Jews and Freemasons. Such mistreatment would stop if suitable propaganda were made over German reprisals. The Jews and Freemasons of the world knew "that we don't treat the Jews with kid gloves and that in the east already many a Jew no longer lives." The Jew-oriented governments ought to be informed that the Jews still alive could have it much worse. This would have the desired effect, especially in view of the "tempting offers" made by American Jews when they heard of the "mass killings" (*Massentötung*) of Jews in Rumania at Jassy and in Bessarabia. Weizsäcker circulated Hübner's memorandum among the old guard, and no one indicated surprise at the information it contained. However, Weizsäcker withheld it from *Abteilung Deutschland.*[13]

Rumors of significant change in German Jewish policy reached as far as South America at this time. The Montevideo embassy wrote on September 2, expressing objection to the possible emigration of a teacher from Warsaw who might strengthen Jewish propaganda "on the basis of her insight into the newest developments of the Jewish question in eastern Europe."[14]

Precisely when the Foreign Office was beginning to learn of these newest developments in eastern Europe, it also learned of an intensification of domestic persecution as well. On August 21, 1941, Rademacher received a telephone call from Eichmann, who confidentially informed Rademacher that Hitler had just approved the marking of Jews in Germany. Eichmann wanted to know if foreign Jews could be included. Rademacher reported the conversation to Luther and suggested proposals to be submitted to Ribbentrop for final decision. Jews from occupied countries were to be marked immediately. Agreement would be sought from friendly European governments, which would also be urged to carry out similar measures of their own. Once agreement had been secured, the marking regulations could be formally extended to all Jews, with non-European Jews exempted by internal instructions. The expected protests of European neutrals like Switzerland and Sweden were to be ignored. Heydrich reacted favorably to these proposals, and Luther then submitted them to Ribbentrop.[15]

On August 29, 1941, an interministerial conference was held in the Interior Ministry to finalize the marking ordinance. Rademacher had not yet received a reply from Ribbentrop but attended the conference anyway. No exception for foreign Jews was made in the text of the law, but the police were authorized to exempt through internal instruction those groups of foreign Jews requested by the Foreign Office.[16] Two days later Ribbentrop's decision arrived, postponing the marking of any foreign Jews for the moment. Luther was to resubmit his proposals in six weeks.[17]

The marking ordinance was published on September 5, but the anonymous letter writer obviously had an inside source of information. On August 30, just one day after the conference, the Foreign Office received two letters complaining that people who had been Christians for several generations as well as front veterans were being branded as common criminals. Once again, however, the Gestapo could not find the sender.[18]

The anonymous letter writer was much better informed than Weizsäcker, for all correspondence over marking had passed directly between Luther and Ribbentrop's staff. Weizsäcker wrote to Luther on September 15 that he had been asked whether the marking law had been issued in agreement with the Foreign Office. Weizsäcker had replied that he knew nothing of any consultation with the Foreign Office but now asked Luther if in fact the Foreign Office had been consulted without the matter's ever being submitted to the state secretary. Luther answered that he had learned verbally from Heydrich about the Führer's decision, that the conference had been called and the ordinance issued very quickly, and that he had informed the foreign minister directly because speedy action was required. Weizsäcker frostily told Luther to adhere to official channels in the future.[19]

Thus in late August and early September various members of the Foreign Office received many indications of an intensification of German Jewish policy. Since Luther and Weizsäcker seemed more intent on withholding information from one another than pooling it, neither *Abteilung Deutschland* nor the old guard received a complete picture. Moreover, the Foreign Office was not directly involved in any significant way yet. It was consulted about the marking of Jews only after the basic decision had been made; it had received reports from both the army and the Bucharest embassy on events in Rumania, but again only after the fact. However, the days of Foreign Office detachment from the Final Solution were at an end. When the Jewish question became acute in Serbia, an area within which the Foreign Office was still striving to make its influence felt, it was drawn into the decision-making process.

## Rademacher in Serbia

Germany had invaded Yugoslavia on April 6, 1941, and the quickly conquered state had been dismembered. Macedonia was awarded to the cooperating Bulgarians; Slovenia was annexed to the Third Reich; Hungary received the Backa and Baranja; Croatia and Montenegro became satellite states; and the Dalmatian coast became an Italian zone of occupation. Serbia, the old core of Yugoslavia, remained as a German zone under military administration. In addition, a Foreign Office plenipotentiary, Felix Benzler, was installed by Ribbentrop to handle all questions emerging in Serbia that touched upon foreign affairs, especially to prevent activity of Serbian political elements that was detrimental to German interests. Jews and Freemasons were as usual included in the political elements to be watched.[20] From the very beginning, not only Benzler but also Rademacher was involved in settling the Jewish question in Serbia. In May 1941, Rademacher had flown to Belgrade to attend a conference on the Jewish question at which he successfully insisted on Foreign Office guidelines for handling the property of foreign Jews.[21]

When the Yugoslav partisan war broke out in the summer of 1941, Benzler recommended to the Foreign Office in mid-August that his operations against Serbian nationalists be subordinated to an all-out struggle against the communists. A simultaneous attack on both communists and nationalists would lead to a united front, while a precondition for success against the communists was the support of the Serbian people and the help of the Serbian police. "As an immediate measure I have demanded the sharpest proceedings against captured communists as well as generally against Jews, who incontestably cooperate with the communists. In addition to this I request the decision, whether the deportation of the Jews can take place down the Danube or to the General Government."[22]

Benzler's first request for a decision to deport the Serbian Jews was ignored. But the general tenor of Benzler's letter, urging close cooperation with Serbian nationalists, fired Luther's mistrust. He did not like Benzler in the first place. Now he suspected him of trying to create a Serbian government, to which he could be appointed a regular ambassador.[23]

Ribbentrop sent Edmund Veesenmayer to look into the partisan activities in Serbia.[24] On September 8, 1941, Veesenmayer and Benzler together repeated the request to ship at least all the male Jews, some 8,000, downriver to an island in the Danube delta within Rumanian territory.[25] Two days later they sent an even more urgent request. "Quick and draconic settlement of the

Serbian Jewish question is the most urgent and expedient requirement. Request appropriate instruction from the foreign minister to be able to exert the most extreme pressure upon the military commander in Serbia."[26]

The impetus for these two appeals in September to deport the 8,000 male Jews from Serbia came from an unlikely source, Dr. Harald Turner, the chief of the military administration but also a high-ranking SD officer. In the course of the partisan war in Serbia, hostages had frequently been shot, including many Jews.[27] Turner approached Benzler and asked him to help arrange the deportation of the male Jews to Rumania, otherwise they would all be shot as hostages.[28] It must be kept in mind that Turner's proposal to deport the Jews did not mean their death. At this time the death camps had not yet been constructed in Poland, and Turner preferred deportation to Rumania, outside immediate German control, in any case. The real danger to Jews at this time was to reside in military and partisan areas, where army and SS units could shoot them as hostages or under the guise of antipartisan activities. Turned needed Benzler's help because deportations to Rumania touched upon foreign affairs and thus lay within the competency of the Foreign Office. Moreover Turner did not wish to reveal any lack of "toughness" on the Jewish question, which might be reported to Heydrich and Himmler to the detriment of his career, so he used Benzler as a stalking horse. The suggestion for deportation would come from the Foreign Office, not from Turner himself.

The Foreign Office knew that previous attempts to dump Jews in France and Rumania had been bitterly contested. Moreover, the Foreign Office had accepted the policy of forcing other countries to keep their Jews, as a means of facilitating the creation of a *judenfrei* Germany. Wholesale deportations from other areas, soon to be a major goal of Foreign Office Jewish policy, was not yet a welcome suggestion. Upon receipt of the September 8th telegram from Belgrade, Woermann, head of the Political Division, turned the matter over to *Abteilung Deutschland* with the instruction that deportation to Rumania was out of the question because of the adverse effect it would have on Rumanian relations.[29] Luther then talked by telephone with Ribbentrop, who likewise rejected deportation to Rumania.[30] Therefore Rademacher drafted a reply on September 9, sent on the following day, which stated that the deportation of Jews to foreign territory could not be agreed to. "A solution of the Jewish question will not be reached in this way." Instead he proposed putting the Jews into labor camps.[31]

Benzler was not at all satisfied with this suggestion. Because of the partisan activity, the security of the Jews could not be guaranteed. One camp at Sabac, with 1,200 Jews, had been evacuated because it was in a military area where thousands of partisans were active. It was proven, he claimed, that the Jews contributed to the unrest in the country. He repeated his request for the deportation of at least all male Jews to Rumania as the essential precondition for the restoration of order. If this were rejected, the only remaining possibility was immediate deportation to Russia or the General Government. "Otherwise Jewish action must be temporarily postponed, which is contrary to the instructions given me by the foreign minister." Luther instructed

Rademacher to discuss Benzler's second alternative, deportation to the General Government or Russia, with the RSHA.[32]

Rademacher telephoned Eichmann from Luther's office, with the latter present. As Rademacher later recalled:

> I still remember exactly, that I sat across from him [Luther], when I telephoned the RSHA, and that I jotted down handwritten notes about Eichmann's answer and shoved them over to Luther during the telephone conversation. Eichmann said roughly, that the military was responsible for order in Serbia and had to shoot insurgent Jews. To my inquiry he simply repeated "Shoot" and hung up.[33]

Rademacher's handwritten notes stated: "According to the information of *Sturmbannführer* Eichmann RSHA IV D VI [sic] residence in Russia and GG impossible. Not even the Jews from Germany can be lodged there. Eichmann proposes shooting."[34]

Eichmann's proposed solution of shooting was of course a suggestion, not an order. Eichmann had the authority to reject deportation to the General Government or Russia, but not to determine the fate of the Jews, if they remained in Serbia. However, by then he knew very well how the Jewish question was being handled by the *Einsatzgruppen* in Russia, as well as what was planned for the rest of the European Jews in the future. If the army would not give the SS the same leeway in Yugoslavia as in Russia, then the army should do the dirty work themselves.

It was a suggestion, however, that Rademacher could not fully accept just yet. After his telephone call to Eichmann, he prepared a memorandum for Luther. He could not understand the necessity of Benzler's proposal of deporting abroad the 1,200 male Jews evacuated from Sabac.

> In my opinion it must be possible with the necessary toughness and determination to keep the Jews in camps in Serbia. If the Jews there foment unrest as before, they must be proceeded against with intensive martial law. I cannot imagine that the Jews will conspire further, if only a large number of hostages are shot.[35]

While Eichmann wanted the "insurgent" Jews, presumably those in the camps whose deportation to the General Government or Russia he had vetoed, shot, Rademacher felt a large number of hostages would suffice.

Even this was hardly suitable language for a telegram to Benzler that would first go through the official channels of the Foreign Office. Luther thus had Rademacher draft a milder version. Deportation to Russia or the General Government was impossible. By "tough and uncompromising" methods, it must be possible to keep the Jews from spreading unrest. Those already in the camp must serve as hostages for the good behavior of their racial comrades.[36]

The persistent Benzler would not quit. He wrote again from Belgrade on September 28, this time "for the foreign minister personally." He complained that his repeated calls for support for the deportation of all male Jews from Serbia had been rejected, though Ribbentrop had earlier promised him help in getting rid of Jews, Freemasons, and pro-English Serbians, whether to German concentration camps, the General Government, or down the Danube. Not only he, the Foreign Office plenipotentiary, but also the military requested the immediate deportation of the 8,000 male Jews. They could cope with the 20,000 Jewish women and children if the men were sent on barges down the Danube. According to his information, deportation of Jews from Czechoslovakia had already been tried with success.[37]

Luther received his own copy of this telegram to Ribbentrop and discussed it with Rademacher. Neither professed to understand how Benzler could insist on the deportation of 8,000 Jews on one hand and say he was able to cope with the remaining 20,000 on the other.[38] Very irritated, Luther drew up his own memorandum to be submitted through Weizsäcker to Ribbentrop.

> If the military commander is agreed with Benzler to the effect that these 8,000 Jews prevent pacification action in the Serbian Old Kingdom in the first place, then in my opinion the military commander must take care of the immediate elimination of these 8,000 Jews. In other areas other military commanders have dealt with considerably greater numbers of Jews without even mentioning it.

Luther requested authorization to discuss the question with Heydrich, due to return shortly from Prague. "I am convinced that in agreement with him we can come very quickly to a clear solution of this question."[39] From Rademacher's telephone contact with Eichmann and his own recent experience with Heydrich over alleged Rumanian *Judenfreundlichkeit,* Luther could have been under absolutely no illusions as to what a "clear solution" in agreement with Heydrich was going to mean.

Weizsäcker initialed Luther's request for authorization to discuss the question with Heydrich. He did not send it to Ribbentrop, however, for he simultaneously received instructions from the foreign minister. Having received Benzler's last complaint, which reproached him for insufficient support, Ribbentrop now wanted to contact the *Reichsführer-*SS to clarify the question, "whether he could not take over the 8,000 Jews, in order to move them to East Poland or anywhere else."[40] Luther's idea of a "clear solution" and Ribbentrop's belated desire to reopen the deportation question were not at all the same, but Luther had secured his authorization to contact Heydrich. He used it to achieve his own aims, not Ribbentrop's.

Luther's meeting with Heydrich must have taken place almost immediately, for on October 4 he already informed Benzler of its first results. Heydrich and Luther had agreed that a special deputy of the RSHA would come to Belgrade to settle the questions raised in Benzler's telegrams. On October 8, Benzler was informed that the RSHA special deputy would be Eichmann, and that he would be accompanied by none other than Franz Rademacher. A week later Benzler learned that not Eichmann but two of his assistants, *Sturmbannführer* Suhr and *Untersturmführer* Stuschka, would accompany Rademacher.[41]

Other than the agreement to send these representatives from Berlin, there is no written record of the talks between Heydrich and Luther at this time. But according to Rademacher, Luther said that Heydrich had his own sources of information in Serbia, who cast considerable suspicion on Benzler's evaluation of the urgent need to deport Jews. Heydrich, like Luther, had little use for Benzler and called him a "Father Christmas" who did not want to work with the RSHA's local representative, SS-*Standartenführer* Wilhelm Fuchs, chief of the *Staatspolizeistelle* in Belgrade. Both Luther and Heydrich would send a representative to examine the situation.[42]

But Rademacher later summarized the reason for his trip: "Purpose of the service trip was to check on the spot, whether the problem of the 8,000 Jewish agitators, whose deportation had been urged by the embassy, could not be settled on the spot."[43] Rademacher went to Serbia not only to examine the problem but also to work for a local solution. That he was actually ordered to see that the 8,000 Jews were shot was neither likely nor necessary. As the representative of the Foreign Office, he had only to block their deportation. It would then be up to his SS travelling companions, Suhr and Stuschka, to see that the local authorities drew from this the conclusion desired by Luther, Eichmann, and Heydrich. But that Rademacher was unaware not only of the possibility but even the likelihood that all the Jews would be shot was utterly impossible, given his earlier talk with Eichmann and his own suggestion of September 13th to shoot large numbers of hostages.

Rademacher and his two companions left Berlin on October 16, stopped over briefly in Budapest, and arrived in Belgrade on October 18.[44] He first talked with Felix Benzler, who told him how precarious the situation had been in Belgrade because of the partisan uprising. Benzler also disparaged Fuchs, the chief of police in Belgrade, for having supplied him with false information about Freemasons in Serbia. He would have nothing more to do with Fuchs. On the following morning Benzler took Rademacher to see *Staatsrat* Dr. Harald Turner, chief of the military administration.

From Turner, Rademacher learned that the problem of the 8,000 Jews was already three-quarters solved. Through an unexplained mix-up, it turned out that there had only been about 4,000 male Jews, "of which moreover only 3,500 can be shot" because 500 were needed by the police to maintain the ghetto they were planning to build. Of the 3,500 available for shooting, over 2,000 had already been shot in reprisals for attacks on German soldiers. The chief of the OKW (High Command of the Armed Forces), Field Marshall Keitel, had issued an order on September 19, 1941, whereby for every German soldier killed by partisans 50 to 100 communists were to be shot.[45] On October 2, the partisans had ambushed a group of German soldiers, killing and mutilating 21 of them. Two days later, the plenipotentiary commanding general in Serbia, Franz Böhme, ordered reprisals on the 100 to 1 ratio. Turner was "requested to designate 2,100 inmates in the concentration camps Sabac and Belgrade (predominately Jews and communists) and to determine the place and time, as well as burial site."[46] Fifty communists and over 2,000 Jews were shot. On October 10, 1941, Böhme expanded this order. All communists and suspected communists, all Jews, and a certain number of nationalistically and democratically inclined inhabitants were to be seized. One hundred were to be shot for every German soldier killed and 50 for each one wounded.[47] Thus it was General Böhme who took Keitel's reprisal order, which mentioned only communists, and turned it on the incarcerated Jews. Just as Luther had previously hoped, the military was eliminating the Jews without even mentioning it.

The problem of the remaining 1,500 Jews would have solved itself if Turner had simply turned them over to the army firing squads. Two further attacks had occurred, which by Böhme's ratios together required over 4,000 reprisal shootings. To the army the problem now was not that there were too many Jews but that there were too few. They were continually short of the required number of hostages, because the partisans defied capture. Moreover, at least some of the lower officers were reluctant to round up Serbs in the towns, for many of the townspeople had cooperated with the army and welcomed protection against the communists. The mass execution of pro-German townsmen would have a "catastrophic psychological effect" and lead to even more trouble for the German army.[48] The simplest course for the army, since they could not catch communists, was to shoot Jews who had been incarcerated since early September and in no way could have participated in the partisan attacks.

But one obstacle stood in the way of the quick dispatch of the remaining 1,500 Jews eligible for execution, and this was *Staatsrat* Turner. In September he had tried to arrange the deportation of the male Jews through Benzler. When this had failed, he resigned himself to their execution. On October 17, one day before Rademacher's arrival, he wrote the Higher SS and Police Leader in Danzig, Richard Hildebrandt:

> That the devil is loose here you probably know. . . . Five weeks ago I put the first 600 against the wall, since then in one mopping-up operation we did in another 2,000, in a further operation again some 1,000 and in between I had 2,000 Jews and 200 Gypsies shot in accordance with the quota 1:100 for bestially murdered German soldiers, and a further 2,200, likewise almost all Jews, will be shot in the next 8 days. This is not a pretty business. At any rate, it has to be, if only to make clear what it means even to attack a German soldier, and, for the rest, the Jewish question solves itself most quickly in this way. Actually, it is false, if one has to be precise about it, that for murdered Germans—on whose account the ratio 1:100 should really be born by Serbs—100 Jews are shot instead; but the Jews we had in the camps—after all, they too are Serb nationals, and besides, they have to disappear. At any rate, I don't have to accuse myself that on my part there has been any lack of necessary ruthless action for the preservation of German prestige and the protection of members of the German armed forces.[49]

But when Rademacher arrived, Turner saw the chance once again to push for the deportation of the male Jews. He expressed to Rademacher his bitterest disappointment that Benzler's first cries for help had been ignored. Rademacher dutifully discharged his obligations, explaining why the Jews could not have been sent to either Rumania, the General Government, or Russia. "*Staatsrat* Turner could not close his mind to these reasons. However he urged as before the deportation of the rest of the Jews from Serbia."

Unable as yet to overcome Turner's insistence on deportation, Rademacher went on to visit Turner's expert for Jewish affairs in the military administration, SS-*Sturmbannführer* Weinmann, and then to the chief of police, Wilhelm Fuchs, and his entourage of Jewish experts. They explained to him that orders by Hitler, Keitel, and Böhme were already at hand, whereby extensive reprisal shootings could be carried out. The problem of the male Jews could be settled within a week by having them shot as hostages. Already the number of incarcerated Jews did not suffice. They assured Rademacher that the Jews had participated in the uprising and carried out acts of sabotage. To climax his presentation, Fuchs drove Rademacher out to an open grave and showed him mutilated bodies of German soldiers who had been tortured to death by the partisans. Fuchs then invited Rademacher to come to a meeting next morning between the SS people and Turner, to which Rademacher agreed.

On the following morning of October 20, Rademacher met with Turner, Fuchs, Weinmann, and his travelling companion from Berlin, Friedrich Suhr. At the meeting Rademacher once again explained that foreign policy considerations made a deportation to Rumania impossible. Suhr explained that there was neither means of transportation to Poland or Russia nor any possibility of lodging the Jews there. Fuchs then once again proposed to have the Jews shot within the framework of the reprisals ordered by General Böhme. Faced with this united front, Turner made no objection. Rademacher could thus report: "The male Jews will be shot by the end of the week, so that the problem broached in the embassy's report is settled."

If the problem of the male Jews was solved, there still remained the 20,000 women, children, and old people, whom the army was not prepared to shoot as hostages. The SS men wanted to collect them in a ghetto in the old gypsy quarter of Belgrade, but Turner said that this was a center of epidemic and had to be burnt down for hygienic reasons. The surviving Jews as well as gypsies would be collected in the gypsy quarter but then moved to the island of Mitrovica. "Then as soon as the technical possibility exists within the framework of the total solution of the Jewish question, the Jews will be deported by waterway to the reception camp in the east." This was the first occasion that Rademacher had heard of a plan involving reception camps in the east in connection with the Final Solution. It obviously made an impression on him, otherwise he would not have mentioned it in his report written five days later.

Rademacher left Belgrade the morning of October 21, stayed over three days in Budapest, and arrived in Berlin the morning of October 25. By his own account he visited a friend where they drank an entire bottle of cognac, and he then wrote his report in an inebriated state. When he filled out his travel expenses form, he wrote next to purpose of business: "liquidation of Jews in

Belgrade" and conversations in Budapest.[50] Luther severely censored the portion of Rademacher's report which made a very negative evaluation of Benzler and Turner in comparison with Fuchs and Weinmann, who from the beginning had optimistically assessed the possibility of a local solution to the entire question. But Luther left completely intact Rademacher's account of the solution of the Jewish question in Belgrade.

Luther did not pass the report on to Weizsäcker until November 7. But word had already gotten around the Foreign Office. Von Hassell wrote on November 1:

> Hans Berndt Häften gave me a gruesome example of the Nazi way of "governing." Benzler, the German Counselor in Belgrade, had desperately inquired what to do with the 8,000 Jews herded together in that city, and made suggestions as to how he thought the problem might be handled. In the Foreign Office (this is, Luther) there was indignation over such softness. Luther got in touch with Heydrich, who immediately sent a "specialist" down to Belgrade to clean out those poor people.[51]

The report itself was widely circulated. Karl-Johann von Schönebeck, a mere assistant in Section VIII of the Legal Division, remembered eleven years later reading it.[52] The episode earned Rademacher the title of "Jew-butcher" (*Judenschlächter*) at least in certain circles within the Foreign Office.[53]

Weizsäcker was not favorably impressed either and asked that Rademacher's report be supplemented with the text of the powers Benzler had received for his duties in Serbia. Rademacher replied that the text was not known, but that Benzler's powers encompassed the entire political sector. On Rademacher's supplement Weizsäcker noted that in his opinion Benzler had exceeded his competency in the treatment of the problem as described in the report. "The same applies in my opinion then also for the Foreign Office," by which Weizsäcker obviously meant Luther and Rademacher themselves.[54]

Weizsäcker did not let the matter drop and discussed it directly with Benzler, who was visiting Berlin at that time. Benzler told Weizsäcker that he was responsible for handling all questions of a foreign policy nature that emerged in Serbia. Weizsäcker then wrote back to Luther that while Benzler and the Foreign Office were justified in concerning themselves with deportations of Jews from Serbia to other countries, it went entirely beyond their task or competency to involve themselves actively in how the competent military and internal authorities coped with the Jewish question within Serbian borders. Weizsäcker instructed Luther to deliver a written reprimand to Benzler.[55]

Benzler, who in fact had nothing to do with the shootings in Belgrade, was caught in the crossfire between Weizsäcker and Luther. Luther realized perfectly well that Weizsäcker's reprimand was really aimed at himself. As he often did when very angry, Luther drafted his own reply. He had received instructions from the foreign minister himself to discuss the entire affair with Heydrich. "I must assume, therefore, that it is in agreement with the foreign minister, when the Foreign Office involved itself in this certainly delicate matter." For this reason and because he considered the matter settled, Luther did not consider it appropriate to write Benzler.[56]

While Weizsäcker was making his rather feeble attempt to assert discipline over Luther, the rest of the program decided upon at the October 20th conference in Belgrade was also encountering difficulties. The island of Mitrovica, which had been intended as the concentration camp for the Jewish women, children, and old people, turned out to be flooded. Benzler then asked the German ambassador to Croatia, Siegfried Kasche, to secure permission to use the exhibition grounds of Semlin, across the river from Belgrade in Croatian territory, for the camp. The Croatians agreed on the condition that the camp was under German and not Serbian administration.[57] Benzler relayed this information to Berlin with the request once again to take the remaining Jews to the east as soon as possible. Rademacher replied on December 8, that this was impossible before spring, for at the moment the deportation of Jews from Germany took precedence.[58]

The Belgrade massacres were not exactly parallel to the Final Solution as it was being carried out in Russia at that time. The executions were carried out by the army within the framework of Keitel's reprisal order, and only the men were shot. In Russia the executions were primarily carried out by *Einsatzgruppen* units, though often with army cooperation and assistance, and they were aimed at all Jews, regardless of age and sex. Though many massacres in Russia were carried out under the guise of antipartisan activities and the commissar order (to execute communist cadres), the *Einsatzgruppen* also operated under an explicit order to exterminate all Jews, an order which as yet had no parallel in Serbia. Thus the Belgrade massacres in themselves were not conclusive evidence to the Foreign Office that such a racial extermination program in fact existed.

Yet the Belgrade massacres marked a turning point for the Foreign Office. For nearly a year the SS had pursued its own Jewish policy, in almost total disregard of the Foreign Office, even when this caused foreign policy complications such as occurred with the expulsion of Jews into France and Rumania. While this may have been caused in part because Luther and Heydrich were not on good personal terms, the most important causes were more likely the belief in the SS that the Foreign Office lacked the requisite "toughness" and its traditional reluctance to share any of its competency. In Serbia, however, the SS did not have sufficient power to deal with the Jewish question on its own. When Luther did display the necessary toughness by coming *unsolicited* to Heydrich and asking his help in forcing the military to shoot the Serbian Jews, a bond of cooperation between the SS and the Foreign Office in the Jewish question was forged.

Luther's decision was crucial. From below, Benzler was merely urging that the Jews be taken out of Serbia. From above Ribbentrop had asked Luther to contact the SS in order to see if the Jews could not be sent somewhere else. Thus Luther was not succumbing to pressure from others, but was shaping a policy in contradiction to both the guidelines of his superior and the advice of the Foreign Office representative on the spot. Luther knew that many Jews were being shot in the east, though he apparently was not fully aware of the authority for and extent of the genocide policy. Whatever their personal differences, he was like Heydrich in the respect that he wanted "clear solutions." Thus Benzler's incessant requests to get the Jews out of Serbia had precisely the opposite effect from what Benzler desired. Irritated, Luther decided that the simplest solution was to follow Eichmann's earlier suggestion and shoot the Jews on the spot. If Benzler and the military would not do it on their own, Luther would see Heydrich about devising a way to force them into a local solution.

Rademacher was only a pawn in the scheme of Luther and Heydrich. He was sent in part to spy on Benzler and Turner, but more importantly to convey the final and irrevocable veto of any deportations to Rumania. Heydrich's emissaries would do the same concerning any deportations to the General Government or Russia, as well as reinforce Fuchs and Weinmann in urging a local solution. By sealing the Jews in Serbia, they would force the military to take care of the Jews themselves. Moreover, when Rademacher arrived, the task proved to be much simpler than previously expected. The military was no obstacle and in fact clamoring for more Jewish hostages than were available. The sole resistance came from Turner. Rademacher dutifully explained the impossibility of deportation to Rumania to Turner, but he still held out. In fact, Rademacher too may have wavered, for Fuchs and the local SS-men worked hard to explain to him the alleged connection between the Jews and the partisans and even took him to view the mutilated corpses of German soldiers. Thereupon Rademacher agreed to attend the meeting between Turner and the SS-men the following morning, knowing full-well that he would be part of a united front aimed at forcing Turner to hand over 1,500 Jews to be shot as hostages. Thus by the end of October both Luther and Rademacher were not only aware that many Jews were being shot, but also became personally entangled in the killing process for the first time.

How much did Luther and Rademacher know at this time about the process in which they were getting entangled? On July 31, 1941, Heydrich had received the authorization from Göring to prepare the next phase of the Final Solution, which extended the extermination program beyond Russia to the rest of European Jewry.[59] Eichmann was informed shortly thereafter, in the late summer of 1941, as best he could remember.[60] He tipped off Rademacher and Luther that something new was coming, on August 28, 1941, when he added on to the old formulation of "in view of the imminent final solution" the additional phrase "now in preparation."[61] But certainly in early October neither Luther nor Rademacher had any idea that this new Final Solution meant the deportation of Jews from the various countries in Europe. In September Eichmann had confirmed that there was no room for even German Jews in the General Government. Also when Rademacher inquired in Bratislava about rumors that Slovakia was going to expel Jews into Poland,

Ludin had assured him that this was false. The Slovaks were building ghettos on the model of the General Government, on the advice of SS adviser Wisliceny.[62] Neither of these incidents had indicated that the SS had large deportation plans.

Whether Heydrich took Luther into his confidence in October and revealed the ultimate goal of the Final Solution "now in preparation" cannot be determined. One incident at this time is revealing, however. A number of Spanish Jews had been arrested and interned in France. This led the Spanish to suggest the possibility of evacuating all Spanish Jews, some 2,000, from France to Spanish Morocco. Abetz wished to know what attitude he should take to the Spanish offer. On October 13, 1941, Luther prepared a memorandum on the subject. He viewed the Spanish proposal as a possibility for a final solution to the question of the treatment of Spanish Jews in France and therefore proposed that Abetz be instructed to work for the removal of the Jews to Spanish Morocco.[63] A week after his meeting with Heydrich, Luther was still thinking of the Final Solution in terms of deporting Jews from Europe, which was in line with the underlying principles of the Madagascar Plan. It would then appear that Heydrich had not discussed other aspects of the Jewish question with Luther beyond the Serbian problem. However, on October 17, 1941, Luther wrote a second memorandum on the question of the Spanish Jews in France. He noted that in a telephone conversation, the RSHA had opposed the evacuation to Spanish Morocco. The RSHA perceived no solution therein, as the Spanish government had neither the will nor the experience effectively to guard the Jews there. "In addition these Jews would also be all too much out of the direct reach of the measures for a basic solution of the Jewish question to be enacted after the war."[64] It was now perfectly clear to Luther that the Final Solution of the Jewish question no longer meant the removal of the Jews from Europe. And he well knew Heydrich's inclinations concerning a local solution.

Much more substantial written evidence survives to prove that Rademacher discovered at least the general outlines of the Final Solution immediately upon his return from Belgrade. We have seen that on October 25, 1941, Rademacher wrote his Belgrade report, including the portion referring to Jewish women, children, and aged that stated: "Then as soon as the technical possibility exists within the framework of the total solution of the Jewish question, the Jews will be deported by waterway to the reception camp in the east." Rademacher had heard of reception camps in connection to the newest total or final solution of the Jewish question. There was as yet no attempt to disguise these camps as work camps; they were to receive women, children, and old people incapable of heavy labor. Nor was there any reason for Rademacher to doubt the authenticity of the plans for reception camps. Friedrich Suhr, one of Eichmann's right-hand men straight from Berlin with the latest news, was present at the meeting.

On this same day that Rademacher returned from Belgrade and wrote his report, he must also have received a letter from Paul Wurm, his old friend of *Der Stürmer,* written on October 23. Wurm had visited Berlin but missed seeing Rademacher, who was absent in Belgrade. He dropped a friendly note to Rademacher on a topic of mutual interest, the Jewish question:

> Dear Party Comrade Rademacher! On my return trip from Berlin I met an old party comrade, who works in the east on the settlement of the Jewish question. In the near future many of the Jewish vermin will be exterminated through special measures.[65]

Wurm's acquaintance referred to special measures in the future, while the *Einsatzgruppen* massacres had already been going on for three and a half months. Nor did he refer merely to Russian Jews or *Ostjuden,* but to the Jews in general. He was making a veiled reference to the next phase of the Final Solution, which was then being planned in Berlin, namely the deportation of the other Jews of Europe to the death camps. Wurm said nothing about camps, but Rademacher had already heard of the plans for reception camps in the east for Jews incapable of heavy labor. Now he also knew the intention to exterminate many Jews through special measures. It is impossible to escape the conclusion that from October 25, 1941, Rademacher realized that deportation to the east within the framework of the Final Solution meant death. Nothing in the future occurred to change this realization, while much happened to strengthen it.

## November Interim

The month following Rademacher's and Luther's first direct encounter with the Final Solution was a very busy one. The deportation of German Jews to the east had begun on October 15, 1941, the day before Rademacher left for Serbia. Two days after his return, October 27, he received a telephone call from Eichmann, who wanted to know if Slovak and Croatian Jews could also be included in these deportations. Rademacher did not think that there would be any objection, as both these states had enacted harsh Jewish measures within their own countries. Thus Rademacher suggested to Luther that the Croatian and Slovak ambassadors be informed orally that the Jews of their countries' citizenship would have to be recalled within a reasonable space of time or otherwise face deportation to ghettos in the east along with the German Jews. Luther however felt that the issue was sufficiently important that official communications to the governments concerned had to be made via the German embassies. Weizsäcker, Woermann, and Albrecht of the Legal Division were informed and approved this procedure.[66] Luther's insistence on the most formal procedures, both in approaching the foreign governments and in securing the approval of the other heads of the Foreign Office, would indicate that he realized the importance of the course upon which the Foreign Office was embarking. Previously preferring solo ventures, Luther this time wanted responsibility and participation as widely spread as possible.

Because the Rumanians had likewise demonstrated what in German eyes was a positive attitude to the Jewish question, they too were approached. Both the Rumanians and Croatians quickly refused to take back their Jews and left it up to the Germans to deport them to the east.[67] Only the Slovak government did not reply immediately to Luther's inquiry. Ludin's contacts reported to him that while the Slovak government preferred to see its Jews deported directly from German to the east rather than return to Slovakia, they were very interested in the property of these Jews and supposed it would be easier to recover this property if the Jews in question were brought to concentration camps in Slovakia than if they were deported to the east "never to be seen again" (auf Nimmerwiedersehn).[68] Ultimately the Slovak government agreed to the deportation of its Jews in Germany, but only on the condition that its legal claim to the property of these Jews was in no way endangered. Ludin replied that within the realm of possibility, the justified Slovak interest in Jewish property would be protected by Germany.[69]

Because a question of legal claims to property had emerged, both the Legal and Economic Divisions within the Foreign Office claimed the right to participate. Luther's draft reply to Eichmann took three weeks to make the rounds before it could be officially dispatched. Thus it was not until January 10, 1942, two and a half months after his inquiry, that Eichmann was told that he could include the Croatian, Slovak, and Rumanian Jews. Luther warned him, however, that the Slovak government had insisted on the protection of its property rights, and the other two would probably do likewise in the near future. All the property of these Jews had to be impounded upon their deportation.[70] The delay turned out to be significant. The deportations from Germany were well underway, and the local Gestapo agencies had already received instructions to deport only German and stateless Jews. At least in the case of the Rumanian Jews residing in Germany, they were not arrested until 1943 and were then sent to German concentration camps instead of death camps in the east.[71]

Surprisingly, the beginning of deportations from Germany preceded rather than followed a change in emigration policy. In late August, Heinrich Müller of the Gestapo had reaffirmed the policy of facilitating Jewish emigration from Germany itself. Many South and Central American consulates were making a business of selling visas to Jews, on the promise that they would not actually enter the visa-granting country. But at least this helped them get transit visas necessary to get out of Germany. Since these consulates were breaking no German laws and were aiding Jewish emigration, Müller told the Foreign Office that no police measures would be taken against their fradulent sales of visas.[72] Emigration was still being pursued in October, when the Foreign Office arranged for the visa of a travel agent commissioned by the RSHA to accompany Jewish transports to Lisbon, which was virtually the last escape line for Germany Jewry. The visa was to be valid for repeated trips through Spain and Portugal throughout October, November, and December.[73]

On November 12, 1941, however, the German ambassador to Portugal recommended that Jewish emigration through Lisbon be stopped, for the Jews were allegedly giving information on bomb damage and recommending new worthwhile targets to the British. Luther concurred and asked Rademacher immediately to contact the RSHA. Rademacher replied that he had already learned from Eichmann ten days earlier (November 4) that the RSHA had forbidden the further emigration of German Jews to the west.[74] As in the case of the Serbian Jews, once again Luther demonstrated his willingness to take the initiative in the Jewish question. This time, however, the RSHA had been a step ahead of him.

The month of November was confusing in some ways for Luther and Rademacher. They knew that German *Judenpolitik* was taking a new and fatal direction. The SS, the army, and now the Transportation Ministry were officially involved, but as yet the Foreign Office was not. Luther had already had trouble from Weizsäcker on his free-lancing efforts in the Jewish question, both over marking and the Belgrade affair. Until the new Jewish policy became more official, Luther and Rademacher had to proceed very cautiously. This was already seen in Luther's handling of Eichmann's inquiry about the inclusion of Croatian and Slovak Jews, where Luther approached the foreign governments through the most official channels and then only after the approval of Weizsäcker, Woermann, and Albrecht. Also in other actions during the month of November, Luther and Rademacher were solicitous of both official Foreign Office procedures and the Foreign Office point of view.

The SS was causing the Foreign Office no small embarrassment through its careless handling of Dutch Jews in German concentration camps. Over 600 Dutch Jews had been brought to Germany in the first half of 1941. The Jewish Council in Amsterdam had then received lists showing that over 400 of them—all young men—had died, mostly on specific days. Since Sweden represented the diplomatic interests of the Netherlands in Germany, the Swedish ambassador repeatedly applied to the Foreign Office to visit the surviving Dutch Jews in their camps. This request was of course rejected.

When Luther found out about the SS miscue, he wrote Heinrich Müller a sharp letter stating that the issue was quite difficult and unpleasant for the Foreign Office, because Sweden also represented German interests in enemy countries. Swedish requests in Germany could not be rejected without the fear that Sweden in turn would not represent German interests abroad with the necessary energy. Luther assured Müller that "in principle the Foreign Office held the same viewpoint as the RSHA and advocated on its part reprisal measures against Jews as causers of unrest." But in order to avoid such incidents in the future, he continued, the RSHA should not bring arrested persons back to the Reich but keep them as prisoners in their own territory, so no diplomatic intervention could be made. Furthermore, care should be taken in the notification of deaths that the impression should not arise that the deaths all occurred on certain days.[75]

When mass round-ups of Jews took place in France in reprisal for attacks on army personnel, many foreign Jews were included. This led to foreign protests, but both the military commander and the RSHA representative in

Paris refused to release a single foreign Jew for fear of setting a precedent.[76] Rademacher and Weizsäcker worked together to secure the release of the non-European Jews involved. While Rademacher appealed directly to Eichmann, Weizsäcker wrote Ribbentrop about the problem. Weizsäcker had no objection to the arrest of European Jews, for he did not fear any diplomatic developments arising from this. But the arrest of Jews from North and South America brought with it the danger of reprisals. Here Germany was pulling on the short end of the lever, because the number of Germans in the Americas far exceeded the number of American Jews in the German sphere. Ribbentrop agreed with Weizsäcker, and Luther passed the appropriate instructions along to Abetz. Later Eichmann telephoned that the American Jews had been released.[77]

Luther's willingness to follow official channels during this period gave the state secretary the opportunity to counter Luther with opposing opinions from other division heads. Luther was subject to continual inquiries from the RSHA on the question of marking foreign Jews and needed to coax the procrastinating foreign minister into a decision. On November 3, 1941, he drafted a proposal, suggesting that marking now be extended to all foreign Jews in Germany. In order to avoid intervention by the United States, however, all North American Jews would be expelled first.[78] Weizsäcker circulated this proposal through the Political, Economic, and Legal Divisions, where it encountered unanimous opposition.[79]

War broke out between Germany and the United States before the marking question finally got back to D III. In the face of the solid opposition of the rest of the Foreign Office, Fritz-Gebhardt von Hahn, in his first stint with D III at this time, decided that the state of war gave no occasion to change the cautious policy which had been pursued vis-à-vis the United States until then.[80] The impatient Eichmann was finally told in late January that the Foreign Office had no objections to the marking of Croatian, Slovak, and Rumanian Jews (whose deportation had just been agreed to), but North and South American Jews were to be exempted.[81] The case of the other European Jews remained in limbo.[82] Luther's initial proposal to expel the North American Jews and mark all the rest was effectively sidetracked.

In another case Weizsäcker and the old guard were also successful in checking Luther. In early August, 1941, *Reichskommissar für das Ostland,* Hinrich Lohse, requested instructions from the Reich Ministry for the Occupied Eastern Territories (*Ostministerium*) on the treatment of foreign Jews. An exit of these Jews was "intolerable" because of the material they could deliver for anti-German propaganda. On the other hand, "these Jews also could not remain in the *Ostland* in the long run." For a start, he wanted to extend his police measures to the Jews of Slovakia as well as countries occupied by Germany.[83] Lohse had not explained what he meant by police measures, though the paradoxical comment that the foreign Jews could neither leave nor stay indicated that he meant extermination. His inquiry was forwarded to Luther, where it sat unanswered until Luther's meeting with Heydrich over the Serbian Jews in early October. Luther then suddenly took it up and attempted to give Lohse a nearly free hand by reiterating the Foreign Office line: as in western Europe, Lohse's police measures should be extended to all foreign Jews, with the exception of property questions. Luther submitted his deceptively simple proposal to Weizsäcker, who sent it to the Legal Division.

Erich Albrecht stalled through two more reminders from the *Ostministerium* that its August inquiry had still not been answered. Then he revealed his suspicions. According to "international common law" (*völkerrechtlichem Gewohnheitsrecht*) foreign citizens in a militarily occupied area still had a claim to a certain minimum of rights, and this included the protection of one's person as well as his property. Measures against persons also carried as much danger of reprisals as those against property. The Foreign Office should therefore answer Lohse's inquiry with one of its own over the nature of the police measures intended and the countries involved.[84] Reluctant to follow this course, Luther let the matter drop.

On yet another occasion Weizsäcker tried to use the Legal Division to impede Luther. On November 26, 1941, the Bulgarian Foreign Minister Popov complained to Ribbentrop that foreign Jews residing in Bulgaria were being protected by their countries from Bulgarian Jewish legislation. Popov wanted the treatment of Jewish legislation regulated in common between the European nations. Ribbentrop assured Popov of the Führer's unalterable decision that all Jews would leave Europe at the end of the war. In the meantime, however, he promised to submit Popov's question about a common European handling of Jewish legislation to the Foreign Office.[85]

Rademacher welcomed the Bulgarian suggestion. "The opportunity rendered by this war must be utilized finally to eliminate the Jewish question in Europe." However, he doubted that pan-European Jewish legislation (on the German model, of course) was possible yet. He suggested that at least the European members of the anti-Comintern pact should sign an agreement whereby all their Jews would fall under the legislation of the country in which they resided.[86]

Weizsäcker initialed Rademacher's memorandum but sent it to the Legal Division rather than directly to Ribbentrop. Albrecht was more skeptical than Rademacher. He pointed out numerous legal complications and opined that even an agreement limited to Slovakia, Bulgaria, Rumania, and Croatia would be difficult, for each would fear to lose the property of its Jews residing abroad through foreign aryanization. Albrecht recommended a series of bilateral treaties instead.[87]

Luther brushed aside the more timid proposals of both Rademacher and Albrecht. Despite anticipated difficulties he felt that as many European countries as possible should be induced to adopt German legislation.[88] Ribbentrop either lost interest in the question when confronted with the complications raised by the Legal Division or had not been very interested in the first place and had consulted the Foreign Office merely out of courtesy to Popov. He neither decided between the conflicting proposals of Luther and the Legal Division nor authorized further activity concerning Popov's suggestion.

However, Luther could not be thwarted entirely. Six months later, he would refer to Popov's suggestion and the Legal Division's endorsement of bilateral treaties to suggest an agreement with Bulgaria on the Jewish question.

The time in which Weizsäcker could assert any authority over Luther in the Jewish question and delay or block his proposals was fast coming to an end. Even up to this point, Weizsäcker's behavior in the matter had alternated between moderate and extreme passivity. He was the model "bureaucrat without backbone."[89] In the spring of 1941, when the military in France had sought his aid to protect American Jews from recently introduced legislation, Weizsäcker had simply turned the matter over to *Abteilung Deutschland* to formulate a negative reply. When many European countries had protested the arrest of their Jews in France, he dismissed their protests as being without diplomatic danger for Germany and limited his intervention solely to the Jews of the Americas. Twice in the fall of 1941, however, Weizsäcker found the energy to reprimand Luther, once over his failure to notify the state secretary about the Foreign Office role in the marking edict and once over his exceeding the authority of the Foreign Office in Serbia. Luther had then obediently complied with official channels in dealing with the deportation of Slovak, Croatian, and Rumanian Jews from Germany, the marking of foreign Jews, and the treatment of foreign Jews in the east. In all these cases Luther either met delays or saw his proposals whittled away by objections from other Foreign Office divisions. As long as the Foreign Office was not officially initiated into the newest phase of the Final Solution, Luther avoided a confrontation with Weizsäcker. Once the Foreign Office was officially brought into the Final Solution, this abruptly changed. On the one hand, Luther no longer feared a showdown with Weizsäcker, knowing he was carrying out official Reich policy. On the other hand, Weizsäcker became even more timid and cautious in his attempts to obstruct Luther. He even stopped insisting on Luther's following proper channels, probably hoping that Luther would in fact bypass him, so he would not have to initial Luther's proposals. The year of 1942 would be Luther's year of triumph over Weizsäcker.

### The Einsatzgruppen Reports

For some months various members of the Foreign Office had learned of the massacres of the Russian Jews through unofficial sources. But the Foreign Office had never been officially informed of these events. This official silence was broken when the Gestapo chief, Heinrich Müller, on the orders of Heydrich, sent the first five "Activity and Situation Reports of the *Einsatzgruppen* of the Sipo-SD in Russia" to Ribbentrop on October 30, 1941.[90] They reached Ribbentrop's staff on November 11. A presentation to the foreign minister was not felt to be necessary, and Johann Georg Lohmann of Ribbentrop's staff sent them on to D II, Luther's liaison office for the SS and Police. Werner Picot received them on November 15 and sent them to Luther and D III. Luther initialed the covering letter on November 17, Rademacher the following day.[91]

The reports covered the entire activities of the *Einsatzgruppen* in Russia, and included such topics as the activities of communist functionaries and the clergy as well as nationalistic strivings of the non-Russian peoples in the Ukraine, White Russia, Latvia, Estonia, and Lithuania. But the most sensational parts of the reports concerned the Jewish question. The first report, covering the month of July, reported that many Jews had been liquidated around Riga and another 8,000 by *Einsatzgruppe* B in White Russia. In the Ukraine 7,000 Jews had been shot. The construction of ghettos had begun. *Einsatzgruppe* D, operating out of Rumania, complained that the Hungarian army was basically pro-Jewish and that "the Rumanians proceed against the Jews haphazardly. There would be no objection to the very numerous shootings of Jews if the technical preparation and execution were not so inadequate. The Rumanians usually leave the executed persons on the spot without burial."[92] The second report, covering the first half of August, recorded many executions of Jews, though only in Latvia did the number reach as high as 1,550 for one massacre. Once again complaints were made against the Rumanians. "Only sporadically do the Rumanian police proceed sharply against Jews. The number of liquidations carried out by them cannot be ascertained."[93] These reports were no doubt the source of Heydrich's earlier complaints about the Rumanians which he had voiced to Luther in late August.

In the first two reports, the executions of Jews had been mixed indiscriminately with accounts of shootings of partisans and communists. Beginning with the third report, covering the last half of August, the Jewish question received its own subheading, clearly ending any pretense that the Jewish massacres were antipartisan measures. The third report told of the shoving match between Rumania and Germany on the Dniester River, of which the Foreign Office had already learned. It also noted that over 4,000 Jews had been liquidated by *Einsatzgruppe* D.[94] The fourth report had little new on the Jewish question, but the fifth contained the biggest numbers of all. In the Ostland, one *Sonderkommando* of *Einsatzgruppe* A had liquidated over 75,000 Jews by the end of September, and another had even surpassed this with a total of 85,000 executions. The areas of both these units were now *judenfrei.* Individual massacres of 1,025, 2,278, and 1,668 were reported in White Russia and the Ukraine.[95]

Rademacher received these reports on November 18 and read them immediately and carefully. Earlier the German embassy in Bucharest had complained that the Hungarian intelligence service was sending reports and photos concerning the Rumanian treatment of Jews to the U.S. State Department. Jagow in Budapest had denied this accusation. On the day after he received the *Einsatzgruppen* reports, Rademacher excerpted three paragraphs from the first one which complained of Hungarian pro-Jewish behavior and asked Jagow to check the matter once again.[96]

On November 25, 1941, Heydrich forwarded to Ribbentrop the sixth report, covering the month of October.[97] According to it, in the Ostland *Kommissariat* all male Jews over 16 years of age, with the exception of doctors and elders, had been executed. Only five hundred Jewesses and children were left. In Kiev, nearly 34,000 Jews were shot on September 29th and 30th. Other massacres included 3,000 at Vitebsk, 3,145 at Zhitomir, and 4,891 on the Dnieper River.[98]

On December 8, 1941, Dr. Bruns of the foreign minister's staff requested the compilation of a short summary of the six lengthy reports, to be submitted to Ribbentrop.[99] Luther had just received the sixth report and wrote a summary of it himself on December 10. It was intialed by Weizsäcker on the 12th and sent on to Ribbentrop.[100] It duly recorded all the vital statistics on Jewish executions.

Apparently Luther had no desire to write a similar summary for the first five reports. Legation Secretary Fritz-Gebhardt von Hahn had just begun work at D III in early December, and he was given the task of summarizing them. In giving the task to D III and not D II, it is clear that Luther felt the reports pertained most significantly to the Jewish question rather than to SS and Police affairs. As Hahn had to cover much more material than Luther, a statistical litany of executions was omitted. An exact overview of the number of Jews that had been liquidated could not be ascertained from the reports, Hahn noted. But he calculated that on the average, 70–80,000 Jews had been liquidated by each *Sonderkommando* in the time period covered by the reports.[101] As there were several of them in each of the four *Einsatzgruppen,* the reader was free to make his own staggering extrapolation. The report was then forwarded to Luther by Dr. Herbert Müller, who had joined D III one month before Hahn.

Ribbentrop was not the only one in the Foreign Office who saw the summaries of Hahn and Luther. In the last half of December, Luther's summary of the sixth report was circulated to Woermann, his deputy Erdmannsdorf, the Military and Russian desks in the Political Division, the Russian desk in the Economic Division, D III, and the Information and Radio Divisions.[102] In January Luther's summary along with Hahn's was circulated through the Balkan, Russian, and Scandinavian Desks of the Political Division, and to the Cultural and Information Divisions.[103] The original reports were returned from D III to D II on December 29. Picot gave them to Weizsäcker on January 8, who in turn sent them to Woermann on January 10.[104] Despite their highly confidential classification (*geheime Reichssache*), there was little attempt to keep the contents of the reports secret. The reports and summaries taken together were initialed by no fewer than twenty-two different people and could have been seen and talked about by far more than that. Clearly, by January 1942, it was no secret to the higher officials in the Foreign Office that the Russian Jews were being systematically decimated. What had been unofficial rumor for several months was now officially confirmed.

The massacres in Russia continued, as did the stream of reports to the Foreign Office. Increasingly, the pretense of treating the executions as counterinsurgency measures was dropped in favor of proclaiming the solution of the Jewish question. The seventh and eighth reports were sent by Heydrich to Ribbentrop on January 16, 1942, and were forwarded to D II by Lohmann on the 26th.[105] The seventh report, covering the month of December, stated: "The Jewish question in the Ostland can be regarded as solved. Great executions have severely decimated the Jewry and the remaining Jews were ghettoized." It also cited three other massacres of 3,100, 3,726, and 1,865, and announced that as a result of one of these the area around Mogilew was *judenfrei*.[106] The eighth report made no attempt to disguise the shootings as spontaneous retaliation. "In Rowno the long-planned Jewish action was carried out, by which 15,000 were able to be shot." It also cited other massacres of 5,281, 1,113, 835, and 2,365.[107] No summaries were made. Instead the original reports were circulated by Picot and Pusch to Luther, Weizsäcker, Woermann, Tippelskirch, Bismarck, the Military Desk, the Information Division, and D III, D VIII, and D IX. In D III, Rademacher and Herbert Müller initialed both reports.[108]

The ninth report, for the month of January, never arrived, but the tenth report was sent by Heinrich Müller to Ribbentrop on March 5, 1942, and forwarded by Lohmann to D II on March 11.[109] It stated succinctly: "Now that the Jewish question in the Ostland can be regarded practically as solved and settled, the clarification of this problem progresses further in the other occupied territories of the east. . . . Again and again Jews . . . are seized and shot."[110] Luther wrote a short summary of this report, and circulated it to Weizsäcker, Schulenburg, Hilger, Grosskopf, Ditmann, Wüster, Rühle, and Schmidt.[111] This was a different circulation list than any previous and was the only one which was not initialed by at least one member of D III.

The eleventh and final report, for the month of March, was sent by Heydrich to Ribbentrop on April 23.[112] It announced that the Ostland was for the most part *judenfrei* and reported further massacres of 3,412, 2,007, 1,224 and in Rakow 15,000, which was now also *judenfrei*.[113] This report was circulated to Luther, Woermann, Bismarck, Tippelskirch, Triska of D VIII, Grosskopf of D IX, Rademacher, Wüster of the Information Division, Schulenberg, and to the Military, Russian, and Scandinavian Desks of the Political Division as well as to the Radio Division.[114]

These later reports did provide the Foreign Office with more information for those who were reluctant to draw conclusions earlier. No one reading these reports could any longer view the Jewish massacres in Russia as counterinsurgency measures related to the fact that Russia was a military area. The executions were viewed as a solution to the Jewish question and aimed at making the occupied eastern territories *judenfrei*. Also important for the Foreign Office role in future deportations, the later reports repeatedly emphasized that in the Ostland the solution to the Jewish question had been achieved earliest. Yet it was to Riga in the Ostland that many trainloads of German Jews had been shipped in the last months of 1941. If the territory was *judenfrei*, it was obvious that the fate of the deportees differed in no way from that of the native *Ostjuden*. As early as December 21, 1941, Bernhard

Lösener of the Jewish *Referat* in the Interior Ministry had received an unofficial and secondhand, but nonetheless quite detailed and accurate, description of the massacre of German Jews who had been deported to Riga.[115] That the Foreign Office did not have similar unofficial sources, in addition to the official reports they received, is quite unlikely. The second phase of the Final Solution, the deportation of European Jewry to the death camps, would be treated with a great deal more secrecy than the almost public *Einsatzgruppen* operations in Russia. It has already been seen how widely circulated were the single Foreign Office copies of the "top secret" reports, and that copy was always merely one of the often one hundred copies of each report that had been made and distributed. Thus while the death camps would be shrouded in secrecy, every high-ranking official in the Foreign Office now knew well to what extent the Nazi regime was prepared to go in order to solve the Jewish question.

## The Wannsee Conference

On November 29, 1941, Luther received a letter from Heydrich inviting him to a meeting of the major government agencies concerned with the Jewish question in order to make all necessary preparations for a "total solution." The meeting was especially necessary since deportations of Jews from the Reich had been underway since October 15. The meeting was to be held on December 9. Heydrich included the guest list which showed that the state secretaries of the Ministries of the Interior and Justice as well as the General Government and Four Year Plan would attend, yet he, Undersecretary Luther rather than Weizsäcker, received Heydrich's personal invitation to the conference. Luther fell ill, however, and asked Rademacher to inform Heydrich that he was sick but would attend if possible. He also requested Rademacher to prepare a memorandum of "our desires and ideas" and to inform Weizsäcker of the meeting. On December 8, Rademacher told Luther that Weizsäcker had been informed but that the meeting was postponed.[116]

It was more than a month after Rademacher's and Luther's initial involvement in the killing process that the Foreign Office was officially solicited to help prepare the Final Solution to the Jewish question. Since the Belgrade massacres the Foreign Office had learned of Himmler's decision to halt Jewish emigration from Germany, reversing an SS policy dating back to Eichmann's expulsions from Austria in the spring of 1938. It had learned of the initial deportations to the east when asked to approve the inclusion of Croatian, Slovak, and Rumanian Jews residing in Germany. And it had learned in great detail of the *Einsatzgruppen* operations in Russia courtesy of Heydrich's first five Activity and Situation Reports. Thus Heydrich's invitation came when all the higher officials of the German Foreign Office had ample information not only to conclude that Jewish policy was entering a new and more radical phase but also to envisage the basic outline of this new policy.

Just how clearly D III realized that deportation was a key word of the new

*Judenpolitik* is shown by the memorandum of "our desires and ideas" that had been requested by Luther. It was unsigned and may possibly not have been written by Rademacher. In any case Rademacher initialed the covering letter and instructed that the memorandum be resubmitted when the postponed meeting was rescheduled. There is no evidence, however, that Luther did in fact read it. The memorandum outlined eight "desires and ideas."

1. Deportation to the east of all Jews of German citizenship residing in the Reich as well as Croatian, Slovak, and Rumanian Jews.

2. Deportation of all Jews living in the territories occupied by us who are former German citizens but became stateless through the recent supplementary decree to the Reich citizenship law.

3. Deportation of Serbian Jews.

4. Deportation of the Jews handed over to us by the Hungarian government.

5. Declaration of our willingness vis-à-vis the Rumanian, Slovak, Croatian, Bulgarian and Hungarian governments, likewise to deport to the east the Jews living in these countries.

6. Influencing the Bulgarian and Hungarian governments to introduce Jewish legislation on the Nürnberg model.

7. Influencing the other European governments to introduce Jewish legislation.

8. Execution of these measures as hitherto on friendly terms with the Gestapo.[117]

Clearly D III did not want Luther appearing at the conference with proposals any less positive or less zealous than the others.

The Jewish experts were uncertain on only one point—the way in which one could speak of the fate which awaited the Jews after deportation. No mention was made of deportation in connection with labor. This disguise apparently did not become official until it was articulated by Heydrich when the conference was finally convened. Thus nothing was said at all on this subject, though at least Rademacher already knew that the goal was extermination.

On January 8, 1942, Heydrich wrote Luther once again. The postponed meeting on the Final Solution was rescheduled "with lunch included" for January 20 at noon. It would be held at 56-58 Am Grossen Wannsee, a villa on the outskirts of Berlin.[118]

The Wannsee Conference, as it became known, was recorded in a long protocol written by Eichmann.[119] He later did not contest that its essential points were correct, but admitted that official euphemisms (*dienstliche Worte*) had been substituted for plainer speech.[120] The conference began with a long monologue by Heydrich. He discussed the order of *Reichsmarschall* Göring for a plan for the Final Solution, a copy of which had been sent to each participant at the conference. This required prior treatment in common by all the organizations directly involved, so that the policy would be properly coordinated. But Heydrich made it clear that despite the participation of other agencies, the central authority lay with the *Reichsführer*-SS (Himmler) and the chief of Security Police and SD (Heydrich himself). He then reviewed German *Judenpolitik* up to Himmler's prohibition of further emigration. On the order of the Führer, evacuation to the east had now replaced emigration "as a further solutional possibility" (*als weitere Lösungsmöglichkeit*). By Heydrich's calculation, eleven million European Jews in all had to be taken into consideration. This included Jews even from Spain, Portugal, England, Ireland, Switzerland, Turkey, and Sweden, as well as from Germany's allies, satellites, and vanquished enemies.

> Under proper direction the Jews should in the course of the Final Solution be brought to the east in a suitable way for use as labor. In great labor columns, with separation of the sexes, the Jews capable of work are brought to these areas and employed in road building, in which task undoubtedly a great part will fall out through natural diminution.
>
> The remnant that finally survives all this, because here it is undoubtedly a question of the part with the greatest resistance, will have to be treated accordingly, because this remnant, representing a natural selection, can be regarded as the germ cell of a new Jewish reconstruction if released.

In carrying out the program, Europe would be combed through from west to east. However, the Reich would come first. Here Jews over 65 years old and those wounded or decorated in war would be sent to an old people's ghetto at Theresienstadt. Many interventions would thus be eliminated in one blow.

> Concerning the treatment of the Final Solution in the European territories occupied and influenced by us, it is proposed that the relevant experts of the Foreign Office confer with the competent specialists of the Security Police and SD.

Heydrich anticipated no difficulties with Slovakia, Croatia, or Rumania. Hungary would have to accept a Jewish adviser, and Heydrich anticipated establishing contact with the police chief in Italy to prepare the settlement of the Jewish question there. No great difficulties were foreseen in France. At this point Heydrich was interrupted, apparently for the first time. Luther pointed out that:

> . . . in a basic treatment of this problem in some countries, such as the northern countries, difficulties would emerge, and it is thus recommended to postpone these countries for the time being. In view of the small number of Jews in question here, this postponement constitutes no significant restriction anyhow. On the other hand, the Foreign Office sees no great difficulties for southeast and west Europe.

In his own account Luther said that he requested that all questions concerning non-German territory should be harmonized with the Foreign Office, and that Heydrich promised to act accordingly.[121] The protocol, however, made no mention of such a request on Luther's part, only Heydrich's proposal that the experts from the Foreign Office and RSHA confer with one another.

The discussion then shifted to the problems of "half-breeds" (*Mischlinge*) and mixed marriages in Germany, with sterilization and compulsory divorce as the most frequently mentioned solutions. State Secretary Bühler of the General Government requested that the Final Solution begin in his area, for the majority of the 2.5 million Jews there were already incapable of work. It was quite obvious to Bühler, as it must have been to the others, that work camps were just a cover for the ultimate goal of extermination. "In conclusion the different types of solutional possibilities were discussed." Eichmann later confirmed that this meant "killing possibilities" (*Tötungsmöglichkeiten*).[122]

The plan of the ultimate Final Solution, the outline of which Luther and Rademacher were aware since the end of October, had now been officially promulgated. The Foreign Office was now officially involved, and the rules for cooperation between the Foreign Office and SS had been discussed and mutually agreed upon. The Jewish experts of the RSHA and Foreign Office, Eichmann and Rademacher, would confer before carrying out the Final Solution not only in countries under German influence but also in German-occupied territories. All questions relating to deportations from non-German territories would be harmonized with the Foreign Office. Luther had gained recognition from the RSHA for an extensive Foreign Office role in the Final Solution. But it was in fact no more than Weizsäcker earlier considered proper when he had stated that internal Jewish measures in Serbia were not a Foreign Office concern but deportations from Serbia would have been.

If Luther learned something new at the Wannsee Conference, it was not the fate in store for the Jews, but rather that the deportations would begin in the west instead of the east. The memorandum of the "desires and ideas" of the Foreign Office had mentioned deportations from Germany, Serbia, Rumania, Slovakia, Croatia, and Hungary, but it had not broached the topic of deportations from western countries like France, Holland, and Belgium. The timetable envisioned by Heydrich was thus the opposite of the original viewpoint of *Abteilung Deutschland.*

Luther must have quickly confirmed to Rademacher that the conference went nearly as expected, for Rademacher lost little time in burying the now defunct Madagascar Plan. On February 10, 1942, he wrote the head of the Colonial Desk in the Political Division, Bielfeld, that the plan he had given him for his files in August, 1940, was no longer operative. The war with the Soviet Union had placed other territories at the disposal of the Final Solution. "Therefore the Führer had decided that the Jews shall be deported not to Madagascar but to the east. Madagascar thus no longer needs to be provided for the Final Solution."[123]

Bielfeld told his division chief of the change which came as news to Woermann. He immediately asked Rademacher about the source of this significant decision. Rademacher informed Luther of Woermann's inquiry and asked him to inform Woermann of the conference with Heydrich. Luther subsequently assured Rademacher that he had personally answered the inquiry.[124] It is unlikely that Luther told Woermann anything more than that the Führer's decision to deport the Jews to the east rather than to Madagascar had been relayed by Heydrich. There is no written record that Luther told Weizsäcker anything at all after the state secretary had been informed by Rademacher in early December of Heydrich's invitation.

Luther was well aware that Heydrich had personally invited him rather than Weizsäcker. He was thus personally charged with securing Foreign Office cooperation. There is little reason to believe he would have told Weizsäcker and Woermann anything that would have caused them to place obstacles in his way and render his task more difficult. That Weizsäcker and Woermann could have and should have realized, given the *Einsatzgruppen* reports, that deportation to the east meant death is clear. But to presume that Luther would have drawn these conclusions for them is not logical.

Luther was reticent not only with Weizsäcker and Woermann; there is also evidence that he neither consulted Ribbentrop before the Wannsee Conference nor informed him of the proceedings immediately afterwards. At no time prior to the conference was any reference made to instructions from the foreign minister. Moreover, by Luther's own account Ribbentrop was not informed of the conference at the time and did not receive a copy of the protocol until the following August![125] Thus within the Foreign Office the Wannsee Protocol did not receive anything like the open treatment of the *Einsatzgruppen* reports.

In the aftermath of the Wannsee Conference, several other conferences, attended by lower-ranking officials, were held to settle minor questions pertaining to the Final Solution. The first of these was held in the Reich Ministry for the Occupied Eastern Territories on January 29. Dr. Leibbrandt of the *Ostministerium* wished to discuss a draft of an ordinance defining the concept of Jew for the eastern occupied territories. The Nürnberg Laws provided no adequate model, because the documentary proof of ancestry was unavailable. Likewise, there was no need to preserve the legal position of half-Jews, as in Germany; in the east they could be equated with full Jews. Half-Jews were "racially just as undesirable as full Jews" for in the east no German "blood infusion" (*Bluteinschlag*) had to be taken into consideration. As for foreign Jews, they would still be subject to German law.[126]

Herbert Müller was assigned to deal with the question. He had no objection but consulted the Legal Division.[127] There Conrad Rödiger referred to Albrecht's position of the previous November. If it was not merely a matter of definition but a situation in which practical consequences were to ensue for foreign Jews, the Foreign Office would first have to ask the nature of the intended police measures and the citizenship of the foreign Jews involved.[128]

At the conference on the 29th, a revised Foreign Office position was presented. It would be inexpedient to make any explicit mention of foreign Jews, thus allowing the question to become a topic of propaganda attack and the basis for diplomatic representations by foreign countries. By internal instruction all foreign Jews could be exempted with the exception of Rumania, Croatia, and Slovakia. The Foreign Office viewpoint was accepted.

The discussion then shifted to the topic of half-Jews, in which Müller had the opportunity to gain a fuller insight into the nature of the Final Solution. Dr. Bernhard Lösener of the Interior Ministry opposed equating half-Jews with full-Jews in the east. On January 20th it had been decided that German half-Jews would be sterilized. Since a concept of Jew common to all Europe was desirble, this distinction between Jew and half-Jew should be preserved in the east as well. Dr. Alfred Wetzel cryptically replied that "as a result of the awaited solution of the Jewish question, political danger from the equalization of half-Jews from the eastern territories was not to be expected." In short, Lösener's fear of two conflicting definitions of half-Jews was groundless, for after the Final Solution no half-Jews would exist in the east.[129]

The second post-Wannsee meeting concerned the question of sterilizing German *Mischlinge* (one-half and one-quarter Jews). When Heydrich sent Luther a copy (one of thirty) of the Wannsee Conference protocol on January 26, he asked Luther in his cover letter to provide a specialist for a further conference on March 6 at the Gestapo headquarters on the Kurfür-stenstrasse. The Foreign Office representative was to contact Eichmann about the details. Luther kept the cover letter for over a month, and then on February 28 scribbled a note on the bottom: "Party comrade Rademacher. Please notify in writing that you are the specialist and will participate." Heydrich's cover letter did not receive a D III stamp until March 2.[130] As it was filed along with the Wannsee Conference protocol, it is most probable that this was the first occasion at which Rademacher was able to read the minutes for himself.

At the conference Rademacher apparently observed but took no part. The issue of German *Mischlinge* was primarily an internal one and concerned the Interior and Justice Ministries more than the Foreign Office. Various possibilities were discussed. Compulsory sterilization, as advocated at the January 20th conference, was impractical in wartime because it would have overburdened the hospitals. Other possibilities were offering a choice between sterilization and evacuation as well as ghettoization of all *Mischlinge,* postponing the sterilization question until after the war. No final decision was reached. Rademacher submitted his report to Luther, and it was further initialed by Woermann and Gaus.[131]

### The Jewish Experts at the Crossroads

Between October 1941 and March 1942, the role of the Foreign Office in the Final Solution was transformed from that of a virtually excluded outsider to an active participant. This affected the people involved with Jewish policy in *Abteilung Deutschland* in varying ways. Luther had not particularly con-cerned himself with the Jewish question until the Serbian affair arose in the fall of 1941. But as Jewish policy played an increasingly important role, Luther gravitated toward it with his sure instinct for power. His amazing rise had been due in no small part to his ability to anticipate which tasks Ribbentrop would need performed, to fill vacuums before others even realized they existed. When Luther sensed a turn in *Judenpolitik* in the late summer of 1941, he quickly aligned himself with the direction events were taking. If Jews were being massacred in Russia, he would help out in seeing that Jews were massacred in Serbia as well. If Hitler had ordered the deportation of European Jewry to the east to be murdered, he would make sure that the Foreign Office facilitated these deportations. The more important the policy being carried out, the more eager Luther was to be involved, and unquestionably *Judenpolitik* had now become very important. This technician of power brought to bear upon the Jewish question his considerable energy, ruthlessness, and organizational skill.

Luther intervened in the work of his subordinates to an unusual degree. He always wanted to know everything that was going on, down to the last detail.[132] Thus it was not surprising that as Luther's interest in the Jewish question grew, he increasingly took it upon himself to give detailed instructions and sign all important correspondence concerning this question. This was facilitated by the fact that, though the offices of *Abteilung Deutschland* were dispersed among five different buildings in Berlin, by coincidence Rademacher's office was directly above Luther's at Rauchstrasse 11, the former Norwegian embassy. Thus immediate and personal contact between Luther and Rademacher was possible at all times. The result was that Rademacher's room for individual initiative and maneuver rapidly diminished. In 1940, he had wanted to keep his hands free to deal with the big questions, like the expulsion of the Jews from Europe, and had eschewed routine paperwork. He had compiled one memorandum after another, dealing with the Madagascar Plan, all which went out under his own signature, not Luther's. But now Rademacher's personal initiative was no longer so visible. He was reduced to the capacity of Luther's clerk, receiving instructions, drafting telegrams accordingly or even more frequently passing the instructions along to his own assistant, and then submitting the draft for Luther's approval and signature.

Rademacher did not resist this diminution in power. The zealous anti-Semite, who in 1940 wrote that "victory gives Germany . . . the obligation to solve the Jewish question in Europe," was losing his enthusiasm. By Rademacher's own account, when his cherished Madagascar Plan was officially abandoned in February 1942, he went to Luther and asked to be relieved of the *Judenreferat*. In one account Luther allegedly agreed to let Rademacher go, once he had trained a suitable replacement.[133] In another account, Luther promised to divide D III, leaving Rademacher to deal with national revival movements in other countries and assigning the Jewish question to Rademacher's assistant, once he had been trained.[134] Also according to Rademacher, while waiting to get out of D III, he refused Ribbentrop's suggestion to join the SS.[135]

Such postwar accounts were of course commonplace, but Rademacher's story was supported by a number of witnesses. Hans Schröder, the Personnel Division chief, Walter Büttner, and Walter Gödde, Luther's personal secretary in 1942, all testified that Rademacher requested to be relieved of his duties and permitted to join the armed forces.[136] Likewise both Schröder and Büttner confirmed that Rademacher had refused to join the SS.[137] Karl Klingenfuss also stated that Rademacher had spoken to him of the possibility of separating D III into two parts and that Rademacher would have given up Jewish affairs.[138] While such supporting testimony in the postwar period was also quite common, it must be pointed out that among the witnesses at least Schröder was not well-disposed toward Rademacher. Before the American tribunal in Nürnberg, he had called Rademacher "our Eichmann," and in his affidavit for the Nürnberg-Fürth State Court had stated that in his view Rademacher, before anyone else in the Foreign Office, should be charged with criminal responsibility.[139] Moreover, it was Schröder who discovered Rademacher's postwar address and informed the allies, which led directly to Rademacher's arrest.[140] It is most probable that there is a core of truth in Rademacher's allegations that he did at least ask to be let out of D III and that he did refuse Ribbentrop's suggestion to join the SS.

If Rademacher in fact wanted to get out, it was not that he no longer believed in solving the Jewish question. He was still touting his Madagascar Plan to Klingenfuss in the fall of 1942.[141] Rather he merely wished to wash his own hands of responsibility for the course of events which had outrun even his own fertile anti-Semitic imagination. He would now leave the initiative to others and content himself with following Luther's instructions. In the meantime he would seek an assistant to train as his replacement. On March 24, 1942, he wrote to Schröder that the nature of his *Referat* required that its work not be delayed, and thus he needed a new assistant to replace the departing Herbert Müller.

The stronger the German victory looms, the greater and more urgent become the tasks of the *Referat,* because the Jewish question must be solved in the course of the war, for only so can it be solved without a world-wide outcry. After the settlement of the Jewish question in Germany it will become necessary to approach the other European countries in order, as it is now happening already with Slovakia and Croatia.[142]

For a man who himself wanted out, he showed little inclination to see that the "dirty work" was not faithfully and thoroughly carried out as long as he was still at his post.

Rademacher needed a new assistant because Herbert Müller, who had been with him since November 11, 1941, had in fact succeeded in escaping from D III into the army. When Müller was appointed to D III, he had protested vigorously to the deputy of the Personnel Division, Bergmann, who threatened to report him for disobedience. Müller had heard fearful rumors about Luther's dictatorial regime. He was a "bandwagon" Nazi, not a party activist, and thus he did not want to be expelled from the "old" Foreign Office into the strange atmosphere of *Abteilung Deutschland.* But instead of seeing Luther, he was received by Rademacher, an acquaintance from his law-clerk days. Rademacher, it turned out, had personally requested Müller and received him like an old friend, using the informal pronoun *du,* which Müller thought unusual until he discovered that this was normal jargon within *Abteilung Deutschland.*[143]

Müller was under the impression that the goal of German *Judenpolitik* was emigration, but Rademacher told him that Jewish emigration had now been halted. Rademacher also told him about the Madagascar Plan, which he had personally worked on, but explained that this could not be carried out during the war. It had been decided to send the Jews to ghettos in the east. When Müller questioned this, Rademacher tried to make it plausible that emigrating Jews provided the enemy with propaganda material, and then merely said it was based on orders from the top.[144]

Müller had been out of Germany between December 1939 and October 1941, so his exposure to the latest developments of the Jewish question must have been quite abrupt. Rademacher had told him immediately of the switch from emigration to ghettoization in the east. Two weeks after he began work in D III, Müller received a report from an agent in the Italian embassy who was informing the Germans about what the Americans were telling the Italians. The report told how over 100 German Jews had already committed suicide when faced with compulsory evacuation. The situation in the ghettos in Poland was hopeless; "downright dreadful living conditions held sway over the ghettos, which equaled a sentence to slow death!"[145] Shortly thereafter, Müller received a press clipping from the New York *Post* of October 23, 1941. It was headlined: "German troops masscre thousands of Jews in the Ukraine. . . . Corpses floating in the Dniester River." Based upon the reports of Hungarian officers returning from the front, it reported mass executions of Jews in both the Ukraine and Galicia.[146]

Müller talked with Schröder about getting out of D III, but this was in vain. In early December he saw an old friend in the army about pulling strings to get himself drafted.[147] But meanwhile the work in D III went on, and Müller performed his job like the meticulously trained bureaucrat he was. By the beginning of February, he had handled 48 requests for Jewish emigration. Emigration was still permitted in individual cases in which a positive Reich interest was involved.[148] But Müller requested such exceptional treatment from the RSHA in only four cases and rejected the others.[149]

Müller's exposure was not restricted to minor matters only. He submitted Hahn's summary of the first five *Einsatzgruppen* reports to Luther, filed Heydrich's January invitation to the Wannsee Conference, and noted on it after the meeting that a protocol was expected. He attended the *Ostminis-terium* conference on January 29, 1942, and he read the seventh and eighth *Einsatzgruppen* reports on February 16.

None of this involved any initiative on Müller's part. But Müller was not totally deprived of a chance to leave his mark. In January 1942, the German Red Cross informed the Foreign Office that it had been approached by a Portuguese relief committee named *Relico* about the possibility of sending supplies to the Jews in the Litzmannstadt (Lodz) ghetto. (In fact, *Relico* was a Jewish relief organization based in Geneva, which had been advised by a sympathetic German Red Cross to send its packages from Lisbon.)[150] This inquiry of the German Red Cross to the Foreign Office was handled by Section VIII of the Legal Division, where Dr. Conrad Rödiger invited representatives of *Abteilung Deutschland* and the Economic Division to attend a meeting on February 17 to discuss the question.[151]

Herbert Müller wrote back to the Legal Division on February 5:

> D III askes that the question of permitting aid shipments from abroad to Jews in Litzmannstadt not be clarified in an interdivisional meeting. The planned Final Solution for the European Jewish question, known to you, does not permit that food shipments be made from abroad to Jews in Germany and in the General Government.

The Red Cross should be told not to answer the *Relico* request, or if necessary, to answer that insurmountable technical difficulties made it impossible. Rademacher was quite satisfied with this, and the final Foreign Office reply to the German Red Cross followed Müller's suggestion completely.[152]

By mid-February Müller had his draft notice in his pocket. He passed the first half of March on courier duty to Portugal, and entered the army on April 1, 1942.[153] While his efforts to escape D III by getting into the military had been successful, he certainly did not leave behind the impression that he had found either the work or the company repulsive. In November 1942, Rademacher wrote to Luther that he had learned that "my friend and colleague" Dr. Herbert Müller was seriously wounded in Africa and could not be transported. It was feared that he must now be an English prisoner, and Rademacher asked Luther to find out what he could. It turned out that Müller had escaped capture and was in a military hospital in Bavaria. Luther wrote him a friendly letter, noting: "Uncle Franz waits, I believe, already quite yearningly for your return. In the meantime he has used up a number of candidates in your work area, who however either quickly took to the field or found other employment."[154] But the dissolution of *Abteilung Deutschland* before Müller recovered from his wound spared him further duty in D III.

The Jewish experts of the Foreign Office reacted to the murder of the Jews in different ways. The ambitious Luther saw the rising importance of Jewish policy as a signal to take charge. Here was a program which the old guard would not pursue with the proper enthusiasm and ruthless efficiency, and it would give him ample scope once again to demonstrate his indispensability. It perfectly suited the nature of the double-edged weapon he had forged in creating *Abteilung Deutschland.* On the one hand, he would overcome what timid opposition the old guard of the Foreign Office might offer to this important national-socialist policy. On the other hand, in so doing, he would protect the Foreign Office from further encroachments and attacks by other competence-hungry organizations like the SS. It was by ensuring that the Foreign Office played its role in all important programs of the Nazi regime that Luther hoped to keep his own personal fortunes advancing.

Luther's lieutenants in the *Judenreferat* did not fully share his new-found enthusiasm for the Jewish question. Franz Rademacher, the naive and dilettante anti-Semite, suddenly found himself in over his head. The "natural diminution" of the Jews through the rigors of deportation and resettlement in the swamps of Madagascar was one thing, and Rademacher still showed the plan to every captive audience he could find; systematic extermination was something else. But Rademacher was trapped in the mesh of his own anti-Semitism. He firmly believed that a final solution to the Jewish question was necessary. When his particular "pet" plan could not be realized, it may have taken the joy out of his work but not the necessity. For many Nazis the Madagascar Plan became a big alibi after the war; for Rademacher it was already an alibi in 1942. He could tell himself that he had personally preferred sending the Jews to their own island, but the war situation made this impossible. Some solution had to be found, and in any case orders were orders. This deprived Rademacher of either the imagination or the will to get out. Luther put off his request to be relieved of Jewish affairs until a successor had been groomed for the job. But work in D III was not terribly popular, and Rademacher was unable to find a suitable replacement very quickly. He remained at his job, passing most of the dirty work on to his assistants but continuing to make sure that the operation ran smoothly. After all, he still felt that "the Jewish question must be solved in the course of the war." Herbert Müller—more inventive than Rademacher and without the same anti-Semitic background—did succeed in extricating himself. But like Rademacher, while he was on the job, he performed his duties to the fullest satisfaction of his superiors, so well in fact that they eagerly awaited his return. *Abteilung Deutschland* thus began its murderous work through the driving ambition of Martin Luther, the fatal anti-Semitism of Franz Rademacher, and the bureaucratic reliability of Herber Müller.

# 6. The First Wave of Deportation: March–July 1942

## The Structure of the Foreign Office in German-dominated Europe

At the Wannsee Conference, Heydrich and Luther had agreed that all measures of the Final Solution in non-German territory would be harmonized between the SS and the Foreign Office, but the details of this cooperation were not spelled out. In fact the Foreign Office position in German-dominated Europe was such a crazy quilt that no explicit agreement delimiting the Foreign Office role in the Final Solution could have been worked out in the confines of a single meeting.

In the course of the war, Ribbentrop had faced the dilemma that, as German domination increased, the importance of the Foreign Office diminished. Sovereign nations were reduced to subordinate allies, outright satellites, and occupied territories. In the jungle war of Nazi politics, Ribbentrop rushed for the spoils like everyone else but came out on the short end more often than not. The result of each scramble was different. When Luther secured the "right of participation" of the Foreign Office in the Final Solution, it was not a single, clearly defined right, but one which varied with almost every country. By the time Luther reached the zenith of his powers, the ramshackle structure of the Foreign Office in Europe was already a fait accompli. He would have to tailor his activities in the Final Solution to work within the framework of the structure he inherited.

The position of the Foreign Office was weakest of all in Norway. Ribbentrop had failed to achieve a peaceful occupation of the country and was henceforth excluded entirely. The Foreign Office had no representative whatsoever in the domain of the *Reichskommisar* for Norway, Josef Terboven.[1] Its position in eastern Europe was likewise very weak. When Poland was crushed, the Warsaw embassy was disbanded. A "Deputy of the Foreign Office" (*Beauftragter*) was assigned to the General Government, but it was a position without significance. He was asked to relay inquiries concerning the treatment of foreign citizens to the Foreign Office, but otherwise was totally ignored by the officials of the General Government. In 1941 even the hapless Alfred Rosenberg bested Ribbentrop, when he was named Reich Minister for the Occupied Eastern Territories and charged with the management of civil affairs in occupied Russia.[2] The *Reichskommissaren* for the Ostland and the Ukraine, Hinrich Lohse and Erich Koch, each received a "Representative of the Foreign Office" (*Vertreter*), but these emissaries played as insignificant a role as the *Beauftragter* in the General Government. In both areas Jewish affairs were no exception to the general rule. Except for a few cases when foreign Jews were involved, the Foreign Office was neither informed nor consulted about Jewish measures in Poland and Russia. Here the Jews were not deported but killed locally, and the Nazi authorities there viewed it strictly as an internal affair.

The Foreign Office also had a *Vertreter* in the Protectorate. His role was more significant only because of the large number of foreign Jews, particularly Slovak, Hungarian, and Italian, residing there. Although there were no diplomatic representatives of third states in the General Government or eastern occupied territories, many countries had consulates in Prague to oversee the interests of their citizens. The treatment of foreign Jews in the Protectorate was a much more delicate affair than in the rest of eastern Europe, and the influence of the Foreign Office in Jewish matters correspondingly higher. But, even in this case, deportation of native Jews was viewed as an internal matter not requiring Foreign Office approval and had been carried out simultaneously with deportations from Germany. In contrast with Poland and Russia, however, the Foreign Office was kept reasonably well informed by its representative about internal Jewish measures in the Protectorate.

The position of the Foreign Office in the occupied territories of western and southeastern Europe was much stronger than in eastern Europe. In France, divided between the German-occupied zone and the unoccupied zone administered by the Vichy government, Otto Abetz had been designated as head of the "German Embassy in Paris" responsible for all political questions. His competency in Jewish affairs was shared with the military administration and the Paris Sipo-SD (Security Police and Security Service of Heydrich's RSHA), for Jewish affairs were felt to touch upon military and security as well as political matters. The Netherlands was the satrapy of Artur Seyss-Inquart, but this *Reichskommissar* did not have the autonomy from the Foreign Office that Koch and Lohse enjoyed in the east. Otto Bene had the same title of *Vertreter* as the Foreign Office representatives in the Ostland and Ukraine, but he played a much more active role, being consulted and sending back reports on Jewish affairs as well as other matters. Rosenberg's ministry did not stand as an insulator between the Foreign Office and the Netherlands as it did in the east. Belgium, completely under military administration, had yet another setup—an agency (*Dienststelle*) of the Foreign office under Werner von Bargen, which was attached to the military administration. Bargen played a lesser role than either Abetz or Bene, with his activities mostly confined to keeping the Foreign Office informed.

The two occupied zones in southeastern Europe, Serbia and Greece, each had a plenipotentiary (*Bevollmächtigter*) from the Foreign Office. Felix Benzler's powers in Serbia were never clearly defined and rapidly diminished when the outbreak of the partisan war led to the appointment of a plenipotentiary commanding general in Serbia in September 1941. Benzler had tried to manage Jewish affairs in Serbia but had been quickly bypassed by the army and SS. They were abetted in this by Martin Luther, who thus maintained Foreign Office participation despite Benzler's personal eclipse. Greece was divided between German and Italian zones centering on Salonika and Athens respectively. The Foreign Office plenipotentiary, Günther Altenburg, remained in Athens in the Italian zone, while a German consulate was maintained in Salonika. As Altenburg was not even stationed in the German military zone, he had even less influence on internal measures there, including Jewish affairs, than did Benzler in Serbia. His major duty, apparently, was to maintain relations with the Italians and the Greek puppet government. Despite his grandiose title, he was really little more than a liaison man.

In the two satellites, Slovakia and Croatia, the Foreign Office had full-fledged embassies headed by the SA-men Ludin and Kasche. But in Slovakia the adviser system had enabled internal German agencies to bypass the Foreign Office and deal directly with native collaborators, thus diminishing the importance of the embassy there. Even before the Wannsee Conference Luther had gone through the ambassadors to get official permission to include Croatian and Slovak Jews residing in the Reich in the deportations from Germany. After the Heydrich-Luther agreement the ambassadors would continue to play a similar role, securing basic agreement from the satellite governments but leaving the detailed negotiations up to the Jewish advisers.

Germany's client allies in southeastern Europe—Hungary, Rumania, and Bulgaria—likewise had embassies headed by SA-men (Jagow, Killinger, and Beckerle respectively). Of these only Rumania as yet had a complete adviser system, including the Jewish specialist Gustav Richter. Unlike the satellite states, these countries were not created by Germany, though the extent of their boundaries depended upon German generosity. Their slightly greater degree of independence from Germany made it more difficult to impose Nazi policies, including *Judenpolitik*, but at the same time this insured a greater role for the Foreign Office. Arm-twisting diplomacy was the order of the day.

In only two countries in the German sphere of influence—Italy and Denmark—did the Foreign Office maintain embassies headed by career diplomats. Italy was the only country which approached the status of an equal ally with Germany. It was Ribbentrop's last chance to act like a real foreign minister. He would zealously protect his prerogative to deal with Italy, not only against the other top Nazis, but eventually even against Luther. Thus the Foreign Office position in Italy was comparatively very strong, but paradoxically Luther's room for independent maneuver was not. Denmark was a unique case—a country which had capitulated to Germany but had been granted a large degree of internal autonomy. There was no system of advisers or brow-beating SA ambassador. Relations with Denmark were carried out by a regular embassy in Copenhagen under Cecil von Renthe-Fink. Thus the Foreign Office position in Denmark was strong vis-à-vis its Nazi rivals, but again its ability to impose German *Judenpolitik* was weak.

At the Wannsee Conference Heydrich had assured Luther that the Jewish experts of the Foreign Office and the RSHA would discuss the handling of the Final Solution in the territories occupied and influenced by Germany, but it was apparently understood by both sides that this did not mean a substantial alteration in the status quo of Foreign Office competency. The *Einsatzgruppen* campaign had been mounted in Russia without prior consultation with the Foreign Office, though it was belatedly informed. The construction of the death camps and the extermination of the Polish Jews would likewise not be matters of consultation with the Foreign Office, though they were certainly integral parts of the Final Solution occurring in German-occupied territory. Luther accepted this exclusion from eastern Europe as a fact of life and wrote Ribbentrop later that Heydrich had loyally kept to his promise.[3]

The Foreign Office right to participate was thus only in proportion to the power it already held in the various countries in Europe and was understood as such by Luther from the beginning. In eastern Europe the Foreign Office was competent only for matters affecting foreign Jews. In the areas under military occupation in the west and southeast, it also had the right to object to deportation measures if they were felt to be unacceptable within the framework of Germany's foreign policy interests. This veto power had already been exercised in Serbia, though not to the benefit of the Jews involved. In the satellites the Foreign Office would secure the official permission for deportation from governments already prepared to adopt Germany's radical Jewish measures. Among the allies the Foreign Office would attempt to do much of this preparatory work itself. Thus Foreign Office participation in the Jewish question did not enlarge Foreign Office competency; it did however protect its already diminishing position from declining further.

## Preparations

*Trial Runs.*    At the Wannsee Conference neither Heydrich nor Luther had professed to foresee any difficulties in deporting Jews from western and southeastern Europe. There must have been some apprehension behind this bravado, for the first steps of the deportation program were of a cautious and exploratory nature. The source of this initial caution was the SS, which approached the Foreign Office with very limited requests. In all likelihood Heydrich was not only testing the response abroad to the deportation measures, but also the reliability of the Foreign Office. Luther had asked that all measures be harmonized with him. Yet the earlier request from Eichmann about the inclusion of Croatian, Slovak, and Rumanian Jews in the deportations from Germany had required two and one-half months for an answer. Luther would have to show that he could do better.

In mid-February Eichmann presented a request from Himmler, that the Foreign Office ask the Slovak government to make available 20,000 strong, young Jews to be sent to the east to provide labor. Luther relayed this request to Ludin on February 16, after getting it initialed by Weizsäcker and Woermann. Luther informed Ludin that once he had secured the basic agreement of the Slovak government, the details would be settled verbally by the Jewish adviser. Four days later Ludin replied that the Slovak government had "eagerly snatched up" (*mit Eifer aufgegriffen*) the proposal, so preparatory work could begin.[4]

The trial run had gone very smoothly. For several years the Germans had been doing all in their power to prevent the emigration of Slovak Jews, for this would have diminished the emigration possibilities of German Jews. When they now offered the Slovak government the chance to dump 20,000 Jews to work in the east, it was eager to seize the opportunity, especially as the specific request for "strong, young" Jews made the labor disguise sound very plausible. Not only the Slovak government but also the Foreign Office had performed as well as could be expected. Luther had secured the approval of Weizsäcker and Woermann as well as the Slovak government in a very short time. There was no two and one-half month delay as before.

Following this success in Slovakia, a trial-run was also made in France. In December 1941, General Stülpnagel had requested permission to deport 1,000 Jews and 500 communists "to the east" in retaliation for terrorist attacks on German soldiers. Hitler had approved, but the deportations were not immediately carried out.[5] At the *Mischlinge* sterilization conference on March 6, 1942, Eichmann had a brief chat with Rademacher, informing him of the intention to deport these 1,000 French and stateless Jews to the Auschwitz concentration camp in late March. Rademacher asked for a written communication.[6] Eichmann provided this three days later, concluding: "I would be grateful for a communication, that no objections exist on your side against the execution of this action." Rademacher prepared a telegram to Paris, relaying Eichmann's inquiry and asking for the embassy's position. It was sent after being signed by Luther and initialed by Weizsäcker and Woermann.[7]

No sooner had this been dispatched than Eichmann asked the Foreign Office "to express its agreement" to the deportation of an additional 5,000 French and stateless Jews to Auschwitz. Kurt Weege prepared a second draft to Paris, which again went out with the signature of Luther and the initials of Weizsäcker and Woermann. Abetz's deputy, Rudolf Schleier, declared that there was no objection on the part of the Paris embassy to either inquiry.[8] A message drafted by Weege, signed by Rademacher, and initialed by Luther, Weizsäcker, and Woermann was then sent to Eichmann on March 20, 1942, assuring him that the Foreign Office raised no objection to the deportation of 6,000 stateless and French Jews to Auschwitz.[9]

The trial runs in both Slovakia and France were successful. As promised, the RSHA had undertaken prior consultation in each case. The Foreign Office had satisfactorily participated to the extent of its competency both times. In Slovakia it had achieved the basic agreement of the government, leaving further details to the adviser. In France it had waived its right to pose objections to the planned deportations. In both cases Luther had acted swiftly and with the passive approval of Weizsäcker and Woermann. The machinery was indeed working very well.

*Blocking Undesired Deportations.*    Ironically, when the first deportations were being planned in the spring of 1942, almost as much effort was required to prevent unwanted deportations as to carry out those that were desired. In the fall of 1941, the Germans had grudgingly permitted the Rumanians to deport Jews into Transnistria but not over the Bug River into the Ukraine. On February 10, 1942, the *Ostministerium* complained to the Foreign Office that, according to reports of a local commander, the Rumanians had sent 10,000 Jews over the Bug River into the Ukraine and another 60,000 were said to be following. Because of the danger of epidemic, the *Ostministerium* requested urgent negotiations with Rumania to stop the "wild deportations." Luther urged Ribbentrop to accede to this request. Antonescu should be prevailed upon, "that in the future the Rumanians only deport Jews when this has been arranged with Germany in an orderly way through the Foreign Office." But Ribbentrop replied that the unprecise allegation of a local commander could not be made the object of diplomatic action. Further details should be requested from the *Ostministerium.*[10]

Dr. Bräutigam in the *Ostministerium* complied with the request for details by sending a mass of reports from the Ukraine. Some 15,000 Jews had been concentrated on the Rumanian side of the Bug River, but without sufficient guard to prevent individual crossings, and a further 60,000 were approaching the Bug. An entire resettlement was taking place in Transnistria. The Jews were kept in insufficient quarters and daily perished in large numbers without adequate burial. "There can scarcely be a better functioning set-up for infecting an entire region." This area on the Rumanian side of the Bug also contained many *Volksdeutsch* settlements and German military personnel guarding railways and lines of communications. They were threatened by epidemic, and the danger would increase with warmer weather. The Rumanians, Bräutigam urged, must be persuaded "to stop this type of organization of Jewish camps on the Bug under all circumstances and to find another form for liquidating [*eine andere Form der Liquidierung*] the Rumanian Jews."

The Rumanians claimed that they were acting in accordance with the Tighina Agreement of the previous fall, but Koch, the *Reichskommissar* Ukraine, denied this. The concentration of Jews on the west bank of the Bug was practically the same as deportation over the Bug, because the Jews were insufficiently guarded to prevent crossings over the frozen river. He thus requested that a 50 kilometer stretch on the west bank of the Bug be cleared of Jews.[11]

Eichmann likewise urged the Foreign Office to induce the Rumanians to halt immediately these "illegal" shipments of Jews. "Even if the efforts of Rumania to rid itself of Jews are laudable in principle," they were not desirable at that time. The "planless and premature" deportation of Rumanian Jews into the occupied eastern territories endangered the evacuation of German Jews then in progress and threatened German troops and *Volksdeutsche* with epidemics.[12]

Killinger had already requested Mihai Antonescu to stop the unorganized Jewish deportations into the Ukraine on March 26, 1942, but failed to get any assurances from him. Finally on May 1, the Rumanian Deputy Premier told the Germans that the governor of Transnistria was being recalled to Bucharest to discuss the business, after which he would present the Rumanian point of view. At the very end of May Mihai Antonescu finally conceded that no further deportations of Jews into the Ukraine would be undertaken without first consulting the Germans.[13]

The "wild deportations" were stopped not only because of German pressure but also because so many of the Jews had already died. Helmut Triska of D VIII (*Volksdeutsch* affairs) had made a tour of German settlements in Transnistria and reported to Rademacher: "Some 28,000 Jews were brought to German villages in Transnistria. Meanwhile they were liquidated."[14] And on May 19, 1942, ten days before the Rumanians promised to stop, Dr. Bräutigam wrote Rademacher that no border crossings by Jews had been reported in the last few weeks. "A considerable portion of the Jews in Transnistria have died."[15]

The RSHA showed a marked reluctance to deport Jews from areas where they were being exterminated on the spot. Rumania was not the only country originally targeted for deportation at the Wannsee Conference but one where the Germans found it expedient to prevent any early deportations, as long as the killing process was going on locally. On Rademacher's trip to Belgrade in October 1941, his train had passed through Zagreb, where he talked briefly with Siegfried Kasche. Kasche informed him that the Croatian government had asked that the Germans take their Jews away. Rademacher informed the RSHA of this, but was told that it was out of the question. Again in May 1942, the Croatians formally requested the deportation of their Jews. Luther instructed Rademacher to undertake negotiations with the RSHA "over the earliest possible deportation of Croatian Jews to the east." The RSHA answered that it would not take them at that time.[16]

The RSHA was in no hurry to take up the question, for the longer they waited, the more Jews the *Ustashe*, the Croatian fascist organization, killed on its own (often aided by *Volksdeutsch* units). The *Ustashe* had begun interning Jews in the summer of 1941, and most did not survive the local concentration camps. Other Jews were massacred outright. By itself the *Ustashe* murdered close to 30,000 Jews.[17] It was only in the summer of 1942, when the Foreign

Office reported that Jews were being protected from the *Ustashe* murder squads by the Italians, that the RSHA suddenly became interested in deporting Jews from Croatia. Similarly, it would later interest itself again in deportations from Rumania when it became clear that the Rumanians were sending no further Jews to die in Transnistria.

In Serbia deportations were not only delayed but in the end not required at all. In December 1941, Rademacher had listed deportations from Serbia as one of the "desires and ideas" of the Foreign Office, and he had told Benzler at that time that deportations would take place from Serbia the following spring. In the meantime the Jewish women, children, and aged, whom the army would not shoot as hostages, were concentrated in the camp at Semlin, which was under SS, not army, administration. By the next summer they were all dead. Many had fallen victim to hunger or exposure and overwork, shovelling the air field. Those that survived the winter were killed in a gas van which was returned to Germany in June 1942.[18] No written reports of the Semlin gassings have been found in the Foreign Office files, but Kurt Heinburg, the head of the Southeast Europe Desk, testified that he had seen reports on gassings in Belgrade.[19] Presumably Rademacher had seen these reports too, when he wrote on May 23, 1942: "The Jewish question in Serbia is no longer acute."[20]

## Slovakia

*Deportation.*   Following the trial runs, no immediate action was taken in France, but in Slovakia the Germans moved to complete their task. On March 23, 1942, following a proposal of Himmler, Luther took the crucial step. Ludin was instructed to inform the Slovak government that Germany was prepared to deport the rest of its Jews and make Slovakia *judenfrei.* Weizsäcker initialed the instructions. On April 6, Ludin replied: "Without any German pressure, the Slovak government has declared itself in agreement with the deportation of all Jews from Slovakia."[21]

Two difficulties faced the Foreign Office initially—clerical opposition in Slovakia and the financial demands of the SS. The first was sidestepped. Ludin was explicitly instructed to avoid internal political difficulties concerning the deportations, and the Germans did not oppose restrictions placed upon the deportations by the Slovak government in response to clerical opposition. Jews baptized by the spring of 1939 or living in mixed marriage by the fall of 1941 were to be exempted. This was sufficient to overcome the scruples of Father Tiso, chief of state and a Catholic priest. Ludin reported: "Even the President of the State personally approved the deportation, despite steps of the Slovak Episcopacy."[22] A protest note of the Vatican against Jewish deportations was turned back with the excuse that they were no different than the employment of 120,000 Slovak workers in Germany. Ludin noted, however, that "it is obviously clear to people here that the comparison of the Jewish deportation with the employment of Slovak workers in Reich territory is far fetched."[23]

Perhaps even more crucial to Germany's success in undermining potential clerical opposition than the labor disguise and the minor concessions over baptized Jews and Jews living in mixed marriage was the internal political situation in Slovakia. The Hlinka Guard faction of Tuka and Mach was losing ground to the clerical faction of Father Tiso. To gain needed German support once again, Tuka jumped at the possibility of abetting the deportations. In order not to give Tuka the political advantage, Tiso likewise endorsed them.[24]

The financial problem arose from Heydrich's request to Luther that the Slovak government be induced to pay the Germans 500 *Reichsmark* per deported Jew in order to defray the alleged costs of lodging, food, clothing, and retraining. The Slovak Premier, Vojtech Tuka, countered with a request for a bilateral treaty in which Germany promised neither to return the deported Jews to Slovakia nor to make any claim on the property of the deported Slovak Jews beyond the 500 RM per head. Ludin rejected the form of a bilateral treaty but conceded Tuka's demands in a *note verbal* of May 1. It was not until June 23, 1942, that the Slovak government agreed in principle to paying 500 RM per deported Jew, while reserving the method of payment for later negotiations.[25]

By this time, however, a more serious problem had arisen for the Germans. On June 26, 1942, Ludin reported that the deportation of Jews from Slovakia had "hit a dead spot." Through the influence of the Church and the corruption of individual officials, some 35,000 Jews had received special exemption from deportation. "The Jewish resettlement is very unpopular in wide circles of the Slovak people." Nevertheless Tuka wished to continue the deportations and "requested support through sharp diplomatic pressure of the Reich."[26]

A reply was drafted in D III that authorized Ludin to help Tuka overcome his internal opposition. Ludin was to tell Tuka that the halt in the Jewish resettlement and especially the exemption of 35,000 Jews would "leave a very bad impression in Germany, particularly as the previous cooperation of Slovakia in the Jewish question had been very much appreciated." Weizsäcker changed the text from "would leave a bad impression in Germany" to "would cause surprise in Germany." This apparently satisfied Weizsäcker that he had served both country and conscience, and he sent it on to Ludin.[27]

Whether Ludin had already received Weizsäcker's telegram by the time he attended a meeting with Wisliceny and Tuka on June 30 is not known. In any case there is no record that he made use of his authorization to pressure Tuka at either this meeting or any later time. He was a silent spectator while Wisliceny secured Tuka's assurance that the exemptions would be revised. Allegedly, Ludin had just learned the truth behind the deportations, probably from Wisliceny, and lost his appetite for further work in the Jewish question. Even Wisliceny let it be known that he was open to bribery and that he would not insist on more deportations, if Slovakia itself did not exert pressure. The result was that the Jewish deportations sharply tapered off and then came to a complete halt. Between March and June 1942, 52,000 Jews had been deported, but only 4,000 more had left by the time of the last deportation at the end of September.[28] The Foreign Office role in Slovak deportations was for the moment at an end.

*The Problem of Jewish Property.*    Even with the deportations from Slovakia temporarily halted, negotiations with that country over Jewish property continued to vex Foreign Office Jewish experts. Slovakia was the bellwether of opposition to German policies on Jewish property. On the one hand it was the first satellite and, as such, always the first approached to accept German policies. On the other hand the presence of large numbers of Slovak Jews residing in territory under German control, especially the Protectorate, insured that the property of these Jews would be a matter of substantial contention between the two countries. The Germans were to discover very quickly that no matter how acquiescent Slovakia was in Jewish affairs, in at least one respect Bratislava could be quite stubborn. Regardless of what else Germany did with Slovak Jews, they were not going to make a profit out of them.

Slovakia had sounded the warning as early as September 1941. For some months Slovakia had been protesting the employment of trustees to run the businesses of Slovak Jews in the Protectorate, obviously a thin veil for aryanization. Any restrictions by Germany on Slovak property, even if it was Jewish, had no legal base and had to be suspended until an agreement between the two countries was reached. Slovakia envisaged two possibilities: 1) the "personality principle" whereby each country claimed the property of its Jews, regardless of location, or 2) the "territorial principle" in which each country claimed all the Jewish property located in its territory, regardless of the citizenship of its owners. Since Germany was acting in accordance with the personality principle and intervened for the property of its Jewish citizens in Slovakia, Slovakia would have to do likewise.[29] Again in November 1941, when Luther gave the Slovak government the alternative of recalling its Jews from Germany or permitting their deportation to the east, the Slovaks agreed to the deportations, but only on the firm guarantee from Germany that Slovak claims to the Jewish property left behind would be endangered in no way.

The Germans complicated the question of property rights in November 1941 when they issued the 11th Decree to the Reich Citizenship Law, by which all German Jews residing abroad lost their citizenship, and their property was forfeited to the Reich. This law was issued primarily to facilitate the deportation of Jews from Germany and the subsequent confiscation of their property, but it had repercussions elsewhere. German Jews residing abroad now suddenly became stateless. While Germany claimed that all their property, even that abroad, had been forfeited to the Reich, Germany's ability to lay claim to the property of such stateless Jews located in foreign countries was in fact quite tenuous.

Rademacher invited both the Economic and Legal Divisions to a meeting with D III on February 10, 1942, to establish a common Foreign Office position on Jewish property. There it was decided that despite the sweeping nature of the 11th Decree, it would be expedient to register German property claims for the moment only in countries which already had Jewish legislation. This included Slovakia, Croatia, Rumania, Hungary, and Italy. (The omission of Bulgaria was unexplained and probably accidental.) Furthermore, it would not be a blanket claim to all the property of ex-German Jews in these countries but only to specific properties. A further meeting with other German ministries was scheduled for February 23.[30]

This interministerial meeting, attended by the RSHA, Finance and Economic Ministries, and Office of the Four Year Plan, scaled down German ambitions even further. Individual properties of special significance would be claimed at first only in Rumania and Croatia. Special negotiations would be held with Slovakia, which had already claimed all Slovak Jewish property in Germany. No other countries would be approached yet.[31]

When the deportation of Slovak Jews began in March 1942, both from Slovakia and the Reich, the Slovak government asked that the latter deportations be postponed until its diplomatic representatives in Berlin, Vienna, and Prague were included in the identification of Slovak Jewish property and all this property was impounded.[32] In Prague the Slovak general consul also demanded property lists for all the Slovak Jews deported. When the Germans proceeded to deport Slovak Jews without meeting this requirement, the general consul insisted that all deportation of Slovak Jews from the Protectorate be postponed.[33]

These Slovak interventions and the threatened delay in deportations caused Rademacher to rethink the whole problem. In a lengthy memorandum prepared in May 1942, he advocated a complete turnabout in German policy. Difficulties had arisen, he noted, because property inventories were not always available in time for the scheduled deportations. Even when they were, it proved impossible to reach quick agreement on the value of this property, often businesses whose activities had partially ceased for some time. Long negotiations would be required to ascertain the value of each country's Jewish property in the other's territory. Meanwhile, Dieter Wisliceny and Friedrich Suhr, Rademacher's traveling companion to Belgrade, had talked with Sano Mach, Germany's most faithful collaborator in Slovakia. Mach had indicated that the Slovaks did not want to drive a bargain and were willing to settle on the basis of the territorial principle. Rademacher noted that the property of Slovak Jews in German territory was probably much higher than vice versa, so Germany stood to gain from the territorial solution.

Rademacher went on to discuss the property question in a European-wide perspective. The 11th Decree to the Reich Citizenship Law had deprived German Jews abroad of their citizenship and property, but there was no way to register or confiscate this property without the aid of foreign government authorities. Such help might be forthcoming only in Slovakia, Croatia, and Rumania. But here the authorities were unreliable, and the figures they compiled would be imprecise in comparison to those on the German side. Furthermore German claims to the property of ex-German Jews abroad had been considerably weakened because these Jews were now stateless, while on the other hand foreign Jews living in Germany, with the exception of the Slovaks, had not yet lost their citizenship. Rademacher concluded, therefore, that Germany would suffer considerable disadvantage unless the territorial principle was applied to settle all property questions.[34]

The RSHA was in immediate agreement with Rademacher, and a second interministerial meeting was called for July 30, 1942, officially to reverse the decision reached in February. At the meeting the newly-arrived Karl Klingen-fuss summarized the various arguments in favor of the territorial principle and particularly emphasized how difficulties in establishing the property value and even the real citizenship of many Jews had led to repeated delays in the deportation of Slovak Jews. The reciprocal renunciation by Germany and other states of all claims to the property of their Jews living abroad was the only way to avoid a chain of endless difficulties endangering the settlement of the Jewish question in Europe. All participating ministries gave their agreement to the territorial principle.[35]

By the time the Germans reached common agreement on the territorial principle, however, the Slovaks were already hedging. A week before the interministerial meeting at the end of July, Klingenfuss learned from the economic specialist of the Slovak embassy in Berlin that his government now opposed the territorial solution, which at one time it had favored and Germany had opposed. "I had the impression that on the Slovak side the suspicion exists that the Germans have now changed their point of view because in the meantime the territorial settlement has turned out to be financially more beneficial to the Reich."[36]

Slovak opposition to the territorial solution was confirmed by their ambassador in Berlin on September 22, 1942. He noted that Slovak agreement to the deportation of its Jews from Germany had been based on the assurance that its claim to the property left behind would in no way be endangered. Furthermore, Slovakia had agreed to pay 500 RM per deported Jew and intended to use the Jewish property in question to cover this expense. Thus Slovakia could not renounce its claims to the property of its Jews in Germany.[37]

Klingenfuss felt the Slovak objection was justified. In order to remove the Slovak mistrust that they were being "commercially damaged" so that agreement on a territorial solution could be reached, he recommended that Germany reduce the per capita levy on Slovakia from 500 RM to 300 RM. Luther agreed, but they were unable to persuade the Economic Ministry. It had already reckoned the 500 RM per deported Jew into Germany's difficult foreign exchange balance and thus adamantly opposed its reduction.[38]

In January 1943, the Slovaks requested a German reply to their still unanswered notes of March and September 1942. Until a settlement was reached, they insisted, any further deportation of Slovak Jews would have to be postponed.[39] Luther then tried to enlist Weizsäcker to put added pressure on the Economic Ministry. He noted that it blocked agreement on the basis of the territorial principle, even though the amount of Slovak Jewish property in

Germany probably far exceeded that of German Jewish property in Slovakia. More important than this economic consideration, however, was the over-riding political factor. An agreement with Slovakia on the basis of the territorial principle was of fundamental importance for further negotiations with all other states to settle the question of Jewish property.[40] Whether Weizsäcker complied with Luther's request to pressure the Economic Ministry is unknown. Two weeks later Luther was gone and any coherent effort within the Foreign Office to reach a solution to the property question collapsed. It was not until the summer of 1944 that the Germans answered the Slovak note of September 1942, and asked for a meeting to discuss the matter. By then the outcome was irrelevant.[41]

The Germans stumbled over their own greed in trying to reach an agreement with Slovakia over Jewish property. At first they could not conceive of renouncing their own claims in Slovakia at a time when the Slovaks were ready to accept a territorial solution. They further complicated the situation by pressuring the Slovaks into paying 500 RM per deported Jew. When the Jewish experts finally realized that the territorial solution was not only economically advantageous to Germany but also, more importantly, the only way to reach a quick settlement and avoid delays and postponements in deportations, it was too late. The Economic Ministry would not give up the blood money which Germany had exacted to cover the cost of deporting the Slovak Jews, and the Slovaks justifiably felt that the Germans were not only trying to get their Jews but to make money out of it as well. It cannot be determined if any Slovak Jews residing in German territory were in fact saved by the Slovak insistence on halting the deportations until a property settlement had been reached. If they were, it was one of the few times in which greed outweighed the zeal and efficiency of the killers.

## France, Belgium, and the Netherlands

*Deportation.* The Germans did not follow up their trial run in France as quickly as they had in Slovakia. One reason for this was that preparatory Jewish legislation was not yet complete. In particular, marking ordinances were still lacking. Among the triumvirate for Jewish affairs in France (Sipo-SD, military, and embassy), apparently Abetz had been dragging his feet on the issue. But in early May, the embassy expert for Jewish affairs, Carltheo Zeitschel, informed the Sipo-SD and military administration in Paris that Abetz not only withdrew his objections to introducing the Jewish star but also urged that it be carried out immediately.[42]

While the military proposed exempting all American and British Jews as well as those of neutral and allied countries, Rademacher wished to mark all European Jews. Woermann noted that according to a recent decree in the Netherlands, all foreign Jews were exempt and that even in Germany the only foreign Jews marked were those of Slovakia, Croatia, and Rumania. Luther then ruled that as in Germany the formal law should include all Jews, but internal instructions would exempt foreign Jews except those whose home-lands carried out similar marking measures. In addition to Slovakia, Croatia, Rumania, and now the Netherlands, Rademacher added the Yugoslav Jews in this category. While no marking decree had been issued in Serbia, this was only because the territory had been made *judenfrei*. Shortly thereafter the military authorities in Belgium issued their own marking edict.[43] That the Foreign Office was consulted in France but not in the Netherlands or Belgium once again demonstrates the irregular position and varying competencies that it held.

In accordance with Heydrich's promise to hold discussions between Foreign Office and RSHA experts on measures of the Final Solution, Eich-mann invited Rademacher to attend a meeting with his own men from France, Belgium, and the Netherlands, which was held on June 11, 1942. According to Rademacher the meeting consisted mostly of technical instructions from Eichmann to his subordinates on deportations from these three countries. Rademacher left the meeting before the end and asked Eichmann for a written communication before the deportations began.[44] Eichmann once again dis-cussed the deportations with Rademacher by telephone on June 20 and sent an official letter two days later. He informed Rademacher of the plan to begin deporting 40,000 Jews each from France and the Netherlands and 10,000 from Belgium in mid-July "for labor in the camp at Auschwitz." The Jews of the Americas and Great Britain as well as allied and neutral countries would not be included. As he had discussed the matter with Rademacher twice already without Rademacher's raising any problems, Eichmann added: "I . . . assume also that no objections against these measures exist on the side of the Foreign Office."[45] Luther then asked the Foreign Office representatives in France, Belgium, and the Netherlands for their opinions on the pending deportations.[46]

In France, Zeitschel had already learned of the imminent deportations from Theo Dannecker, Eichmann's deputy with the Paris Sipo-SD. Instead of 40,000 Jews from all of France, as Eichmann had indicated to Rademacher, Dannecker wanted 50,000 from the unoccupied zone alone in addition to 50,000 from occupied France. Zeitschel discussed the question with Abetz and Rudolf Rahn, another Foreign Office official, on June 27. Rahn was instructed to discuss the deportation of 50,000 Jews from unoccupied France with Pierre Laval.[47]

In early May, René Bousquet, the French chief of police, had alrady informed the visiting Heydrich of the French desire to deport the stateless Jews, primarily refugees from Germany, Poland, Austria, and Czechoslo-vakia, who were interned in unoccupied France. Heydrich had left the question open because of transportation difficulties.[48] Laval must have again emphasized to Rahn the French willingness to cooperate with deporting stateless Jews, for when Abetz replied to Luther's inquiry that in the Paris embassy there were no objections to the deportation of 40,000 Jews from France, he strongly urged that it would be psychologically more effective if the foreign Jews in France were taken first. This would not concede a privileged position to the French Jew, "because in any case he must likewise vanish in the course of the release of the European countries from Jewry."[49]

Luther answered that giving priority to the deportation of foreign Jews from France was not possible.[50] But Luther had already been bypassed by events in Paris. Following Rahn, the Higher SS and Police Leader Kurt Oberg had also pressured Laval, who had agreed to the participation of French police in the deportation measures on the condition that for the moment only non-French Jews were taken.[51] Bousquet informed the Germans on July 4 that Petain had approved Laval's bargain,[52] and the early deportations from France contained only non-French Jews, as Abetz had proposed.

As in France, the Foreign Office *Vertreter* in the Netherlands learned of the planned deportations before receiving Luther's inquiry. Bene reported that the deportation of approximately 25,000 stateless Jews from the Netherlands would begin in mid-July and take about four months, after which the deportation of the Dutch Jews would begin.[53]

The response from Werner von Bargen in Belgium was the only one definitely unenthusiastic. While the military administration intended to carry out the deportation of 10,000 Jews, there were many difficulties. Understanding of the Jewish question was not widespread in Belgium, and the Jews of Belgian citizenship were considered by the population as Belgians. Measures against these Jews could thus be construed as part of a general forced deportation of all Belgians. Luther found this a "peculiar point of view." Furthermore, Bargen warned, the Jews were integrated into the local economy, so that labor difficulties were to be feared. Eggert Reeder, the chief of the military administration, had gone to the Führer's headquarters to discuss these difficulties with Himmler. The military could defer its objections, however, if the deportations began with Jews from eastern Europe but avoided Belgian Jews. Bargen also warned that there was a great deal of unrest among the local Jews, and the police power on hand was insufficient for compulsory measures.[54]

According to Bargen's later account, it was General Falkenhausen who most strongly opposed any deportations from Belgium. Reeder told him that they would be difficult to stop, but something could be done at least for Belgian citizens. Thus he went to argue the case successfully with Himmler for exempting Belgian Jews for the moment.[55]

Eichmann had told the Foreign Office that the deportations would begin in mid-July and that he assumed there were no objections on the side of the Foreign Office. Thus the first trains had departed from France and the Netherlands by July 17 before any official Foreign Office reply.[56] Only on July 27 did Rademacher pass along Luther's instructions to Klingenfuss to draft an answer to Eichmann. It confirmed that the Foreign Office had no objection to the planned deportations but suggested that, in view of the psychological repercussions, stateless Jews be taken first. At this time Luther knew that this was the intended procedure in the Netherlands and that Abetz and Bargen had likewise requested this arrangement. He did not yet know that in France and Belgium arrangements had already been taken to this effect.[57]

The Foreign Office had little influence on the course of the deportations from France, Belgium, and the Netherlands. It had been consulted beforehand, but once the deportations were underway, it had little more to say. Luther had belatedly joined the movement to deport stateless Jews first, but only after it had been arranged at the local level. This limited role was due not to any lack of zeal on Luther's part, but rather to the intrinsic limitations on Foreign Office competency in militarily occupied areas. When special problems arose that touched the competency of the Foreign Office, Luther was given a chance to prove his mettle.

*The Problem of Foreign Jews.*   One such problem was the presence of numerous foreign Jews in the western occupied territories. Could they be marked? Could they be interned and deported? What was to happen to their property? Each of these questions had to be answered separately for each country whose Jews were involved. The problem was not unimportant, for in Paris alone Abetz reported 500 Italian, 1,570 Hungarian, 3,046 Turkish, 3,790 Rumanian, and 1,416 Greek Jews.[58] A failure to create some intelligible system out of the potential chaos would have seriously disrupted the efficiency of the killing process. The task lay entirely within the Foreign Office domain, and the success of the Foreign Office in dealing with this complex of problems testifies to the zeal and efficiency with which they sought to facilitate the frictionless operation of the Final Solution.

Before the western deportations began, the Foreign Office had already gained permission to deport from Germany the Jews of Slovakia, Croatia, and Rumania. These Jews were marked in Germany and, according to the Foreign Office, could be marked in France as well. But this covered only a very few contingencies. Now the Foreign Office was deluged with inquiries and protests about the treatment of foreign Jews. The Rumanian consuls in the west, followed by the ambassador in Berlin, hotly protested discriminatory treatment of Rumanian Jews. They were not to be marked until the Jews of Italy, Hungary, and Switzerland were treated in the same way. The Rumanian consul in Prague went even further and demanded that Germany abstain from deporting Rumanian Jews from the Protectorate, denying any knowledge of the fact that the Rumanian government had agreed to just such deportations the previous fall.[59] In Belgium the Italian consul demanded that the Greek Jews there be exempted from Jewish measures, because Italy had ordered no such measures in Greece.[60]

On the home front Friedrich Suhr of the RSHA requested that Bulgarian Jews in Germany be marked and deported.[61] Abetz asked that the foreign Jews in France be deported first for psychological reasons, and Bene inquired about the foreign Jews in the Netherlands, in particular 193 Hungarian Jews.[62] Finally, on July 9, 1942, Eichmann, who had earlier stated the intention to deport only stateless and native Jews, asked for a "quick, basic, and comprehensive" communication on the viewpoint of the Foreign Office to subjecting foreign Jews to German Jewish measures.[63]

If this did not give Luther enough problems to sort out at one time, he promptly added some of his own. Though he had no authorization whatsoever from the Hungarian government, Luther told Abetz that he could include Hungarian Jews in the measures being carried out in France. And though he had not yet resolved the Rumanian protest against the marking of Rumanian Jews, at the end of July he informed Eichmann that not only Hungarian but also Rumanian Jews could be included in the deportations.[64] Incredibly, both Weizsäcker and Woermann initialed this letter, though they had irrefutable grounds for stopping it.

To work his way out of this morass of complications, Luther first tackled the problem of the Bulgarian Jews. On June 19, 1942, in a telegram drafted by Rademacher, Luther told Beckerle of the German desire to deport Bulgarian Jews from the German sphere, thus exceeding the RSHA request to mark and deport Jews in Germany. Noting the earlier suggestion of the Bulgarian foreign minister, Popov, for the common treatment of Jews by all European nations, Luther asked Beckerle to find out if the Bulgarian government would agree to an understanding between the two countries that neither would call upon any existing treaty rights to protect its Jews from the Jewish measures of the other country when they were residing there. Jewish property would be impounded until its disposal was mutually agreed upon. Since the German measures included deportation, Beckerle should broach the question of Bulgaria's compensating Germany for the costs arising from deportation and "retraining," as was the case with Slovakia. If the Bulgarians inquired whether Germany was ready to deport Jews from Bulgaria as well, Beckerle was to answer affirmatively but make no commitment as to when, for pending deportations already so completely claimed the available means of transportation that any deportations from Bulgaria were probably impossible that year.[65]

On July 6, 1942, Beckerle replied that the Bulgarians were ready to enter the proposed "understanding." Furthermore, they agreed to the deportation of Bulgarian Jews living on German territory provided they received in advance an exact list of the deported Jews. To the question of payment, however, the Bulgarians had reacted negatively.[66]

When Klingenfuss attempted to notify the RSHA that it was free to deport the Bulgarian Jews in the western occupied territories and in Germany, he encountered brief resistance from Dr. Stahlberg of the Legal Division. Stahlberg noted that the text of the note exchange referred only to German but not occupied territory. Klingenfuss was aware, of course, of the fuller discussions which surrounded the note exchange. He brushed aside the legal technicality and ordered the original draft dispatched.[67] In early August the Bulgarian Jews became vulnerable to all Jewish measures in Germany and the western occupied territories.

After receiving the protests of the Rumanians, Luther moved quickly on this front as well. On June 22, 1942, Luther instructed Killinger to secure Rumanian agreement that its Jews in the German sphere be subjected to all Jewish measures.[68] The Rumanians apparently wished to discuss the matter in Berlin, not Bucharest, and on July 19, 1942, the first secretary of the

Rumanian embassy, Valeanu, delivered a note reaffirming that Rumanian prestige did not permit discriminatory treatment of Rumanian Jews in comparison with those of other states like Hungary. Valeanu was received by Klingenfuss, who complained that the note did not correspond with the previous sense of cooperation between Germany and Rumania on the Jewish question.[69]

A week later the Rumanian ambassador, Raoul Bossy, called upon Woermann and repeated his concern that Hungarian and Italian Jews held a privileged position vis-à-vis Rumanian Jews. Woermann noted that Rumanian Jews would be treated on par with German and Croatian Jews but urged Bossy to see Luther.[70] Luther requested a memorandum in preparation for this visit, and Rademacher passed the assignment to Klingenfuss. The new assistant noted that the brunt of the Rumanian complaint, that Hungarian Jews were favored, was now removed, for all measures had been extended to them as well. He could not understand why the Rumanians were suddenly making difficulties. "The entire burden of the work and the psychological repercussions in the previously affected areas lie on our shoulders. We can scarcely assume that Rumania, which previously displayed excellent understanding in the Jewish question, now wants to be inferior where possible to Hungary in its attitude." Subsequently, however, Luther decided it was fruitless to deal with Bossy in Berlin and shifted the negotiations back to Bucharest.[71]

By this time, in fact, Killinger had achieved the desired Rumanian concessions. After repeated complaints about how Rumanian Jews in Germany and the western occupied territories were being treated worse than the Jews of Hungary, Italy, Switzerland, and Spain (only in Belgium had the German authorities been somewhat friendly toward Rumanian Jews, it was alleged), the Rumanian Foreign Office agreed on August 8, 1942, that Rumanian Jews abroad could be subjected to all German Jewish measures.[72] In a message drafted by Klingenfuss and initialed by Rademacher, Luther informed Eichmann and the Foreign office representatives in France, Belgium, the Netherlands, and the Protectorate on August 20, 1942, that the Foreign Office had no objections to including Rumanian Jews in all Jewish measures.[73]

The attempt of the Italian consul in Belgium to protect the Greek Jews there from German measures was perhaps the first but certainly not the last time that local Italian diplomatic or military authorities took a private initiative to protect Jews from German persecution. Elsewhere the Italian position would be strong enough to be effective, but in Belgium this was not the case. Klingenfuss cryptically dismissed the Italian arguments, and Luther instructed Bargen to treat Italian protests politely but dilatorily, without postponing measures against the Greek Jews in Belgium.[74]

Thus by mid-August the deportation net in the western occupied territories had been spread considerably wider. The local German authorities in France, Belgium, and the Netherlands had all agreed to deport stateless Jews before native Jews. Through the efforts of the Foreign Office, the Jews of Slovakia, Croatia, Rumania, Greece, and Bulgaria were now added to the list of deportable Jews.[75] But the Foreign Office record was not without setbacks. Two German allies, Italy and Hungary, put up more determined resistance. In France Abetz had welcomed Luther's news of July 2 that the Hungarian Jews could be included, but he perceived a pressing political interest that other pro-German governments, especially Italy, follow the same path. It was deplorable that in French eyes the Axis did not pursue a unified Jewish policy. Every effort should be made to induce the Italians either to permit their Jews in France to be deported, or, failing that, to recall them to Italy. Luther endorsed Abetz's suggestion to Ribbentrop, with Weizsäcker's approving initial. Ribbentrop refused to be hurried into any precipitous action involving the Italians and requested an opinion from the Political Division as well. Woermann supported Abetz's proposal.[76]

While Ribbentrop was delaying a decision on the Italian question, Luther's unilateral and unwarranted declaration that the Hungarian Jews could be subjected to all German measures backfired. Luther had probably taken this risk to defuse the Rumanian criticism that it was being discriminated against vis-à-vis Hungary. But on August 10, 1942, the day before Luther learned that the Rumanians had dropped their protest and left their Jews in the German sphere unprotected, the Hungarian reaction came. The Hungerian ambassador, Döme Sztojay, visited Luther. His government protested that in France its Jews were being forced to wear the Jewish star while those of Rumania and Italy were not. Personally, Sztojay added, he found this task very unpleasant, as he characterized himself as a "pioneer" of anti-Semitism. Luther expressed his astonishment that the Hungarians should complain of dicrimination vis-à-vis Rumania, when the Rumanians had just done likewise. It was the will of the Führer to solve the Jewish question as soon as possible, but one could get nowhere with such protests. Sztojay indicated that Hungary would comply with German desires when Italy did.[77]

Luther wished to pressure the Hungarians and therefore had Klingenfuss draft a telegram for Budapest. It was wrong to speak of discrimination, Klingenfuss argued, because German measures were aimed at international Jewry, not individual nations. Because Germany had taken upon itself the entire burden and psychological repercussions of carrying out these measures, it expected a "certain obligingness" on the part of Hungary. If Hungary continued to make difficulties, it would have to take back its Jews from the western occupied territories, "a settlement that is indeed just as unpleasant to us as to Hungary itself, because from out point of view the affected Jews are for the moment withdrawn from a radical solution in this way."[78]

This telegram was never sent, however. At the end of August, Ribbentrop finally made up his mind in regard to Italy and also cracked down on Luther's free-wheeling with the Hungarians. The foreign minister accepted the policy endorsed by Luther, Woermann, and Weizsäcker to induce the Italians either to recall or to surrender their Jews in the western occupied territories. Concerning the Hungarians, however, he ordered that no initiative be taken on the German side.[79]

Perhaps stunned by this rebuff (reflecting a wider estrangement developing between Luther and Ribbentrop at this time), Luther did not even move to deal with the Italians. Only following further complaints from Abetz did he finally instruct Mackensen, the ambassador in Rome, on September 17, 1942, to inform the Italian government that it was indispensable that all Jews in the occupied western territories be subjected to all Jewish measures by the end of the year. If the Italian government felt itself unable to agree to the inclusion of its Jews in these measures, including deportation to the east, it should recall them before the deadline.[80]

Ribbentrop may have instructed Luther to take no further initiative with the Hungerians, but this did not stop the Hungarians from keeping the issue alive when Luther did little to remedy their complaints. Indeed, the Hungarian protests were fully justified. Klingenfuss had asked the RSHA to refrain from marking and deporting Hungarian Jews.[81] Apparently neither the Foreign Office nor the RSHA relayed these instructions further, and in mid-September the Hungarian general consul in Paris was forced to protest against the continued marking and internment of Hungarian Jews as well as damage to Hungarian Jewish property in France.[82] In Berlin, Sztojay delivered a similar protest note, demanding most-favored treatment for Hungarian Jews. He was particularly incensed over the damage to Hungarian Jewish property and proposed the use of a Hungarian-created trusteeship association, if property measures were required.[83]

The German response was provocatively insufficient. Luther told Abetz that insofar as Hungarian Jews were already interned, they should be not deported at the moment.[84] On September 17, 1942, Bene reported that the local Security Police had interned the Rumanian and Hungarian Jews at the Westerbork camp, where they stood ready for further deportation. A week later Rademacher belatedly asked Bene temporarily to refrain from deporting the interned Hungarian Jews. On October 8, Bene nonchalantly noted that the message had arrived too late to prevent the deportation of some of the Hungarian Jews who had been shipped out with the regular weekly transport.[85]

The continued Hungarian protests, which Luther did nothing to avoid, served his purpose. They kept alive the issue of Hungarian Jews in the west, so that he could reopen the topic despite his earlier rebuff from Ribbentrop. In accordance with instructions passed on by Rademacher, Klingenfuss drafted a progress report for Luther to Ribbentrop on September 19, 1942. The Rumanian, Bulgarian, and Greek Jews were now included in all Jewish measures. The Italians had been approached to recall their Jews by the end of the year or agree to their inclusion as well. The position of the Hungarian and Turkish Jews, however, had yet to be clarified. The Hungarians, for their part, demanded most-favored treatment. Hungary and Turkey should be given the same chance as Italy to withdraw their Jews before the January 1 deadline, when exceptional treatment for foreign Jews would end. To strengthen his case, Luther secured the initials of Weizsäcker, Woermann, and Wiehl for his proposal. Ribbentrop gave his consent.[86]

On October 5, 1942, Luther informed Sztojay of Hungary's option and assured him that Italy had been treated in the same way. As for the Jewish property left behind by the Hungarian Jews, whether they were recalled or evacuated to the east, Germany was ready to agree to the participation of trustees appointed by the Hungarian government. Sztojay said his government would make no difficulties, if the Italian government likewise gave its consent to these measures.[87] A week later the German ambassador in Ankara was instructed to present the same option to the Turkish government.[88]

Hungarian acquiescence depended upon Italian agreement, but this was not forthcoming. On October 10, 1942, the Italians handed their reply to Mackensen in Rome. It noted that Jews of Italian citizenship in the Mediterranean area held significant financial and economic positions vital to Italy's national interest. Therefore the Italian government protected them despite their race. If it agreed to the German proposals for Italian Jews in the western occupied territories, its ability to protect Italian Jews in the rest of the Mediterranean would be seriously endangered. Therefore the Italian government could not agree to either the deportation of these Jews or their subjection to economic measures. The Italians made only one concession; their Jews in the western occupied territories could be marked. The Marchese D'Ajeta, Ciano's deputy, added that the Duce himself had been personally involved in the preparation of the Italian answer.[89]

Luther was not satisfied and had Klingenfuss draft further proposals for Ribbentrop. The Italians should be told that the German measures were in no way an attack on Italian property. In every single case the property of Italian Jews would be impounded for disposal by the Italian government. Since the Duce had been personally involved and the Italians had explicitly rejected deportation, they should be requested to withdraw their Jews to Italy.[90] But Ribbentrop did not respond to Luther's proposal, and no further steps to pressure the Italians were taken at this time.

The Germans were more successful with Turkey and Hungary. The Turkish consulates were informed by their government to induce all Turkish Jews to return voluntarily before December 31, 1942. Those who had been abroad for an unbroken term exceeding five years, however, would be deprived of their citizenship on the basis of Turkish law and not allowed to return. Luther promptly ordered that all denaturalized Turkish Jews be deported.[91]

The Hungarians notified the Germans that they would set up an agency in the western occupied territories to organize the trusteeship of Hungarian Jewish property and would in certain individual cases recall Hungarian Jews. But Hungarian consent was still attached to the most-favored principle; Hungary accepted this settlement provided the removal of all other foreign Jews was also carried out.[92]

Since Ribbentrop refused to press the Italians further for the moment, the deadline of December 31, 1942, came and went without any action being taken by anyone. The Hungarians and Turks waited upon the Italians, the Italians did not withdraw their Jews, and the Hungarian and Turkish Jews remained also. Without Ribbentrop's approval, the Foreign Office could not give the RSHA permission to deport these Jews, even though the deadline had passed.

The attempt to clear the western occupied territories of the Jews of all allied and pro-German countries did not succeed completely. Luther had been quite successful in securing the deportation of Greek, Bulgarian, and Rumanian Jews. But the large contingents of Italian, Hungarian, and Turkish Jews remained. His attempt to have these Jews deported foundered on the combination of Italian resistance and Ribbentrop's reluctance to allow Luther to push him into a confrontation with Italy. The problem remained unresolved into the following year.

# 7. *Judenpolitik* in Southeast Europe

The deportations from Slovakia, France, Belgium, and the Netherlands had begun on the initiative of the SS. The Foreign Office readily cooperated, but ultimately played a secondary role. Southeast Europe presented a different problem. German domination was not so great, and hence conversely the prerogatives of the Foreign Office were greater. Allied governments like Rumania, Hungary, and Bulgaria could not be treated like occupied territories and had to be approached through proper diplomatic channels. Satellite Croatia could not be dominated like Slovakia, for Italian interests had to be respected there. Even where the Germans had military occupation zones in Yugoslavia and Greece, the situation was vastly complicated by the presence of Italian occupation zones in the same two countries. German desires concerning the Italian zones could only be channeled through the Foreign Office. The situation in southeast Europe presented the Germans with far greater challenges than they had hitherto encountered in carrying out the Final Solution. It also offered Martin Luther and the Foreign Office a star role for the first time.

## Complications

The German effort to annihilate the Jews in southeast Europe was not completely successful. During Luther's tenure in office, in fact, it failed more often than it succeeded. This was not due to any lack of zeal on Luther's part but happened rather in spite of it. Two factors combined to thwart the Germans on occasion. The first was the behavior of Germany's allies. The Italians refused to surrender the Jews from their zones of military occupation in Greece and Yugoslavia (as they did later in southern France as well). In Hungary, Rumania, and Bulgaria a delicate political balance determined the relations of each government to Germany and its policy toward the Jews; in 1942 this balance began to tilt away from full cooperation with Germany. The second factor in Germany's incomplete success was Luther's growing estrangement from Ribbentrop, which hampered the former's efforts to exert pressure on the increasingly uncooperative allies for a German solution to the Jewish question.

*Germany's Allies.*   Italy, Germany's least unequal ally, had adopted racial legislation in the late 1930s under the impact of the rise of a new generation of radical or "totalitarian" Fascists and in the wake of Italy's African conquests and rapprochement with Nazi Germany. But anti-Semitism had not been earlier and did not then become widespread among the Italian people. The simplistic identification between an alien modernity and the Jews, which made them the focus of anti-liberal, anti-capitalist, anti-Marxist, and ultra-nationalist fervor in central and eastern Europe, found no echo in Italy, where a humanistic, sophisticated, bourgeois society was an integral part of the historical tradition. Nazi Jewish policy was incomprehensible to most Italians, and they spontaneously refused to cooperate with it. Though obstruction of German plans began at the local level, ultimately even Mussolini, caught between military dependence on his German ally and the revulsion of his own countrymen toward participation in the Final Solution, played a double game, promising the Germans his cooperation while tolerating the sabotage of these promises by his army, police, and diplomats.[1]

Hungary and Rumania, though not Bulgaria, had an indigenous tradition of anti-Semitism.[2] Yet this anti-Semitism was not identical to the Nazi type; it was predominately nationalistic rather than racist.[3] The Jew as an unassimilated and foreign element in a nation struggling to achieve homogeneity and internal solidarity was the primary object of traditional anti-Semitism in eastern Europe. Traditional conservatives like Horthy in Hungary and Antonescu in Rumania could act toward the Jews according to a double standard which was incomprehensible to the Germans but perfectly reasonable in their own minds. The Magyarized and Romanized Jews were discriminated against but nonetheless grudgingly tolerated and ultimately protected, while the unassimilated Jews of Galicia and Serbia or Bessarabia and Bukovina were the objects of intense hatred and either turned over to the Germans or enthusiastically slaughtered by the Hungarians and Rumanians themselves. The Bulgarians ultimately fell into the same pattern, giving up Thracian and Macedonian but not Bulgarian Jews.

A selective, nationalistically oriented anti-Semitism was the major factor in eastern Europe and ultimately determined which groups of Jews would be killed, either massacred locally or turned over to the Germans, and which would be protected from extermination though not from persecution. While the Nazis wished to murder all Jews, their east European allies were eager to kill only certain groups of Jews. "Violent nationalism might lead to mass murder of Jews . . . but the bureaucratic cold-blooded 'Final Solution' was a German and not an Eastern European invention."[4]

Political expediency was also a major factor in determining the response of

Germany's southeast European allies to the Jewish question. Internally, the dominant traditional conservatives or Old Right were challenged by a radical New Right (Iron Guard in Rumania, Arrow Cross in Hungary, Ratnitsi in Bulgaria) which focused on anti-Semitism as one of its major themes. This had a radicalizing effect on the Old Right, which intensified its own anti-Semitism in an attempt to take the wind out of the sails of the New Right without making any concessions on social-economic issues.[5] As German domination and influence grew, the radicalization of Old Right anti-Semitism continued. In order to deter excessive German interference in internal politics, especially outright support for the New Right, the conservative regimes adopted anti-Jewish legislation based on the German model.

Calculations of political expedience in foreign affairs had the same effect. Territorial ambitions obsessed the governments of both Hungary and Bulgaria before 1940 and Rumania as well thereafter. As German power grew and her favor became decisive in redrawing the map of eastern Europe, Hungary, Rumania, and Bulgaria vied with one another for this favor. The Jews were an expendable pawn in this game, and intensification of anti-Jewish measures was considered a cheap price to pay for German goodwill leading to territorial gain.

Political expediency turned out to be a double-edged weapon for the Germans vis-à-vis their southeast European allies. As long as the German war machine appeared invincible, the Jewish policies of these countries followed in Germany's footsteps. When the Germans first approached these countries in the summer and fall of 1942 to march the last mile on the road to the Final Solution, the German war machine was already beginning to show wear. The defeat at Stalingrad shortly thereafter rudely shattered the pretence of inevitable German victory. Regimes which had hitherto accommodated themselves to German Jewish policy first became hesitant and then pulled back. Protecting Jews now became political insurance for an uncertain future where previously sacrificing Jews was easy payment for territorial gain.

The hesitancy caused by the stalled German war effort opened the way for renewed efforts by the Jewish communities themselves. Appeals to leading politicians and churchmen no longer fell on deaf ears, and frequent resort to that elixir of Balkan politics, bribery, played no small role. Even the excessively modest interest expressed by the allies in the fate of the Jews now carried weight.

The destiny of the Jews in southeast Europe, then, was determined neither by German power and influence overwhelming the strong resistance of reluctant allies nor by fanatical native anti-Semites eager to outdo the Germans. There was a strong, indigenous, nationalistic anti-Semitism which led to harsh persecution and frightful atrocities, but it did not lead to complete cooperation with Germany's Final Solution. There were many collaborators and extremists who wholly committed themselves to doing the Germans' bidding in all matters, including Jewish affairs, but more predominate were the traditional conservatives who put considerations of nationalism first, trying to get more out of the Germans than they gave. To the Old Right the Jews were expendable, but they were not the ultimate enemy nor was their extermination the ultimate goal.

*Luther vs. Ribbentrop.*    This was the delicate and complicated situation vis-à-vis Germany's allies which Luther faced in the summer of 1942. If Germany's military position had just reached its high-water mark, Luther's personal position in the German Foreign Office was already beginning to ebb as the result of a growing estrangement from Ribbentrop. The foreign minister became increasingly reluctant to allow his protégé a free hand in dealing with Jewish affairs. Ribbentrop's attempts to rein in Luther would slow down the latter's attempts to pressure other countries to give up their Jews. At a point when time was of the essence, before the German war effort stalled, dissension in the German Foreign Office caused vital delays and played into the hands of those factions among the German allies who were becoming increasingly hesitant to commit their regimes to German Jewish policy.

This internal dissension, which would climax in early 1943 with fatal consequences for Martin Luther's career, had its origins in two separate developments. The first was the burgeoning disaffection among the young men of Luther's group toward the Ribbentrop regime and their decision finally to take up resistance and oust the incompetent foreign minister. The second was Luther's deteriorating personal relationships with both Herr and Frau Ribbentrop, his growing political isolation, and the resultant undermining of his position of power, which made him ready to turn against his erstwhile protector.[6]

The young men whom Luther recruited to *Abteilung Deutschland,* Party activists before the *Machtergreifung,* were Nazis out of conviction and youthful idealism. They were apt candidates for disillusionment, feeling their idealism had been misused by others rather than misguided by themselves. Luther's deputy, Walter Büttner, became the head of an anti-Ribbentrop group composed of these disillusioned young Nazis, the "betrayed youth" as Walter Kieser of D XII called them.

In 1942 Kieser drew up a so-called "Europe-Plan" on behalf of the Büttner circle, the purpose of which was to lay the foundations for peace talks with the West. The young men pressed the plan upon Luther, who forwarded it to Ribbentrop for submission to Hitler. The Führer's response was utterly negative. Nevertheless, the young men entertained the fantastic hope that the ouster of Ribbentrop would win back sufficient freedom for the Foreign Office to negotiate a compromise peace.

The young men's decision to conspire against Ribbentrop was reached in December 1942, but Luther had been laying the groundwork for such a move long before. He had been in contact with Walter Schellenberg, head of foreign intelligence in the RSHA, since August. Schellenberg himself had plans for peace negotiations; as Ribbentrop was an obstacle, he "begged" Luther to get him material which might enable him "to bring about Ribbentrop's downfall." In January 1943, Schellenberg notified Walther Gödde,

Luther's office manager, that he had made tenuous contacts with the American secret service, and it was "now essential to bring down Ribbentrop if progress was to made with the Americans."[7]

Luther was embarking upon an adventure that was not a mere palace revolt against Ribbentrop but was connected with attempts on the part of both Foreign Office dissidents and Schellenberg to open negotiations for a compromise peace. Luther had risen to power through his ties to Ribbentrop. What was the motivation for his own turning against the foreign minister?

First, the weakness of the Foreign Office in the internal power struggle frustrated Luther. He found himself fighting against not only the SS and various Party organizations but also the "passive and complacent" old diplomats of the Foreign Office. The apathy and resignation of the latter hindered Luther's attempts to preserve Foreign Office prerogatives against the encroachments of the former. Second, following the failure of the first Russian campaign and the entry of the United States into the war, Luther felt a compromise peace had to be concluded. The Foreign Office had the duty to maintain contacts with the enemy, so talks to end the war could be commenced at any time. "But Ribbentrop in his megalomania was smashing the last porcelain" and thus had to be toppled.

Moreover, given Luther's dissatisfaction with Ribbentrop's foreign policy on the one hand and inability to defend Foreign Office prerogatives on the other, it was not surprising that a more personal break also took place. For years Luther had slavishly performed majordomo activities, frequently bordering on impropriety, on behalf of the Ribbentrops. This inevitably took its toll on the self-esteem of a man so sensitive to questions of status and position as Luther. In the summer of 1942, with his relations to the foreign minister already strained, Luther abruptly broke with Frau Ribbentrop, charging her with "corruption" for asking him to entrust Foreign Office legal business to her family lawyer, Dr. Oskar Möhrung. Luther's own record in regard to corruption was scarcely unblemished. He had many enemies, headed by Gustav Adolf Steengracht von Moyland of Ribbentrop's staff, who seized the opportunity provided by this final rupture with the Ribbentrops to carry out an investigation of Luther's own propaganda network. It was found to be a "most highly objectionable conglomerate of graft, careerism, and terror."[8]

Luther's seemingly inpregnable position in the Foreign Office was deteriorating quickly. He was estranged from both the Ribbentrops, and his years of aggressive behavior had created countless enemies both within and outside the Foreign Office who were waiting for revenge. In addition to "the eternal pestering of his young co-workers," sheer desperation over his precarious position delivered Luther into the hands of the conspirators plotting Ribbentrop's ouster.

The attempted coup was a disastrous failure. Luther composed a memorandum describing Ribbentrop as incompetent and mentally unbalanced, incapable of carrying on his duties as foreign minister. According to Schellenberg, the Foreign Office dissidents jumped the gun and delivered this memorandum to Himmler before Schellenberg had had a chance to prepare his boss.

According to the Büttner circle, Schellenberg extracted the memorandum with the promise of Himmler's support and then could not deliver. In any case Himmler ultimately had no interest in seeing the weak Ribbentrop deposed and turned over the incriminating memorandum to him. The enraged Ribbentrop took the matter to Hitler. Luther was arrested on February 10, 1943, and sent to the concentration camp at Sachsenhausen. Luther's men were released from their Foreign Office positions for military service, Büttner and Kieser in Waffen-SS units on the eastern front as a cure for their "defeatist attitude," and *Abteilung Deutschland* was completely dissolved at the end of March 1943.

## The Vindication Report

The rupture between Luther and Ribbentrop was caused by factors utterly unrelated to the Jewish question, but inevitably the tense relations between the two affected the *Judenpolitik* of the German Foreign Office. When Ribbentrop felt that Luther was usurping his own prerogatives in dealing with Italy and not adequately protecting the Foreign Office position in Rumania vis-à-vis the SS, their personal quarrel became a dispute over Jewish policy as well.

Initially, Luther was very cautious in dealing with Italy on the Jewish question. In 1941 the rabidly anti-Semitic German consul general in Trieste, Druffel, had sent a stream of reports to the Foreign Office criticizing the lax Italian attitude toward the Jews. In January 1942, Rademacher let himself be persuaded by Druffel's tirades and gossip, which he summarized in a memorandum for Luther. Rademacher proposed that the Italians be informed of the danger involved in their lax treatment of the Jewish question and the "unfortunate impression" which this made upon Germany. Luther emphatically vetoed Rademacher's proposal. The present moment was the "worst conceivable" for such a move, and the reasons given were insufficient. Moreover, "to me Druffel is anything but competent for such reports!"[9]

Luther dismissed Druffel's reports but soon had other complaints about the Italian attitude toward the Jews from more reliable sources. The German consul in Tripoli, Walther, reported on the situation in Libya, emphasizing the web of corruption spun between the Jews and the Italian officials. From France, Abetz complained that in Tunis the Italians had prevented the application of French Jewish legislation to Italian Jews, who held many key economic positions and almost all trade in their hands.[10]

But the most disturbing report came from Croatia. In mid-July Inspector General Schnell of *Organisation Todt* reported that in Mostar the Jews were the most dangerous source of unrest. But the commander of the Italian occupation forces there had ordered that all inhabitants be treated equally. He had told Schnell, who was trying to take over Jewish apartments, that it would be "incompatible with the honor of the Italian army to take special measures against the Jews. . . ."[11] Thus the Italian army could not agree to their resettlement.

In October 1941 and again in May 1942, the Croatian government had requested the German Foreign Office to arrange for the deportation of its Jews. The RSHA had rejected the first request, and did not immediately act upon the second. In the meantime, the *Ustashe* had killed almost all of the Jews except those in the Italian zone, where the *Utashe* murder squads were not permitted to operate. After receiving the report from *Organisation Todt,* Luther telephoned the German ambassador in Zagreb. Kasche informed him that the Croatian government had agreed to a proposal, this time apparently made from the German side, to begin deportations. Especially important were the 4–5,000 Jews in the Italian zone. This was precisely the policy Luther had urged upon the RSHA two months earlier, and no further negotiations between the RSHA and the Foreign Office had been required.[12]

Luther prepared a memorandum for Ribbentrop, informing him of the pending deportations, the evidence of Italian obstruction, and the importance of the Jews in the Italian zone. "In any case the deportation can only take place with German help, because difficulties must be expected from the Italian side." Luther was of the opinion that they should risk deportations from all of Croatia, including the Italian occupation zone, despite these expected difficulties, but requested Ribbentrop's instructions. Luther submitted this memorandum to Weizsäcker, who suggested that Mackensen in Rome be consulted first. Franz von Sonnleithner on Ribbentrop's staff then sent Luther's memorandum to Rome, without submitting it to Ribbentrop.[13]

While Luther awaited the opinion of the German ambassador in Rome on the Croatian Jews, he was also seeking Ribbentrop's decision on his proposal that the Italians be given the choice of surrendering their Jews in the western occupied territories to German deportation measures or recalling them. Negotiations with the Italians could therefore go no further for the moment. In the meantime the Italian problem was eclipsed by more explosive events in Rumania. On July 26, 1942, Eichmann wrote Luther that the RSHA planned to deport Jews from Rumania, beginning sometime after September 10. Eichmann assumed that there were no objections to these measures on the side of the Foreign Office.[14] Luther instructed Rademacher to have two letters drafted—one to Müller of the Gestapo and one to Killinger. As usual, Rademacher passed the job to Klingenfuss. Killinger was instructed "to clarify" the question of deporting Jews from Rumania. The Gestapo chief was informed that "in principle" the Foreign Office had no objection to the deportations. An investigation was being undertaken in Rumania, and the Foreign Office would return to the question as soon as it was concluded.[15]

Rademacher submitted the drafts to Luther on August 8. He advised Luther that such a quasi-decision (*Zwischenbescheid*) to Müller was contrary to usual practice. Moreover, he had heard from two sources in Rumania, Dr. Emil Hoffman (the press attaché to the German embassy and an adviser to the Rumanian government) and a member of the Iron Guard, that Antonescu in fact had no intention of deporting the Rumanian Jews.[16] Luther amended the draft letter to Müller, stating that no measures should be taken in the meantime, and then decided to scratch the letter entirely.[17] But the request to Killinger to clarify the question was sent on August 11.

Luther received a clarification before this request reached Killinger. A report from Gustav Richter, the Jewish adviser in Bucharest, arrived on the same day. Richter reported that he had met with Deputy Premier Mihai Antonescu on July 22, 1942, and had secured from him a letter, in which Antonescu agreed to the deportation of Rumanian Jews in general and to the immediate deportation of those in Arad, Timisoara, and Turda in particular. Allegedly, this corresponded to the wish of Ion Antonescu as well. Moreover, the Rumanian general commissar for Jewish affairs, Radu Lecca, would arrive in Berlin on August 19 to conduct final negotiations with the RSHA.[18]

The picture now became clear to Luther. Richter had negotiated a deal with the Rumanians behind the back of the Foreign Office on July 22 and reported it secretly to Eichmann, who then requested Foreign Office approval on July 26. This was in complete violation of the spirit of the agreement between Luther and the now deceased Heydrich (assassinated in June, 1942), as well as an infringement upon the Foreign Office right to supervise all negotiations with foreign governments. But Luther was not so angry with the SS as he was with Killinger for letting Richter pull off such a coup right under his nose. To Müller he simply noted that the question of the Rumanian deportations had experienced a positive clarification.[19] But to Killinger he sent a blistering letter, expressing his astonishment that a final agreement had been reached through personal correspondence to the adviser and not through official channels. While he understood the necessity of direct personal negotiations, final agreements of such importance were to be made solely by the ambassador. Killinger was ordered to remedy this shortcoming immediately.[20]

Luther than made a summary report to Ribbentrop on the latest developments in Rumania concerning the Jewish question, but carefully hid the fact that the Foreign Office had been upstaged by the SS and that he, Luther, had failed to prevent this. The report merely noted that Deputy Premier Mihai Antonescu had confirmed Rumania's willingness that German authorities could deport the Jews from that country. Lecca would arrive in the next few days to discuss the details of the practical execution of these deportations in direct agreement with the RSHA *and the Foreign Office*. No mention was made of Antonescu's private letter to Richter.[21]

But Luther's attempted cover-up did not succeed. At Hitler's headquarters Ribbentrop received a copy of a report from Eichmann to Himmler. It stated that the Rumanian Jews would be deported to Lublin, "where those capable of labor would be put to work, the rest shall be subjected to special treatment." Moreover, Eichmann did not refrain from bragging to Himmler about how the agreement had been reached. "Upon instruction of the Reich Security Main Office, the adviser for the Jewish question in Bucharest, SS-Captain Richter, had a personal letter delivered from the Deputy Rumanian Premier Mihai Antonescu, whose photocopy I enclose. ..."[22] As Eichmann's report to Himmler was dated July 26, 1942, the same day that he first contacted the

Foreign Office about Rumanian deportations, it was now also clear to Ribbentrop that the Foreign Office had been excluded from negotiating an important agreement with a foreign government.

Just as Luther had been angry with Killinger, Ribbentrop was now angry with Luther. But while Luther was merely exasperated with Killinger's incompetence, Ribbentrop suspected Luther of playing private games with the SS behind his back in Jewish affairs. This did not happen to be the case in Rumania, where Luther himself had been upstaged, but his attempt at a cover-up must have been most suspicious to Ribbentrop. Moreover, Luther had made other decisions in Jewish affairs without proper authorization, such as informing Eichmann that the Hungarian Jews in the western occupied territories could be deported. More importantly, it was precisely in the month of August 1942, following his quarrel with Frau Ribbentrop, that Luther was making his first contacts with Schellenberg, with the ultimate goal of ousting Ribbentrop, whose suspicions of Luther's disloyalty were not at all unfounded.

On August 19, 1942, Ribbentrop telephoned Luther and demanded an explanation not only of the events in Rumania, but of Luther's conduct in the whole field of Jewish affairs.[23] Luther had the choice of trying to make amends with his boss and place all the blame on the SS, or of defending his own actions and those of the SS in Jewish affairs together. Formerly Luther had made himself indispensable by defending Ribbentrop against the encroachments and ambitions of the other Nazi chieftains. But now he despised Ribbentrop and was laying the groundwork for an alliance with the SS against him.

Using Rademacher and Klingenfuss to assemble the materials, Luther composed his "Vindication Report" (*Rechtfertigungsbericht*) in two days time. Accompanied by supporting documents, it was a comprehensive denial that Luther had ever behaved improperly or independently in Jewish affairs.[24] First it reviewed the prewar policy of emigration, the Madagascar Plan, and early Jewish legislation in France, noting that in all cases the foreign minister had been informed and had given his approval. The approaches to Slovakia, Croatia, and Rumania in the fall of 1941 to permit the deportation of their Jews residing in Germany had been approved by Weizsäcker, Woermann, Wiehl, and Albrecht. However, no mention was made of the Serbian affair, where Luther had considerably exceeded the instructions of the foreign minister in his intrigues with Heydrich.

Luther then related his own version of the Wannsee Conference, stating that Weizsäcker had been informed of the meeting—a distortion of Rademacher's note that he had informed the state secretary of the invitation in December 1941. He gave Ribbentrop the lame excuse that he had not informed the foreign minister at that time because Heydrich had planned a follow-up conference. This had never taken place, however, because of Heydrich's preoccupation with affairs in the Protectorate and then his assassination. Now, for the first time, he sent Ribbentrop a copy of the Wannsee Protocol. Given the context of the Vindication Report, Luther would have emphasized any undocumented conversations with Ribbentrop relating to the

Wannsee Conference, had they taken place. The lack of any such reference clearly indicates the degree to which Luther had been operating on his own initiative.
Luther emphatically defended his cooperation with the SS.

> In the meeting on January 20, 1942, I requested that all questions concerning foreign territory must be coordinated with the Foreign Office beforehand, which *Gruppenführer* Heydrich promised and has also loyally complied with, as indeed the agencies of the Reich Security Main Office competent for Jewish affairs have carried out all measures from the beginning in frictionless cooperation with the Foreign Office. The Reich Security Main Office has proceeded in an almost too cautious way in this sector.

Luther then proceeded to deal with the Foreign Office role in various European countries, trying to prove that he was not guilty of any unwarranted actions and had not been dealing behind Ribbentrop's back. In Slovakia he carefully listed all the documents initialed by Weizsäcker and Woermann. His memorandum to the foreign minister over the Croatian Jews had been sent first to Rome by Weizsäcker, and no answer had yet been received. His memorandum about the Italian Jews in the western occupied territories still awaited a decision from Ribbentrop himself. The foreign minister had commissioned him to examine the suggestion made by the Bulgarian Foreign Minister Popov for common Jewish treatment, but the Legal Division had brought up the problem posed by existing trade treaties to any German-Bulgarian agreement in Jewish affairs. Therefore Luther had instructed the ambassador in Sofia to secure an exchange of notes with Bulgaria whereby each side renounced any protection these treaties might afford to its Jews residing in the other's territories. The way had been prepared for the inclusion of Bulgarian Jews in German measures. Luther maintained that as of yet the Hungarian government had not been approached concerning Jewish deportations, failing to mention of course that he had okayed the deportation of Hungarian Jews in the west without approaching the Hungarian government.
Luther then dealt with the ticklish Rumanian situation. He had asked Killinger to clarify the situation.

> Concerning this matter the embassy appeared to make use of the Jewish adviser Richter assigned to it, to whom the Rumanian government confirmed its earlier agreement to include Rumanian Jews in the German measures and to whom the Deputy Premier Mihai Antonescu communicated the desire of the Marshal, that German authorities could also carry out resettlement from Rumania itself and immediately begin with the deportation of Jews from the districts Arad, Timisoara and Turda.

This in itself was a transparent attempt to give Richter's activities a veneer of Foreign Office sanction and to confuse Rumania's earlier decision about the deportation of Rumanian Jews from Germany with the later decision over deportations from Rumania itself. Moreover, it was a complete distortion in its implication that Luther's request for clarification preceded and caused Richter's activities. But Luther went even further. He tried to strengthen Richter's credentials as an agent of the Foreign Office, not the RSHA, noting that Richter was in Bucharest on the urgent request of the embassy, despite the attempts of the RSHA to withdraw him the previous year. "Because all negotiations with the Rumanian government have gone through the Foreign Office, the report of Captain Richter submitted to the *Reichsführer* SS must be evaluated only as an internal work report to the Reich Security Main Office." Luther assured Ribbentrop that he had "sharply" complained to Killinger about "allowing a final conference to be confirmed through a handwritten letter," thus once again trying to convey the impression that Richter's letter was the result of prior official negotiations. In conclusion, Luther noted, "The planned deportations represent an important step forward on the path of the total solution and are very important in regard to other states (Hungary)." He requested Ribbentrop to approve the continuation of the negotiations and measures already begun.

This report was sent to Ribbentrop on August 21, 1942. While awaiting the answer, Luther chafed impatiently over the Croatian affair. Kasche had visited Berlin at the end of July, and several reports from Zagreb had requested that urgent steps be undertaken in Rome to secure Italian cooperation. All attempts to deal with the Italian authorities in Croatia had failed; they merely replied that the decision had to be made in Rome.[25]

Weizsäcker and Sonnleithner had merely asked Mackensen for his opinion on Luther's memorandum on the Croatian deportations, but no reply had come. Luther was now tempted to take precisely the kind of independent action that he had denied ever doing to Ribbentrop. The day after the *Rechtfertigungsbericht* was dispatched to headquarters, Luther had Klingenfuss draft new instructions for Mackensen. He was to inform the Italian government that Germany had arranged with the Croatian government to deport Jews from that country. The Italians should instruct their troops to support these actions in their zone. Luther then changed his mind, however, and the new instructions were not sent.[26]

Meanwhile, the delay in Mackensen's reply was caused by his decision not to give his own opinion, as requested, but to inquire of the Italian position on deporting the Jews from their occupation zone in Croatia. The inquiry caused consternation. Reluctant officials in the Italian Foreign Office prepared two memoranda, one for Ciano and one for Mussolini. The first stated that Germany must be given a negative answer. The second was more cautiously worded and simply indicated the terrible fate in store for the Jews if they were deported. Mussolini noted cryptically in the margin: "Not against."[27] On August 25, 1942, the Italians informed the German embassy that the matter had been presented to the Duce by Ciano, along with a report from Casertano, the Italian ambassador in Zagreb, over his discussions with Kasche. The Duce had given instructions that the Jews in the Italian zone should be treated in the same way as those in the rest of Croatia.[28]

If Luther was impatient with the Italians, he was furious about the

Rumanians. He had to put up with the double-dealing of the SS for ulterior motives, but he did not have to accept such treatment from the lowly Rumanians. Rademacher's informant in Bucharest, Dr. Emil Hoffman, viewed Radu Lecca, the general commissar for Jewish affairs, as Richter's willing tool, and gave negative reports on him as well as on Richter's independent activities and Killinger's incompetence.[29] The Jewish experts of *Abteilung Deutschland* planned their own special welcome for Lecca, who came to Berlin as a guest of the RSHA. According to Rademacher, Luther and he both agreed that they should not negotiate with him, yet they could not refuse to see him entirely. It was therefore planned that Luther would feign to be busy and send Lecca to Rademacher. "He—Luther—would then immediately have me ostentatiously called away, so that no substantive conversation could take place."[30] This little scenario was played out, and Lecca was properly snubbed.

On August 29, 1942, Luther received his answer from Ribbentrop, which bristled with the foreign minister's displeasure.[31]

1. The foreign minister requests you in the future, before taking up negotiations with any foreign government that falls within the work area of your division, to report or submit the relevant matter to him and await his approval.

2. Concerning the Rumanians the foreign minister is agreed, that the measures already agreed upon be carried out in the way provided for.

3. Concerning Hungary the foreign minister requests you to refrain from any initiative on our side.

4. Concerning Bulgaria for the moment you shall not go beyond the agreement reached in the exchange of notes of July 6–7, 1942.

5. Concerning Croatia you must proceed from the fact that it is a matter for the Croatian government to see that Jews in the territory occupied by the Italians are included in the deportation. Supporting steps by the German embassy in Rome in this affair are to be postponed for the time being.

6. Concerning the Jews of Italian citizenship in occupied France, the Italian government can be approached in order to induce them, in accordance with our measures, to withdraw their Jews from occupied France or agree to their evacuation to the east. A unified treatment is unconditionally necessary for military and other reasons.

Ribbentrop insisted that all further negotiations with foreign governments not only on the Jewish question but in any area of Luther's competency required Ribbentrop's explicit approval. Luther's free-lancing was to come to an end. Moreover, negotiations with Bulgaria and Hungary as well as with Italy over the Croatian Jews were now off bounds. Luther was permitted to proceed with his programs only in Rumania and with the Italian Jews in the west. Not since his temporary dismissal in the fall of 1937 had Luther received such a rebuff or open display of suspicion from his former patron.

No sooner had Luther received this reply from Ribbentrop than he was buffeted by an equally bitter complaint from Killinger.[32] The ambassador was of course reluctant to admit that he had not been adequately supervising Richter's activities. He professed not to understand how the Foreign Office could assume that he had permitted the settlement of such an important question exclusively through an SS officer.

> Herr Mihai Antonescu can write letters to whom he wants, it is all the same to me. That the Jewish adviser did the preliminary work on my orders, is obvious. One can not speak at all about a conclusion to the negotiations. Had *Abteilung Deutschland* received the Rumanian *Ministerialdirektor* Lecca even just briefly (Lecca told me that Undersecretary Luther had been occupied and that Herr Rademacher had been apparently ostentatiously called away from the conference), then this would have given a completely different impression.

After Lecca had returned from Berlin "somewhat piqued" (*etwas verschnupft*), Killinger had tried to remedy the situation through a verbal note to the Rumanian government stating that he considered the preliminary negotiations concluded and he now awaited a final communication from the Rumanian government.

Killinger then returned to his complaints against Luther.

> I request, when such important persons as *Ministerialdirektor* Lecca come to Berlin, they not be put off in such a way that the good relations between Germany and Rumania can be poisoned. I would also like to note that all letters to SS-Lieutenant Colonel Eichmann went via the Foreign Office, so that the Foreign Office had knowledge of all previous correspondence. That naturally Herr Eichmann has not found it necessary to make contact with the Foreign Office is in no way surprising to me, because the methods of the gentlemen of the SS are well known to me. Moreover I would like to note that everything that I report to *Abteilung Deutschland* lands in the SD in the shortest time. I have the impression that Herr Dr. Emil Hoffman has very good friends in the Foreign Office.

Killinger was simply too vain to admit that he had allowed Richter to send secret communications to Berlin without going through the embassy. In fact, Richter had informed Eichmann of Antonescu's letter within four days of the July 22 meeting, but the official report through Killinger to the Foreign Office was not dispatched until August 7. Killinger resented being made the scapegoat by Luther, and in turn attacked the latter's treatment of Lecca. Killinger was not aware, however, that it was Luther, not himself, who was in trouble with Ribbentrop. Luther naturally had no intention of forwarding Killinger's criticisms of himself to Ribbentrop and told Killinger that he had not done so. When Killinger complained that his views on the affair had not been imparted to the foreign minister, Luther scribbled in frustration, "Herr von Killinger obviously does not want to understand."[33]

Luther's spat with Killinger was minor in comparison with his difficulties with Ribbentrop. In the Croatian matter Luther was sitting on a potential bomb. The day before Ribbentrop's directive arrived instructing him to undertake no steps in Rome in support of the Croatians, he had learned from Rome that as a result of the German inquiry there Mussolini had instructed that Jews in the Italian zone would be treated in the same way as Jews in the rest of Croatia. The inquiry which led to Mussolini's decision was caused by Weizsäcker, Sonnleithner and Mackensen, not Luther, but Luther knew that in his present mood the foreign minister was not likely to consider him blameless in the matter. Luther did not immediately inform Ribbentrop of this news. Rather, he kept it quiet until tempers had cooled and something else had come along to distract Ribbentrop's attention.

The opportunity for this came quickly. On September 2, 1942, the Italian embassy in Berlin delivered a note to Weizsäcker, complaining about the endangered position of Italian economic interests in Tunis. Over 5,000 Italian Jews lived in Tunis and played a vital role in Italy's economic position there, which the French had been trying to destroy for years. This attack now took the form of aryanization legislation enacted by the Vichy government. When the Italian government protested to Vichy that the decrees could not be applied to Italian citizens, the French had replied that they were under great pressure from the Germans to enact racial legislation in North Africa immediately. The Italian government therefore requested the Germans not to press the French in this matter.[34]

Weizsäcker forwarded the note to Luther, suggesting that the French government was playing the Germans and Italians off against one another to create dissension within the Axis. But Luther knew from an earlier report that Abetz had indeed concerned himself with Italian-French relations in North Africa, warning the Italians that it was not in the interest of Italian colonial policy for them to appear in the eyes of the Arabs as the protectors and the French as the persecutors of the Jews.[35] Luther was not reluctant to let Abetz take the heat and thus instructed him to report on any pressure exercised on Vichy in regard to the Italian Jews in Tunis. When Abetz admitted that a general pressure had been exerted on the French to solve the Jewish question not only in France but overseas in French colonies and protectorates, Weizsäcker expressed his dismay. He immediately instructed Luther to tell Abetz to disinterest himself in French Jewish policy in Tunis, which after all was claimed by Italy as a war goal.[36]

Perhaps hoping that Abetz would now draw upon himself all of the foreign minister's displeasure for meddling in Italian affairs, Luther belatedly forwarded Mackensen's telegram concerning Mussolini's decision that Jews in the Italian zone would be treated in the same way as those in the rest of Croatia. If he had expected the foreign minister to be distracted, he was mistaken, but at least Luther was not personally singled out. Ribbentop immediately wanted to know "for what reason we have contacted the Italians in this question and thereby interfered in a Croatian-Italian question, which contradicts the principle not to make ourselves the spokesman of Croatian interests in Italy, rather much more to leave to Italy precedence in Croatia in every respect."[37]

Luther now wrote Mackensen that contact with the Italian government had not been requested, only the ambassador's opinion. Luther also wanted a report on the degree to which the decision of the Duce traced back to German initiative. He wrote Kasche as well, asking to what degree the report of the Italian ambassador in Zagreb, which had also been presented to the Duce, traced back to German initiative. Not unnaturally, neither could give a definitive answer as to how much they had influenced Italian decision making.[38] Kasche did inform Luther, however, that neither the Italian ambassador, Casertano, nor the Italian commanding general, Roatta, had received any instructions concerning the Duce's decision.[39]

On September 11, the day after Luther had forwarded Mackensen's telegram about Mussolini, he also tried to put back in motion German negotiations with Bulgaria. Great progress had been made early in the summer, but then Beckerle had reported a disconcerting incident. On the occasion of the crown prince's birthday, the president of the Central Consistory of Bulgarian Jews had sent a telegram of birthday greetings. The king had replied with a thank-you note, and the whole exchange was published in the Jewish *Bulletin.* Luther noted in the margin: "Crazy!" (*Toll*). He planned a memorandum to Ribbentrop on the Bulgarian situation at the end of August, but scratched it entirely when Ribbentrop's bombshell arrived, explicitly forbidding further negotiations with Bulgaria.[40]

After discreetly waiting for two weeks, Luther had another memorandum for Ribbentrop on the Bulgarian situation drafted by Rademacher and Klingenfuss. He reported the incident of the king's reaction to the birthday greetings, but also summarized the flood of Jewish legislation that had recently been enacted. Most important, the Bulgarians were creating a fund out of blocked Jewish capital to finance the resettlement of Jews into special camps and villages. This plan, Luther told Ribbentrop, had caused the RSHA to inquire of the Foreign Office, whether Germany should not intervene and offer its services for deporting Bulgarian Jews. (In fact, no written record of such a RSHA suggestion exists.) Luther thus requested instructions from the foreign minister if Beckerle could pose to the Bulgarians in a proper and cautious form the question of deporting Bulgarian Jews. Weizsäcker initialed the memorandum. He made the sole reservation that the German inquiry should make no reference to the recent incident with King Boris. But Ribbentrop was reluctant to unleash Luther again and scribbled: "Still wait" (*Noch warten*).[41]

Through Ribbentrop's suspicions of Luther, his resentment of the highhanded behavior of the SS in Rumania, and his vanity that did not allow any subordinate to make Italian policy, Foreign Office participation in the Final Solution had come to a virtual standstill. This was the result of an internal Nazi squabble related in no way to any desire on Ribbentrop's part to save Jews. But tactically *Judenpolitik* was the wrong issue for Ribbentrop to employ to reassert his position. Ribbentrop was an insecure sycophant. He had shifted his own headquarters to the east, for fear that if he were too far from Hitler for too long, his competitors would edge him out of the way. According to Steengracht, he spent 60 percent of his time trying to prevent his rivals from interfering in foreign policy.[42] For a man concerned only to remain in Hitler's good graces and fearful of his rivals, it was an entirely untenable position to attempt to thwart the Final Solution. Nothing would have played faster into the hands of the rival Himmler and the intriguing Luther than to be able to paint Ribbentrop as the major obstacle to carrying out the Jewish policies ordered by the Führer. Whatever the magnitude of his other defects, Ribbentrop was not such a fool as to let himself be trapped into opposing the Führer. After he had had his pout, Ribbentrop sensed the danger and worked quickly to extricate himself.

Ribbentrop's realization came on the occasion of back-to-back visits to Hitler's headquarters by Rumania's deputy prime minister, Mihai Antonescu, and Croatia's *Poglavnik,* Ante Pavelic, on September 23 and 24, 1942. The record of the Hitler-Antonescu meeting, attended by Ribbentrop, does not mention any discussion of the Jewish question.[43] But Ribbentrop did discuss it at another meeting with Antonescu, without Hitler present. The Rumanian assured Ribbentrop of his government's complete willingness in the question of Jewish deportations.[44] Ribbentrop undoubtedly reported the results of this conversation to Hitler, upon which the Führer probably displayed such vehemence on the topic of Jewish deportations as to throw a great deal of fear into the foreign minister. He literally rushed to the telephone to retract his earlier instructions, instead of having one of his staff send off written orders. Luther circulated Ribbentrop's latest instructions to Weizsäcker, Woermann, Wiehl, and Albrecht.

> The Reich Foreign Minister has given me instructions today over the telephone to hurry as much as possible the evacuation of Jews from the various countries of Europe, because it is a known fact that the Jews stir up people against us everywhere and that they must be responsible for attempts of murder and acts of sabotage. Upon a brief report concerning the present stage of evacuation of Jews from Slovakia, Croatia, Rumania, and the occupied territories, the Reich Foreign Minister has given instructions now to start contacting the governments of Bulgaria, Hungary, and Denmark with the object of starting the evacuation of the Jews from these territories. With regard to the settlement of the Jewish question in Italy, the Reich Foreign Minister has reserved for himself all the steps to be taken. This question is to be discussed personally either between the Führer and the Duce or between the Reich Foreign Minister and Count Ciano.

Ribbentrop must have made one other reservation besides Italy, however, for Luther explicitly assured Weizsäcker: "The steps being undertaken by us will in each case be submitted to you beforehand for your approval."[45]

The following day Hitler and Ribbentrop met Pavelic, who declared that he had practically solved the Jewish question in most parts of Croatia but not in the Italian occupation zone. Hitler declared that the Jews were an integral part of the partisan movement which had to be stopped. Once again Ribbentrop took his cue. The previous day he had still explicitly reserved the Jewish question in Italy to himself. Italy was not among the countries Luther could approach. Now he authorized Luther to instruct Mackensen once again to inquire about the situation of the Croatian Jews in the Italian zone.[46] Luther was at least partially unleashed, and the Jewish experts of the Foreign Office were back in business.

## Diplomatic Arm-Twisting

*Rumania.* Even while Luther's activities in other countries had been restricted at the end of August 1942, he still had Ribbentrop's permission to follow up the steps already taken in Rumania. In addition to disarray on the German side there, however, the picture on the Rumanian side was quite unclear. In 1940, when Rumania had found itself isolated and caught between the great powers of Russia and Germany, as well as faced by the demands of Hungary and Bulgaria for the return of territory awarded to Rumania following the Second Balkan War and World War I, the Rumanian government had sought security through the closest possible connection with Germany. Already afflicted by a strong, indigenous anti-Semitism, Rumania quickly began adopting anti-Jewish legislation based on the Nazi model in a vain attempt to win German support. This did not prevent the loss of Bessarabia to Russia nor the return of most of Transylvania to Hungary and the Southern Dobrudja to Bulgaria.

Following these catastrophic losses of territory in the summer of 1940, King Carol abdicated. With German support the professional soldier and representative of the Old Right, Marshal Ion Antonescu, formed a coalition government with the radical Iron Guard. This uneasy coalition was rocked by an Iron Guard revolt in January 1941, but on Hitler's orders the Germans sided with Antonescu, whose regime was saved. Not only Rumania's diminished boundaries but also Antonescu's own government were dependent upon Germany. The Iron Guard leaders received asylum in Germany, where they represented a constant threat should Antonescu prove insufficiently pliant to German wishes.

Not free of Rumania's traditional anti-Semitism himself, Antonescu was perfectly willing to accept a Jewish adviser from Germany and approve anti-Jewish legislation as an acceptable means of winning German support. Moreover, like other east European countries, Rumania was still engaged in the nation-building process. The unassimilated Jews of Bukovina and Bessarabia, "accomplices of Stalin" in Antonescu's eyes, constituted an element of the population which he viewed with the utmost hostility as an obstacle to the "Romanization" of these newly won territories.[47] Calculating that he could simultaneously please the Germans, simplify the process of integrating these territories, and take revenge for Rumania's recent national humiliation, Antonescu ordered the deportation of the Jews of Bessarabia and Bukovina to Transnistria in the fall of 1941, where the bulk of them perished.

The German demand to deport the Jews from Old Rumania constituted a problem of a different dimension for Antonescu, however. The double standard of traditional anti-Semitism encouraged persecution of these assimilated Jews but not their extermination. Other factors also influenced Antonescu. The assimilated Jews represented such an important factor in the Rumanian economy that the induction of 60,000 into work battalions in the summer of 1941 had had to be cancelled (with German approval) as too disruptive. Many Rumanians, including traditional anti-Semites who felt that matters had gone too far, voiced to Antonescu their opposition to further deportations. The Jewish leadership had also maintained their contacts (and bribes) with government circles, which they utilized to the utmost. Finally, as the summer offensive of 1942 failed once again to defeat the Russians, it was increasingly apparent to the Rumanian leaders that they had to maintain as much independence as possible and save the little "moral capital" that was still to be saved.[48]

Antonescu was in a delicate position. He could not risk antagonizing the Germans, yet he could not fully meet their demands. The Rumanians therefore played for time. Despite the reluctant promise that Richter had extracted from Mihai Antonescu in July 1942, Rademacher's sources claimed that Rumania had no intention of honoring this commitment. Killinger obviously felt that the deportations were anything but certain, when he told Luther on August 28, 1942, that one could not yet speak of a conclusion to the negotiations. Killinger had tried to secure the more official handling of the matter demanded by Luther, as well as make up for the damage caused by Luther's treatment of Lecca, when he presented the Rumanians with a note on August 27. It simply stated that the German ambassador considered the preliminary negotiations at an end and requested the official communication of Rumania's position for transmission to Berlin.[49]

The impatient Eichmann was warned in mid-September that the Rumanian government had not replied to Killinger's note. Yet he went ahead and held a conference at the end of September in Berlin to discuss various aspects of the Final Solution, including the deportations from Rumania. The Rumanian railway representative whom he expected to come simply did not attend. Nonetheless it was planned to run "special trains" every other day, each carrying 2,000 Jews, to Belzec. A German railway expert was sent to Bucharest to make the arrangements, but no deportations took place.[50]

In early October 1942, Richter reported growing political pressure within Rumania against the deportation of the Jews.[51] Moreover, this internal opposition to the measures demanded by Germany was matched by continued discord within the German ranks. On October 6, 1942, Killinger recommended that Richter be withdrawn. His prediction on Richter's success had proved correct, Killinger gloated. As usual the Rumanians said yes to everything but did nothing. Klingenfuss, however, advised Luther not to endorse Richter's removal while the deportation question was still being negotiated, and Richter stayed in Bucharest.[52]

The Rumanians became increasingly evasive through the month of October. When Mihai Antonescu had visited Hitler's headquarters at the end of September, he had assured Ribbentrop of Rumania's willingness to permit the deportation of its Jews. But back in Bucharest he still had no answer as yet to the German note of August 27. Richter demanded a conference with Mihai Antonescu on October 22, and the latter chided the German inconsistency in demanding deportations now when just last spring they had implored the Rumanians to cease deporting Jews over the Bug River. Richter reported that this alleged inconsistency was merely a pretext seized by Mihai Antonescu to explain the decision of Marshal Ion Antonescu to postpone the deportations to a more advantageous moment.[53]

By early December Luther was resigned to the fact that the Rumanian deportations "had come to a standstill" and that "with regard to the present situation we probably cannot drive the question forward in the sense desired by us." He comforted himself with the fact that deportations were not desirable during the winter months, anyhow, and instructed Killinger to keep things in play so that progress could be made in the spring.[54] One German ally had successfully evaded German pressure for deportation.

*Hungary.* In analyzing this failure in Rumania, Rademacher noted: "For the rest, I do not consider it as excluded, that the very hesitant policy of the Hungarian government in the Jewish question has moved the marshal also to assume a more temporizing attitude on his side."[55] Indeed, the Hungarians had been every bit as evasive in the face of German pressure as the Rumanians, though in this case the pressure was exerted personally by Luther to a much greater extent than in Rumania, where a plethora of Germans had been nullifying one another's efforts through internal strife.

Hungary moved toward Germany in 1938, receiving a slice of Slovakia that autumn and the Carpatho-Ukraine the following spring. The Hungarian government also enacted its first Jewish legislation in those years, motivated in part by the hope of winning increased favor with Hitler. The desire to recover Transylvania from Rumania, partially realized in the Second Vienna Award in 1940, bound Hungary even closer to Germany. Thereafter, fear of the consequences of the German-Rumanian rapprochement and the entice-ment of further territorial expansion at the expense of Yugoslavia brought Hungary into the war on Hitler's side against the U.S.S.R.[56]

In Hungary, as in other countries allied to Germany, ardent Germano-philes struggled with more reluctant collaborators for control. As a result, the Germans received very mixed signals concerning Hungary's intentions in the Jewish question. During the regime of the pro-German Laszlo Bardossy (April 1941–March 1942), the Germans had every reason to believe Hungary would fully cooperate in the Final Solution. In August 1941, the Hungarians rounded up 15–18,000 Jews who had emigrated to Hungary from Galicia and shoved them back over the border, where they were liquidated by German mobile killing units. In January 1942, Hungarian army units executed thousands of Jews and Serbs in Novi Sad, a city on Yugoslav territory awarded to Hungary.[57] Also in January 1942, Hungarian Major General Jozsef Heszlenyi mentioned to Dr. Karl Clodius of the Foreign Office Economic Division the desire of the Hungarian government to resettle in Transnistria all Jews who had illegally emigrated into Hungary. Negotiations took place between the Hungarian military on the one hand and representatives of the *Ostministerium* and SS on the other concerning this suggestion. As a result of transportation difficulties, however, the desire of the Hungarian government could not be accommodated at the time. But the Germans promised to take up the matter again later.[58] The Bardossy regime also enacted considerable legislation on the model of German racial laws and excluded Jews from the army, obligating them to serve in labor units instead.[59]

When Bardossy was replaced by Miklos Kallay in the spring of 1942, it was not immediately clear to the Germans that this meant a significant alteration in official Hungarian Jewish policy. Luther felt quite free to declare in July 1942 that the Hungarian Jews could be deported from the western occupied territories. The Hungarian government had vigorously protested this discriminatory treatment of Hungarian Jews in the German sphere, but even then the Hungarian ambassador to Berlin, Döme Sztojay, the self-styled "pioneer" of anti-Semitism, had been at pains to make clear to Luther how unpleasant he found this task of protecting Jews. Also in July 1942, the Hungarian military attaché, Sandor Homlok, once again brought up the Heszlenyi proposal to deport illegally immigrated Jews to Transnistria.[60]

The matter was turned over to the Foreign Office by the OKW. Klingenfuss noted that "D III would welcome it if the Hungarian government strives to get rid of Jews who fled to Hungary without official approval." He therefore inquired around the Foreign Office as to whether resettlement in Transnistria was possible, but Dr. Schliep of the Russian desk responded that the Rumanian resettlement plan for this area had been postponed.[61]

Klingenfuss then informed Eichmann that the Hungarians had brought up Heszlenyi's suggestion once again. Eichmann ignored the whole question until the OKW requested an urgent answer because of discussions scheduled to take place in Budapest in late September.[62] On September 25, the day after Ribbentrop finally gave Luther permission to approach the Hungarians about deporting their Jews to the east, Eichmann indicated his lack of interest in the Hungarian proposal. It was a mere "partial action" affecting only Jews who had illegally fled to Hungary. Deportation of these Jews would require just as much preparation and effort as the evacuation of all Hungarian Jews. He would consider it "inexpedient" to set in motion the "entire evacuation apparatus" on this basis. It would be better to wait until Hungary was ready to include all Jews in these measures.[63]

Obviously, elements in the Hungarian military were anxious to get rid of the non-Magyarized foreign Jews seeking refuge in their country. Nor were they alone in this. Like Antonescu vis-à-vis the Jews of Bukovina and Bessarabia, the Regent Horthy "openly detested" the Galician Jews.[64] And like Antonescu, the Hungarians must have calculated that such a maneuver would not only win German approval but also forestall greater German demands. It was precisely this ploy Eichmann wished to counter.

Despite Eichmann's manifest lack of interest in Hungary at this time, however, Luther was eager to take the initiative himself. After Ribbentrop had forbidden any dealings with Hungary for a month, in late September he had finally agreed that Luther could approach the Hungarians concerning both their Jews in the western occupied territories and in Hungary itself. In preparation for a meeting between Luther and Sztojay scheduled for October 5, 1942, Rademacher had Klingenfuss draft a list of German "demands." *(Forderungen)*. In addition to the ultimatum that Hungary either permit the deportation to the east of its Jews within the German sphere or recall them by the end of the year, for the first time German demands were formulated concerning the treatment of Jews in Hungary itself. The Jews should be excluded from cultural and economic life through legislation, then marked, and finally resettled in the east.[65]

Luther presented these demands to Sztojay precisely as formulated by Rademacher and Klingenfuss, before clearing them with Ribbentrop or Weizsäcker. He had to admit to Sztojay that this was not yet an "official step" by the German government. Sztojay, the eager collaborator, urged that the German ambassador submit an official note before he returned to Budapest on October 18, so he could then discuss the whole matter with Kallay and Horthy. The Germans could be sure, said Sztojay, that Horthy would have great understanding for their wishes because of his experience with Bela Kun in 1919. However, because there were so many Jews in Hungary, some 8–900,000, who had such a strong economic position, it would not be easy to reach a quick and final settlement. Sztojay then broached one other problem.

> From his previous conversations he [Sztojay] knows that the Prime Minister [Kallay] is especially interested in the question of whether any possibilities of a livelihood would exist in the east for the Jews after their evacuation. Many rumors were being circulated in this connection, which he personally, of course, did not believe, but Prime Minister Kallay was somewhat uneasy about them. He said he did not wish to reproach himself with having exposed the Hungarian Jews to misery or worse after their evacuation. He was visibly calmed by my [Luther's] reply that all the evacuated Jews, and thus also the Hungarian Jews in the east, were employed first in road construction work and would later be accommodated in a Jewish reservation. . . . When he left, Herr Sztojay told me emphatically that he especially welcomed our suggestions, since he had seen . . . what a terribly undermining influence the Jews had everywhere.

Luther immediately urged Ribbentrop to authorize Jagow to present the German demands in Budapest.[66]

Ribbentrop was still far from giving Luther a free hand in Jewish matters. At the end of August he had insisted that all approaches to foreign governments required his prior approval. Even when he had okayed the approach to Hungary, Bulgaria, and Denmark at the end of September, he had instructed

Luther that everything had to be approved by Weizsäcker beforehand. Now the foreign minister requested that Luther send him a copy of the proposed instructions to Jagow. Furthermore, Ribbentrop insisted that Weizsäcker also receive the Hungarian ambassador and discuss the Jewish question with him. Weizsäcker was to impress upon Sztojay "how important it is to secure agreement of the Hungarian government to the deportation of its Jews to the east."[67]

Weizsäcker, who had been excluded from Jewish affairs (except for passively initialing documents put on his desk) until Ribbentrop's belated attempt to resurrect him as a counterweight to Luther, could think of nothing better to do than ask the latter what he should say to Sztojay. Luther obliged him by suggesting that he repeat the three German demands—legislation to exclude the Jews from cultural and economic life, marking, and deportation.[68] On October 14, Weizsäcker met with Sztojay and found the ambassador already acquainted with Luther's three-point program. He "forcefully" conveyed the sense of Ribbentrop's instructions, that is, the importance of deporting the Jews from Hungary. Sztojay, not at all reluctant to be a tool of the Germans in this matter, tried to strengthen his hand vis-à-vis the more hesitant government in Budapest by once again explicitly urging that Jagow officially present the German desires before he returned to Budapest the following week. Weizsäcker asked Luther to insure that this was done.[69]

With Sztojay's urging, Weizsäcker's encouragement, and finally Ribbentrop's approval, Luther instructed Jagow to transmit the German demands.[70] Jagow saw the deputy foreign minister, Jeno Ghyczy, on October 17, and it was quickly apparent that the Hungarians in Budapest were not nearly as obliging as Sztojay in Berlin. Ghyczy did not even want to accept the German communication, as the Jewish question belonged to the competency of the Interior Ministry. Only after a telephone call to Kallay did Ghyczy take the German document, remarking that Kallay had already drafted a "particularly firm program" on the Jewish question which he would present the following week.[71]

Kallay's program did not fully meet German expectations. He did proclaim that not only the property but the spirit of Jewry must be eliminated from Hungary, that all Jews of service age would be inducted into labor camps, and that the Jews must give up all hope. But he said nothing about marking and deportation, and explicitly attacked those who saw no other problem in the country but the Jewish problem. He would go to any extreme, insofar as the interests of the nation permitted, but he would not endanger its honor and good reputation.[72]

Twice in the following month Jagow met with Kallay and broached the Jewish question, but on both occasions Kallay said he had not yet had time to formulate an answer to the German suggestions. He warned, however, that the Jewish question in Hungary was a "purely internal matter."[73] In late November Sztojay returned to Berlin but could tell Luther only that the examination of the subject had not progressed very far. He again noted the problem caused by "rumors of the treatment of the Jews in the east—which he obviously did not believe." The task of his government would be facilitated if the Germans could assure that the Jews would be assigned to a particular district for their residence. Luther replied that he could give this assurance without further ado.[74]

Up to this point Germany's arm-twisting in Hungary had been solely a Foreign Office affair, in fact almost a one-man show on Luther's part. The SS, convinced that the available train capacity was going to be exhausted by deportations from Rumania, had shown no interest in Hungary at all. By late November, however, the SS realized that no deportations would be forthcoming from Rumania. Himmler now sought to break up the Balkan bottleneck elsewhere.

Hungary now beckoned as the most fruitful target for deportations. In early October, while visiting Budapest, the SS-adviser on Jewish affairs in Slovakia, Dieter Wisliceny, was approached by a certain Fay who identified himself as a personal secretary to Kallay. Fay expressed interest in the solution to the Jewish question in Slovakia and Rumania and then asked if Hungary would be considered for a resettlement program as well. It would be a question first of the 100,000 Jews in Carpatho-Ruthenia and the ex-Rumanian territories, "which Hungary would like to resettle," then the Jews of the flatlands and finally those of Budapest. Wisliceny reported the conversation to Ludin and must have informed the RSHA as well.[75]

In a letter to "Dear Ribbentrop," the *Reichsführer*-SS sought to enlist the aid of the Foreign Office to pressure Hungary as if unaware that Luther had already been working on this for some time.[76] Himmler reminded Ribbentrop of Heszlenyi's earlier proposal. He added that "authoritative politicians and statesmen" in Hungary demanded a solution to the Jewish question and were considering as a first step the deportation of 100,000 Jews from eastern Hungary. Himmler had earlier decided to delay such a deportation until the Hungarian government had declared itself ready to include all Jews in Hungary. Now he felt it expedient to send a specialist to the German embassy in Hungary, perhaps Wisliceny, who had prepared the "release" (*Freimachung*) in Slovakia "on most friendly terms with your gentlemen." Himmler estimated that there were as many as one million Jews in Hungary.

> It would therefore be really extraordinarily gratifying, if we were successful in conveying out of this world the question of this burning problem in Hungary also, the more so as in my opinion through this the Rumanian government would doubtless be forced to give up the hesitant attitude that it displays at the moment in regard to the final beginning of the Jewish evacuation. The question in Bulgaria might thereby be automatically clarified, because as is known to me, the Bulgarian government on its side would gladly like to see its Jewish measures coupled with those of the Rumanian government.

On Ribbentrop's instructions Luther asked Jagow to report on the present suitability of an agreement with Hungary to deport some 100,000 illegally immigrated Jews.[77]

Once the attention of the SS was focused on Hungary, it lost no time in establishing its own sources of information apart from the Foreign Office. On December 11, 1942, SS-*Gruppenführer* Gottlob Berger met secretly with Archduke Albrecht of Hungary. "Hopefully the Foreign Office will not learn of it," he reported to Himmler, "because otherwise there will be another letter from Herr *Unterstaatssekretär* Luther." Berger reported that Hungary had rejected the Foreign Office note on the Jewish question.[78]

Luther himself did not learn of the Hungarian answer until three days later, December 14, when Sztojay handed it to him personally. Hungary was ready to remove its Jews in the German sphere, provided German policy was applied equally to all foreign Jews. The Jewish question within Hungary was a different matter, for each sovereign state had to find for itself the most expedient solution. By now the Jews were practically eliminated from the intellectual life of the country. Given the extraordinarily high percentage of Jews in the population (800,000 out of 14 million, compared with 600,000 out of 60 million in old Germany), Hungary had achieved extraordinary results in economic life as well. With 80 percent of Hungarian production connected to German economic interests, however, it would be an error to force a rhythm that the economy could not bear. As for marking, it could not be considered at the moment. Nor did the Hungarian government have the possibility or technical means to carry out deportations, which would seriously disrupt the war economy in any case.[79]

In mid-January 1943, Luther once again returned to his personal campaign of pressuring the Hungarians. He set upon Sztojay with a ferocity unusual even for Luther in his dealings with foreign diplomats.

> I had to remind him once more of the fact that the Führer is determined under all circumstances to remove all Jews from Europe during the war still, because they, as we indeed precisely know, represent an element of subversion and in most cases are guilty of the sabotage acts that occur and moreover occupy themselves above all in enemy espionage. It fills us with very great alarm, that one country alone in the middle of Europe, friendly to us, shelters some one million Jews. We could not view this danger passively in the long run.

Luther found Sztojay's excuses so "lame" that the Hungarian obviously did not believe in them himself. Luther concluded: "In any case he [Sztojay] will report back to Budapest this conversation which was emphatically and very seriously conducted by me, and we can only hope that our constant pressure will for once lead to success."[80]

But Luther's fury and threats of Hitler's wrath could not move the Hungarians in the month of Stalingrad. Even the Hungarian military no longer seemed anxious to do the Germans' bidding. Jagow approached the Hungarian General Staff in order to clarify whether Major-General Heszlenyi had actually been deputized by the government to propose the deportation of the illegally immigrated Jews. He could get no answer.[81] The Balkan bottleneck could not be broken either in Rumania or Hungary. But despite Himmler's fears that the Bulgarians could be brought into line only by cracking the others, German diplomatic pressure in the last half of 1942 succeeded there where it had failed in Rumania and Hungary.

*Bulgaria.* Bulgaria had been well-rewarded for her alliance with Germany, receiving the South Dobrudja from Rumania in 1940 and Thrace and Macedonia from Greece and Yugoslavia in 1941. There was no strong, native anti-Semitism to cater to politically, but the expediency of the German alliance had led the Bulgarians, like the Rumanians and Hungarians, to carry out increasingly severe Jewish measures between 1939 and 1942.[82] This culminated in June 1942 in the agreement surrendering Bulgarian Jews in the German sphere to deportation and the passing of an enabling law which granted the Bulgarian cabinet full powers to handle Jewish affairs. As Luther noted in August, the way had been cleared for the inclusion of Bulgarian Jews in German measures.

Luther had unsuccessfully pressed Ribbentrop to permit him to approach the Bulgarians until the foreign minister relented on September 24, 1942. We have seen that Luther had informed Ribbentrop that this was an RSHA suggestion, though in fact no written record of such RSHA initiative exists. Luther had earlier told Beckerle if the Bulgarians brought up the possibility of deporting their own Jews, he should accept the offer in principle but make no precise commitment on scheduling, because Luther doubted that the train capacity existed. He would hardly have made such a conjectural statement, if he had received an explicit request from the RSHA. German initiative in Bulgaria, as in Hungary, was most likely due to Luther, not the RSHA.

Once Luther received permission from Ribbentrop to approach the Bulgarians, he lost no time. Beckerle came to Berlin and met with Luther for three hours on October 9, 1942.[83] The memorandum on the Jewish question in Bulgaria which Klingenfuss prepared for the meeting stated that since Bulgarian legislation provided for the resettlement of Jews within the country, the proposal should now be made to the Bulgarian government to deport these Jews to the east. Germany was ready to take them over. The question of a Bulgarian contribution (*Beitrag*) to defray the costs of this deportation should be brought up as well.[84]

On October 15, 1942, Luther sent instructions to Beckerle in Sofia, which referred to the discussions held earlier in Berlin. Luther officially requested Beckerle to approach the Bulgarian government concerning the deportation of its Jews to the east. The Jewish property left behind would accrue to Bulgaria, which could then pay Germany for the cost of the deportation. Luther suggested a contribution of 250 RM per head. Between the Berlin meeting of October 9 and the sending of instructions on October 15, Luther must have contacted the RSHA. For the first time he mentioned that Germany was ready to place at the disposal of Bulgaria one of its advisers for the Jewish question. In the margin Luther noted that, according to the RSHA, Wisliceny had been suggested.[85]

Beckerle discussed the question in detail with Prime Minister Bogdan Filov, who claimed that the Bulgarian government was counting upon the use of Jewish labor for road construction. The German offer regarding the rest of the Jews, however, was "welcome," and he promised to discuss the question with the cabinet. Two weeks later, on November 16, 1942, he reported the results of the cabinet discussion to Beckerle. Bulgaria welcomed the possibility of being able to deport its Jews to the east, though Filov reiterated that a portion of male Jews needed for road construction could not be spared for the time being. Filov also expressed gratitude for a Jewish adviser to help carry out the appropriate measures. The proposed contribution of 250 RM per head, however, was felt to be "extremely high."[86]

Klingenfuss reported the Bulgarian agreement to Eichmann, asked whether Wisliceny was still the candidate for the post, and proposed that the question of the Bulgarian monetary contribution be left for the adviser to negotiate after his arrival.[87] Eichmann replied that Wisliceny could not be spared from Bratislava at the moment. In his place he had appointed the very experienced SS-*Hauptsturmführer* Theo Dannecker to be attached to the Police Attaché already in the Sofia embassy. Dannecker had been busy with Jewish affairs in France until illness forced his recall, but he was now fully restored to health. To Eichmann the whole question of Bulgaria's monetary contribution was of "no crucial importance."[88]

Klingenfuss accepted Eichmann's nomination of Dannecker and urged that he be sent as soon as possible, preferably in the beginning of January. Woermann initialed Klingenfuss' draft.[89] Hahn, Klingenfuss' successor, then asked the Personnel Division to assign Dannecker officially. His work was characterized by Hahn as "indispensable." But in the Personnel Division, Dr. Wallenberg was less than enthusiastic. Dannecker was of draft age. Apparently not realizing the full importance of Dannecker's job, Wallenberg assumed that he would be called up if assigned to the Foreign Office. "If the assignment of D[annecker] cannot be avoided," Wallenberg proposed an assignment for only nine months or for the length of the commission given him. "I request clarification, however, if D. or some other person ultimately is being considered." Hahn assured him that only Dannecker was being considered, and the official assignment was made.[90]

The Foreign Office not only took the initiative to extract Bulgaria's consent to the deportations but also made the necessary arrangements to dispatch a RSHA expert to take care of the practical details on the spot. This accomplishment was due primarily to the zeal of Martin Luther, who was well served by his underlings, Karl Klingenfuss and Fritz-Gebhardt von Hahn, as well as his SA-comrade, Adolph Heinz Beckerle. The stage was now set for the beginning of the deportations from Bulgaria.

## Italian Obstruction

If the German allies, Hungary and Rumania, were in a position to resist German demands more effectively than a puppet state like Slovakia or the occupied territories, Italy was even more able to do so. Italy was a less unequal ally than either Hungary or Rumania and could not be subjected to the same arm-twisting diplomacy simply by virtue of its greater power and independence. On the Italian side, instead of eager pro-German collaborators, officials in responsible positions were prepared not only to resist the Germans but to pressure an ambivalent Mussolini as well. The internal situation in Germany's power structure also facilitated Italian resistance. Ribbentrop was extremely jealous about encroachments by his rivals into the area of foreign affairs, and nowhere was he more sensitive than over relations with Italy. Not only did he keep a wary eye on the other Nazi chieftains, but he was also reluctant to delegate authority to negotiate with Italy even to his subordinates within the Foreign Office. As he stated on September 24, 1942, negotiations with Italy were to be conducted by the Führer and himself. While such exclusive control over relations with Italy was impossible to maintain in practice, nonetheless Ribbentrop never gave others a free hand to deal with Italy as with Germany's lesser allies. In particular, as Ribbentrop's relations with Martin Luther deteriorated, the foreign minister was increasingly re-luctant to permit his ex-protégé to take liberties with the Italians as he had done elsewhere. With Luther restrained, direct pressure was not exerted upon the Italians in the Jewish question until Ribbentrop undertook the task himself in 1943. This delay on Ribbentrop's part left the Italians free to flaunt German desires over the treatment of Jews in the Italian military zones in Croatia and Greece, while a frustrated Luther looked on helplessly.

After some delay Ribbentrop had approved approaching the Italians with the choice of recalling their Jews from the western occupied territories or surrendering them to deportation measures. But Ribbentrop had forbidden any approach to the Italians concerning the Jewish question in Croatia until Ante Pavelic had complained to Hitler personally that Italian forces in Croatia had professed no knowledge of Mussolini's decision to treat the Jews in the Italian zone in the same way as in the rest of Croatia. Pavelic had most certainly requested German help in dealing with the Italians, and Ribbentrop had been forced to instruct Luther to inquire about the status of the Duce's decision. Mackensen carried out this inquiry and received the Italian answer on October 8, 1942. The occupation forces in Croatia had been informed of the Duce's decision in August, he was assured.[91]

In fact the Italian Foreign Ministry had not transmitted Mussolini's initial decision but merely informed the Italian military in Croatia that the German approach was being taken into consideration. Leonardo Vitetti, director general of the Foreign Office, requested a report from the military command over the number of Jews who came from territory annexed by Italy or who were in some way connected to these territories and thus not liable to deporta-tion. A verbal understanding was then reached between the Foreign Office and the Italian command in Croatia that it would be necessary to have a census of the Jewish refugees in the Italian zone in order to gain time.[92]

When Luther asked Kasche to report whether the Croatian government had been notified yet of the Italian agreement to deportations from its zone, the answer was negative. In a meeting between General Roatta and Pavelic, the Italian commander said he had received instructions to turn over the Jews not to the Croatians but to the German army. In Roatta's opinion, the German army was not competent for this, and he had once again checked with Rome and expected new instructions at any moment. Kasche advised Luther that either the Italian Foreign Office or Roatta had once more given out false information, which signified a new delay in the business.[93]

Luther immediately instructed Mackensen to report Roatta's talk with Pavelic to the Italians and to request clear instructions to their occupation forces in Croatia that the Jews were not to be turned over to the German army. Rather the Italians were merely to give a free hand to the Croatians, working in cooperation with certain authorized German officials to carry out deportations from the Italian zone.[94]

Croatia was not the only area in Europe where Italian behavior in the Jewish question was bothering Luther. The Italians also had a military zone in Greece, where they were just as uncooperative. As early as July 1942, Friedrich Suhr wrote Rademacher about the RSHA desire to introduce Jewish measures in all of Greece. The local Security Police and Security Service (Sipo-SD) had already asked the Reich plenipotentiary in Athens, Günther Altenburg, to ascertain if the competent Italian authorities were agreed to the marking of Jews in Greece. After consulting the Foreign Office in Rome, the Italian plenipotentiary, Ghigi, had replied that in consideration of the significant economic power that Italian Jews held in the Mediterranean (especially Tunis), Italy wished to postpone marking the Jews in Greece. If Germany decided to mark the Jews in its own zone around Saloniki, Jews of Italian citizenship there had to be exempted. Suhr wished to know if marking and select internment of Jews in Saloniki could be carried out, provided the 2,000 Italian Jews were exempted.[95]

Surprisingly, the fact that Altenburg had initiated negotiations with the Italians on the request of the Sipo-SD in Greece without prior consultation with the Foreign Office did not cause a big uproar, apparently because Rademacher did not immediately inform Luther. Instead he merely had Klingenfuss ask Altenburg to provide an exact report on the negotiations and to give his opinion on the RSHA request concerning marking.[96] Altenburg responded that Suhr's account of the Italian response was correct; in view of the economic position held by Italian Jews in the Mediterranean, measures against Jews in Greece had to be postponed. If the Germans insisted further, Ghigi had suggested that the question should be treated between Rome and Berlin, not locally. In Ghigi's opinion, a unified procedure for all Greece was desirable, but if the Gemans proceeded against the Jews independently in Saloniki, then Italian Jews had to be exempted. Altenburg left it up to the German Foreign Office to seek an agreement with Italy on unified procedure through direct negotiations with Rome. In his own opinion special measures for Jews in Saloniki were not expedient, because Italian Jews there would be exempted and thus their economic power would be unaffected. Furthermore, the Jews living in the capital of Greece, Athens, would not be included.[97]

While awaiting a Foreign Office decision on marking, the German military in Greece began inducting Jews for road construction work, which resulted in a strong emigration of Jews to the Italian zone. In mid-August Suhr once again urged Rademacher to reach a decision on marking.[98] But the attempts of the Foreign Office to negotiate the Greek question through its embassy in Rome were futile. In direct contradiction to Altenburg's earlier report, the Italians in Rome claimed that this question was being treated in negotiations between the two plenipotentiaries in Athens. On September 15, 1942, Luther instructed Altenburg once again to undertake discussions in Athens with Ghigi over marking. Despite waiting a month, however, Luther received no report on the course of these negotiations.[99]

In mid-October Luther decided to urge upon Ribbentrop a full-scale diplomatic offensive against the recalcitrant Italians. He had just received the Italian refusal to agree either to the deportation of its Jews in the western occupied territories or to their recall. In Croatia the Italians had refused to comply with Mussolini's order to treat the Jews in the Italian zone in the same way as in the rest of Croatia. In Greece negotiations over the mere introduction of marking had been going on for over three months without the slightest positive result. The evidence of Italy's massive obstruction to German *Judenpolitik* was overwhelming. Even under a cloud, Luther was not a man to accept such obstruction lightly.

Another factor also played a role in Luther's decision. Heinrich Himmler had discussed the Jewish question with Mussolini on October 11, 1942, during a visit to Rome. Luther knew the details of this conversation because the report from Himmler to Ribbentrop was forwarded through D II.[100] As Luther was trying to cement an alliance with the SS in preparation for ousting Ribbentrop, Italy and the Jewish question seemed to provide the perfect tool for driving a wedge between Himmler and Ribbentrop. Luther calculated that if he succeeded in pushing Ribbentrop into making sharp demands upon the Italians in the Jewish question, and the pressure worked, he would get some of the credit. But if the Italians put up the expected resistance and refused to give in to the German demands, Ribbentrop would be discredited by the failure. "Luther wanted to prove to Hitler that the Italians made a fool of Ribbentrop, that they did not take him seriously."[101] On the other hand, if Ribbentrop showed his usual reluctance to confront the Italians, the foreign minister's hesitancy would stand in marked contrast to Luther's zeal in supporting the Jewish policy of Hitler and Himmler. This was the same trap which Ribbentrop had almost inadvertently fallen into and narrowly extricated himself from in September. This time it was no accident, however, for Luther was consciously baiting the trap.

On October 20, 1942, Luther had urged that Ribbentrop explicitly request the Italians to withdraw their Jews from the western occupied territories, since they refused to agree to their deportation to the east. Two days later Luther submitted to the foreign minister a far more comprehensive memorandum, drafted by Rademacher, which covered all facets of the problem of Italy and the Jewish question.[102] The Italians had showed little understanding about the question in general and were very sensitive when the interests of Italian Jews were disturbed. After complaining about Italy's lax treatment of the Jews in Italy itself as well as its protection of the Italian Jews in the western occupied territories, Luther launched into a discussion of the difficulties caused by Italy elsewhere in Europe. Italy placed extraordinary value on the economic power of Italian Jews in the Mediterranean area, and therefore shrank from Jewish measures everywhere. In Tunis they had protested against France's aryanization measures. In Greece the Italians had asked for the postponement of marking. Local discussions between the German and Italian plenipotentiaries were pending, but "the prospects for unified procedure are very slight." In Rumania as in other southeast European states, Italian Jewish firms maintained their key positions in the economy. Moreover, Jewish salesmen and employees, whose further activities in native firms were made impossible by legislative measures, were hired by Italian firms. The economic advantage thus gained for the Italians naturally made the Jewish legislation in these countries unpopular. In Croatia, the Jews were protected from Croatian deportation measures. The decision of the Duce was not being carried out by the local Italian authorities.

Luther proposed that the entire problem be discussed between Ribbentrop and Ciano or even between the Führer and the Duce. Luther then formulated the German "desires" to be presented at such a meeting. In the German sphere the Italian Jews must be either subjected to German measures or recalled to Italy by a given deadline. In Italy itself Italian legislation must adapt to German principles. "In such an important area as the Jewish question, the Axis must appear unified." Vis-à-vis other states, Italy must coordinate its behavior with Germany beforehand. The essence of the problem was that Italy wanted to treat its Jews abroad only as Italian citizens, not as Jews. To justify this position, Italy always referred to the importance of Italian Jews abroad to the reconstruction of Italy's economic position in the Mediterranean. But this argument was dangerous and resulted in "a strengthening of the resistance of individual governments (for example, Hungary) against our attempt to coordinate Jewish policy." Moreover, it hindered the measures deemed necessary by Germany in Croatia and Greece. Ultimately, it was dangerous to Italy as well, for in the long run the protection of the Jewish economic position in the Mediterranean would not serve the interests of Italy but those of the enemy.

Ribbentrop avoided Luther's trap in the time-honored bureaucratic manner. He neither endorsed nor refused the proposals put forward by his undersecretary. He simply refused to make any decision at all and let the proposals sit. He did not let himself be pushed into an undesired confrontation with Italy nor could he be immediately singled out for blocking Foreign Office pressure to make Italy conform to Germany's Jewish policy.

Meanwhile, Luther had to continue dealing with Italian obstruction. At the very time that his memorandum for Ribbentrop was being prepared, an even more bizarre incident was reported from Croatia. Through the Croatian foreign minister, Lorkovic, Kasche had learned that in Rome the Croatian ambassador, Peric, had been told that Croatia should suggest that the Jews be taken out of the Italian zone to Italy. Lorkovic assured Kasche that the Croatians had replied to the Italian feeler that agreements existed with Germany over Jewish deportations and thus Croatia could not simply begin deportations to Italy without German agreement. Kasche concluded:

> Italian behavior appears ever more clearly to me as a delaying tactic. Obviously we have been falsely informed of the decision of the Duce, or it is not being observed by subordinate officials. . . . A handing over of the Jews to Italy would upset the entire European Jewish policy, as it is advocated by us.

Luther instructed Mackensen that in case the Italian feeler was repeated in negotiations in Rome, he should insist that it contradicted the decision of the Duce.[103]

Peric in Rome was telling the Italians a different story than Lorkovic was telling Kasche in Zagreb. The Croatian ambassador informed the Italians that his government had no objection to the Jews in the Italian zone being transferred to Italy as long as they gave up all their property. "Peric was good enough to add his personal pious hope that this proposal would be accepted by the Government in Rome, so that the Jews would be saved from the terrible fate in store for them in Poland."[104]

Apparently the Italian move had been an entirely unauthorized maneuver by certain of their Foreign Ministry officials to confuse the Croatians with alternative proposals and thus buy time. When the Croatians consented so quickly, the Italians backed out immediately. Italy could not take Croatian Jews, for Italy was no Palestine, Peric was told. But Italy would take responsibility for all Jews of Italian citizenship. The Marquese D'Ajeta, Ciano's deputy, told Mackensen the Croatian move was an attempt to shift its own responsibility for its Jews onto Italy. But the Duce had instructed the military authorities to place all Jews in the Italian zone in concentration camps. There they would be divided into two groups, one which was "duly qualified for Italian territory," and the second which would be turned over to Croatian authorities.[105]

Reports from Croatia confirmed that the Italians were indeed interning the Jews, but over 700, allegedly Italian citizens, had been sent to Italy already. Many others were being shifted to a camp on Italian territory in Istria. Kasche warned, "The Italian refusal to take over the Jews therefore may not have been so vehement." Because of the Italian sorting process, there was no indication as to when deportations could begin.[106]

On November 20, 1942, Kasche again reported. According to his informants, the Italian internment of the Jews resulted solely from German pressure. They reserved the task solely to themselves. They refused an attempt to have the Jews transferred to Germany for labor and likewise blocked any participation by the Croatians, either in internment or seizure of Jewish property.[107] In early December Kasche reported that the Italians were shifting the Croatian Jews in inland cities like Mostar to the coastal town of Dubrovnik and to islands off the coast, where hotels were requisitioned to accommodate them. When the Germans had requested the use of one of these seaside island hotels, the Hotel Kupari, for the recreation and recuperation of German soldiers, the Italians refused. Kasche suggested that since the transfer of these Jews to Germany by rail through partisan-infested territory was too dangerous, they could be taken by ship to Trieste and then brought to Germany from there.[108]

In accordance with Kasche's suggestion, the German embassy in Rome requested the Italians to ship the interned Jews to Trieste. D'Ajeta replied that this was not possible due to lack of shipping capacity. Furthermore, due to the internment of many Slovenes in Trieste, there were no transit camp facilities. The Jews would have to be left in their present camps where they were under control and could cause no trouble.[109]

Despite Mussolini's initial decision to surrender the Croatian Jews in the Italian zone, key people in the Italian Foreign Ministry and army clearly had no intention of surrendering a single Jew to the Germans. The Germans estimated that some 4–5,000 Jews were protected in the Italian zone. The Italians themselves registered 2,662 interned Jews.[110] There were probably a number of others who were exempted from internment. The Germans finally realized the futility of waiting for the inclusion of the Jews from the Italian zone in their deportation measures and proceeded to take small numbers of surviving Croatian Jews from elsewhere. By the end of 1942, 4,927 Jews had been deported, and in March 1943, another 2,000 were brought out in sealed cars attached to regularly scheduled trains.[111] The attempt of the German Foreign Office to coerce the Italians without Ribbentrop's approval for a full-scale diplomatic offensive had failed. The zeal of Luther and Kasche and the cooperation of Mackensen proved insufficient to overcome Italian obstruction.

In Greece the Germans even failed to get the Italians to the negotiating table. After waiting more than a month since instructing Altenburg to reopen negotiations with the Italians in Athens over the question of marking the Jews, on October 23, 1942, Luther requested a report on the course of the negotiations. Altenburg replied that Ghigi had requested instructions from Rome and promised to return to the business as soon as they were received. Since then Ghigi had not mentioned the subject. Luther directed Altenburg to inquire of Ghigi what instructions he had received, and Altenburg replied that Ghigi had still received none. The German plenipotentiary recommended treating the business directly through the German ambassador in Rome.[112]

For the second time the seat of the hoped-for negotiations shifted from Athens to Rome. On December 5, 1942, Luther ordered Mackensen to discuss the matter directly with d'Ajeta because further delay was most objectionable. But the slippery Italians refused to be tied down. D'Ajeta answered that the Italian plenipotentiary had received instructions to enter an agreement with the Italian military commander in Greece concerning the treatment of the Jews, and the results of the agreement would be communicated to Altenburg immediately.[113]

Upon Luther's instructions, Altenburg approached Ghigi once again. This time Ghigi confirmed that he had indeed received instructions, but through a transmission error they could not be deciphered. When he found out what his instructions were, he would inform the Germans. When Altenburg inquired on January 10, 1943, whether an agreement between Ghigi and the Italian military on the Jewish question had yet been reached, the answer was negative once again. General Carlo Geloso, the Italian commander in Greece, was in Rome, and nothing could be arranged until he returned.[114]

Three days later Ghigi held out the prospect of yet further delay. Even when an agreement was reached between him and Geloso, they would first have to report it to Rome, where it would probably experience further revision. But by this time the RSHA had given up waiting for Luther to secure the cooperation of the Italians and was preparing for independent procedures in the German zone. Altenburg had to inform Ghigi that SS-*Sturmbannführer* Rolf Günther, one of Eichmann's staff, had arrived in Greece to make preliminary arrangements for the evacuation of the Jews in the German zone.[115]

Luther's Italian strategy failed completely. First, he failed to widen the net of the Final Solution to include the Jews within the Italian occupation zones in Croatia and Greece. Ultimately, the RSHA decided in each case to proceed with the deportation of those Jews immediately accessible to the German grasp and pass up those under Italian protection. This failure was due to several factors. On the one hand, Italian officials and military officers proved quite inventive in thwarting German pressure, a course of action which Mussolini must have tolerated. On the other, Ribbentrop refused Luther's request for high-level pressure on the Italians that might have compelled Mussolini to extract more obedience from his evasive officials.

Second, Luther's hope to make Ribbentrop carry the blame for this lack of success, for failing either to overcome Italian resistance or to authorize high-level pressure aimed at this goal, also was not realized. Ribbentrop parried Luther's ploy by following the same delaying tactics utilized by the Italians. He neither endorsed nor refused Luther's proposals for direct pressure on Mussolini or Ciano. He simply left Luther's proposals unanswered for months, while the RSHA lost patience, gave up on the Italians, and initiated more limited deportation programs.

## Unfinished Business

While Italy and southeast Europe consumed most of the energies of the Foreign Office Jewish experts in the last half of 1942, several other problems also claimed their attention. First, the Foreign Office continued to be consulted on certain matters concerning internal Jewish affairs, and in this regard the most important problem in 1942 was the regulation of the *Mischlinge* question as well as the related question of mixed marriage. Second, during the deportations from the western occupied territories, there was a hitch in Belgium which provoked Luther to intervene.

*The Mischlinge Question.*    At the Wannsee Conference Heydrich had proposed that, with few exceptions, first-degree *Mischlinge* (half-Jews who neither had a Jewish spouse nor practiced the Jewish religion) would be equated with full Jews, that is deported and exterminated. Second-degree *Mischlinge* (quarter-Jews), with few exceptions, would be allowed to remain in Germany. Allegedly aware of the technical impossibility of his proposal, State Secretary Wilhelm Stuckart of the Interior Ministry suggested compulsory sterilization of all *Mischlinge* as the simplest solution. Heydrich also proposed that Jewish partners in mixed marriages be deported either to the "privileged" ghetto of Theresienstadt or to the east. Stuckart suggested compulsory divorce before deportation in both cases.[116]

Rademacher had attended the subsequent meeting of March 6, 1942, in the Gestapo headquarters, which dealt solely with the *Mischlinge* and mixed marriage problems. As the conference calculated that the compulsory sterilization of 70,000 *Mischlinge,* as proposed by Stuckart, would require 700,000 hospital days, this measure was impossible to carry out during wartime. The conference recommended the internment of all first-degree *Mischlinge* with the sterilization question postponed until after the war. Both the Justice and Propaganda Ministries opposed compulsory divorce in mixed marriages. Rademacher supported the reasoning of the Propaganda Ministry in this, apparently his only contribution to the conference. The conference then recommended that divorce should be automatically granted upon application of the aryan partner; if this was not forthcoming, the public prosecutor would file for the divorce, which would be automatically granted.[117]

The decisions of the conference of March 6 were not final, apparently, for afterwards both the Justice and the Interior Ministries sent circulars to all the participants advocating their respective views. Stuckart favored the natural dying out of the *Mischlinge* on German territory, following their sterilization. State Secretary Franz Schlegelberger of the Justice Ministry advocated offering the choice between sterilization and deportation. The Justice Ministry also opposed divorce upon petition of the public prosecutor. With access to the top-secret Wannsee Protocol, Rademacher compiled a list of all the suggestions made at the Wannsee and March 6 conferences, as well as in the two later letters of Stuckart and Schlegelberger. He then noted in his covering letter for Luther, Gaus, and Weizsäcker: "From the point of view of foreign policy, it ought to be immaterial whether the *Mischlinge* are deported to the east or sterilized and allowed to remain in Germany."[118]

Weizsäcker must not have acted on Rademacher's letter, for on August 12, 1942, Friedrich Suhr reminded Rademacher that the RSHA had still received no opinion from the Foreign Office on the urgent matters discussed at the March 6 conference.[119] Therefore in early September Rademacher and Klingenfuss prepared a detailed memorandum on the problem. The basic criteria which they used for establishing a Foreign Office position were the possible effects of the future regulations on German citizens living abroad and on the Jewish legislation of other countries. The policy choices for *Mischlinge* were: a) compulsory sterilization, or b) their division into those equated with

Jews and included in general Jewish measures, and those equated with Germans (who would undergo "voluntary sterilization in return for conditional permission to remain in the Reich"). For mixed marriage the choices were: a) compulsory divorce, or b) divorce upon application of the aryan partner, or, after a reasonable length of time, upon application of the public prosecutor.

Rademacher and Klingenfuss noted that no matter whether Germany deported or sterilized its first-degree *Mischlinge,* there was no way to force either procedure on German *Mischlinge* abroad. As for the effect of German policy upon the Jewish legislation of other countries, compulsory sterilization would meet great resistance. A unified European Jewish policy could thus be reached sooner along the lines of separating the *Mischlinge* into those equated with full Jews and those freed from discriminatory legislation. Once again the inadequate legislation in foreign countries posed difficulties for a "biologically pure solution," but Germany should strive that "in the other states a legal prevention of descendants is fully assured (Nürnberg laws)."

For general and propaganda reasons, the Foreign Office Jewish experts preferred the simplified procedures for individual divorce over compulsory divorce. For German mixed marriages abroad, compulsory divorce was legally ineffective. But individuals could be given the choice of voluntary divorce or denaturalization. Simplified procedures for individual divorce would also be more suitable as a model for a unified European Jewish policy. The memorandum was submitted to Luther, Woermann, Gaus, and Weizsäcker.[120]

This memorandum reached Weizsäcker at the height of the late summer crisis between Luther and Ribbentrop, during the period in which the foreign minister was severely restricting his undersecretary's activities in the Jewish question. Perhaps emboldened by this turn of events, Weizsäcker reasserted himself in Foreign Office Jewish policy for the first time in nearly a year. The Foreign Office lacked the data and knowledge necessary for a competent opinion on such matters, he stated. "I think we ought therefore to limit ourselves to the general remark that in each case the more lenient solution is the preferable one from the foreign policy point of view," in order not to provide any pretext for enemy propaganda and to facilitate the cooperation of other European states.[121]

Luther passed on to the RSHA Weizsäcker's formulation that the Foreign Office preferred the "more lenient" solutions, but then gave precisely the opinion which Weizsäcker had felt the Foreign Office was not competent to make. Luther, on the basis of Rademacher's memorandum, claimed that for the Foreign Office the "more lenient" solutions were the simplified procedure for individual divorce and the separation of the *Mischlinge* into two categories—those treated like full Jews and those permitted to remain in the Reich.[122] But in fact this latter was precisely the more radical solution which Heydrich had been trying to push upon the reluctant Ministries of Justice and Interior, for treating first-degree *Mischlinge* like full Jews meant their deportation and extermination rather than a policy of mass sterilization which was in fact technically unfeasible. To those who did not know that equating

*Mischlinge* with full Jews meant their death, this policy might indeed appear more lenient, and Rademacher had reasoned that it would be easier to force this upon other countries than a policy of compulsory sterilization. It was precisely because Weizsäcker knew that the superficially more lenient policy recommended by Rademacher was in fact the more radical one advocated by Heydrich and opposed by the other Ministries, that he had disavowed the competence of the Foreign Office to make such a recommendation. A blanket statement for leniency would support Stuckart and Schlegelberger against the SS. But Luther brushed aside Weizsäcker's interference and enlisted the Foreign Office on the side of the SS anyhow.

Shortly after Luther informed the RSHA of the Foreign Office position on the question of *Mischlinge* and mixed marriage, Suhr wrote Rademacher inviting him to a second conference to clarify these questions, and Rademacher sent Klingenfuss to attend on October 27, 1942.[123] Klingenfuss had been in South America during the first round of conferences in early 1942, and therefore this was his first exposure to the interministerial coordination of the Final Solution.

At the conference it was announced that new techniques of sterilization now permitted the operation to be carried out quickly and simply, even during the war. Those attending therefore quickly approved the option of sterilization for all first-degree *Mischlinge,* which would represent "a voluntary recompense by the first-degree *Mischlinge* for his conditionally being allowed to remain in Reich territory." For the previously uninitiated at the conference, like Klingenfuss, it was made clear that in comparison with deportation, "sterilization must be considered a merciful favor." As for those few first-degree *Mischlinge* who decided for deportation over sterilization, care would be taken "that through a separation from the other sex every possibility of procreation would be taken from them." It was already clear to the initiated that "every possibility of procreation" would be ended by prompt extermination.[124]

Luther informed Weizsäcker, Woermann, and Gaus that a quick and simple method for the sterlization of all first-degree *Mischlinge* had come to the fore.[125] However, the RSHA announcement of the new sterilization techniques proved premature. The method was not perfected, and in the end the first degree *Mischlinge* were neither deported and exterminated nor sterilized. The Foreign Office attempt to influence policy in this regard proved academic. But it did demonstrate that even when Weizsäcker once again ventured into the field of Jewish affairs, he was too feeble to thwart Luther, despite the latter's growing estrangement from Ribbentrop.

*Luther and Belgium.* Once the deportations from the western occupied territories were underway, the Foreign Office was not involved except in the question of foreign Jews, for whom it had zealously tried to secure either recall or deportation. Otherwise the deportation machinery ran so smoothly that the Foreign Office had almost nothing to do. Only once did Bene report any serious difficulties in the Netherlands. In mid-August 1942, he wrote: "Since the Jews have found out and know what's going on with the deportation and labor in the east, they no longer line up for the weekly transports." But shortly thereafter he assured the Foreign Office that the general excitement had abated somewhat. The trains kept running, and in his last report before the dissolution of *Abteilung Deutschland* in the spring of 1943, Bene noted that 50,000 Jews had already been deported from the Netherlands to the east.[126]

A more serious difficulty arose in Belgium, where the German military administration was insufficiently eager to murder Jews, who in turn were insufficiently passive, all of which finally provoked Luther's wrath. Bargen's first telegram from Belgium had been unenthusiastic. His following reports continued to depict and emphasize the difficulties involved in deporting the Jews. Roundups were necessary to fill the transports, for the Jews did not answer the orders to report. Many Jews abandoned their apartments and attempted to find accommodation with non-Jews, an effort supported by a considerable portion of the Belgian people. False identity cards and illegal emigration caused further difficulties.[127] In November, when nearly 17,000 Jews had been deported and the operations were ended until the following year, the situation had little changed. Because of "rumors about butchering of Jews" *(Gerüchte über Abschlachten der Juden),* roundups and individual arrests were needed to seize the Jews. Illegal emigration to unoccupied France and Switzerland continued. The curfew and the wearing of the Jewish star were no longer observed. Perhaps as many as one-third of the Jews had false identity cards. The beginning of participation by the Jews in the active resistance had already been detected.[128]

Luther was very irritated by this state of affairs. Previously, Jews of Belgian citizenship had been exempted from deportation, but this was no longer tolerable.

> When the Jews remaining in Belgium today disregard the orders of the military commander, furthermore attempt by all means to conceal their Jewish character and to crawl into hiding places which are difficult to mop up, and when finally traces of participation of these Jews in active resistance against the occupying power are already discovered, then an energetic intervention should prevent further diffusion from this source of danger.
>
> I therefore request you to consider the possibility, in agreement with the military commander, of now extending the existing measures to all Jews in Belgium and to concentrate them in collection camps until deportation is possible. . . . A drastic cleansing of Belgium of the Jews must take place sooner or later in any case.[129]

This letter of December 4, 1942, was drafted by Klingenfuss in accordance with instructions that Rademacher passed to him from Luther. It was sent directly to Brussels and was not submitted to Weizsäcker or Woermann. Luther was well aware that the Foreign Office had no competency to urge the arrest and deportation of Jews by the German military administration in Belgium. But Luther was not a man to listen to an endless litany of difficulties without trying to do something about it. Bargen had unwittingly provoked the same undesired initiative from Luther that Benzler had done in Serbia.

Bargen claimed that he never acted upon Luther's instructions, and the evidence supports his claim.[130] He replied to Luther that he had discussed the problem with the military commander as well as the local Sipo-SD "as instructed." But in fact the results were not at all what Luther had asked for. Bargen reported that no railway cars were available for deportations at the moment. Collection camps were already full with foreign Jews, and no further camps were available. When deportations resumed, the Belgian Jews would be deported only after the foreign Jews.[131]

Luther was not pleased. On January 25, 1943, he wrote Bargen that he wanted all Jews in Belgium, including those of Belgian citizenship, collected in camps immediately. If this was not possible, then at least a certain percentage of Belgian Jews should be interned. Luther was sure that elements among the Belgian Jews could be found whose conduct would appear to justify such immediate measures. But Luther did not stop there. He not only sent this letter to Bargen but also had Rademacher send it to the RSHA, along with a copy of Bargen's report. Eichmann was requested to have Luther's recommendations carried out.[132]

Luther's private campaign against the Belgian Jews abruptly ended with his own arrest two weeks later. Bargen was recalled from Belgium in July 1943, and deportations were renewed from Belgium only in September 1943.[133] The delay may have given some Belgian Jews the opportunity ultimately to escape the German grasp.

# 8. The Last Phase of D III: January–March 1943

## Changing of the Guard

Martin Luther had assured Rademacher that he could be relieved of Jewish affairs once he had trained a suitable successor. The mass of German diplomats returning from South American missions in the spring of 1942 offered Rademacher a wide selection from which to choose, and he requested Karl Otto Klingenfuss, his successor as chargé d'affaires at the Montevideo embassy. Rademacher tried to make the work congenial for Klingenfuss. He apologized that Klingenfuss had to work as his subordinate though having only one month less seniority than his new supervisor. Because of the new influx of personnel, however, there was no other alternative, and Rademacher promised Klingenfuss as much individual activity as possible. He had urged the division of D III into two sections, Rademacher told Klingenfuss, but Luther had vetoed the proposal.[1]

If Rademacher was seeking a suitable successor, the choice was inappropriate. Klingenfuss followed instructions meticulously and did his work well, but without evident enthusiasm. Rather than displaying a take-charge spirit, Klingenfuss asked entirely too many awkward questions. His inquiries manifested a suspicious curiosity instead of the toughness which was a prerequisite for dealing with Jewish affairs. He repeatedly asked Rademacher what happened to the Jews deported through the efforts of D III. Rademacher always gave him the same evasive answer. The Jews had to be treated as potential enemies and therefore removed from areas where they presented a danger behind the backs of the troops. They were lodged in ghettos and put to work, which was only fair as they did not do military service. After the war, the Jews would be resettled.[2]

But this stock answer did not satisfy Klingenfuss' curiosity. He found the whole atmosphere of Jewish affairs rather "sinister" (*unheimlich*). When he visited his family in Mannheim, they told him how the neighboring Jewish family had hanged themselves in the stairwell the night before they were to be evacuated. His brother, back from the eastern front, reported that he had heard of mass executions of Jews there.[3] And then there was Bene's telegram of August 13, 1942, in which the *Vertreter* to the Netherlands reported that the Jews had found out what was going on with the deportations and work in the east and no longer reported for the transports.[4]

Klingenfuss had also heard many rumors in *Abteilung Deutschland* about *Einsatzgruppen* reports and about a protocol from an important meeting held in January 1942. When he asked Rademacher about the *Einsatzgruppen* reports, the latter told him that it was a matter of antipartisan measures by SS and police units and read him an excerpt from one over the partisan war.[5] After repeated inquiries about the notorious protocol, Rademacher finally took it from the files, let Klingenfuss thumb through it just briefly, then took it back before Klingenfuss could analyze it.[6]

Rademacher finally lost patience with Klingenfuss' questions about what happened to the deported Jews and told him to ask for himself at the RSHA. Rolf Günther entertained Klingenfuss' inquiry and told him that the Jews were sent to camps. Women and children also, Klingenfuss asked. No, they were sent to ghettos. What sort of ghettos? "Rather cramped." Was the separation of the sexes permanent, Klingenfuss asked. Günther answered affirmatively. When Klingenfuss concluded that this meant a solution in the sense of a denial of descendants, Eichmann's associate confirmed the observation. When Klingenfuss then asked if he could visit one of the work camps, Günther suggested Theresienstadt. But Rademacher informed him that Theresienstadt was a privileged camp. Because he would not get a true picture of the real camps, Klingenfuss thereupon declined the trip to Theresienstadt.[7]

It was by now quite clear to Klingenfuss that he was participating in a long-term genocidal policy, even if he was not yet aware of the systematic and immediate extermination in gas chambers which faced the deported Jews. In October 1942, Klingenfuss went to Hans Schröder, the head of the Personnel Division, and begged to be released from the *Judenreferat*. But he did not say why, except that the work was "unpleasant" (*unangenehm*). He wanted no discussions which might complicate his release. He only wanted to get out.[8]

For three long months after his request for a transfer, Klingenfuss continued to do his job at D III, aware that he was part of a program whose aim was the extinction of the Jewish race. As before he drafted telegrams and memoranda on Rademacher's instructions and attended the *Mischlinge* conference at the end of October, but there is no evidence that he took a personal initiative in Jewish affairs during this period. Neither Luther nor Rademacher any longer placed hopes on Klingenfuss as a suitable successor to head D III. When Fritz-Gebhardt von Hahn indicated his willingness to return to D III in December 1942, Klingenfuss' request for a transfer was finally granted. He was posted to the German embassy in Bern, Switzerland, at the beginning of the new year.

The departure of Klingenfuss and the arrival of Hahn also changed the situation of Franz Rademacher. In his first two years at D III, Rademacher had been so entranced with his work that he had postponed any thoughts of vacation. He claimed that he was too busy. It was not until the summer of 1942, when work on Jewish affairs was actually increasing, that Rademacher requested his first vacation.[9] By then, of course, he had asked Luther to relieve him of the *Judenreferat* but had been turned down until he could groom a successor. Klingenfuss had proved unsuitable, but Hahn brought enough enthusiasm and ambition to the job that he could be trusted to work independently. In January 1943, Rademacher was already being phased out of Jewish affairs and spent increasing amounts of time away from Berlin, carrying out special duties for Luther.[10]

The failure of the Luther *Putsch* in February 1943, only accelerated the process of Rademacher's disengagement from Jewish affairs, a process that had already begun a month earlier. Rademacher was not among the inner circle of conspirators who plotted the attempted overthrow of Ribbentrop. What he knew of the conspiracy, he learned directly from Luther, not from Büttner and his group. Under increasing pressure from the Büttner clique, Luther apparently turned to Rademacher for an outside opinion and told him all that was going on. As the specialist in *Abteilung Deutschland* for nationalist movements as well as for Jewish affairs, Rademacher attempted to make a contribution to the Europe-Plan in the former field. On Rademacher's suggestion to Luther, the plan incorporated the slogan "respect for foreign peoples" to summarize its attitude to other nationalities. For tactical reasons, no mention of the Jewish question was made in the Europe-Plan.[11]

By Rademacher's own admission, his motivation for being associated with the conspiracy was not any misgiving over the Jewish policy in which he was participating. While Jewish policy "was not to my heart," nonetheless the Jews had declared war on Germany, he later stated. They were a danger for Germany that had to be combatted. In Rademacher's own account, he supported the conspiracy because he shared the view that no coherent foreign policy was being pursued and that Ribbentrop was too feeble to impose a coherent foreign policy against the interests and ambitions of Himmler, Bormann, Goebbels, and Göring. Luther told him of the shrinking competency of the Foreign Office and how it had lost its traditional prerogatives in Norway, Russia, and Holland. He himself had experienced how the SS had grabbed the Madagascar Plan.[12]

There is some dispute over Rademacher's role in the days following the failure of the revolt against Ribbentrop. By Rademacher's own account, he was not immediately arrested because he was not one of Büttner's clique. Instead, Ribbentrop offered him Luther's position as chief of *Abteilung Deutschland*, a nomination which would not have been unusual as Rademacher was by then the most senior *Referat* leader. But Rademacher claimed he refused the offer and declared his solidarity with the conspirators. He was thereupon arrested and interrogated by the Gestapo.[13] This story was confirmed by Walter Büttner, who claimed that during his own interrogation by the Gestapo, Heinrich Müller questioned him about Rademacher's role and then said that Rademacher had been offered Luther's position and had rejected it.[14] Georg Ashton, a low-ranking official in D III at that time, also confirmed the story.[15] On the other hand, Hans Schröder, the Personnel chief, denied Rademacher's account. He claimed that he himself had suggested to Ribbentrop that Rademacher act as Luther's temporary replacement, but that Ribbentrop rejected the suggestion.[16]

However the case may be, what is not in dispute is that Rademacher was arrested and interrogated by the Gestapo, and that he made no attempt to hide his sympathy for the conspirators and his opposition to Ribbentrop. After several days he was released but remained under house arrest. Like Büttner, Kieser and others in the conspiracy, he was forced to sign a statement abjuring his defeatist attitude and any further opposition to government policy.[17] But unlike Büttner and his associates who were sent to the eastern front as a further punitive measure, Rademacher was permitted to join the navy.

While awaiting final induction, Rademacher occasionally returned to D III during the month of March to help clear up uncertainties in special cases.[18] But he no longer worked full-time. At the end of the month, he took official leave of his friend and anti-Semitic colleague, Paul Wurm. After informing him that Jewish affairs would now be handled in a new bureau called Inland II, he wrote: "To my joy I myself have been released for military service."[19] Nor did Rademacher indicate any regret at leaving *Abteilung Deutschland* when he met Karl Klingenfuss in May 1943.[20]

Before he severed his last ties with the *Judenreferat,* however, Rademacher talked briefly with Eberhard von Thadden, the Jewish expert who succeeded Rademacher and Hahn following the dissolution of *Abteilung Deutschland* and the reorganization of the Foreign Office. Rademacher related to Thadden a bizarre incident, which indicates just how much Rademacher had learned even about the specifics of the killing process by the end of his tenure in the Foreign Office. Rademacher told Thadden that on the occasion of a visit of a group of Italian Fascists to Minsk, the visitors had inquired of *Generalkommissar* Wilhelm Kube about the piles of suitcases and parcels they had seen stored in a church that had been secularized by the communists. Kube had answered that they were the sole remains of Jews who had been deported to Minsk and then proceeded to show the Italians a gas chamber in which the Jews allegedly had been killed. Rademacher had learned of the incident from a contact in Rosenberg's *Ostministerium*.[21]

Since taking his post as *Generalkommissar* in Minsk, Kube had been openly critical of Nazi Jewish policy.[22] Many Jews were killed in the Minsk area by firing squad, but there is no record that the Germans actually erected gas chambers there. Kube must have known about the gas chambers elsewhere and used the Italian inquiry about the piles of Jewish baggage to present the Italians with as graphic, complete, and convincing information about the killing of the Jews as he could. Whatever the veracity of the incident in Minsk, it is clear that rumors of the gas chambers circulated unofficially through the German bureaucracy and that Rademacher was privy to such rumors. Even the deepest secrets of the Final Solution could not be kept from those so closely associated with it.

Between the Luther revolt in early February and the reorganization of the Foreign Office, which went into effect on April 1, 1943, one might have expected a lull in Foreign Office Jewish activities. Martin Luther, the driving force behind these activities until then, was in a concentration camp. Franz Rademacher was at first also under arrest and then worked at the Foreign Office only sporadically. It would not have been unusual if in the confusion of this transition period the continuity of Foreign Office Jewish policy had been lost. But in fact this policy continued with utmost efficiency. This was due in part to the extraordinary zeal of Fritz-Gebhardt von Hahn.

Herbert Müller and Karl Klingenfuss had both successfully extricated themselves from D III. Franz Rademacher at least had some aspirations in that direction. To Fritz-Gebhardt von Hahn belonged the dubious distinction that he strove to overcome his debilitating war wound in order to return to the work in D III from which others sought to escape. From the very beginning Hahn was under no illusion as to what this work meant. His first stint in D III actually covered less than four weeks (December 10, 1941–January 5, 1942), but in that time he was given the rare opportunity for a mere legation secretary of preparing a report for submission to the foreign minister himself. This was the summary of the first five *Einsatzgruppen* reports. Despite his later claims of amnesia about the content of this report, he remembered it well enough during the war. Well over a year later, he asked the Foreign Office representative in the Ostland about the possibility of exchanging the foreign Jews in the Riga ghetto. The *Vertreter* replied that they could not be released. It would lead to enemy propaganda, because "many thousands of local and German Jews in the area of Riga have been shot. . . ." Hahn replied that these facts "were known to the Foreign Office."[23]

Hahn underwent lengthy medical treatment for his wound throughout the year of 1942, though he managed once again to work part-time in D III during the summer. When Rademacher was searching for a replacement for Klingenfuss, he wrote Hahn at the military hospital that there was much work to be done in D III and that he should return.[24] Hahn then informed the Personnel Division of the Foreign Office that he had been released from the hospital on December 17, 1942, and had been given four weeks recuperation leave. Though his arm was still in a sling and the doctor had declared him unfit for duty, he was reporting for work in D III.[25] Hahn wanted no one to overlook his zeal and sacrifice as he voluntarily began his third stint at D III.

During his earlier work Hahn had learned of the *Einsatzgruppen* campaign in Russia. The day after he returned he learned that the campaign to exterminate the Jews was not limited to Russia. The Press Division forwarded to D III a Tass release of a declaration of the Russian Foreign Ministry, which was classified as: "Confidential! Forwarding to unauthorized personnel is strictly forbidden." Hahn found it interesting enough to keep in the D III files.[26] The Russian Foreign Office declared that Germany was putting into

effect a "special plan for the complete extermination of the Jewish people."
Aside from detailing the massacres in Russia, of which Hahn was already
aware, the declaration covered the extermination program in the rest of
Europe as well. Poland had been turned into a "slaughterhouse." Over
400,000 Jews had been put in the Warsaw ghetto but only 30–40,000
remained. Jews from the rest of Europe were brought to Poland as well, and
many died from hunger and sickness during the trip. Of the survivors, the men
were put to work and the women and children murdered. "In addition to the
fact that men, women and children are shot with machine guns, they are
murdered in especially erected gas chambers. . . ."

Hahn knew enough from the *Einsatzgruppen* reports not to dismiss the
Russian declaration as mere propaganda. His subsequent actions prove that
he did not. On December 29, 1942, ten days after receiving the Tass report,
Conrad Rödiger of the Legal Division notified Hahn of an inquiry by Dr.
Junod of the International Committee of the Red Cross. Dr. Junod noted that
one function of the Red Cross, approved by both sides, was the transmission of
news between family members living in countries fighting one another. The
Red Cross had received countless requests to transmit news between Jews
deported to the east and family members left behind in occupied territories.
Dr. Junod wanted to sound out the Germans informally as to how they would
receive an official ICRC request to undertake such a function.[27] Hahn
drafted a prompt reply.

> Obviously the unreasonable request which was submitted can in no way be
> accommodated. Were the International Committee of the Red Cross engaged in
> the transmission of news in the proposed way, then the members of the
> committee active in Geneva would possess the possibility at any time, to
> visualize approximately the number of deported Israelites as well as their fate at
> the place of deportation and on the way there.

This material would then be forwarded to Germany's enemies through their
agents in the Red Cross. In any case the Red Cross activities were pertinent
only to the transmission of news between family members in opposing
countries, not in two different areas of the German sphere. The request thus
overstepped the competency of the Red Cross. Hahn's memorandum was
approved by Rödiger, Rademacher, and Luther.[28]

From the beginning, Hahn had far greater independence in his activities
than Rademacher's previous deputies. Rademacher was increasingly absent
from the *Judenreferat* in January 1943. Unlike Klingenfuss, who had received
all his instructions from Rademacher and met Luther only once, Hahn
regularly received his instructions from the undersecretary directly.[29] But
because he was officially on leave from the navy and still wore his uniform, he
was classified only as temporary help and his name was never entered on the
organization chart of the Foreign Office.[30] When the Luther *Putsch* failed,
Hahn was not arrested and interrogated along with the other officials of
*Abteilung Deutschland.* He arrived at the office to find all the men gone and

the secretaries weeping. He was summoned to Luther's office, where he encountered Schröder's deputy, Bergmann, who had just been named acting division head. Bergmann told him of the arrests and that he, Hahn, was the only available ranking official in the entire division and would have to help Bergmann until the division was dissolved and a reorganization took place.[31] Hahn had thus gained a free hand in Jewish affairs, for the overworked Bergmann had neither the time nor previous knowledge to interfere in Hahn's activities.

Even when Rademacher was released, he returned to the Foreign Office only occasionally and then occupied himself primarily with matters concerning nationalist movements abroad. According to Dr. Walter Pausch, who was temporarily recalled from the consulate in Trieste at the beginning of March to fill out the depleted staff of *Abteilung Deutschland* by working in both D III and *Referat Partei,* Hahn made the decisions in Jewish affairs.[32] Hahn himself admitted that after the Luther revolt he was "almost exclusively occupied with Jewish affairs."[33]

Hahn was proud of his position as the new Jewish expert of the Foreign Office and wished to impress his former patron, Ernst Bohle, with both his new status and his commitment to his work. On March 4, 1943, he wrote Bohle:

> In my present activity as expert for Jewish questions in the Foreign Office, I have several times had to recognize, that not only a number of governments friendly to us, but also some of our own officials abroad do not muster sufficient understanding for the necessity of a quick final European solution of the Jewish question.
>
> I am endeavoring to do all that is suitable in order to afford relief in this matter. I would therefore be very gratefully obligated to you, if on your side you would instruct speakers travelling abroad to national celebrations to leave no opportunity unused to throw light upon the subject of the Jewish question.[34]

Hahn carried on his indoctrination campaign within the Foreign Office as well. When the German ambassador to Finland warned that Germany's Jewish policy estranged it from the Finnish people, Hahn drafted Luther's reply:

> Please leave no opportunity unused again and again to remind the government and influential people there of the fact that the struggle against Bolshevism also represents in every regard the struggle against Jewry. In the same way as the defense against Bolshevism is a vital question for Finland, so for Europe the ruthless destruction of Jewish political and economic power represents the unalterable precondition for the freedom and future of the continent.[35]

When Walter Pausch asked Hahn what happened to the Jews evacuated to the east, the latter replied that they would be interned there until the end of the war. Pausch argued that the deportation of Jews to the east was economically senseless because the addition of so many people there would lead to considerable difficulties in providing food and lodging. "Thereupon Herr von Hahn explained to the effect that harsh living conditions in the east would already provide for a decimation."[36]

Hahn took a short vacation in late March 1943, leaving Jewish affairs in the hands of Walter Pausch, who could still call upon Rademacher for assistance.[37] When Hahn returned in early April his situation had radically changed. The reorganization of the Foreign Office had gone into effect at the beginning of the month, and Jewish affairs were now managed by Eberhard von Thadden within the new bureau Inland II under Horst Wagner. Hahn was asked to stay on and help orient Thadden, but given his ambition and sudden demotion to a subordinate position, it was no surprise that Hahn did not get along with his new boss. Thadden soon requested Hahn's transfer. Hahn was assigned to the Political Division in early May and then returned to "home duty" in the navy that summer, where he remained for the rest of the war.[38]

With the transfer of Hahn, the last of the Jewish experts from D III departed the scene. Jewish affairs were now handled by new personnel within a new organizational framework. The old tandem of Martin Luther and Franz Rademacher gave way to the team of Horst Wagner and Eberhard von Thadden. In the transition period, Fritz-Gebhardt von Hahn may not have served as long as either his predecessors or successors but he was second to none in his zeal.

## Shipping Home the Foreign Jews

One piece of unfinished business facing the Jewish experts of the Foreign Office in 1943 was the question of the foreign Jews within the western occupied territories. Luther had secured the inclusion of Rumanian, Bulgarian, and Greek Jews in the deportations. Permission to include the Jews from the puppet states of Slovakia and Croatia had been taken for granted, and their deportation had elicited no protest. Turkey, Hungary, and Italy had been approached with the choice of recalling their Jews or permitting their deportation. Turkey and Hungary had agreed to recall some of their Jews and forsake the rest, though Hungary did so only on the condition of equal treatment with Italy. However, when the Italians had declined both options, Luther had been unsuccessful in his attempt to push Ribbentrop into a confrontation with the Italians by delivering an ultimatum to withdraw their Jews by December 31, 1942, or accept the consequences.

The deadlock was finally broken in mid-January, when after three months of delay, Ribbentrop replied to Luther's proposal of the previous October. The foreign minister dealt only with Luther's memorandum of October 20, 1942, which urged an ultimatum to Italy on the question of its Jews in the German sphere. However, he still ignored Luther's far more drastic memorandum of October 22, which had urged German interference in Italian Jewish policy internally and in regard to other countries in Europe as well, and which Luther had concocted as part of a scheme to discredit Ribbentrop. The foreign minister approved the ultimatum to Italy, but with a new deadline of March 31, 1943. Mackensen informed Ciano immediately, and the Italians acquiesced on January 27, 1943.[39]

Luther then began contacting the neutral governments of Europe. Switzerland had already agreed to withdraw its Jews in early January.[40] On January 22, 1943, the Foreign Office informed the governments of Spain, Portugal, Denmark, Finland, and Sweden that they had the opportunity to remove their Jews from the western occupied territories by the end of March. Otherwise these Jews would be subjected to all German measures.[41] In February the Germans extended this policy to cover the eastern occupied territories as well. However, Hahn insisted to the RSHA that, regardless of deadlines, deportations could only take place after explicit instructions from the Foreign Office. For the two countries whose deadlines had already expired, Hungary and Turkey, it was still necessary to abstain from deportation. The new head of the RSHA, Ernst Kaltenbrunner, complied with this demand.[42]

The various countries which had received the German ultimatum reacted differently. The Hungarians had protected their Jews abroad primarily to assert their equality vis-à-vis Italy, not for humanitarian reasons. They withdrew selected Jews, but the Hungarian consul general in Paris gave the Germans a list of over 400 families in which the Hungarian government fully disinterested itself and whom it would no longer protect.[43] The Spanish initially indicated they would not permit their Jews in the German sphere to return to Spain. If Germany would not allow their emigration elsewhere, they would be left "to their fate." Hahn drafted a message, approved by Rademacher and Bergmann, notifying the Spanish that the emigration of Spanish Jews to other than their homeland was not possible. The Spanish thereupon reversed themselves and permitted the return of their Jews.[44] The Portuguese not only agreed to recall their Jews but indicated they might also be willing to take the colonies of Jews in Saloniki and Amsterdam that had emigrated from Portugal and spoke Portuguese, but were not Portuguese citizens, if the Germans were interested in getting rid of them in that way. Rademacher, in one of his last gestures before leaving D III, declared flatly that the emigration of these Jews to Portugal was out of the question.[45] The Danish and Finnish governments likewise accepted the return of their Jews.[46]

The cases of two countries, Turkey and Sweden, were much more complicated. The Turks had earlier explained to the Germans that any of their citizens who had been abroad for an unbroken term of five years would be denaturalized by Turkish law, and Luther had thereupon ordered the deportation of all Turkish Jews so treated. Luther then reversed himself in late January and cautiously ordered that no internment and deportation should take place until further notice.[47] In early February the Turkish consul general in Paris submitted a list of only 631 Jews whose return the Turkish government valued. This left over 2,400 Turkish Jews unprotected, and the Paris Sipo-SD immediately pressed for their internment and deportation.[48] In addition to the Turkish consul general in Paris, neither the Turkish ambassador in Berlin nor the Turkish government in Ankara could be moved to express interest in the unlisted Jews, but no one would provide the German government with the written confirmation of this disinterest which the Germans requested.[49]

The zealous Hahn urged immediate approval of the Paris Sipo-SD request to intern and deport unprotected Turkish Jews. The Turkish Jews were saved, however, by the actions of a single man, Wilhelm Melchers of the Near East Desk in the Political Division, who demonstrated what one man could do with the proper courage, invention, and determination. He had earlier saved Palestinian Jews in German hands by raising the specter of reprisals against German colonists in Palestine. He now intervened for the Turkish Jews who had been abandoned by their own government. He requested that the deportation of these 2,400 Jews not be carried out. They posed no security risk, but their deportation would be exploited by enemy propaganda and raise a storm of indignation in the Turkish press. It was of no significance that Turkish diplomatic representatives had shown no interest in them. Germany had to be especially cautious to create no pretext which could bring difficulties with Turkey. The disadvantage of 2,400 Jews remaining in the western occupied territories was less than the political disadvantages that would arise from their deportation. Woermann did not fully endorse Melchers' reasoning, but was at least sufficiently moved to recommend waiting until the Turkish position was clearer. Their silence in the face of German requests for written confirmation of disinterest did not yet offer sufficient foundation to approve the deportations.[50]

The Turks continued to refuse to make a declaration of disinterest as requested by the German government, and in July, 1943, Rademacher's successor, Thadden, urged giving the Sipo-SD a "free hand" with the Turkish Jews. But Melchers successfully reiterated his opposition to taking any action that might burden German-Turkish relations. Finally, in September, 1943, the Turkish government moved to rescue its previously abandoned Jews, instructing its consuls to permit the return of all Turkish Jews who so desired.[51] Wilhelm Melchers had single-handedly thwarted the will of the Paris Sipo-SD, Hahn, and then Thadden to deport the Turkish Jews to the east, buying time until the Turkish government at last regained its conscience.

It was over the withdrawal of Swedish Jews that the men of D III ran into their greatest complications. Even before the Swedish government was aware of the German ultimatum, it had demanded the release of two alleged Swedish Jews, Alexander and Heinz Bondy, interned in Theresienstadt. Both had been born in former Czechoslovakia and had been interned in the fall of 1942. Their widowed mother had escaped earlier, however, and married a Swede in December 1942. The Swedes promptly conferred Swedish citizenship on the man's two new stepsons, and the Swedish consul in Prague demanded their release from Theresienstadt. The Foreign Office *Vertreter* in the Protectorate, SS-*Oberführer* Dr. Werner von Gerlach, refused the request on the grounds that their alleged acquisition of Swedish citizenship took place only after their resettlement in Theresienstadt and exit approval could no longer be granted.[52]

When the Germans promised to permit the recall of all Swedish Jews up to the March 31 deadline, the Swedes jumped at this as a means to extricate the Bondy children. On February 5, 1943, the Swedish ambassador Richter called upon Martin Luther and demanded the release of the Bondy brothers from Theresienstadt as well as the release of three other children, the Kalter sisters, likewise recently naturalized by Sweden, who were interned in Westerbork in Holland. This meeting took place only five days before the Luther revolt, which may explain Luther's unprecedented behavior. Without even consulting the RSHA, which after all had control of the children, Luther promised the Swedish ambassador that they would be allowed to return to Sweden before the deadline. Rademacher wrote on the margin of the Swedish note: "Von Hahn for settlement. Undersecretary Luther has replied to the Swedish ambassador, that the return of the five children to Sweden is promised by April 1, 1943." Both Eichmann and Gerlach were then informed of Luther's unilateral decision. Hahn saw the Swedish chargé d'affaires, Otter, on February 16, confirmed Luther's promise in accordance with the written note he had received from Rademacher, but warned the Swede that other such cases would be subjected to the most exacting examination because the naturalizations were very recent.[53]

The Kalter sisters in Holland were released, but the local authorities in the Protectorate did not abide by Luther's decision. Gerlach reported that the RSHA had sent no instructions for the release of the Bondy children, and that great objections existed against their departure from the Theresienstadt ghetto, where they had been interned before being naturalized by Sweden. He requested the Foreign Office to discuss the matter with the RSHA in Berlin. Upon receiving Gerlach's telegram, Woermann tried to reverse what had been the only recorded charitable act by the now-departed Martin Luther in his entire activities on the Jewish question. Woermann wrote that he could not close his mind to Gerlach's arguments and that he felt the exit of the Bondy brothers was "undesirable" *(unerwünscht)*. He instructed that the entire affair be handled dilatorily.[54]

At the beginning of March, Eichmann contacted Hahn and complained that the children interned in Westerbork and Theresienstadt were just two among many cases in which the Swedes were systematically trying to thwart German Jewish measures through precipitate naturalizations of people who had never even been in Sweden. He wanted the Foreign Office to agree to the RSHA desire to include in Jewish measures all persons naturalized in this tendentious form. The Scandinavian Desk balked at this, however, noting that in the cases of Westerbork and Theresienstadt, the Swedes had already been promised their release. The Swedes therefore should be told that these two cases would be treated as exceptions but all further naturalizations would not be recognized. Sweden was informed on the basis of this formulation.[55]

While the Germans delayed, in accordance with Woermann's decision to treat the matter dilatorily, the Swedes continued to demand the release of the Bondy children, referring explicitly to the promise made by Hahn to Otter on February 16, 1943, but not to Luther's earlier promise of February 5, since the undersecretary had meanwhile fallen from power. Hahn was already on vacation, and his stand-in, Walter Pausch, who had just arrived and knew nothing about the background, confessed to Eichmann that he did not know on what grounds Hahn had made the promise to the Swedes.[56]

Pausch urged Gerlach to drop his objections to the immediate release of the Bondy children. But Rademacher had only a few days left to work in D III and wanted nothing to do with a quarrel with the RSHA, especially as he had just recently been arrested by the Gestapo. He urged that the matter continue to be handled dilatorily.[57] The Swedes continued to press the matter, however, constantly referring to Hahn's promise of February 16. When Pausch oriented Wagner and Thadden to the problem, he once again concluded that dilatory treatment was useless.[58]

When Hahn returned from vacation, he found himself in a ticklish situation. Wagner and Thadden not unnaturally wanted to know why and on what authority Hahn had promised the release of the Bondy children to Otter on February 16. He was required to write a long, explanatory memorandum. Hahn said that he had merely acted upon Rademacher's instructions in the margin of the Swedish note, following Luther's meeting with Richter on February 5, and that he had only been confirming a promise Luther had made earlier.

> On February 5, 1943, I had already expressed to Legation Counselor Rade-macher my astonishment over the fact that Herr Undersecretary Luther had promised the exit of the Jewish children without consulting the RSHA. Legation Counselor Rademacher shared my objections. He said that Herr Luther had made the promise without asking him beforehand.

Hahn went on to surmise that the Swedes only referred to his promise because they did not wish to support their demand with the promise of a man who had been deposed from office.[59] The documents supported Hahn's explanation, and he cleared himself of suspicion.

The Bondy affair dragged on for the rest of the war. Eichmann continued to refuse their release from Theresienstadt, but the Swedes incessantly de-manded their release on the basis of the promise they had received. In the fall of 1943, Thadden actually went over Eichmann's head and met with Heinrich Müller personally to discuss the matter. A compromise was finally reached between the Foreign Office and the RSHA whereby the Bondys were removed from Theresienstadt and brought to Bergen Belsen, a camp for "prominent" Jews and political prisoners who might be exchanged. They survived there until the end of the war and then finally went to Sweden.[60]

## Caution in Denmark

Apart from his concession to the Swedish ambassador in the question of the Bondy brothers, Luther was consistently cautious in dealing with another Scandinavian country, Denmark, over the Jewish question. In contrast to

Norway, where the Foreign Office had been excluded entirely following its failure to negotiate peaceful acquiescence to German occupation, Denmark had surrendered without a struggle in April 1940. The Danish government continued to function with considerable autonomy, and the career diplomat and long-time ambassador to Copenhagen, Cecil von Renthe-Fink, remained at his post with the additional title of plenipotentiary. While determined to coordinate Denmark's economy and foreign policy with Germany's, Renthe-Fink also believed that Germany should avoid any actions, including a radical Jewish policy, that would undermine the Danish government and provoke greater resistance to German occupation.[61]

In early January 1942, two weeks before the Wannsee Conference, Renthe-Fink reported on the condition of the Jewish question in Denmark. Following Denmark's signing of the Anti-Comintern Pact, rumors were circulating about German pressure for the introduction of Jewish legislation. Propaganda broadcasts from England claimed that pro-German ministers had submitted such legislation to the king, who had thereupon threatened to abdicate. A lively discussion in the Danish press had arisen over the Jewish question. Renthe-Fink proposed that Germany not interfere in this internal discussion, but that he would continue trying to awaken a greater understanding for the Jewish question.[62]

Luther shared Renthe-Fink's perception about the lack of understanding of the Jewish question in Denmark. At the Wannsee Conference he warned Heydrich that difficulties would emerge in the northern countries and urged that German measures there should be postponed. Because of the small number of Jews involved, Luther concluded that this constituted no significant restriction on the Final Solution. Luther's stand was reinforced by a second report from Renthe-Fink, written on January 20, 1942.

> For us it is scarcely conceivable, how backward wide circles in Denmark still are today in regard to the Jewish question. . . . As long as it is urgent from the standpoint of our direction of the war and our entire political interests that the peaceful development in Denmark is not disturbed, a basic taking up of the Jewish question in Denmark ought not be considered.[63]

As Luther and the Foreign Office were in an exceptionally strong position vis-à-vis other Nazi organizations to control the pace of Jewish measures in Denmark, in fact the Germans undertook no further steps in the direction of implementing the Final Solution. This reticence elicited strong criticism from the Danish Nazi leader, Fritz Clausen, in the summer of 1942. Rademacher and Dr. Werner von Grundherr of the Foreign Office Scandinavian Desk discussed Clausen's complaint and concluded: "Actually a further impetus can only be expected, when through soft but constant pressure Denmark can also be persuaded to tackle the Jewish question." Luther agreed and requested a memorandum for submission to Ribbentrop.[64]

Klingenfuss drafted the memorandum, suggesting that Germany's hands-off policy had reached its outer limit, and that timely measures now could prevent the need for sharper measures in the future. "It may therefore be submitted for consideration, to get the Jewish question in Denmark underway through a soft but constant pressure, in which the government would be induced to some immediate measures—as the beginning of an intensifying program." But Rademacher and Grundherr felt that such a policy of soft, constant pressure did not yet mean broaching the Jewish question with the Danish government, and that no basic instruction from the foreign minister was necessary.[65] Luther was at that time already at odds with Ribbentrop over Jewish policy elsewhere in Europe and apparently agreed with Rademacher not to submit the memorandum on Denmark.

When Ribbentrop suddenly dropped his opposition on September 24, 1942, to Luther's proposals for Bulgaria and Hungary, he likewise urged that Denmark be approached for the purpose of deporting its Jews. This was not due to any initiative or pressure on Luther's part, for the Foreign Office Jewish experts were still shying away from far less radical measures vis-à-vis Denmark. Nothing demonstrated more clearly that Luther, not Ribbentrop, determined the pace of Foreign Office Jewish policy than the fact that Luther felt free to disregard this unsolicited and unwanted authorization to press for deportations from Denmark. While Luther moved with alacrity to press for deportations from Hungary and Bulgaria, countries where his previous efforts had been restricted by Ribbentrop, in Denmark he did nothing more than approve very limited proposals by Renthe-Fink to diminish the influence of Jews in Danish industry by refusing to supply Jewish distributors with coal and fuel from Germany.[66]

In the late fall of 1942, Ribbentrop replaced Renthe-Fink with an SS-General, Werner Best. In December Rademacher travelled to Copenhagen to discuss the question of future Jewish measures with Best, but Luther advised yet a further postponement.[67] Best then met with both Luther and Rademacher on January 7, 1943, in Berlin, and discussed the Jewish question once again. There is no indication that Best required any persuasion to follow Luther's cautious line. Upon his return to Copenhagen he submitted a report on the Jewish question which represented no break with past Foreign Office policy. Best warned that the Danes viewed the Jewish problem as a constitutional one, and a German demand for a discriminatory treatment of Jews on the German model would lead to the resignation of the government. The king and parliament would no longer cooperate with the Germans. "Norwegian measures" would be required; the country would have to be taken over by a *Reich Kommissar,* reinforced with additional military and police strength. Even Fritz Clausen, the Danish Nazi leader, admitted that if the Jewish star were introduced, 10,000 Danes would wear it in protest. Best therefore recommended milder measures that would not annul Denmark's constitutional system, such as the removal of Jews from public life and German-Danish economic relations as well as the seizure of individual Jews that could be justified on criminal grounds.[68]

Luther submitted Best's evaluation and proposals to Ribbentrop, recommending their approval in order to "gradually" (*schrittweise*) solve the Jewish question in Denmark. Ribbentrop assented.[69] Throughout his tenure, Luther consistently pursued a moderate line in Denmark, which contrasted sharply with his radical stance in the rest of Europe.[70]

### The Second Wave of Deportations: Greece and Bulgaria

The Foreign Office had cooperated in the first wave of deportations in 1942 from Slovakia, France, Belgium, and the Netherlands. It had been excluded only from the Norwegian deportations, which took place in the fall of 1942. After the New Year, the Foreign Office took part in a new wave of deportations, this time from Greece and Bulgaria.

Since the summer of 1942 the Germans had sought to introduce common Jewish measures in both occupation zones in Greece but had been thwarted by the stalling tactics of the Italians, who repeatedly shifted the seat of negotiations between Athens and Rome. After a delay of six months, both the Foreign Office and the RSHA finally lost patience. On January 7, 1943, Luther informed Altenburg, in a telegram drafted by Hahn, that the Foreign Office was interested in the quickest possible introduction of Jewish measures in Greece.[71] Less than a week later, Eichmann's deputy, SS-*Sturmbannführer* Rolf Günther, arrived in Athens and informed Altenburg of the imminent deportation of the Jews from the German occupation zone. He then went on to Saloniki, where Luther assured Consul General Schönburg that Günther was there in agreement with the Foreign Office and was to receive the support of the consulate.[72]

Günther's trip was merely a preparatory one, however. Even before his return to Berlin, negotiations opened between the Foreign Office and the RSHA for the assignment of a full-time RSHA specialist to carry out the Greek deportations. Karl Klingenfuss had just returned from Switzerland to fetch his family and had to report to the Foreign Office, where he was hurriedly pressed into service to handle these negotiations.[73] Klingenfuss talked with Otto Hunsche, another member of Eichmann's staff, on the telephone on January 20, 1943. According to Hunsche, the temporary delegation of Dieter Wisliceny from Slovakia was necessary. Wisliceny would carry out the deportation measures in agreement with the Foreign Office plenipotentiary in Athens and consul in Saloniki, as well as with the military commander.[74] The Foreign Office checked Wisliceny's nomination with Altenburg in Athens and Ludin in Bratislava, for as in the case of Dannecker's assignment to the Bulgarian embassy, Wisliceny was attached to the embassy in Slovakia, and his temporary reassignment required the active cooperation of the Foreign Office.[75]

Once the Foreign Office had approved and arranged Wisliceny's assignment to Saloniki, the Jewish experts in D III were no longer involved in the Greek deportations except when foreign complications occurred. Once again the major problem was Italian obstruction. In early February the RSHA complained that the Italian consulate in Saloniki was conferring Italian citizenship upon wealthy Jews. The RSHA wished the Foreign Office to negotiate an agreement with Italy, whereby all Jews who had gained Italian citizenship after July 1, 1942, the date of the first Jewish measures in the German zone, would not be recognized as Italian citizens. Hahn was so attracted by the idea that when he forwarded the request to the German embassy in Rome, he selected the much earlier cut-off date of Italy's entry into the war.[76] In Rome the Italians emphatically denied that any naturalizations had taken place in Greece since the occupation.[77]

Perhaps with the hope of avoiding further German pressure, the Italians put forward their own plan for the Jews in the Italian zone. Jews of Italian citizenship would be treated exactly as in Italy. Greek Jews would be interned, either in camps on the Ionian Islands or in Italy itself. Jews of friendly and neutral countries would be ordered to leave.[78] In short, the Italians were preparing to follow the same strategy as had been used in Croatia. The Greek Jews would be interned beyond the German reach and would provide no easy pretext for further German pressure on the grounds of military security.

Ribbentrop requested an evaluation by the Foreign Office Jewish experts, in agreement with the SS, as to whether the Italian plan was sufficient. With Hahn on vacation, Rademacher had to help Walter Pausch draw up a memorandum for the foreign minister. Rademacher and Pausch noted that both they in D III and Eichmann in the RSHA considered the Italian plan as insufficient, for these same measures had already proved unsatisfactory in Italy. Moreover, past experience made it very doubtful that they would be executed sincerely, for the Italians always exempted the most influential and dangerous Jews.[79] This rejection of the Italian plan was the last initiative taken by the men of D III in the Greek deportations, which began in mid-March and ultimately sent over 50,000 Greek Jews to the death camps.

The deportations in Bulgaria began almost simultaneously with those in Greece. In response to an RSHA request to arrange for the deportation of Bulgarian Jews in Germany, Luther had secured an agreement with Bulgaria in July 1942, permitting such deportations from the entire German sphere. Luther deemed the moment opportune for broaching the question of deportations from Bulgaria itself, but Ribbentrop ordered him to wait. When the foreign minister reversed his position, the Foreign Office extracted Bulgarian consent to the deportation of its Jews in November 1942, and arranged for the assignment of one of Eichmann's deportation experts, Theodor Dannecker, as Jewish adviser in the Sofia embassy at the turn of the year. The Bulgarian consent was not unqualified, however, as Prime Minister Filov had mentioned the need to use a portion of the Jewish male population for road construction. The Bulgarians became increasingly hesitant thereafter, as the Germans suffered defeat at Stalingrad and internal opposition grew in Bulgaria against total compliance with German Jewish policy. Ambassador Beckerle talked with interior minister Gabrovski on January 22, 1943, on the eve of Dannecker's arrival. Gabrovski vetoed the idea of an anti-Jewish exposition which the Germans were urging. More importantly, he told Beckerle that as far as deportations were concerned, for the moment only the Jews of Thrace and Macedonia, the "newly liberated" territories awarded to Bulgaria by Germany, came into question. Awaiting Dannecker's imminent arrival, Beckerle did not explore this issue further.[80]

When Dannecker met Gabrovski on February 2, 1943, the Bulgarian again expressed his readiness to deport the Jews of Macedonia and Thrace but insisted that the deportation of Jews from Old Bulgaria was not possible at the moment, as they were needed for labor on public works projects. Gabrovski sent Dannecker to see Alexander Belev, the commissar for Jewish affairs, to plan the operation. Belev proved more eager. Upon Dannecker's suggestion, he agreed to the deportation of 20,000 Jews, while the new territories contained a total of only 14,000. An additional 6,000 "undesirable" Jews from Old Bulgaria would have to be included in the initial operation, which was to be a prelude to the eventual deportation of all Jews. Without even awaiting the final approval of the cabinet for the Dannecker-Belev plan, Belev sent his deputies into Thrace and Macedonia to begin preparations.[81]

On February 16, 1943, Beckerle urged the Foreign Office to do all in its power to bring about the quick deportation of the Jews being offered by Bulgaria at that moment, so that an end-of-March deadline could be met. Hahn made Beckerle's request his own, urging Eichmann: "I would be grateful, if also everything were done at your end so that the end-of-March deportation deadline can be met."[82]

Events moved very quickly, as all those advocating the deportations, both German and Bulgarian, felt the urgent need to carry them out before the situation in Bulgaria deteriorated further and made them impossible. On February 22, 1943, Dannecker and Belev signed the written agreement over the deportation of 20,000 Jews. Dannecker noted that the prompt execution of this deportation might make possible further deportations in the future.[83] Beckerle likewise laid great value on the fact that the railway cars necessary for the deportation be procured by the end of March. Once again Hahn forwarded Beckerle's request to Eichmann and added his own encouragement: "The Foreign Office herewith forwards this renewed request with its own endorsement."[84]

The initial phase of the deportations went as planned. On March 2, 1943, the Bulgarian cabinet formally approved the Dannecker-Belev agreement and authorized the procurement of the transport and camps for the Jews in Thrace and Macedonia as well as in Old Bulgaria which were necessary to fulfill the agreement. Despite the critical situation on the eastern front, the strenuous efforts of Hahn and Beckerle among others to secure the transport necessary to fulfill the German side of the agreement also prevailed. In early March the Jews of Thrace and Macedonia were interned in camps. On March 20 and 21, 1943, four Bulgarian ships carried 4,150 Thracian Jews to Vienna, where the Germans put them aboard trains for Treblinka. Between March 22 and 29, 1943, three trains carried 7,144 Macedonian Jews from Skopje to Treblinka. None survived.[85]

The Germans and their Bulgarian collaborators were not mistaken in their sense of urgency. Even as the action got underway in Macedonia and Thrace, it was already unravelling in Old Bulgaria. Though the preparations for the deportation of Jews from there had been treated as top secret, word got out almost immediately. The Jews sought the intervention of their Bulgarian friends and raised money for bribes. The most effective help came from a group led by Deputy Prime Minister Dimiter Peschev, comprised of members of the government majority in Parliament including Bulgarian chauvinists and Macedonian terrorists, who pressured and even threatened Gabrovski to rescind the order for the seizure and deportation of Jews from Old Bulgaria. Gabrovski consulted Prime Minister Filov, who agreed to postpone the deportations from Old Bulgaria on March 10, 1943. Peschev then presented a petition on March 17, signed by 42 members of Parliament, which protested even against the Jewish measures in Thrace and Macedonia, because, as Walter Pausch phrased it, "the fate that awaited the Jews in the German eastern territories violated the most elementary commandments of humanity." This move was unsuccessful, however. Filov held his majority together, and Peschev was stripped of his position as deputy prime minister on March 26.[86]

Though Peschev's effort to save the Macedonian and Thracian Jews failed, the postponement of the plans to include 6,000 Bulgarian Jews broke the momentum of the deportation program, and it never recovered despite further German pressure. Beckerle's incessant demands upon Filov did extract the reassurance that all the Jews would be deported from Bulgaria.[87] But when King Boris met with Hitler and Ribbentrop at Klessheim Castle in early April 1943, the Bulgarian monarch merely said that he would put the Jews in local concentration camps, where they were needed for road construction. He remained unmoved in the face of Ribbentrop's observation that "in our opinion in the Jewish question the most radical solution is alone the right one."[88] Ultimately, no Jews from Old Bulgaria were ever turned over to the Germans. Despite the continued Foreign Office support maintained by Hahn and Beckerle and even Ribbentrop personally for the Final Solution in Bulgaria, it nevertheless stalled before completion.

## Italian Obstruction Continues

The Italian refusal to cooperate with German Jewish policy was not restricted to Croatia and Greece. As preparations were being made for the deportations from Bulgaria, Dannecker complained that the Italians were granting citizenship to former German, Austrian, Czech, and Polish Jews residing there.[89] And when the Macedonian Jews were interned in Skopje, the German consul reported that the staff of the Italian consulate and the Italian commandant of the train station spent entire days in the area of the camp trying to contact Jews within. Only firm action by the Bulgarian police had prevented their entry into the camp.[90] But in the spring of 1943, the real center of Italian resistance shifted from the Balkans to southern France.

In November 1942, following the allied landings in North Africa, southern France was occupied by Axis troops. Nice and eight departments in the southeast corner of France formed the Italian zone of the newly occupied territories. Once again the problem of conflicting Jewish policies in German and Italian military zones arose, and the Foreign Office became the conduit for the complaints of the German police in France over the behavior of the Italians toward the Jews there.

At first it did not appear as if a conflict would arise. In early December 1942, the Italian High Command notified the Germans that all Jews in their zone would be interned.[91] When the Sipo-SD in France prevailed upon the Vichy government to accept a plan, whereby French authorities would remove all Jews from the coastal regions and intern all unprotected foreign Jews for the purpose of deportation to the east, they did not anticipate that the French authorities would be prevented from carrying out these measures within the Italian zone.[92] But very quickly evidence accumulated of systematic Italian obstruction.

On December 20, 1942, the French prefect of the department of the Alpes-Maritime, located in the Italian zone, ordered the removal of the Jews to two other departments, one of which was in the German zone. Angelo Donati, a prominent Jew with connections to high places in Italy, appealed to the Italian consul general in Nice, who in turn asked authorization from the Italian Foreign Office to block the activities against the Jews of the French authorities in the Italian zone. On December 29, 1942, the Foreign Office authorized the consul general to forbid French authorities from resettling not only Italian but all foreign Jews residing in the Italian zone. Measures concerning Italian and foreign Jews were the exclusive prerogative of the Italian occupying forces.[93] The following day, December 30, the Italian armistice commission likewise lodged a protest with the Vichy government against the internment of Jews by French authorities within the Italian zone.[94]

On January 13, 1943, the French premier, Pierre Laval, informed Rudolph Schleier of the German embassy in Paris that the Italians had taken not only their own Jews but all foreign Jews under protection, and had prevented their resettlement as well as the stamping of their identity cards or their incorporation into labor battalions.[95] After a second report ten days later, Luther instructed Schleier to negotiate with the Italians to secure their permission to evacuate Jews from the coastal areas. Schleier replied that both he and the local Sipo-SD felt that such an agreement could only be obtained through direct negotiations between Berlin and Rome.[96]

Luther was not reluctant to pressure the Italians. He immediately informed Mackensen of the urgent desire of the German government that the Italian military in southern France be instructed to support the French authorities in carrying out measures against all non-Italian Jews and to cooperate with German military and police authorities in preventing an expected Jewish migration into the Italian zone. Woermann approved these instructions, which had been drafted by Hahn, initialed by Rademacher, and signed by Luther.[97]

In reply the Italians insisted that all Jews in the Italian zone had been interned in the interior, so that the Germans had no reason to complain on the basis of military security.[98] Hahn, temporarily on his own following the arrest of Luther and Rademacher, accepted this claim at face value, but still urged the German embassy in Rome to insist that the Italians withdraw the letter of December 30, 1942, from their armistice commission to the Vichy government, and to arrest and surrender to the Germans all people attempting to cross into the Italian zone.[99]

At this point the negotiations with Italy over the Jewish question were taken out of the hands of D III to be managed directly by Ribbentrop himself. Since the previous November, Luther had been urging Ribbentrop to confront Italy on the issue, on the calculation that regardless of the outcome he stood to gain personally. But Ribbentrop, sensing that he was being pushed into a dangerous venture, had ignored the recommendation of his undersecretary. Nor did he immediately respond to a personal letter from Heinrich Himmler on January 29, 1943, in which the *Reichsführer*-SS noted that as long as Jews remained in the Italian sphere, other countries had a pretext to proceed more leniently against the Jews.[100] After the Luther revolt, however, Ribbentrop's behavior changed markedly. The possibility of an alliance between the SS and dissidents within his own Foreign Office had been demonstrated all too graphically. He had been saved because Himmler had sided with Ribbentrop instead of Luther, but it had been a close call. Ribbentrop no longer dared ignore an issue to which Himmler attached so much importance. Moreover, with Luther now in a concentration camp, Ribbentrop had no cause to fear that he was playing into the hands of the unscrupulous former protégé whose ambition had outgrown his usefulness. Just as Ribbentrop had made a quick and expedient reversal the previous September, when the restraints he had put upon Luther threatened to alienate him from Hitler, he now adopted the very policy which Luther had been advocating unsuccessfully since October in order to reinforce his ties with Himmler.

Ribbentrop's turnabout was very sudden. On February 23, 1943, he asked Himmler's personal adjutant, Karl Wolff, to forward all the desires of the SS concerning the Jewish question and Italy. He wished these desires to be communicated in full detail, so that he could discuss the issue with the Duce personally during his impending visit to Rome. The material was to be compiled within twenty-four hours, so that it reached Ribbentrop before his meeting with Mussolini.[101] Within the time limit, Bergmann and Hahn could only compile a general outline of the relevant desires of the SS. For Italy itself, Jewish measures analogus to those in Germany were desirable. Outside Italy, the SS emphatically requested that Italian military commanders cease sabotaging German Jewish measures in Greece and France. The attitude of the Italian government was also judged detrimental to the deportation programs in Croatia, Rumania, Bulgaria, and Slovakia. A Sipo-SD report over interventions by the Italian military in Lyon and Grenoble, which forced the French police to release hundreds of interned Jews destined for the east, was included, and further details were promised later.[102]

Ribbentrop's newfound sense of urgency was demonstrated when he telephoned on the morning of February 25, to complain that the promised elaboration of the initial outline of SS desires had not arrived. Bergmann had to promise it by evening, when Ribbentrop was scheduled to confer with Mussolini.[103] Apparently Rademacher's house arrest had been sufficiently relaxed to permit him to work at the Foreign Office at this point, and he and Hahn worked together to meet the foreign minister's deadline. They noted that Italy had informed the Vichy government that not only Italian Jews but all foreign Jews in the Italian zone were exempt from measures of the French authorities. The Italian commander in Nice had intervened with the French prefect, so that Jewish ration cards were not stamped with a "J." In gratitude for Italian protection, the Jews of Nice had raised a collection of three million francs to aid Italian victims of Anglo-American air raids. The removal of Jews from the coastal areas and their internment inland, as previously promised by the Italian military in early December, had not taken place. Finally, deportations from Croatia had been ruined by the hostile attitude of the Italian military authorities there.[104] A day later a further report was forwarded to Ribbentrop's train on the sympathetic attitude of Italian officers to the Jews and how more Jews than ever were now sheltered in Nice.[105]

The mass of material apparently did not reach Ribbentrop in time. When he conferred with Mussolini on February 25, 1943, he talked only in generalities. As the Duce knew, Germany was radically minded in regard to the Jewish question. Therefore the Jews were being deported from the German sphere to a reservation in the east. France was likewise adopting very useful Jewish measures. Unfortunately, the foreign minister was aware that Italian military circles (and sometimes the German army itself) lacked a proper understanding of the Jewish question. This could be the only explanation for the order of the Italian High Command cancelling the Jewish measures undertaken by French authorities in the Italian zone. Mussolini refused to believe that his military had intervened against Jewish measures in France which were advocated by Germany. He suspected a French intrigue to disrupt German-Italian relations but promised to check the matter.[106] Because Ribbentrop's decision to broach the Jewish question with Mussolini had been so sudden and belated, he was not properly prepared and was unable to deliver the litany of evidence on Italian obstruction which Rademacher and Hahn had tried to prepare in time.

Despite Ribbentrop's visit, Italian obstruction continued. As they had done earlier in Lyon and Grenoble, Italian troops surrounded the French police barracks in Annecy and forced the release of 2,000 Jews that had been seized for deportation. On March 2, 1943, General Avarna, the Italian military liaison in Vichy, delivered a note to his French counterpart, Admiral Platon, which expanded the range of Italian protection for the Jews. Until then, the Italians had only protected non-French Jews and left French Jews under the jurisdiction of French authorities. As the French police were only cooperating in the deportation of non-French Jews, this in practice had served the purpose of blocking virtually all deportation from the Italian zone. But now the Italians theoretically widened their claim, demanding that the French refrain from any measures concerning the arrest and internment of any Jews, French or non-French. The German consul general in Marseille also reported, in regard to the Italian claim that they had interned the Jews themselves, that great numbers of Jews moved about unhindered in the Italian zone and that additional Jews from the German zone arrived constantly.[107]

Ribbentrop received the reports of further Italian obstruction with great irritation. On March 9, 1943, less than two weeks after his talk with Mussolini, he drew up a memorandum for Mackensen to deliver to the Duce personally. It listed all the events compiled by Rademacher and Hahn on February 25, as well as the events that had transpired since then. Ribbentrop reminded Mussolini that he had refused to believe Ribbentrop's claims about the activities of his military, but here was clear evidence that it pursued a policy diametrically opposed to the intentions of the Duce. He would thus be grateful if the Duce would personally intervene and take the necessary "draconic" measures to remedy the intolerable situation. Ribentrop suggested three possibilities: 1) Mussolini could order the Italian High Command to leave all Jewish affairs of the French police; 2) he could withdraw Jewish affairs from the jurisdiction of the military and assign them to the Italian police (this was the personal suggestion of Himmler); 3) or he could permit the German police, with the assistance of the French police, to deal with the Jewish question in the Italian zone. In closing, Ribbentrop remarked that the Führer himself had approached the foreign minister on this matter.[108]

Before Mackensen could deliver this note to Mussolini, however, he received an answer from the Italian Foreign Office to his earlier inquiries. The Italian Foreign Office knew of the letter of the Italian armistice commission of December 30, 1942, and the note of General Avarna of March 2, 1943. These letters had been approved by the Duce, it was claimed. They did not alter the fact that the Jews in the Italian zone would be interned, only that it would be done solely by Italian authorities. The Duce had insisted that any significant police measures could be undertaken only by Italian authorities. The withdrawal of these letters was not possible for reasons of Italian prestige. Mackensen asked Ribbentrop whether he wished to attune his message to Mussolini to this latest Italian response.[109]

Ribbentrop left his three alternatives intact, but noted that the first was scarcely feasible as it would require Mussolini to disavow his own military vis-à-vis the French. But the foreign minister could not conceal his astonishment that the Italian military had intervened, when they ought to have been very satisfied that the French police themselves were undertaking the necessary "cleansing action." Ribbentrop confidentially told Mackensen that he already knew the attitude of the Italian military to the Jewish question from its behavior in Croatia, and that without strict instructions from the Duce, it would continue to sabotage his and the Duce's intentions in this matter.[110]

When Mackensen made his presentation to Mussolini on March 17, the latter emphatically agreed that it was incomprehensible why the Italian army had tied the hands of the French police when it should have been very content that the French were doing the necessary work themselves. He agreed that the need for drastic measures against the Jews was "obvious and imperative." If his generals thwarted these measures, it was not out of evil intention but because their way of thinking was directed to other things. They not only lacked understanding for the significance of the action but were affected by "mistaken sentimental humanitarianism that did not correspond to our harsh era.'" Mussolini promised that he would instruct General Ambrosio to give the French police a free hand. When Mackensen noted that Ambrosio would protest this disavowal of the Italian military vis-à-vis the French, Mussolini shrugged and said he was the one who gave orders. Mackensen thus reported to Ribbentrop that Mussolini had opted for the first alternative.[111]

Three days later Mackensen was invited to the Italian Foreign Office by Ciano's successor, Giuseppe Bastianini, and informed that the Duce had in fact opted for the second alternative. Mackensen expressd his surprise, because in his discussion with Mussolini, the latter had clearly decided for the first alternative. Bastianini informed him that his initial impression had been correct, but that Mussolini had changed his mind. He had summoned General Ambrosio and ordered him not to interfere with the Jewish measures of the French police. But Ambrosio convinced him that the French police could not be relied upon. They gave the appearance of taking drastic action, but in many cases the influence of Jewish money and the Jewish "female world" (*Damenwelt*) had corrupted the French police, and many Jews had eluded their grasp. Mussolini had therefore decided on the second alternative and appointed the energetic police inspector from Bari, Guido Lospinoso. In the presence of Ambrosio, Mussolini had made Lospinoso fully independent of the military. Lospinoso would remove the Jews from the coast to remote areas of the interior, as the Germans had requested. As there were no concentration camps available there, they would be lodged in houses and hotels requisitioned for the purpose. To Mackensen's blunt inquiry about the possibility of deportations to the east, Bastianini replied that none were intended.[112]

In fact Mussolini's reversal can be traced back to the energetic efforts of the Italian Foreign Office, not to arguments by General Ambrosio over the unreliability of the French police to carry out sufficiently drastic measures. When it appeared that Mussolini was about to permit the French police to hand over Jews from the Italian zone to the Germans, officials in the Italian Foreign Office collected documentation on the massacre of the Jews. The documents were passed on to Mussolini with the note "that no Power—not even allied Germany—could make Italy a partner to such crimes, for which the Italian people would one day have to pay the reckoning." Mussolini wavered and chose an alternative that allowed his subordinates not to turn over the Jews to the Germans.[113]

The Italian authorities on the spot made the most of Mussolini's indecisiveness. They converted Lospinoso to their point of view, and he went into hiding on the Cote d'Azur while the Germans vainly sought to contact him in order to coordinate Jewish measures.[114] The Italian authorities requisitioned numerous hotels for the Jews, as they had earlier in Croatia. Rather than substitute concentration camps, however, they were administered by the Jewish committee as refugee centers,[115] and the Italian zone in France remained a sanctuary for the Jews.

During his visit to Rome, Ribbentrop had not limited his importuning on the Jewish question to the Italian zone in France. He also renewed German pressure to secure the long-sought deportations from the Italian zone in Croatia. Just as Mussolini had initially given way in regard to France, he likewise agreed to take the Croatian Jews to Trieste and turn them over to the Germans. He summoned General Robotti, commander of the Italian 2nd Army, along with the Italian governor in Montenegro, Pirzio Birolli, and informed them of Ribbentrop's pressures and his own decision. General Robotti argued that such measures would cause painful repercussions among the Yugoslav population, whose initial favorable disposition toward Italy had already been hurt by Italy's support of Pavelic and the Germans. Mussolini allowed himself to be persuaded and let Robotti know that he was free to find suitable excuses, such as the lack of means of transport to Trieste, to avoid surrendering the Jews.[116]

While Italian resistance to German Jewish measures began at their lower echelons of Foreign Office and military, it ultimately spread to the center of the Italian government. Ribbentrop's original refusal to confront the Italians, as Luther advised, bought time for the resisters. When Ribbentrop finally brought pressure to bear upon the Italians, the German opportunity had been lost. The resisters were able to persuade the increasingly discouraged and ailing Duce to turn a blind eye to their activities. Ribbentrop, like Luther before him, had totally failed to overcome Italian resistance to German Jewish policy.

## Blocking Jewish Emigration from Southeast Europe

In 1942 Luther had been on the offensive in southeast Europe, pressing Bulgaria, Rumania, and Hungary to deport their Jews to the east. By the spring of 1943, the German Foreign Office was clearly on the defensive in this region. Of the governments concerned, only Bulgaria had even partially acquiesced to German demands. Now the Germans feared that all three had become involved in plans to permit the emigration of their Jews to Palestine. Unable to deport these Jews for the moment, the Jewish experts of the German Foreign Office strove at least to prevent their permanent escape to enemy territory.

The first warning over the danger of massive Jewish emigration to Palestine was sounded by Killinger on December 12, 1942, at a time when the failure of German pressure to produce deportations from Rumania had become obvious. Radu Lecca told Killinger that he had received instructions from Marshal Ion Antonescu to organize and carry out the emigration of 75–80,000 Jews to Palestine and Syria. Each emigrant would have to pay a sizeable fee to the state before departure, so that the Rumanian government would make money and get rid of Jews simultaneously. Killinger warned Lecca that the German government could scarcely approve of this project, especially when it was a question of Jews capable of military service. Moreover, it contradicted German policy toward the Arabs. Lecca assured Killinger that he would not carry out this order until he knew the official German position and that there was no urgency due to lack of shipping capacity.[117] Klingenfuss, with the approval of Luther as well as Woermann of the Political Division, concurred with Killinger's arguments against the Rumanian emigration plan and added some of his own. It was an "intolerable partial solution" when judged in terms of German policy to solve the Jewish question in Europe. Moreover, there would be serious repercussions throughout Europe if Rumania, one of Germany's allies, concluded an agreement with the enemy.[118]

On January 15, 1943, the Foreign Office received information from the OKW that Jewish emigration from Rumania was in fact already taking place. The Jews had purchased ships and planned to resell them in Palestine to recoup their investment. Five ships had sailed, and permits for ten more had already been granted. The OKW therefore requested that the Foreign Office take appropriate steps with the Rumanian government to avoid the loss of indispensable shipping capacity. Hahn dispatched the corresponding instructions to Killinger, and the Rumanians ordered a halt to all such shipping at the end of February.[119] German Foreign Office pressure was successful in plugging one leak in southeast Europe, but even before this others had already sprung.

On February 3, 1943, the Foreign Office received press reports on a meeting of the House of Commons, in which Colonial Minister Oliver Stanley claimed that agreement had been reached with Bulgaria to permit the immigration of 4,000 Bulgarian Jewish children accompanied by 500 adults to Palestine. Earlier an agreement had been reached to take 270 Jewish children from Rumania and Hungary, and some of these children were already on the way. Ultimately, the British government was ready to admit 29,000 Jews into Palestine by the spring of 1944. The following day Beckerle reported that through the Swiss embassy Britain had offered to take 5,000 Jews from Bulgaria, but at the moment it was only an informal inquiry.[120]

Hahn drafted a reply to Beckerle, which was lost in the confusion surrounding the Luther revolt of February 9–11, 1943. But the efficient and meticulous bureaucrat double-checked on whether his telegram had been sent. Upon discovering that it had not, he had two telegrams dispatched on February 13. In the first he asked about the discrepancy between the press reports which said that an agreement had been concluded and Beckerle's report which said only an informal inquiry had been made. In the second he instructed Beckerle to advise the Bulgarians against such an agreement, giving the same reasons as had been sent to Killinger earlier.[121] All this was done on Hahn's own initiative. *Abteilung Deutschland* was in a chaotic state following the arrest of all its top personnel, and business had come to a temporary standstill. Only in Jewish affairs, thanks to Hahn, did the orderly flow of business continue.

Beckerle reported that he had spoken to Prime Minister Filov on the issue. Filov wanted to act in accordance with Germany's suggestion, but Bulgaria did not want to take upon itself the odium of inhumane action. It would agree officially to the Swiss inquiry made on behalf of Great Britain, but in reality would insure that technical difficulties rendered the transport fully impossible.[122]

On March 2, 1943, the Foreign Office received further distressing press reports. The British ambassador to the United States, Lord Halifax, in an address to the American Jewish Congress in New York, had again announced that an agreement with Bulgaria for the immigration of 4,000 Jewish children and 500 adults to Palestine had been reached.[123] Hahn received the news in the evening, rushed in great excitement to the office where the newly arrived Walter Pausch was still working, and declared that something had to be done very quickly through the Sofia embassy in order to prevent the exit of the Jews to Palestine. When Pausch replied that it would be very good to get rid of the Jewish children in this way, Hahn insisted that it had nothing to do with children but men of military age who would be used as soldiers against Germany.[124]

Hahn dispatched an inquiry to Sofia about Halifax's speech, and Beckerle replied that the Bulgarian government had released an official announcement (in response to a Swiss radio broadcast of Halifax's speech) that technical difficulties had prevented the realization of the negotiations.[125] But even before Hahn received Beckerle's assurance, further distressing news arrived. According to Eichmann, representatives from Rumania were negotiating with Turkey for transit visas for 1,000 Jewish children and 100 accompanying adults to travel from Rumania through Turkey to Palestine. And a German News Bureau report of March 4, 1943, confirmed that 400 Jewish children of unspecified nationality had already arrived in Tel Aviv and two more groups were expected.[126]

On March 6, 1943, Hahn drafted a telegram, approved by Rademacher, for all south European embassies, asking them to report on the position of their respective governments to the issue of Jewish emigration and exert pressure to prevent negotiations with the enemy to this end.[127] Two days later another report from the German News Bureau reported the arrival in Palestine of another 72 Jewish children, this time specifically from Hungary, and that a total of 500 were expected.[128] Rademacher then contacted Budapest and Bucharest again, stating that evidence was now at hand that Stanley's statement in early February that agreements over Jewish emigration had been reached not only with Bulgaria but also with Rumania and Hungary was true. Once again Rademacher emphasized that the exit of Jews from Germany's allies could not be condoned. These negotiations with the enemy had to be broken off.[129]

Despite the continual flow of telegrams from the German Foreign Office demanding an end to the exit of Jews, reports over further Jewish emigration reached epidemic proportions. On March 10, 1943, Rolf Günther of the RSHA reported that 150 Jewish children were to emigrate from Rumania via the land route through Bulgaria to Palestine. Günther urged that all possible pressure be exerted on Rumania to desist from this "incomprehensible" policy and that Bulgaria be induced to make difficulties for the transit. On the same day Killinger dispatched news about this imminent departure of 150 Jewish children from Rumania through Bulgaria, and also that Turkey would probably grant a total of 1,000 transit visas for Jewish children from Rumania.[130] As if a further round of telegrams could stem the flow, Pausch drafted yet another message to Budapest and Bucharest, demanding that the exit or transit of any Jews to Palestine must be met with the "greatest possible resistance."[131]

On March 13, 1943, Killinger wrote that a transport of 75 Jewish children was leaving the next day. Transit visas had been granted by the Bulgarian embassy in Bucharest on instructions from the government in Sofia. Beckerle wrote that the RSHA request to exert pressure upon the Bulgarian government to prevent this transit could not be accommodated, because there was no prospect of success. Such importuning would only arouse mistrust and endanger Germany's relations to Bulgaria. He could take action only if German sources in Rumania could verify that the transport actually consisted of adult males instead of children.[132] Rademacher thereupon requested Killinger to check whether the transport consisted of male youths obviously intended for military service. If so, German protests could be facilitated. Frustrated by his helplessness, Rademacher also repeated the Foreign Office requests to Sofia and Budapest, the fourth in ten days, to prevent Jewish emigration.[133]

But Foreign Office efforts to get to the bottom of the "conspiracy" behind Jewish emigration did not succeed. Killinger repeated that the transports consisted of Jewish children, despite Rademacher's request that he find otherwise. He could only urge that the issuance of Bulgarian transit visas be blocked in some way by Dannecker, the German adviser in Sofia. But in his own report, Beckerle relayed the denial of the Bulgarians that any transit visas had been issued to the Rumanian Jewish children.[134]

Meanwhile the German embassy in Hungary discovered through an agent in the Rumanian embassy there that the Hungarian Ministry of the Interior, without informing its own Foreign Office, had approved the exit of Jewish children of both sexes between the ages of 12 and 15. The Rumanian embassy had been instructed by Bucharest to grant up to 500 transit visas, and 126 Hungarian Jewish children had already left. The Budapest embassy could only suggest that pressure be exerted in Sofia and Bucharest to prevent the issuance of transit visas.[135]

The efforts of the German Foreign Office to stem the trickle of Jewish children emigrating from southeast Europe to Palestine was unsuccessful. The embassies in Budapest, Sofia, and Bucharest acknowledged their inability to coerce their respective governments on the issue. Each could only suggest that pressure be exerted by the others.

The episode is instructive not only of the ability of Germany's allies to evade German demands if they cooperated with one another, but also of the mentality within D III even in the last days before its dissolution. Luther was no longer there to drive on his underlings. Even by Hahn's own admission, the temporary head of *Abteilung Deutschland,* Schröder's deputy Bergmann, was not an anti-Semite.[136] Rademacher and Hahn had a free hand to follow their own inclinations. Nothing could have been easier, in the confusion following Luther's fall, than to sit back and passively allow the emigration of Jewish children from Hungary, Rumania, and Bulgaria.

Both Rademacher and Hahn knew that Germany was pressing all of these countries to surrender their Jews and the fate that was in store from them if German pressure were successful. Yet Rademacher and Hahn undertook what amounted to a personal crusade to prevent the escape of any Jewish children. Telegram after telegram issued from D III, exhorting the embassies to stop this emigration. Not a single embassy or press report gave credence to the allegation that male adults of military age rather than children were involved, despite Rademacher's leading question to Killinger on the subject. This was an excuse made up by Hahn to overcome the objections of Walter Pausch and later used by both himself and Rademacher in their postwar trials. Martin Luther may have been the prime mover behind the Jewish policy of the Foreign Office, but he clearly had eager helpers who were not reluctant to carry on even when he was no longer present.

In Hahn's case this is not surprising, for he was out to prove himself on all fronts. But Rademacher was leaving the Foreign Office in disgrace for his defeatist attitude. His career was in shambles. In March 1943, during his "lame-duck" period of service in the Foreign Office, Rademacher did not work full-time, nor did he display any enthusiasm for the other facets of the Jewish question at that time, leaving the work and decisions mostly to Hahn. But the issue of the emigration of Jewish children rekindled Rademacher's interest, as if only emigration schemes competing with his cherished Madegascar Plan still had the power to arouse him.

## After Luther's Fall

Foreign Office Jewish policy suffered no disruption or break after the fall of Luther not only because of his dutiful underlings like Hahn and Rademacher, but also because Joachim von Ribbentrop himself began to play a more aggressive role. For the most part Ribbentrop had passively accepted Luther's actions or even actively restrained him, as when he had forbidden Luther to approach Hungary, Bulgaria, or Italy in August 1942, or later when he refused to act upon Luther's proposals for a confrontation with Italy in October 1942. But this behavior on Ribbentrop's part was not expedient for a man constantly toadying to Hitler's whims and fearful of rivals like Heinrich Himmler. Immediately following Luther's fall, Ribbentrop had adopted the very policy of confrontation with Italy over the Jewish question which Luther had vainly urged upon him earlier. Ribbentrop had seen what an alliance between Foreign Office dissidents and the SS could mean for himself, and he was determined not to be maneuvered into such a vulnerable position again. Moreover, with Luther out of the way, he no longer had to fear that he was playing into the hands of his unscrupulous protégé. The fall of Martin Luther meant a sharp increase in Ribbentrop's personal participation in Jewish policy.

Ribbentrop's trip to Rome in late February 1943, and the ensuing negotiations with Mussolini that he personally conducted, were only one manifestation of this increased participation. Hitler and Ribbentrop held a series of conferences in April at Klessheim Castle in Salzburg with various allied leaders, and Ribbentrop prominently displayed his newfound zeal for the Jewish question. When King Boris of Bulgaria told Ribbentrop that he was interning the Jews in camps because he needed them for road construction labor, it was Ribbentrop who said, "according to our view in the Jewish question the most radical solution is alone the right one."

On April 17, 1943, Hitler and Ribbentrop met with Admiral Horthy, the regent of Hungary. Hitler began pressing Horthy on the Jewish question.

> To Horthy's counterquestion as to what he should do with the Jews, now that he had deprived them of almost all possibilities of livelihood—he could not kill them off—the Reich Foreign Minister declared that the Jews must either be exterminated or taken to concentration camps. There was no other possibility.

Inspired, Hitler launched into a monologue on how the Jews "had to be treated like tuberculosis bacilli. . . ."[137]

Nor were Ribbentrop's activities restricted to personal diplomacy. Jagow suggested from Budapest that when Martin Bormann was going to receive Hungarian government party leaders in Munich in mid-March 1943, he should broach the Jewish question. Rademacher endorsed this suggestion because of the difficulties Hungary was making on the issue. Though Ribbentrop had formerly been extremely jealous of any of his rivals mixing in foreign affairs, he must have approved; *Abteilung Deutschland* dispatched a memorandum to Bormann to form the basis of such a conversation. As in Italy, Luther's policies outlasted his career, and once again his three-point program was pushed upon the Hungarians. They should eliminate the Jews from cultural and economic life, introduce marking, and agree to their immediate deportation to the east.[138]

The reorganization of the Foreign Office following the fall of Martin Luther also reflected a changed relationship between Ribbentrop and Jewish affairs. Previously Luther managed *Abteilung Deutschland* as his own empire, and Ribbentrop learned about Jewish affairs only what Luther wanted him to know. Only occasionally, as in Rumania, did Ribbentrop receive information from other sources. Luther had set the pace for Jewish affairs, either exceeding the foreign minister's authorization, as in Serbia, or ignoring it, as in Denmark.

Only after Luther's personal estrangement from Ribbentrop did he have difficulty doing as he pleased.

When Luther's empire was broken up, Jewish affairs were placed in a new section known as Inland II A. The head of Inland II, Horst Wagner, was directly responsible to the foreign minister and indeed spent much of his time at Ribbentrop's headquarters while the head of Inland II A, Eberhard von Thadden, deputized for him in Berlin. While Luther had operated with almost complete independence, ultimately controlled by neither Ribbentrop nor the state secretary, the activities of Inland II would be under the close scrutiny of the foreign minister.

Ribbentrop's break with Luther over Jewish affairs had come about because Ribbentrop felt that the activities of the SS in Rumania had not been properly supervised and that Luther had not properly protected Foreign Office prerogatives against SS encroachment. In fact, in SS circles Luther was resented as a much too ardent watchdog for Ribbentrop. Ironically, when Luther attempted his coup against Ribbentrop through an alliance with the SS and Himmler had balked to the latter's benefit, Ribbentrop now became more dependent upon Himmler than he had ever been when Luther was around. The new personnel in charge of Jewish affairs, Wagner and Thadden, were both members of the SS, a state of affairs that had never existed under Luther. It was Ribbentrop, not Luther, who brought about the deepest SS penetration into Foreign Office *Judenpolitik.*

Even with Luther gone, his programs continued to be pursued by Ribbentrop out of political expediency. For example, Ribbentrop immediately adopted Luther's policy toward Italy and continued his policies toward Hungary and Bulgaria. Likewise, the Foreign Office continued its attempts to block Jewish emigration to Palestine and to either deport or repatriate foreign Jews in the German sphere. Only in Denmark was a radically different policy adopted, and the resulting fiasco proved Luther's earlier prognosis on the need for caution there.

Furthermore, Foreign Office *Judenpolitik* did not change significantly after Luther's fall because there was little maneuvering room left. With the war turning against Germany, the Foreign Office had little diplomatic leverage with which to pressure reluctant allies. Those that had not succumbed to Luther's bludgeoning during the high tide of Germany's war effort, were not going to give way when Germany's defeat appeared imminent. In the areas of complete German domination, the deportation programs were already underway. In the areas of more tenuous German influence, the new Foreign Office experts could not now succeed where Luther had failed.

New deportation programs therefore depended not upon Foreign Office policy, but upon the changing military situation. When Italy dropped out of the war in the fall of 1943, German troops occupied northern Italy and the old occupation zones in France, Croatia, and Greece. That these former sanctuaries for the Jews were finally subjected to deportation measures was not due to any breakthrough by the Foreign Office. Likewise, in 1944 both

Hungary and Slovakia were occupied by German troops with the same results. In Hungary, however, the Foreign Office did play a significant role in securing a puppet government that would assist the German deportation program.

The Jewish policies of the German Foreign Office in the last two years of the war were largely a legacy of Martin Luther. His policies survived despite the collapse of his career. His underlings, Rademacher and particularly Hahn, kept these policies on track during the transition period before the reorganization of the Foreign Office. Finally Ribbentrop, despite his previous differences with Luther on the Jewish question, followed the course of political expediency and continued the policies of his fallen protégé. In fact, after the reorganization of the Foreign Office, the new personel appointed by Ribbentrop assured an even closer coordination of Jewish policy between the Foreign Office and the SS than before. The combination of Ribbentrop's new aggressiveness and his closer ties with the SS in Jewish affairs compensated for the absence of Luther's drive and dynamism. Despite the absence of its originator, Foreign Office *Judenpolitik* continued as before.

# 9. Conclusion

This case study of the Jewish experts and the Jewish policy of the German Foreign Office sheds light on three problems: the nature of the personnel involved, their motivations, and the policy making process from which the Final Solution arose.

Rademacher and his assistants—Müller, Klingenfuss, and Hahn—were aspiring career civil servants who opportunistically joined the Nazi Party immediately after it came to power. Only Rademacher, a member of the SA since the summer of 1932, had committed himself to the Nazi movement earlier. Even he demonstrated that he viewed the Party as a means to enhance his career, not as an outlet for ideological convictions, by leaving the SA in February 1934, when it was becoming too radical and even somewhat "disrespectable" by careerist standards.

As the actions of the Wilhelmstrasse officials in the first months of 1933 attest, anti-Semitism was not the monopoly of long-time Party members. It also afflicted the conservative-nationalist bureaucracy. As ambitious young men anxious to conform to the standards of both Party and bureaucracy, Rademacher, Müller, Klingenfuss, and Hahn were certainly not immune to this pervasive anti-Semitism. However, none of these four men displayed any strong predilection for Nazi racial theory—none was an anti-Semitic "activist"—before taking up his task in D III. Müller and Klingenfuss remained unenthusiastic in this regard. Hahn, a political chameleon totally without convictions of any sort, put on the best display of ideological zeal once on the job, but was equally adept at wearing the mask of benign moderation when it suited him. For Hahn, Nazi ideology was but another weapon in the arsenal of career advancement, a calculating attitude that was detected in at least one evaluation at the Bad Tölz NSDAP civil service school. Rademacher was the most problematic of the four. A self-made man, he eagerly strove to train himself as a Jewish expert and be recognized as such by established anti-Semitic authorities like Paul Wurm. He sincerely believed that it was Germany's obligation to achieve a final solution to the Jewish question. When this solution evolved into systematic extermination, however, his anti-Semitism did not prevent a loss of zest for personal participation and a half-hearted attempt to extricate himself. He did not, however, abjure the conviction that a Final Solution was necessary. Of the four, therefore, only Rademacher was motivated, though only in part, by the anti-Semitic ideology he embraced when appointed head of D III in 1940. The anti-Semitic climate of the Third Reich may have dulled the moral sensitivities of the others, making them less susceptible to a crisis of conscience, but it was not the mainspring behind their actions. Anti-Semitism was a contributing factor but not the decisive one.

Fanatical obedience provides even less a key for understanding these men than ideological conviction. Klingenfuss and Müller displayed a literal-minded obedience to carrying out the duties of their position, faithfully performing the tasks assigned them. But they actively worked to get themselves out of D III instead of accepting their assignments there as the "Führer's call." Rademacher, at least during the early phase, and Hahn displayed an enthusiastic obedience in the performance of their duties, not limiting themselves to carrying out explicit assigments but often taking the initiative. On the other hand, Rademacher was affiliated with the conspiracy against Ribbentrop and openly admitted his opposition to the foreign minister during his Gestapo interrogation, hardly the mark of blind obedience. Hahn could be enthusiastic about anything which he deemed would impress his superiors. The obedience of these men in carrying out Jewish policy was calculated, not fanatical. It was not the fundamental cause of their behavior but rather a symptom.

These men arrived in D III through entirely fortuitous factors, not through any systematic process of recruitment. Rademacher had left Uruguay because of a marital tiff. Müller had missed a posting to Sofia because of amoebic dysentery. Klingenfuss was picked because Rademacher remembered him from South America, and there was an opening in D III when the South American embassies were closed down. Hahn originally came to D III because his war wound made impossible the long hours as adjutant in the Economic Division. None was chosen because he had displayed any previous expertise in Jewish affairs. None volunteered or connived to get into the agency. They were a random cross-section of German bureaucracy who just happened to draw the assignment to handle Jewish affairs.

As might be expected from such a chance selection process, the Foreign Office Jewish experts differed in their personal feelings toward their job. Müller and Klingenfuss actively and successfully sought to escape from D III. Rademacher was originally enthusiastic but later lost his zest for the job. Though he perceptibly curbed his own initiative and requested to be relieved of the *Judenreferat,* he nevertheless did not exert himself forcefully enough to escape. Hahn on the other hand was so attracted by the work in D III that he voluntarily came back for more.

Despite the difference in their personal feelings about handling the Jewish question, all these men uniformly carried out their duties in D III with meticulous efficiency. Hahn acted above and beyond the call of duty because the work agreed with him, but Klingenfuss and Müller never did less than was expected of them, even though the work was disgusting. Two months after he began efforts to enter the military, Müller was blocking the shipment of food to Jewish ghettos in Poland. On a weekend trip to Berlin to pick up his family after he had already been transferred to the embassy in Bern, Klingenfuss helped out understaffed D III by negotiating the appointment of Dieter Wisliceny to organize the deportations from Greece.

These men seem to have been totally enthralled by their status as civil servants. Whatever else they may have felt or desired personally, any action that might have tarnished their reputation as efficient and reliable bureaucrats was unthinkable to them. If one wanted to get out of *Abteilung Deutschland* at all costs, one could do so instantly by displaying the slightest disloyalty or insubordination to Luther. Even a lesser offense could suffice. Werner Picot, the head of D II, slandered Ribbentrop before it was the fashionable thing to do in *Abteilung Deutschland,* and he was transferred out immediately. It cost him a derogatory letter from Luther in his file, but nothing more.[1] Yet Rademacher, Klingenfuss, and Müller spent months delicately and covertly maneuvering to extricate themselves from D III with their records unblemished. In the meantime, they continued to help the killing process run smoothly.

These men were not coerced by any external physical threat to behave the way they did. They were dominated by an internal compulsion to keep their records unstained. This compulsion was so strong that it blotted out any sense of individual responsibility. They viewed their activity in D III solely from the point of view of how it affected themselves, not what they were doing to others. In short, they had become dehumanized.

After the war Rademacher himself summed up this ideal of dehumanized bureaucratic subservience.

> My will was exclusively directed toward doing my duty as an official to the best of my knowledge and conscience.... My entire education from childhood aimed at serving the state, irrespective of the political opinion of the state leadership of the moment.[2]

No doubt Rademacher correctly calculated that a German court would be much more lenient toward one motivated by a sense of duty rather than racial hatred. But even intended as a rationalization, it stated the very crux of the problem: the conscience of the official applied solely to how he executed his tasks, not to the content or meaning of the tasks he performed. His sense of individual responsibility extended only upwards to those who set policy and evaluated how well he implemented this policy, never downward to the victims of the policy.

Klingenfuss was the only one among them who openly admitted after the war that he continually asked himself if he could have acted differently. Such was his self-centered bureaucratic mentality still that the only answer forthcoming was that he ought to have kept his name off documents where possible!

Otherwise, he concluded, there was nothing he could have done differently.[3] It apparently never occurred to the others even to ask themselves the question.

Every modern bureaucratic state has no shortage of amibitious careerists anxious to serve the leadership of the moment as the most obvious mode of personal advancement. But the careerists, with their excessive willingness to allow themselves to be used, become dangerous or criminal only when used by politicians of even greater ambition and less moral scruple than themselves. Such was the combination of Martin Luther and the reliable bureaucrats of D III.

Martin Luther was an amoral technician of power who thrived in the atmosphere of the Third Reich. The Nazi chieftains, Hitler's vassals, were engaged in a perpetual struggle to build up their power bases or fiefs. Each Nazi chieftain needed his own "private army" led by sub-vassals, directly loyal to him, who constantly guarded the domain from encroachments by others and expanded it when possible. The ideal sub-vassal had to be vigilant, ruthless, efficient, and loyal. Until he developed a weakness in this last category, Martin Luther was Ribbentrop's most valuable subordinate.

Martin Luther's career was so meteoric because he filled a desperate need on Ribbentrop's part. Ribbentrop was not the most successful competitor in Nazi Germany's internal struggle. A rising star before the war, he found that the German conquest of Europe disastrously diminished his power base. The Foreign Office simply did not have as significant a role to play when war and occupation replaced diplomacy. While others performed deeds for the Führer, Ribbentrop relied increasingly upon cultivating Hitler through fawning personal attendance at his court. He needed someone in Berlin to watch over his domain and to preserve intact what prerogatives he still had. Among Ribbentrop's associates, most were as unsuited for such a task as Ribbentrop himself. They remained in Ribbentrop's personal entourage, carried about in the special train always in close proximity to Hitler's headquarters, playing the same role toward the foreign minister as he did toward Hitler. The task of defending the domain in Berlin fell to Luther not only because the job matched his talents and inclinations, but because he had virtually no competition from Ribbentrop's other toadies.

While Luther fought a defensive battle for Ribbentrop to preserve the latter's shrinking domain, he also fought an offensive battle on his own behalf, carving out and constantly enlarging his own territory within the German Foreign Office. To carry out this dual role as his own empire builder and Ribbentrop's defender, he forged a two-edged weapon in the form of *Abteilung Deutschland*. On the one hand, it was Luther's own power base in the Foreign Office, constantly expanding and gaining new jurisdiction. On the other hand, it was designed to nazify and revitalize the Foreign Office, enabling it to fend off attacks by Ribbentrop's rivals. The old guard in the Foreign Office viewed *Abteilung Deutschland* as a foreign body, a cancer growing inexorably in their midst. The Nazi rivals tended to view it as a staunch defender of the insufficiently nazified Foreign Office bureaucracy and hence a betrayer of the Nazi revolution.

Luther was in a very difficult position. His boss was vain, insecure, and incompetent. The bulk of the Foreign Office, the enemies within, feared and hated Luther, while Ribbentrop's rivals, the enemies on the outside, resented his vigilance. In this tortuous situation it is perhaps surprising not that he finally fell but that he kept his balance so well for so long. What is certain is that Luther never could afford the luxury of extraneous ideological causes. He was totally absorbed by the continual struggle for power and survival. If he suddenly became personally involved in the fall of 1941 in the program to annihilate the Jews, it was not because of any ideological commitment to Nazi racial theories but because his political instincts detected that Jewish policy had become too important to be ignored.

Luther had constantly to study and evaluate the politial situation within the Third Reich and decide what course of action best served the interests of his boss and himself. When important Reich policies touched upon foreign affairs or involved foreign territory in any way, he had to insist upon the right of the Foreign Office to participate in that policy. But this participation had to take the form of constructive and helpful cooperation, not obstruction. Otherwise the Foreign Office risked total exclusion if the matter were taken to Hitler for arbitration. Luther understood much better than Ribbentrop that one competed with one's rival best by sharing and cooperating effectively in programs deemed important by the Führer if they were primarily under a rival's jurisdiction. Luther's strategy in the struggle for power within Nazi Germany lay not in establishing exclusive monopolies or competencies, a goal for which the Foreign Office power base was simply inadequate. At best he could defend Ribbentrop's domain, not expand it, and as new problems arose, whether it be the extermination of the Jews or the importation of foreign workers or even something as innocuous as pan-European veterans organizations, Luther was on guard to preserve the Foreign Office right to participate and thus ward off encorachment by his competitors.

Both Luther and his Jewish experts were motivated primarily by careerism, though not of the same type. The careerism of the bureaucrats of D III was passive. They stood ready to implement the policies of their superiors with meticulous efficiency, irrespective of their own personal feelings, in order to keep their records untarnished and enhance their prospects for advancement. They sought the security and status of the civil servant. Luther, on the other hand, sought the power of the successful politician. His careerism was dynamic. It required initiative and aggressiveness in order to survive in a fierce and often squalid struggle. The Jewish experts of D III were professional bureaucrats; Luther was a professional infighter.

In her book *Eichmann in Jerusalem,* Hannah Arendt portrays Eichmann as a mundane figure who could not think or feel from anyone's viewpoint but his own and whose conscience applied only to the manner in which he obeyed orders, not to the effect of his actions on others.[4] Eichmann presented "the dilemma between the unspeakable horror of the deeds and the undeniable ludicrousness of the man who perpetrated them. . . ."[5] It was a dilemma that could only be understood by realizing the "banality of evil." In their frightfully limited perspective and conscienceless reliability, the Jewish experts of D III fit Arendt's model of the banal bureaucrat better than Eichmann himself. But this does not explain the Jewish policy of the Foreign Office. These men implemented this policy, but they did not initiate it. This was the achievement of Martin Luther. He was extraordinarily ruthless and unscrupulous. He was unsurpassed in his ambition and energy. The only things mundane about Luther were his health and his incurable Berlin accent. He was anything but a banal bureaucrat.

To understand the decision-making process behind the Jewish policy of the Foreign Office, it must be approached from Luther's point of view, that of the perpetual struggle for power. As this struggle was played out before Adolf Hitler, the supreme arbiter, it was shaped by his own personal obsessions, including anti-Semitism. No one could hope to be competitive if he proved inadequate when the Final Solution of the Jewish question was at stake.

This was the matrix into which Martin Luther was drawn. At first he did not consider Jewish matters to be of vital importance. True, he did recommend Rademacher's Madagascar Plan to Ribbentrop; and within a few days it won the fancy of the Führer and also attracted the jealous attention of Heydrich, who insisted that Jewish affairs lay within his own jurisdiction. But Luther did not effectively resist the usurpation of the plan by Heydrich. He halted Foreign Office preparations on the plan as soon as it became apparent that Great Britain was not defeated, long before Eichmann's activities in the same direction had ceased. And while Luther quickly established *Abteilung Deutschland*'s monopoly over Jewish affairs within the Foreign Office, he showed little concern in either combatting or aiding the unilateral expulsion measures of the SS in France, though this unquestionably touched upon foreign affairs.

Luther was not mistaken in his calculations that neither the Madagascar Plan nor the SS expulsions were of great significance. In the end neither plan was a viable solution to the Jewish question, and each was abandoned. When the ultimate Final Solution began in the summer of 1941 with the massacres of the Russian Jews, Luther immediately sensed that something of significance was afoot. It was no longer advisable to stand aloof from the Jewish question. If Jews were being massacred in Russia, then the Foreign Office would follow that lead and help out where it could.

The opportunity came in Serbia. Luther went unsolicited to Heydrich and, contrary to Ribbentrop's explicit instructions to ask the SS about the possibility of deporting the Serbian Jews, concocted a plan to force the military to execute the male Jews on the spot. He thereby established his credentials with Heydrich as a proven collaborator in the Final Solution. This earned Luther an invitation to the Wannsee Conference, where he and Heydrich worked out an understanding for cooperation between the Foreign Office and the RSHA on carrying out the Final Solution within Ribbentrop's sphere.

It is important to note that in his later Vindication Report to Ribbentrop of

August 21, 1942, Luther made no mention of the Serbian affair at all. Moreover, he made no mention that he had been authorized by Ribbentrop to negotiate with Heydrich at the Wannsee Conference or that he had even informed Ribbentrop immediately afterwards. All he wrote was that he had informed Weizsäcker of the meeting, i.e., that it would take place, that he had insisted upon the Foreign Office right to be consulted, that the SS had complied with its promise in this regard, and that he was sending Ribbentrop a copy of the protocol for the first time. If he had discussed Jewish policy and the meeting with Ribbentrop either before or immediately after the fact, he surely would have mentioned it. Since he did not, it is clear that Luther had acted on his own, with no guidance or authorization from the foreign minister.

Both in Serbia, when the Foreign Office first became entangled in the killing process, and at the Wannsee conference, when this entanglement was formalized, Luther was not acting on the basis of orders from above. He was acting out of his own sure instinct for power that participation in the Final Solution was necessary to preserve the position of the Foreign Office. There was no love lost between Luther and Heydrich. As the conscientious guardian of Foreign Office prerogatives against SS encroachment, Luther had earned the extreme enmity of Himmler's deputy. On one occasion the latter had gone so far as to threaten the entire Luther gang with the concentration camp for obstructing SS plans.[6] With the Final Solution, however, Luther realized that he either provided effective collaboration or risked further aggrandizement by his rival in the RSHA at the expense of the Foreign Office. Luther's relationship with the RSHA in this regard was not "fusion" (Hilberg's term for the cooperation of the party, army, industry, and ministries in carrying out the Final Solution) but symbiosis. Heydrich and Luther worked together only when it was in both their best interests. Heydrich's task was greatly facilitated by Luther's help, while the latter knew he stood to gain more by offering than withholding it.

Luther obviously had little faith that Ribbentrop could be brought to see the necessity of this policy in time and proceeded behind Ribbentrop's back. To what extent other organizations became involved in the Final Solution through the spontaneous initiative of ambitious and clever subordinates (such as Heydrich vis-à-vis Himmler) is beyond the scope of this study. But it clearly shows that when zealous subordinates like Luther were desperately trying to anticipate the will of the Führer in the Jewish question in order opportunistically to advance their own careers, a chain of command requiring obedience to the Führer's orders was superfluous. Initiative from below obviated the necessity for orders from above.

If Luther's struggle with Ribbentrop's rivals shaped his initial decision to involve the Foreign Office in Jewish policy, Luther's later decisions on Jewish policy were increasingly affected by his growing estrangement from Ribbentrop himself. Luther's quarrel with Ribbentrop began to take precedence over his previous quarrels on Ribbentrop's behalf. Trying to ally himself with the SS as a preliminary to deserting the foreign minister, Luther did not protest when the SS violated the Luther-Heydrich understanding by conducting private negotiations with the Rumanian government on the Jewish question. Instead, he tried unsuccessfully to cover it up. Ribbentrop suspected Luther of disloyalty and selling out to the SS, not mistakenly, and for the first time deprived him of a free hand in Jewish affairs.

Ribbentrop's action threatened to cement the alliance between the SS and Luther as well as place him in direct opposition to Hitler, and he quickly abandoned the untenable position. Luther was given permission to push forward the deportation program under the supervision of State Secretary Weizsäcker, whom Ribbentrop was trying to resurrect as a counterweight to Luther. With his usual brutality, Luther once again worked for the fulfillment of the Final Solution.

Luther also began striving to enhance his own image in the eyes of the SS while discrediting Ribbentrop. He urged upon Ribbentrop a hardline against Italian resistance, a course he knew Himmler favored. If Ribbentrop acted accordingly and succeeded, Luther proved his own value as the man who could get Ribbentrop to act. If Ribbentrop tried and failed to overcome Italian resistance, he stood discredited. If he refused even to confront the Italians, he was guilty of obstructing important policy. Luther planned to gain, regardless of the outcome.

Ribbentrop became evasive and delayed any action on Luther's Italian proposal. Luther then took the offensive in Belgium, He made a private approach to the RHSA, in defiance of Ribbentrop's order to consult Weizsäcker beforehand, which was remarkably similar to his behavior in the Serbian affair. But before his last initiatives in the Jewish question bore fruit, Luther was pushed by Schellenberg into the premature and unsuccessful coup against Ribbentrop which ended his career. However, the same political calculations that compelled Luther to pursue the Jewish policy that he had were now operative upon Ribbentrop. The foreign minister now personally took up the same policy toward Italy that his disgraced undersecretary had advocated in vain and also exerted pressure on Hungary and Bulgaria. And though Ribbentrop had accused Luther of insufficiently preserving Foreign Office prerogatives in the Jewish question against SS encroachment, he now appointed two SS men to replace Luther and Rademacher. Foreign Office Jewish policy remained Luther's policy without Luther, for the political factors which had moved him in the first place were more overriding than ever, given the further deterioration of Ribbentrop's position.

The Foreign Office personnel involved in the Jewish question were a combination of opportunistic professional bureaucrats and an excessively ambitious and ruthless politician who was Ribbentrop's number-one political infighter. They were primarily motivated by considerations of careerism, not racial ideology or fanatical and blind obedience to higher authority. The decisions which led to the original involvement of the Foreign Office in the Final Solution and later to pressing forward the Final Solution with increased urgency resulted from the pressures exerted upon the Foreign Office by virtue of the intense internal political rivalry which was the essence of the Nazi system of government.

# Appendix I

## THE POSTWAR FATE OF THE JEWISH EXPERTS

In the aftermath of the dissolution of *Abteilung Deutschland,* the fate of the men who had shaped Foreign Office *Judenpolitik* varied greatly. The prime mover, Martin Luther, suffered the most severe fate. After the failure of the revolt against Ribbentrop, Luther was sent to the concentration camp at Sachsenhausen, just north of Berlin, where he was housed among the more prominent prisoners and was free to leave his cell and move about the camp. He occupied himself with herb gardening and bookkeeping, and at first told the other prisoners that he was only "in" for a short spell and would be released soon. Even though he was eventually allowed to live with his wife in a house on the edge of the camp, the realization that his incarceration was permanent, in addition to the death of one son and the capture of the other on the eastern front, so plunged him into depression that he attempted suicide several times.[1] As the Russians closed in on Berlin, Luther was released. In failing health he was hospitalized and died of a heart attack shortly after the war's end.[2]

Luther's death at the age of 49 freed him from the inevitable postwar judicial proceedings. Secretary of State Weizsäcker and Undersecretary Woermann were both tried by the Americans in the ministries trial in Nürnberg in 1948 and convicted for "crimes against humanity." Each was sentenced to five years for approving the Foreign Office response of no objection to Eichmann's request to deport 6,000 Jews from France to Auschwitz in March 1942, and for "like instances."[3] Undoubtedly, Luther would have fared far worse. With Luther dead and Weizsäcker and Woermann convicted by the Americans, the German courts were left only Rademacher, Klingenfuss, Hahn, and Müller (and their successors Horst Wagner and Eberhard von Thadden) to deal with.

Following his release from the Foreign Office, Rademacher enlisted in the navy. He served on a mine sweeper based in France and Norway for the duration of the war and even continued to assist British minesweeping operations immediately after the war. His wife and two children had moved from Berlin back to Mecklenburg in 1943, when Rademacher entered the navy. But Rademacher did not rejoin his family in the Russian zone after the war. Instead he settled in Hamburg, where he worked as a journalist.[4]

During the pretrial interrogations for the American war crimes trials in Nürnberg, Hans Schröder, the former Personnel chief, told the American prosecutor Robert Kempner that the Jewish business in the Foreign Office had all been Rademacher's fault and that he could find him. Schröder was successful in tracing Rademacher's whereabouts, and the latter was arrested in September 1947. He was brought to Nürnberg for interrogation where he refused to cooperate as a witness against his superiors, Weizsäcker and Woermann. Kempner found him one of the most stubborn men he had ever questioned.[5] Rademacher consistently denied any knowledge or invented wildly untruthful accounts of his activities. He refused to incriminate even Luther, placing all blame solely upon Ribbentrop, Hitler, and Himmler.[6] After it was clear to Rademacher that he was not going to be put on trial by the Americans, a subsequent interrogator, Dr. Max Mandellaub, got him to confess once: "I have committed great crimes, I do not know how I can ever make up for that."[7] But he signed no such statement. In July 1948, Rademacher did give Mandellaub written notes on the Belgrade affair as well as on Luther, the Europe-Plan, and the conspiracy against Ribbentrop.[8] That was the extent of his cooperation with the prosecution, and he was not called as a witness during the trial.

Karl Otto Klingenfuss, who had spent the last half of the war in Bern and Paris, voluntarily accepted the prosecution's invitation to come to Nürnberg to be interrogated in the fall of 1947. Unlike Rademacher, who denied everything even when the documentation was laid before him, Klingenfuss freely gave information before being confronted with the incriminating documents. Of course, Klingenfuss had less to hide. Yes, he had heard from soldiers returned from the eastern front that the native Jews there had been shot. His family had told him, upon his return from South America, that the Jews in Germany had been taken from their homes and deported. From Rolf Günther of the RSHA, he had learned that a propagation of the Jewish race was to be prevented through a permanent separation of the sexes. Thereupon he had requested a transfer from D III, which after some delay had been granted. Only in Switzerland in 1943, did he read about systematic killing, which he found so unbelieveable that he dismissed it as propaganda. Then he had a visitor from Germany who used the word "gassing" (*Vergassung*). When Klingenfuss asked him if that were really true, the visitor replied: "Yes, that is generally known." Only then, Klingenfuss claimed, did he clearly see what the activity of D III had meant. Earlier, while in D III, he had asked to see the Wannsee protocol. He had finally been allowed to thumb through it but then had to give it back almost immediately. Therefore he had learned nothing from it. Because Klingenfuss had been cooperative and was in poor health, suffering from heart and gallbladder conditions, he was not arrested.[9]

While the Americans did not try Rademacher or Klingenfuss, they did turn over to the Germans a report which summarized the evidence against them as well as that against Wagner and Thadden. All four cases were given over to the jurisdiction of the German courts in August 1948, and the State Court of Nürnberg-Fürth issued arrest orders for them immediately.[10] Actually, only Rademacher was arrested, for he merely had to be transferred from American to German custody. Wagner had left Germany already, and the charges against Thadden were dropped. Klingenfuss was residing in the French zone, and for their own reasons the French authorities blocked his arrest and extradition to the American zone. Once the pretrial investigations of the *Landgericht* Nürnberg-Fürth were completed, Rademacher was released as well in May 1949.[11]

In 1950 another attempt was made to arrest Klingenfuss. It was discovered that he had left for Argentina via Switzerland in December 1949, and the proceedings against him were temporarily halted.[12] After several years of legal maneuvering over the content of the charges to be brought against Rademacher, a new arrest order was issued for him in August 1951. He had quit his earlier job as private secretary at the Reemsta cigarette firm in Hamburg but was found working in Bonn as a journalist in a press service directed by a Frau Juliana Geis.[13]

When Rademacher's trial opened on February 4, 1952, the prosecution was severely hampered in trying to prove its case. All the original documents of the Foreign Office were in allied hands. The prosecution could therefore only work with photostat copies of Nürnberg documents selected by the American prosecution, which had not been interested in trying low-ranking personnel like Rademacher. By virtue of the selection process of the American prosecution, the German prosecution was deprived of much relevant evidence that would only come to light later when the entire Foreign Office files were returned to Germany in 1958. But an even more serious problem was to get the Bavarian court to consider a former Foreign Office official accused of participating in the genocide of the Jews as a serious criminal. In the end, the prosecutor attained only a most limited conviction.

In all the charges brought against Rademacher, the court immediately concluded that at worst Rademacher could only be considered an accessory, not the main perpetrator. To be guilty of accessory to murder, he would have to have known that murder was committed. Even to be found guilty of accessory to deprivation of freedom, he would have to have known that the deportations were illegal. Rademacher, of course, claimed that he had been completely ignorant of the extermination program and that he had thought the deportations were legally justified at the time.[14]

The court concluded that it was very probable that Rademacher did not belong to the inner circle of those who knew about the extermination program, because he could run his *Referat* without being officially informed, and it was Hitler's order that no one was informed who did not have to know. The court granted that Rademacher could have deduced the facts, given his constant contact with the Jewish question, his associations with Eichmann and Luther, and his trip to Belgrade, but this did not prove that he knew. The suspicion existed that he had seen the Wannsee protocol, but Rademacher's denial could not be positively contradicted. It was possible that he had attended the March 6 conference without knowing the details of the preceding conference on January 20, as Rademacher claimed. The compilation of the various suggestions for the *Mischlinge* question, including those summarized in the Wannsee protocol, could have come from the RSHA, as Rademacher claimed, because his signature was only on the covering letter, not on the document itself. And though Rademacher admittedly initialed the circulation sheets of many of the *Einsatzgruppen* reports, the court found it "believable" that he had not read them. After all, both the accused Rademacher and the witness Hahn conveniently agreed that Rademacher had given the *Einsatzgruppen* reports to a mysterious Mr. Peters, allegedly a young apprentice clerk, who prepared the summary for Ribbentrop. Neither Rademacher, who initialed the circulation sheet, nor Hahn, who touched up Peters' notes and signed the report, had any reason to remember the contents of the reports themselves. Likewise the convenient Mr. Peters, according to Rademacher, prepared the "Ideas and Desires" memorandum for Luther before the Wannsee Conference. Rademacher had found this memorandum "unsuitable" and had buried it in the files.

The court put itself in the ludicrous position of believing on the one hand that Rademacher need not have seen the Wannsee protocol or known of the extermination program because they were top secret, and on the other hand that the *Einsatzgruppen* reports, likewise stamped top secret, could be treated so casually that Rademacher could pass them to an apprentice clerk without reading them. Furthermore, the whole story of the mysterious Mr. Peters required the court to accept that two of the most important documents ever prepared in D III, a direct report to the foreign minister himself and a memorandum preparing Luther for an interministerial conference with Heydrich and the state secretaries, were both assigned to an apprentice clerk, while Rademacher and Hahn busied themselves with such earthshaking matters as rejecting emigration applications of German Jews. Having no access to the archives of the Foreign Office, the prosecution was not able to disprove the existence of Mr. Peters.

But the court had not yet completed its display of monumental gullibility. Rademacher did not deny that he eventually learned that the native Jews in Russia had been killed, but the court found it quite believable that Rademacher had not drawn the conclusion that Jews deported to the east for "labor" were also systematically killed. As for the death of almost all the Dutch Jews sent to Mauthausen in 1941, the court also found believable Rademacher's explanation that Luther had told him that it was the result of an epidemic. There were various letters stamped and filed "D III," which contained awkward phrases. The Sipo-SD report of July 26, 1942, over the proposed Rumanian deportations told how the capable Jews would be put to work and the rest would be subjected to "special treatment." On August 13, 1942, Bene had reported that the Jews had found out what went on behind the resettlement and work in the east and no longer reported to the transports. On

November 11, 1942, Bargen had reported about rumors of "butchering." Though these were all found in the D III files, none contained Rademacher's initial, and he naturally denied having seen any of them. Just how business could have been conducted in D III if Rademacher did not know what was in his own files, was not clear. But the court once again concluded that only the suspicion, not proof, existed that Rademacher had read these reports.

While refusing to recognize that Rademacher had to have known that the Jews deported to the east were going to be killed, the court did conclude that Rademacher knew that the deportations in themselves were illegal and not justified by international law. All cases in which it could be proved that he had aided the deportation program were to be evaluated as accessory to deprivation of freedom, but not accessory to murder.[15]

The court then proceeded to deal with the various charges brought against Rademacher. The most difficult one for a court bent on exonerating him was the Belgrade massacre. Because of Rademacher's own report, there was no way to deny that he had attended the meeting at which the decision was taken to shoot the Jews. The fact that Rademacher voluntarily accompanied Weimann and Fuchs to the meeting with Turner and remained there until Turner changed his mind constituted support of their position, even if, as Rademacher claimed, he played no active role in the debate. Turner had to evaluate his behavior as signifying the agreement of the Foreign Office with Weimann and Fuchs, and the court was convinced that Rademacher was aware of the effect of his behavior upon Turner. But Turner's decision to shoot the Jews constituted not first-degree but second-degree murder. He did not act out of base and cruel motives; the Jews were not shot solely because they were Jews but because in Turner's mind they represented a threat to security. In forcing Turner's decision, Weimann and Fuchs were guilty of incitement to second-degree murder. Rademacher was an accessory to this incitement and therefore himself guilty of accessory to second-degree murder of 1,300 Serbian Jews.[16]

With the worst behind it, the court quickly dispatched all but one of the other charges. Rademacher was accused of participating in the negotiations which led to the deportation of Rumanian and Bulgarian Jews residing in Germany and the occupied territories. Evidence was presented that the Rumanian Jews in Germany had been interned but not deported, so there was no crime committed in this case. The deportation of Rumanian Jews from France, Belgium, and Holland was not conclusively proven because the prosecution did not have access to the Foreign Office archives yet. The total absence of any surviving Bulgarian Jews from Germany or the occupied territories led the court to conclude not that the crime had been carried out with frightening thoroughness but that no proof existed that a crime had been committed. The complete destruction of the victims legally erased the crime.[17]

The court quite correctly acquitted Rademacher of any responsibility for the deportation of Rumanian Jews to Transnistria in the fall of 1941. It also concluded that Rademacher's effort to block the emigration to Palestine of Rumanian and Bulgarian Jews was based on sound political reasons and was not racially motivated. As this had not been done to further deportations to the east, no crime had been committed.[18] Rademacher was acquitted of any connection with the Croatian deportations as well, though he had passed on the Croatian request to deport its Jews in May 1942. Because the deportation of the few thousand surviving Jews (who had not been killed locally) began at the earliest in the fall of 1942, the court concluded that there was no proof that Rademacher's action in May was in any way involved.[19]

Rademacher had facilitated the deportation of 6,000 Jews from France to Auschwitz in March 1942. But these Jews were already interned in France, so shifting them from one camp to another did not involve any deprivation of freedom.[20] Concerning the further deportations from France, Belgium, and Holland, Eichmann had merely told Rademacher that he assumed there were no Foreign Office objections. Since the prosecution had not proved that Rademacher was aware of grounds for protest to the RSHA that could have effectively prevented the deportations, there was no accessory through omission or neglect.[21]

Rademacher was found guilty of only one charge arising out of the entire deportation program. This involved Luther's letter to Bargen of December 4, 1942, urging the deportation of the rest of the Jews in Belgium. Klingenfuss had drafted the letter and Rademacher had initialed it. Bargen had not complied with Luther's letter, but the letter itself was an incitement to commit the crime of deporting the Jews. As Rademacher was an accessory to the sending of the letter and it would have affected at least 10,000 Belgian Jews, he was guilty of accessory to incitement to commit the crime of depriving 10,000 Jews of their freedom.[22]

Rademacher was sentenced to three years for the Serbian case and eight months for the Belgian case and given a combined sentence of three years and five months.[23] Both the defense and the prosecution immediately appealed the case to the German Federal Court at Karlsruhe. As Rademacher had already served a large portion of his term while interned first by the Americans and then by the Germans from September 1947 to May 1949 and again since September 1951, his attorney requested that he be let out on bail pending the appeal.[24] On July 25, 1952, Rademacher was released. The prosecution protested the lifting of the arrest order, for if its appeal were upheld, Rademacher still would have a substantial part of his sentence to serve. The *Oberlandsgericht* Nürnberg agreed and issued a new arrest order on August 29, 1952.[25] It was too late; Rademacher had already gone into hiding.

Though Rademacher had disappeared, the appeals were heard in Karlsruhe in the spring of 1953. Rademacher's appeal was rejected, but the prosecution's appeal was upheld.[26] In the Serbian case, the Federal Court challenged two conclusions of the *Landgericht* Nürnberg-Fürth. First, the Federal Court was not convinced that the massacre of the Serbian Jews was second-degree murder. The 1,300 Jews had been interned for weeks, and there was no perceptible reason why they could not have been kept there without endangering military security. If the Jews had been killed solely because they were Jews, as the Federal Court suspected, this constituted first-degree murder. Second, the Federal Court challenged the evaluation of Rademacher's role as an accessory. As he had come to Serbia to achieve a local solution, he was imparting his own will to others and was thus at least guilty of incitement and could possibly even be classified as one of the perpetrators.[27]

Judicial errors or inadequate examination of the evidence was also found in most of the State Court's acquittals regarding Rademacher's involvement in the deportation program. In particular, the whole question of how much Rademacher knew of the government's murderous intentions during the deportations had to be reexamined.[28] The Federal Court showed its displeasure with the lower court decision by ordering that a new trial should be held not in Nürnberg but in the neighboring State Court in Bamberg. Furthermore, not only the Serbian case but all charges on which Rademacher had been acquitted were opened to reexamination, even those which the Federal Court had not specifically overruled. The only point in the judgment of the lower court which was left intact was the conviction for accessory to incitement in Belgium.[29]

However, a new trial could not be held without Rademacher, who made good his escape from Germany. At first Rademacher hid in the house of a Frenchman in Bad Neuenahr and communicated with his friends through Frau Geis in Bonn, the director of the press bureau where he had worked briefly before his second arrest. Rademacher remained in hiding in Germany for more than a year. Then in August 1953, he wrote a friend from his navy days, Kurt Gunkel, that he had papers and foreign currency but needed someone with a car to get out of Germany. Gunkel had worked briefly as an editor for the neo-Nazi newspaper, *Die Anklage,* founded by Robert Kremer. Gunkel therefore enlisted Kremer to drive Rademacher to France. Rademacher, who spoke fluent Spanish, had secured a Spanish passport under the name Tomé Rosello, as well as a visa for Syria, his ultimate destination. The trip went flawlessly until Marseille. There Rademacher had to procure a Lebanese transit visa. An official in the Lebanese consulate, who had worked previously in Berlin, recognized Rademacher but did not give him away. The fugitive reached Damascus, where he was joined by Frau Geis. He then began his new life as a journalist and free-lance economic adviser.[30]

In September 1952, a month after Rademacher's sudden disappearance, an arrest order was issued for Karl Klingenfuss. It was followed two months later by an extradition request to Argentina, though no extradition treaty existed between it and the new Federal Republic of Germany. On November 7, 1952, Klingenfuss appeared at the German embassy in Buenos Aires, after learning of the extradition request in the newspaper, to protest the action. He had left Germany in 1949 under his own name with regular papers in order to take a job in Argentina. He was still working under his own name and had openly explained his past activities in the Foreign Office to his employer, who had thereupon corresponded with the former American prosecutor, Dr. Kempner, before hiring him. Klingenfuss said that he was ready to return to Germany to stand trial on the conditions that the travel costs were paid for by the German government and that he was not immediately arrested upon arrival, so that he could visit relatives and find a lawyer. These conditions were granted. The Bavarian *Obersten Landgericht* then decreed that the Rademacher and Klingenfuss cases should be tried jointly.[31]

Because Rademacher could not be extradited from Syria, whose government thoroughly approved of anyone convicted of crimes against the Jews, the trial could not take place, and Klingenfuss remained in Buenos Aires. In 1958, extremely irritated that the charges were still hanging over his head, Klingenfuss wrote an indignant letter to a member of the *Bundestag,* Prof. Gülich. He had been given a job in D III through no initiative on his own part. He had escaped from it as soon as possible. He had been charged with accessory to deprivation of freedom, though he was the lowest-ranking man, who had merely drafted telegrams on others' orders. Higher-ranking men who initialed their approval of these instructions and ambassadors who carried them out had not been charged. When he came to Berlin in 1942, he had found his own apartment and furnished it. He had not wanted to live in an evacuated Jewish apartment, to sleep in their beds, eat off their plates, relax in their arm-chairs and read their books, like many other Foreign Office officials who after the war became ambassadors and then claimed never to have heard of the persecution of the Jews. He was being prosecuted, while Kurt Georg Kiesinger had also worked in *Abteilung Deutschland* and was now the "star" of the CDU. Rademacher had had other assistants also, one of whom was a high-ranking official back in the Foreign Office. (Klingenfuss was referring to Herbert Müller, though he did not mention him by name.) Klingenfuss concluded: "Now I have truely paid enough."[32]

While Klingenfuss was waiting, informal negotiations were undertaken with Rademacher through a German merchant in Damascus. If he returned, the Bamberg court promised to issue no arrest order until the verdict in the new trial was reached. In 1956, Rademacher went so far as to get a passport at the German embassy in Damascus that was valid only for entry into the Federal Republic. He then changed his mind, however, and did not return.[33]

In 1960 the statute of limitations expired for all war crimes other than first-degree murder and accessory or incitement to first-degree murder. The public prosecutor of the *Landgericht* Bamberg did not feel that he could charge Klingenfuss on this basis and asked that the charges be dropped. The court approved this request.[34] To uphold a charge of accessory to murder the public prosecutor would have had to prove that Klingenfuss knew that the deported Jews were being killed. This he could not have done, certainly not to the satisfaction of a Barvarian court.

Just as Klingenfuss was finally freed from the legal entanglements resulting from his activities in D III, the net began to close around Fritz-Gebhardt von Hahn. In the postwar period Hahn had continued to display his extraordinary dexterity. He applied for reappointment to state service, not listing the *Judenreferat* among his past activities in the Foreign Office. The first denazification proceedings, however, refused his request. Hahn then lodged an appeal. He remembered how the events surrounding the case of the two Bondy children interned in Theresienstadt had put him in an awkward position because the Swedes kept referring to his promise for their release without mentioning Luther's earlier promise, making it appear that Hahn had acted without authorization. Hahn cleverly exploited the incident, claiming that during his service in the Foreign Office he had intervened to save Jews, including the Bondy children, at great risk to his own safety and career. This was accepted as clear proof of Hahn's anti-Nazi attitude, and he was exonerated and permitted to reenter state service.[35]

Hahn worked first in the Economics Ministry and then in the Defense Ministry, and rose to the rank of *Oberregierungsrat.*[36] The potentially dangerous Rademacher trial in 1952 did not affect Hahn's career. On the one hand, the American-selected Nürnberg documents did not include those most incriminating of Hahn. On the other hand, he cleverly corroborated Rademacher's tale about Mr. Peters and the *Einsatzgruppen* reports. Rademacher claimed he had given the reports, without reading them, to Peters, and Hahn confirmed that the summary for Ribbentrop, which he had signed, had in fact been prepared by Peters, so he too was not familiar with the reports.

It was not until the 1960s that the past finally caught up with Hahn. In 1958 the Foreign Office archives were returned to Bonn, at last providing the German courts with the complete evidence on the activities of lesser personages in whom the allies had had little interest. Horst Wagner, who had fled Germany after the war but returned to Germany in 1956, after living in Argentina, Italy, and Spain, was arrested in February 1958. Proceedings began in the *Landgericht* Essen. The *Landgericht* Cologne had earlier indicated Ebernard von Thadden in 1950, but the case had been dropped. A new investigation of him was now also undertaken in Essen. This latter investigation was cut short by Thadden's death in an automobile accident in November 1964.[37]

During the preliminary investigation of Wagner and Thadden, a court official interrogated Hahn in September 1962, particularly focusing on what Hahn had known of the extermination program during his activities in D III and might have been able to pass on to Wagner and Thadden when they began their work in April 1943. Twenty years had passed since Hahn's work in D III, and ten years since he had escaped unimplicated from the Rademacher trial. It was apparently inconceivable to Hahn, basking in the success of his new career, that he might still be vulnerable to legal proceedings. The desire to please others, to be zealously cooperative in the task at hand, finally backfired on Hahn. He could not resist displaying his cleverness rather than playing dumb. In an amazing two-day interview he revealed to the court investigator the full extent of his knowledge of the extermination process at the time, as requested.

Hahn admitted drafting and signing the summary of the first five *Einsatzgruppen* reports. Naturally he had had to read them first and had drawn the conclusion that the SD units were carrying out a plan for the extermination of all Jews living in occupied Russia. There was no mention of the mysterious Mr. Peters. From other circumstances Hahn had also concluded that "the Jews' lives were no longer safe, as soon as they were evacuated to the east." He supposed "that I, just like all other officials occupied with preparing these cases, drew this or similar conclusions at this time." As for the foreign press reports, he could not imagine that they would spread propaganda reports that were totally false. "Where there's smoke, there's fire." He had no exact knowledge of the fate of the Jews but "a more general conception, that after their deportation the Jews died in mass." From the beginning he was very much involved in Jewish affairs because Rademacher was often gone. After the fall of Luther, he was almost exclusively occupied with Jewish matters. "Through this activity I naturally received an extensive look into the Jewish measures of the Third Reich. . . . More and more it appeared that the destruction of the European Jews had to have been decided at the highest level." But he did not tell Thadden what he knew, for no confidential relationship existed between the two of them.[38]

Hahn's testimony may have been of some help to Thadden, but it was of no help to himself. The *Landgericht* Frankfurt opened proceedings against him the following year, and he was suspended from his government job. But the trial did not take place immediately. Adolf Heinz Beckerle, the former German ambassador to Bulgaria, had been captured by the Russians and did not return to Germany until 1955.[39] He was under suspicion for crimes in connection with the Bulgarian deportations, which also comprised one of the counts against Hahn. It was decided to prosecute the two cases together. But due to Beckerle's bad health, he was repeatedly judged unfit to stand trial. The cases were separated, and Hahn finally came to trial alone in 1968.[40]

Before this trial opened, however, unexpected developments had occurred in the case of Franz Rademacher. His Syrian sanctuary suddenly became a nightmare. In July 1963, he was imprisoned by the Syrians and accused of being a NATO spy and slandering the Syrian state.[41] Apparently Rademacher's activities in Syria had extended beyond journalism and economic counseling. When weapons shipments to Algerian rebels, of which Rademacher had prior knowledge, fell into French hands, he was suspected of having betrayed the information.[42] Rademacher spent two years and three months in prison, including seven and one half months in a darkened cell. During his imprisonment he suffered two heart attacks. He was tried first before a military tribunal for spying and then in a civil court for slandering the Syrian state, but was acquitted in both cases. The Syrians released him in October 1965.[43]

Penniless and in extremely poor health, Rademacher decided to return to Germany and face a second trial there. But the Syrians would not let him return even of his own free will, unless Germany dropped its extradition request for him. They would not even permit the appearance of surrendering to the Germans a man wanted for crimes against the Jews. In an ironic twist Rademacher threatened to seek asylum in the German embassy in Damascus unless the German government insisted that the Syrian government no longer withhold an exit visa from a German citizen who had been acquitted of all legal charges brought against him by the Syrian authorities.⁴⁴ The German government thereupon withdrew its extradition request. Rademacher secured his exit visa and, accompanied by a German Foreign Office official, flew from Damascus to Nürnberg on September 30, 1966. He was arrested upon arrival and taken to the hospital section of St. George prison in Bayreuth.

In June 1967, Rademacher was judged medically fit to stand trial, if the sessions were limited to three or four per week. But his lawyer, Rudolph Aschenauer, an expert in war crimes cases who had begun this specialty by defending Ohlendorf before the American tribunal in 1948, was busy with an euthanasia case in Frankfurt and an *Einsatzkommando* case in Darmstadt.⁴⁵ The trial did not begin until February 21, 1968, while Hahn's was still pending in Frankfurt.

The public prosecutor in Bamberg had plenty of time to prepare his case and now also had the full archives of the Foreign Office open to him. Nonetheless he did not comb through the archives but merely ordered eight files which contained the originals of the most important Nürnberg document photostats used in the 1952 trial.⁴⁶ Only when by accident these eight files contained some new evidence did the public prosecutor benefit from the restoration of the German Foreign Office Archives. Unfortunately much other new evidence that was available was not utilized.

In his preparation the public prosecutor focused mainly on the question of Rademacher's knowledge of the extermination program and did substantially strengthen his position. First he secured testimony from Karl Klingenfuss, given in the German embassy in Buenos Aires. In confirmation of what he had told Kempner in 1947, Klingenfuss said that after much importuning on his part Rademacher had taken the Wannsee protocol from his files but allowed him only the most fleeting glance through it.⁴⁷ This directly contradicted Rademacher's claim, uncontested by the *Landgericht* Nürnberg-Fürth in 1952, that Luther had kept the protocol from him. Second, in one of the files lent to him by the Foreign Office Archives, the public prosecutor found not one but four copies of the compilation of the various suggestions on the *Mischlinge* question, which was based in part on the Wannsee protocol. The copies were numbered in pencil from one to four. This destroyed Rademacher's contention that this document had not been prepared in D III but had been sent to him by the RSHA.⁴⁸

Unfortunately, many important documents were still not in the hands of the prosecutor. For example, he did not have Paul Wurm's letter of October 23, 1941, which spoke of "special measures" in the near future to "exterminate" the Jewish "vermin." He did not have Rademacher's letter to Jagow of November 18, 1941, containing excerpts from the *Einsatzgruppen* reports, that would have contradicted Rademacher's claim that he had not read them carefully. Nor did he have Thadden's memorandum on his conversation with Rademacher over the incident when Kube showed alleged gas chambers used for killing the Jews to the visiting Italians.

In the case of the Belgrade massacres, the State Court of Bamberg initially followed the lead given by the Federal Court in its appellate decision of 1953. While Serbian hostages had at least been screened to find the most suitable candidates for reprisal executions, the judgment noted, the Jews were shot indiscriminately. Turner himself recognized that shooting the Jews not only filled reprisal quotas but also solved the Jewish question. By German law such shootings were basely motivated and constituted first-degree murder. But the Bamberg court did not follow the Federal Court suggestion of reevaluating Rademacher's role from accessory to incitement or coperpetration. Under German law Rademacher was a coperpetrator only if he willed the criminal act as his own deed. The court concluded that there was insufficient evidence for such an interpretation, as it could not be proven that Rademacher had zealously worked upon Turner, Fuchs, and Weimann to have the Jews shot. Strangely, the judgment of the court gave no explanation as to why it had not felt that Rademacher's actions at least constituted incitement. Rademacher was found guilty of accessory to the first-degree murder of 1,300 Serbian Jews.[49]

Because of the new evidence which the prosecution found in one of the eight files it borrowed from the Foreign Office Archives, it was able to get a conviction on one count upon which Rademacher had been acquitted in 1952. This involved the deportation of Rumanian Jews from occupied France. In early August 1942, Killinger had extracted a promise from the Rumanians to drop their objections to the inclusion of Rumanian Jews in the German sphere in all Jewish measures. On August 20, 1942, Luther informed the German missions in France, Belgium, Holland, and Prague that the Foreign Office had no objection to resuming the previously interrupted deportation of Rumanian Jews from the German sphere. This message was drafted by Klingenfuss and initialed by Rademacher. Furthermore, a document was found from the records of the Sipo-SD in Paris, which stated that the deportation of the Rumanian Jews had been carried out on the basis of a communication from the German embassy in Paris. Finally, the Centre de Documentation Juive Contemporaine provided evidence that at least 2,000 Rumanian Jews had been deported from France, of which at least 1,930 did not survive.[50] The link between Rademacher's initial and the death of 1,930 Jews was thus firmly established.

In evaluating this incident, the court sidestepped the issue of Rademacher's knowledge of the extermination program, an issue the Federal Court had instructed it to reexamine. The prosecution had put much emphasis on it, knowing that Rademacher could be convicted for accessory to murder for his involvement in the deportations only if it were proven that he had been aware of the fate of the Jews. Accessory had to be conscious. The efforts of the prosecution centered mainly upon proving that Rademacher had read the Wannsee protocol. Karl Klingenfuss had testified in 1947 and again in 1967 that Rademacher had taken the Wannsee protocol from his files. Klingenfuss was asked to come to Bamberg as a key witness. But face to face with Rademacher in court, Klingenfuss decisively weakened his testimony. He had assumed at the time that the document in question was the Wannsee protocol, but he could no longer say with certainty that it was.[51] The court concluded only that a "considerable suspicion" existed that Rademacher had read it.

The court then followed the line of reasoning that even if Rademacher did not have positive knowledge of systematic extermination, he at least knew with certainty that a pitiless and cruel fate awaited the Jews, that with insufficient food and lodging and the most difficult forced labor, a large portion of them would die. The court had "no doubt" about this because Rademacher had read the *Einsatzgruppen* reports, had seen Triska's notation about the liquidation of 28,000 Jews in Transnistria, had attended the *Mischlinge* conference on March 6, 1942, which made it clear that even the *Mischlinge* were not to be allowed to propagate, and knew that most of the Dutch Jews at Mauthausen had died. Rademacher had to have reckoned in August 1942, when he initialed the telegram, that most of the Rumanian Jews involved would die as a result of the deportation. As Rademacher was merely carrying out Luther's orders and displayed no initiative of his own, he was only an accessory. He was therefore found guilty of accessory to the first-degree murder of at least 1,930 Rumanian Jews and accessory to the deprivation of freedom and attempted murder in the case of the survivors.[52]

The court did not convict Rademacher for the Rumanian Jews deported from Belgium and Holland. In the same letter of November 11, 1942, in which Bargen had reported the rumors about "butchering the Jews," he also said that Rumanian Jews were among those who had been already deported from Belgium, though he did not give an exact number. A witness from the State Institute for War Documentation in Amsterdam testified that by the end of September 1942, exactly 45 Rumanian Jews had been deported from the Netherlands. The court also acknowledged that both Bene and Bargen had received the August 20 letter, initialed by Rademacher, notifying them that the Rumanian Jews could be deported. However, the court refused to convict Rademacher on the grounds that there was no proof that this message had been relayed by Bene and Bargen to the Sipo-SD and thus directly promoted these deportations.[53]

The court did not have to resort to such reasoning regarding the deportation of Bulgarian Jews from the German sphere, because the prosecution had not found all the relevant evidence. It did not have a copy of Luther's letter to Beckerle of June 19, 1942, drafted and initialed by Rademacher, containing instructions to secure an agreement with Bulgaria whereby it would not protect Jews of Bulgarian citizenship residing in the German sphere. A photostat of Klingenfuss' draft message of July 14, 1942, initialed by Rademacher, planning to inform the RSHA that Bulgarian Jews could be deported, was presented in court, but this was merely for internal circulation to the other branches of the Foreign Office and did not prove that the message was actually sent. Klingenfuss' note of August 3, 1942, ordering the dispatch of the message despite the objections of the Legal Division, was not presented in evidence. Moreover, there were no Bulgarian survivors to testify that they had indeed been deported in the summer of 1942. The court concluded that insufficient evidence existed either to prove that Rademacher had helped inform the

RSHA that the Bulgarian Jews could be deported or that this message had been acted upon. Rademacher therefore had to be given the benefit of the doubt and was acquitted.[54]

Rademacher was acquitted of any role in the deportation of Croatian Jews. The only existing evidence was a note from Luther instructing him in May 1942 to negotiate with the RSHA over the quickest possible deportations from Croatia. Deportation of the few surviving Jews in Croatia was not undertaken until the fall of 1942. Though Rademacher admitted forwarding a report from Kasche that Croatia was agreed to deportations, his actual communication to the RSHA, in response to Luther's instructions, did not exist. There was no proof that Rademacher either gave Foreign Office approval or urged the RSHA to act. As far as facilitating deportations simply by passing the information of Croatian willingness, this was already known to the RSHA since September 1941, and Rademacher's message played no decisive role. There was insufficient proof that Rademacher's actions constituted incitement to commit first-degree murder, and the statute of limitations had expired on attempted incitement. As for German pressure on Italy to give up the Jews from its occupation zone in Croatia, this pressure was unsuccessful. No murder was committed, and hence Rademacher was no accessory.[55]

Rademacher was acquitted on all remaining counts concerning Rumania. Neither the Foreign Office in general nor Rademacher in particular had been involved in the deportations to Transnistria in the fall of 1941. Rademacher had initialed Luther's letter to Killinger of August 11, 1942, to "clarify" the question of deportations. But no deportations took place thereafter, so Rademacher was no accessory. When Rademacher helped block the emigration of 75,000–80,000 Jews from Rumania, he already knew that the Rumanian government had decided not to permit deportations by the Germans, so it was merely a question of whether the Jews remained in Rumania or went to Palestine. The same held for the emigration of Jewish children from Rumania. Thus Rademacher had committed no action injurious to the Rumanian Jews.[56]

An important question was not raised in regard to Rademacher's involvement in blocking the emigration of Jewish children. Due to its incomplete research, the prosecution had Rademacher's telegrams to Bucharest only, and the Rumanian Jews were not murdered because they had been unable to emigrate. The court ruled that Rademacher had committed no crime. But Rademacher had also initialed three telegrams to Budapest, urging all efforts to block the emigration of Jewish children from Hungary. And later several hundred thousand Hungarian Jews were murdered. Rademacher's activities in this regard, undertaken on his own initiative, clearly should have been examined by the court.

The most controversial section of the judgment concerned the deportations from France, Belgium, and Holland. First, the court considered the deportation of 6,000 French and stateless Jews to Auschwitz in March 1942. Weizsäcker's and Woermann's initials on the Rademacher telegram informing Eichmann of no Foreign Office objections had led to their conviction before the American tribunal. But the Bamberg court acquitted Rademacher. The 6,000

Jews were already interned in France, so Rademacher did not contribute to depriving them of their freedom. According to the court, Auschwitz was not yet operating as a death camp. Because it was on German territory in Upper Silesia, and because the transfer to it of the 6,000 Jews from camps in France took place within the framework of a reprisal measure, the court concluded that Rademacher need not have viewed the action as a deportation "to the east" and part of the Final Solution. He was therefore not guilty of accessory to murder.[57]

Likewise, Rademacher was acquitted of any criminal responsibility for the subsequent deportations from France, Belgium, and Holland. On June 22, 1942, Eichmann had written Rademacher that he assumed no Foreign Office objections existed against the deportation of 90,000 Jews from these three countries. On July 27, 1942, Rademacher initialed Luther's response (dispatched on July 29) that no such objections existed. The court concluded, however, that since the deportations began in mid-July before the Foreign Office response, this proved that the Foreign Office response was of no interest or importance to the RSHA. Eichmann's June 20 letter was a mere formality (*Formsache*). The eventual Foreign Office answer did not assist or promote the deportations in any way and was thus without significance. At most, Rademacher's initial on the letter could have made him an accessory. But the letter itself did not further or promote the deportations in any way. And attempted accessory was no longer punishable. Finally, Rademacher was not guilty of accessory through omission when he did not object to the deportations, for the prosecution had not demonstrated that there was any type of protest that he could have formulated that would have had the least effect upon the RSHA's determination to carry out the deportations.[58]

On May 2, 1968, Rademacher was sentenced to three years and six months imprisonment for each of the two counts on which he had been convicted of accessory to murder. The minimum sentence for each count was three years, but because of the "very high" number of victims involved, the judge slightly exceeded the minimum. By German law the two individual sentences did not have to be served consecutively but were combined to form a total sentence of five years. As Rademacher had already served more than two-thirds of this total sentence during pretrial arrest, the judge had the discretionary power to release Rademacher. Because of his age, bad health, and lawful conduct since the Nazi era (apparently his jumping bail and leaving the country under false papers was not considered), the judge ordered him set free.[59]

The contrast between the trials of Rademacher and Hahn was stark. In Bamberg the prosecution clearly did not present as strong a case as it could have, simply through lack of thorough preparation. And it was faced with a court anxious to acquit Rademacher on as many counts as possible, so that he would not have to serve further time in prison. In Frankfurt the prosecution combed through every scrap of material that was available and presented an extremely thorough case against Hahn. It charged Hahn on two counts, got convictions on both counts, and failed only in its attempt to have him convicted for murder rather than merely accessory to murder. Hahn, who had served in D III less than six months and was technically subordinate to

Rademacher, received an eight year term, while Rademacher himself, the head of D III for nearly three years, had been sentenced to only five years by the Bamberg court.

Hahn was charged with murder for his involvement in the deportations from Bulgaria and Greece. First the prosecution convinced the court that due to the unusual events that occurred in *Abteilung Deutschland* in February 1943, affecting both Luther and Rademacher, Hahn had unusual scope for independent action despite his low rank of legation secretary. Hahn himself had confirmed this, styling himself as the "expert for the Jewish question" in his letter to Bohle. His activity in D III was not, as Hahn claimed, without significance.[60] Moreover, Hahn worked with such zeal and industriousness, that he clearly did more on his own than was required of him.[61]

The prosecution shattered Hahn's claim to have saved the Bondy children at great personal risk. It presented Rademacher's marginal note, telling Hahn of Luther's promise to the Swedish ambassador on February 5, 1943, long before Hahn repeated this promise on February 16. Hahn then claimed that after February 16 he had asked Rademacher to cover him by inventing back-dated instructions from the then departed Luther. But the prosecution presented correspondence with Prague and Stockholm that was based on Luther's promise of February 5 but preceded Hahn's of February 16.[62]

Most important, the prosecution convinced the court that by the end of 1942, Hahn clearly knew that the deported Jews were being killed. Hahn claimed that he did not remember the details of the *Einsatzgruppen* reports, a summary of which he had signed in December 1941, because the summary had allegedly been prepared by the apprentice clerk Peters. But no witness from *Abteilung Deutschland*—Walter Büttner, Walter Gödde, or Herbert Müller—could remember the existence of Peters, with the exception, of course, of Franz Rademacher. The court refused to believe that, even if Peters had existed, he could have been assigned to prepare two top secret memoranda, one for Ribbentrop and another for Luther, as Rademacher and Hahn claimed. Also, the court noted, Hahn had made no mention of Peters in his 1962 interrogation. The court further concluded that any informed reader, such as Hahn, would have concluded from the *Einsatzgruppen* reports that the planned extermination of the Russian Jews was underway.[63] Hahn, in fact, had admitted to just such a conclusion in his 1962 interrogation. He denied the validity of this interrogation, saying that it represented his later postwar knowledge, not conclusions made at the time. The court rejected this excuse, noting that the interrogator had specifically focused on his knowledge at that time, for the whole purpose of the interrogation then had been to determine what Hahn might have passed on to Wagner and Thadden.[64]

Despite his knowledge of the massacres in Russia, Hahn had voluntarily returned to D III. From the Tass report, he learned that the extermination program applied not only to Russian Jews but to the Jews in the rest of Europe as well. Hahn said he could not remember reading the Tass report, that when he marked it to be filed, that merely meant it was "uninteresting." The court dismissed this explanation. Other witnesses testified that any press reports that were filed were of importance, as most were thrown away. Hahn clearly studied the foreign press reports, as witnessed by his urgent reaction to the news of Jewish emigration to Palestine. His reaction to Dr. Junod's inquiry on behalf of the Red Cross demonstrated that he believed the Tass report. Finally, he admitted in the 1962 interrogation that he did not dismiss such press reports as wholly unfounded. The court therefore concluded that as of December 1942 Hahn knew the Jews were being killed according to plan.[65]

The court then dealt with Hahn's subsequent activities in the deportations from Bulgaria and Greece. In both cases, Jewish advisers were dispatched by the RSHA to organize the deportations, but only after their nomination had been cleared by the Foreign Office. In the Bulgarian case the nomination of Dannecker was discussed between Klingenfuss and Eichmann but was finalized only after Hahn's negotiations with the Personnel Division within the Foreign Office. Later Hahn twice added, on his own authority, the endorsement of the Foreign Office to Beckerle's urgent pleas to procure sufficient means of transportation to carry out the deportations before the end of March.[66]

In the case of Greece, Hahn had drafted a telegram for Luther on January 7, 1943, which declared to Altenburg the interest of the Foreign Office in the quickest possible solution of the Jewish problem. The initial negotiations for the nomination of Wisliceny were carried out between Klingenfuss and Otto Hunsche of the RSHA. But once again Hahn became involved, drafting the telegram to Bratislava instructing Ludin to release Wisliceny for temporary duty in Greece.[67]

The court concluded that Hahn acted with the foreknowledge that the deported Jews would be killed, and that his actions contributed to the carrying out of the deportations. The court also accepted the evidence presented by the prosecution that 7,132 Jews from Macedonia, 4,150 Jews from Thrace, and a minimum of 20,000 and possibly as many as 56,000 Greek Jews were killed as a result of the deportations.[68] The court therefore found Hahn guilty of accessory to murder for his part in both the Bulgarian and Greek deportations. He was sentenced to five years for the Bulgarian case, six years for the Greek case, and given a combined total sentence of eight years.[69]

The court rejected, however, the suggestion of the prosecution that Hahn be judged a "coperpetrator" of the murders. A coperpetrator in German law is one who viewed the crime as his own act. The prosecution argued that Hahn's zeal and especially the attitude displayed by his voluntary return to D III indicated Hahn's acceptance of the crimes as his own acts. But the court concluded that in both cases the deportations had already been decided upon when Hahn's activities began and that his role in the deportations was not extensive enough to constitute coperpetration.[70]

Through the Hahn trial the previously immune Herbert Müller was finally caught in the legal web as well. Following recovery from the wound he had suffered in North Africa, Müller went back to the Foreign Office and was assigned to the Paris embassy for the rest of the war. Not mentioning his assignment to D III on his application form, he entered the Foreign Office of the Federal Republic in 1951. In 1953, with the support and encouragement of the Foreign Office, he changed his name to Müller-Roschach, adding his wife's last name. The Foreign Office did not suggest him as a possible witness at the 1952 Rademacher trial. Müller-Roschach experienced rapid promotion, becoming ambassador to Afghanistan in 1960, *Ministerialdirektor* and head of the planning staff of the Foreign Office in 1962, and ambassador to Portugal in 1966.[71]

In the course of their preparation for the Hahn case, however, the Frankfurt prosecution came across Müller's name, traced him and summoned him as a witness at the Hahn trial. Following his appearance in Frankfurt, the public prosecutor in Cologne opened an investigation of Müller's own activities. Müller retired from the Foreign Office in 1969, when the investigation began.[72]

The investigation uncovered 48 Jewish applications for emigration that had been handled by Herbert Müller. The Foreign Office had the right to ask for exceptions to Himmler's ban on Jewish emigration, when it lay in the interests of the Reich. Müller recommended such exceptional treatment in only four cases.[73] In sixteen cases where Müller did not intervene and the applications were rejected, it could be established that the Jews in question were deported to the east. The question to be examined was whether, in facilitating the rejection of these applications, Müller was facilitating their later deportation and was thus guilty of accessory to murder.[74]

However, Müller's activities were criminal only if it could be proven that he was aware that deportation to the east meant the death of those whose emigration applications he had not recommended. Müller naturally denied any such knowledge. While Jewish affairs were so counter to his feelings that he had joined the army rather than remain in D III, he maintained that this did not mean he had known that the Final Solution meant the extermination of the Jews.[75]

The public prosecutor in Cologne did not find Müller's denial convincing. Müller had read the New York *Post* article on massacres behind the Russian front and handled the report of the agent within the Italian embassy over starvation in the Polish ghettos. The former might have been dismissed as foreign propaganda; the latter could not be. Müller had initialed and submitted Hahn's summary of the first five *Einsatzgruppen* reports to Luther. Müller denied reading it, but the prosecutor did not believe that anyone submitted to the much-feared Luther something so important as a report destined for the Foreign Minister without reading it. However, the prosecutor conceded that Müller may have concluded from all these incidents only that the Russian Jews were being killed, without realizing that the same fate awaited the German Jews whose emigration requests he failed to recommend.[76]

Müller later had ample opportunity to realize that the Final Solution meant the death of all European Jews. On January 29, 1942, he attended the *Ostministerium* conference, and he already knew that a special meeting of the state secretaries had been held on January 20. The telegram that Müller drafted on February 5, 1942, rejecting the *Relico* request to send food shipments to the ghettos clearly showed that Müller either felt that starvation of the Jews was part of the Final Solution or that extra food was senseless in view of the systematic murder planned for them. The prosecutor concluded that as of February 5, 1942, Müller definitely knew the fate which awaited the deported Jews.[77]

The last emigration case handled by Müller in which subsequent deportation to the east could be proved was on February 2, 1942. At this point in time, three days before the *Relico* telegram, the prosecutor did not have sufficient evidence to prove Müller's awareness of the extermination program. As prior knowledge of the crime was essential for a conviction of accessory, the prosecutor realized that he had insufficient evidence to prove his case. The proceedings were halted, and Müller was never brought to trial.[78]

This whirlwind of legal activity in 1968 and 1969 did not close the book on the personnel of D III. The legal odyssey of Franz Rademacher continued. In the summer of 1968 both the prosecution and the defense appealed the verdict of the *Landgericht* Bamberg. Once again the Franz Rademacher case came before the Federal Court in Karlsruhe. In January 1971, for the second time in as many appeals, the Federal Court overruled part of the verdict of a Bavarian State Court. The ruling of accessory instead of incitement for Rademacher's role in Belgrade was upheld. But Rademacher's acquittal regarding the deportations from France, Belgium, and the Netherlands was rejected.

The Federal Court found a contradiction in the lower court's evaluation of the deportation of 6,000 Jews from France to Auschwitz in March 1942. Rademacher had been acquitted on the grounds that it had not been proven that he knew the Jews would be killed in Auschwitz. He may have thought it simply a transfer from one camp to another. Yet, in evaluating the deportations of Rumanian Jews from France in August 1942, the court concluded that it had "no doubt" that Rademacher knew a cruel and pitiless fate awaited them. It had so concluded because of his trip to Belgrade, the mass deaths of the Dutch Jews at Mauthausen, the *Einsatzgruppen* reports, the *Mischlinge* conference of March 6, and finally Triska's marginal note that 28,000 Jews had been liquidated in Transnistria. Only the last of these took place after March 1942. The Federal Court could not understand why Rademacher did not already know in March what the Bamberg court was sure he knew by August. The Federal Court noted that the Wannsee protocol and Rademacher's access to it was a key consideration in this question. But the Bamberg court had refused to evaluate the evidence provided on this point, claiming that it was not essential. The acquittal of the defendant was not justified.[79]

Furthermore, Rademacher's acquittal in the subsequent deportations from France, Belgium, and the Netherlands was invalidated by judicial error. The Bamberg court had claimed that the letter of July 29, 1942, initialed by Rademacher, had no influence on the deportations which had already begun, and that Rademacher was not an accessory. The Federal Court ruled that this was an erroneous conception of accessory. Accessory did not have to make a causal contribution to the success of the crime. Rather the simple act of providing support for the commission of a crime, even if it was not essential to the success of the crime, constituted accessory. This support merely had to facilitate or help the commission of the crime in some way. The whole charge had to be reexamined in light of the proper definition of accessory.[80]

It was also not clear to the Federal Court why the Bamberg court had ruled that Eichmann's initial letter of June 22, stating that he assumed that the Foreign Office had no objections, was merely a formality. Considering that Rademacher had already had one meeting as well as a telephone conversation with Eichmann on the subject, the letter could also be interpreted to mean that Eichmann already had Rademacher's agreement and was ready to go ahead with the deportations unless subsequent objections arose on the side of the Foreign Office. The fact that Luther made an official response on July 29 to Eichmann's letter of June 22 also indicated that it was considered an official inquiry. It was incumbent upon the Bamberg court to explain why it dismissed Eichmann's letter as a formality of no significance. As for accessory through omission, the Bamberg judgment left the Federal Court unconvinced. It felt that almost any sort of objection based on foreign policy considerations could have been made.[81]

Despite the evidence submitted by the State Institute for War Documentation in Amsterdam that 45 Rumanian Jews had indeed been deported from the Netherlands, the Federal Court upheld Rademacher's acquittal concerning the deportation of Rumanian Jews from Belgium and the Netherlands. It still felt that insufficient evidence was at hand to prove that the Rumanian Jews had actually been deported. Without proof of the crime, there was no accessory.[82]

Rademacher was scheduled to go on trial once again on the issue of the deportations from France, Belgium, and the Netherlands. However, he suffered a relapse in his heart condition in November 1971. He never recovered sufficiently to stand trial and died in Bonn on March 17, 1973.[83] With his death the last of the legal proceedings against the Jewish experts of D III was closed.

# APPENDIX II

## ORGANIZATION OF THE GERMAN FOREIGN OFFICE
December 1941

### REICH FOREIGN MINISTER
Joachim von Ribbentrop

*Foreign Minister's Secretariat:*      Paul Otto Schmidt
Lohman
Sonnleithner
Bruns
Weber
Bergmann
Hilger

*Personal Staff:*      Hewel
Steengracht

*Ambassador for Special Duties:*      Ritter

### STATE SECRETARIES
*State Secretary of the Foreign Office:*      Weizsäcker
*Head of the Auslandsorganisation:*      Bohle
*State Secretary for Special Duties:*      Keppler

### PROTOCOL DIVISION
*Head:*      Dörnberg
*Deputy:*      Halem

## ABTEILUNG DEUTSCHLAND

| | | |
|---|---|---|
| *Head:* | | Luther |
| *Deputy:* | | Büttner |
| D I | *(Party liaison)* | Luther |
| D II | *(SS and Police)* | Likus |
| *Deputy:* | | Picot |
| D III | *(Jewish question, national movements abroad)* | Rademacher |
| D IV | *(printing)* | Klatten |
| D V | *(travel abroad)* | Graben |
| D VI | *(special construction)* | Luther |
| D VII | *(geographic service)* | von zur Mühlen |
| *Deputy:* | | Winz |
| D VIII | *(ethnic Germans)* | Triska |
| D IX | *(ethnic Germans-economics)* | Grosskopf |
| D X | *(foreign workers)* | Kieser |
| *Referat Organisation* | | Luther |
| *Deputy:* | | Krümmer |

## PERSONNEL DIVISION

| | |
|---|---|
| *Head:* | Schröder |
| *Deputy:* | Bergman |

## POLITICAL DIVISION

| | | |
|---|---|---|
| *Head:* | | Woermann |
| *Deputies:* | | Rintelen, Erdmannsdorf |
| Pol I M | *(military)* | Kramarz |
| Pol II | *(Great Britain, Ireland, France, Belgium, Netherlands, Switzerland)* | Strack |
| Pol III | *(Spain, Portugal, Vatican)* | Haidlen |
| Pol IV | *(Italy, Hungary, Rumania, Bulgaria, Greece, Serbia, Montenegro, Albania, Slovakia)* | Heinberg |
| Pol V | *(Soviet Union, General Government)* | Schliep |
| Pol VI | *(Scandinavia)* | Grundherr |
| Pol VII | *(Near East)* | Melchers |
| Pol VIII | *(Far East)* | Braun |
| Pol IX | *(N. and S. America)* | Freytag |
| Pol X | *(Africa)* | Bielfeld |
| Pol XI | *(war guilt questions)* | Schmieden |
| Pol XII | *(boundaries, treaties)* | Schmieden |

## ECONOMIC DIVISION

| | |
|---|---|
| *Head:* | Wiehl |
| *Deputy:* | Clodius |

## LEGAL DIVISION

| | | |
|---|---|---|
| *Head:* | | Gaus |
| *Deputy:* | | Albrecht |
| R I | *(international law, Red Cross, laws of war)* | Conrad Rödiger |
| R V | *(police questions, civil and trade law)* | Gustav Rödiger |
| R IX | *(treatment of foreign property in Germany and German property in foreign countries)* | Schiffner |

## CULTURAL DIVISION

| | |
|---|---|
| *Head:* | Twardowski |
| *Deputy:* | Nöldeke |

## PRESS DIVISION

| | |
|---|---|
| *Head:* | Paul Karl Schmidt |
| *Deputy:* | Braun von Stumm |

## INFORMATION DIVISION

| | |
|---|---|
| *Head:* | Wüster |
| *Deputy:* | Rahn |

## RADIO DIVISION

| | |
|---|---|
| *Head:* | Rühle |
| *Deputy:* | Schirmer |

## FOREIGN OFFICE REPRESENTATIVES

| | |
|---|---|
| *Belgium* | Werner von Bargen |
| *Bulgaria* | Adolf Heinz Beckerle |
| *Croatia* | Siegfried Kasche |
| *Denmark* | Cecil von Renthe-Fink (until Oct. 1942) Werner Best |
| *France* | Otto Abetz |
| *Greece* | Günther Altenberg |
| *Hungary* | Dietrich von Jagow |
| *Italy* | Hans Georg von Mackensen |
| *Netherlands* | Otto Bene |

### FOREIGN OFFICE REPRESENTATIVES (continued)

| | |
|---|---|
| *Protectorate* | Werner von Gerlach |
| *Rumania* | Manfred von Killinger |
| *Serbia* | Felix Benzler |
| *Slovakia* | Hans Elard Ludin |

# Appendix III

## CHRONOLOGY

| *Germany* | *Jewish Policy* | *Foreign Office* |
|---|---|---|

### 1933

*January 30*
Hitler Comes to Power

*February 27*
Reichstag Fire

*March 20*
Referat Deutschland
established

*March 23*
Enabling Act

*April 1*
Boycott of Jewish Stores

*April 7*
Legislation Restricting
Jews in the Civil Service
and Legal Profession

*April 25*
Legislation Restricting
Jewish Students and
Teachers

*April 30*
First Referat Deutschland
Circular on the Jewish
Question

## 1933 (continued)

*August 7*
Haavara Agreement

*October 14*
Germany Leaves the
League of Nations

## 1934

*June 30*
Blood Purge

*October 16*
Bülow-Schwante
Opposes all Negotiations
on Jewish Question, a
Policy Adopted by
Foreign Office Circular
of October 30

## 1935

*January 13*
Saar Plebiscite

*March 16*
Hitler Announces Rein-
troduction of Conscription

*June 18*
Anglo-German Naval
Agreement

*July 15*
Kurfürstendamm Riots

*August 20*
Schacht Conference on
the Interference of Party
Radicals in the Economy

*September 15*
Nürnberg Laws

## 1936

*March 7*
Occupation of the
Rhineland

*August*
Luther Joins Bureau
Ribbentrop

*September*
Göring Made Plenipo-
tentiary of Four Year
Plan

**November**
Luther Forms Party
Liaison Office

# 1937

**January 7**
Referat Deutschland
Begins Opposition to
Haavara Agreement and
Jewish Emigration to
Palestine

**November**
Luther Temporarily Fired
From Bureau Ribbentrop

# 1938

**February 4**
Ribbentrop Made Foreign
Minister

**March 7**
Anschluss with Austria

**March**
Luther Reinstated by
Ribbentrop

**April 26**
Göring Decree on Regis-
tration of Jewish Property

**July 6–15**
Evian Conference

**September 28**
Munich Agreement

**October 28**
Expelling of Polish Jews
Begins on Ribbentrop's
Request to Heydrich

**November 9**
Kristallnacht

**November 12**
Göring Conference to
Centralize Control of
Jewish Policy

**November**
Luther enters the Foreign
Office as Head of Referat
Partei

**December**
Schacht Trip to London
to Discuss Jewish
Emigration

# 1939

### January 24
Founding of Heydrich's
Reich Central for Jewish
Emigration

### February 2
Schacht-Rublee Plan
Agreed Upon

### March 15
Germany Occupies
Prague

### July 4
Establishment of Reich
Union of German Jews
under SS Control

### September 1
Germany Invades Poland

### September 21
Heydrich Memo on
Making the Incorporated
Territories *Judenfrei*

### October 12
First Transports to
Lublin Reservation

### October
Schumburg Inquiries to
RSHA over Lublin
Reservation

# 1940

### February 15
Stettin Deportation

### March 12
Schneidenmühl
Deportation

### March 23
Göring Bans Further
Deportation to the
General Government

### April 9
Germany Invades
Denmark and Norway

### May 7
Abteilung Deutschland
Founded

### May 10
Germany Attacks France,
The Netherlands, and
Belgium

*June 3*
Rademacher's First Memo
on Madagascar Plan

*June 18*
Hitler and Ribbentrop
mention Madagascar Plan
to Mussolini and Ciano

*June 21*
France Surrenders

*June 28*
Rumania Cedes Bessarabia
and Bukovina to USSR

*July 2*
Rademacher's First
Detailed Madagascar
Plan

*July 28*
Hitler Demands Political
Realignment in Slovakia;
Killinger sent to install
Adviser System

*August 30*
Rumania Cedes Transyl-
vania to Hungary (2nd
Vienna Award)

*August-September*
Height of Battle of Britain

*September 1*
Wisliceny Arrives in
Slovakia as Jewish
Adviser

*September 27*
Military Adminsitration in
France Decrees Jewish
Legislation Suggested by
Abetz

*October 23*
Baden-Pfalz Expulsions

*November 15*
Sealing of Warsaw Ghetto

# 1941

*March 13*
Hitler Authorizes Himmler
to Carry Out "Special
Duties" in Russia

*March*
Richter Becomes Jewish
Adviser in Rumania

# 1941 (continued)

*April 6*
Germany Invades Greece
and Yugoslavia

*June 22*                          *June 22*
Germany Invades Russia             Einsatzgruppen Activities
                                   Begin

                                   *July 31*
                                   Göring Authorizes
                                   Heydrich to Coordinate
                                   Final Solution

                                                        *July*
                                                        Luther Promoted to
                                                        Unterstaatssekretär

                                                        *August 14*
                                                        Benzler's First Request to
                                                        Deport Serbian Jews

                                   *August 29*
                                   Conference which decides
                                   to mark German Jews

                                   *September 1*
                                   Kamenetz-Podolsk
                                   Massacres

                                                        *September 13*
                                                        Rademacher-Eichmann
                                                        Phone Conversation on
                                                        Serbian Jews

                                   *September 28–29*
                                   Kiev Massacres

                                                        *October 3 or 4*
                                                        Heydrich-Luther Meeting
                                                        on Serbian Jews

                                   *October 15*
                                   First Deportations from
                                   Germany

                                                        *October 18–21*
                                                        Rademacher in Belgrade

                                   *October 23*
                                   End of Jewish Emigration
                                   from Germany

                                                        *October 29*
                                                        Foreign Office asks
                                                        Croatia, Slovenia, and
                                                        Rumania to Include their
                                                        Jews in Deportations
                                                        from Germany

*November 11*

Eleventh Edict to German
Citizenship Law Deprives
Jews Outside German
Boundaries of
Citizenship

*November 11*

Foreign Office Receives
Einsatzgruppen Reports
#1–5

*November 25*

Foreign Office Receives
Einsatzgruppen Report #6

*November 29*

Foreign Office Receives
Invitation to Wannsee
Conference

*December 8*

First Gassings at Chelmno
and Riga Massacres of
German Deportees

*December 10*

Luther and Hahn Write
Summaries of Einsatz-
gruppen Reports

*December 11*

Germany Declares War
on USA

# 1942

*January 20*

Wannsee-Conference

*January 29*

Ostministerium Conference

*February 10*

Ostministerium Complains
of Rumanian Expulsions
from Transnistria

*February 16*

Foreign Office asks
Slovakia for 20,000
Jewish Laborers

*February 23*

Foreign Office Sponsors
First Interministerial
Conference on German
Jewish Property Abroad

# 1942 (continued)

| | |
|---|---|
| **March 6**<br>First *Mischlinge*<br>Conference | **March 6**<br>Eichmann Inquiry to<br>Rademacher about De-<br>porting 1,000 French<br>Jews to Auschwitz |
| | **March 11**<br>Eichmann Inquiry about<br>an Additional 5,000 |
| | **March 23**<br>Foreign Office Asks<br>Slovakia to Deport all<br>Slovak Jews |
| **March 26**<br>Slovak Deportations Begin | **March 26**<br>Foreign Office Asks<br>Rumania to Cease Ex-<br>pelling Jews from<br>Transnistria |
| **March 28**<br>First French Train to<br>Auschwitz | |
| | **May 27**<br>Luther Instructs Rade-<br>macher to ask RSHA to<br>Accept Croatian Request<br>to Deport its Jews |
| **June 5**<br>Death of Heydrich | |
| | **June 11**<br>Rademacher Attends<br>Meeting of Eichmann's<br>Deportation Experts from<br>Western Occupied<br>Territories |
| **June 23**<br>First Gas-Chamber Selec-<br>tions at Auschwitz | |
| | **June 28**<br>Luther asks Abetz,<br>Bargen and Bene about<br>Deportations |
| **July 1**<br>German Troops Reach<br>Don River in Russia, El<br>Alamein in North Africa | |
| | **July 6**<br>German-Bulgarian<br>Agreement to Deport<br>Bulgarian Jews from<br>German Sphere |

*July 17*
Deportations from
France and the Nether-
lands Begin

*July 21*
Hungary Repeats Hesz-
leyni Proposal of January
to Deport Illegally
Emigrated Jews in Hun-
gary to Transnistria

*July 22*
Richter-M. Antonescu
Meeting in Rumania

*July 25*
Luther Requests Ribbentrop
to Approach Italy about
its Jews in Western
Occupied Territories

*July 29*
Luther Replies to Eich-
mann Inquiry about
Western Deportations

*July 30*
Second Interministerial
Conference on German
Jewish Property Abroad

*August 4*
Belgian Deportations
Begin

*August 8*
Rumania Agrees to Depor-
tation of its Jews from
Western Occupied
Territories

*August 10*
Luther-Sztojay Meeting
on Hungarian Protests

*August 19*
Ribbentrop Demands Ex-
planation of Luther's
Actions; Lecca in Berlin

*August 21*
Vindication Report Sent
to Ribbentrop

*August 25*
Mussolini Agrees to
Uniform Treatment of
Jews in Croatia

*August 29*
Ribbentrop Rebukes
Luther, Limits His Actions

# 1942 (continued)

*September 9*
German Army Enters
Stalingrad

*September 11*
Luther's Bulgarian
Proposals Rejected by
Ribbentrop

*September 17*
Germany asks Italy to
Remove its Jews from
West or Permit Their
Deportation

*September 18*
Rademacher Recommends
Against Broaching Jewish
Question with Danish
Government

*September 23–24*
Ribbentrop and Hitler
Meet with M. Antonescu
and Pavelic

*September 24*
Ribbentrop Reverses him-
self, Urges Deportations
from Hungary, Bulgaria,
and Denmark

*September 25*
Ribbentrop Permits Luther
to Inquire about Croatia
too; Eichmann Rejects
Heszlenyi Proposal

*October 3*
End of Warsaw
"Resettlement"

*October 5*
Ultimatum to Hungary on
its Jews in Western
Occupied Territories and
Luther Gives Sztojay his
3-point Program

*October 9*
Luther and Beckerle
Confer in Berlin

*October 10*
Italy Refuses German
Options on its Jews in
West

*October 15*
Germany Requests Bul-
garia to Deport its Jews

*October 22*
Luther Urges Ribbentrop
to Confront Italy on
Jewish Question

*October 23*
British Offensive at El
Alamein

*November 11*
Allied Landings in
North Africa

*November 16*
Bulgaria Accepts German
Request

*November 22*
Russian Counter-Attack at
Stalingrad

*November 25*
Norwegian Deportations

*November 30*
Himmler Writes Ribben-
trop over Hungarian
Deportations

*December 4*
Luther Intervenes in
Belgium

*December 14*
Hungary Rejects Luther's
3-point Program

*December 30*
Italian Armistice Com-
mission Objects to French
Interning Jews in Italian
Zone

# 1943

*January*
Foreign Office Arranges
Assignments of Dannecker
and Wisliceny to Bulgaria
and Greece

*January 16*
Germany Repeats Request
that Italy Withdraw its
Jews from West

*January 18*
Resistance in Warsaw
Ghetto Begins

*January 27*
Italy Agrees to Withdraw
its Jews from West

# 1943 (continued)

*January 28*
Luther Supports Best's
Proposals on Denmark

*January 29*
Himmler Writes Ribben-
trop on Italy and Jewish
Question

*February 2*
German Army Sur-
renders at Stalingrad

*February 5*
Luther Promises Swedish
Ambassador the Release
of Bondy Brothers

*February 10*
Luther Arrested

*February 16*
Hahn Reaffirms Luther's
Promise to Swedes

*February 19*
Melchers Objects to
Deportation of Turkish
Jews from West

*February 22*
Dannecker-Belev
Agreement

*February 23*
Ribbentrop asks for
Material on Jewish
Question and Italy

*February 25*
Ribbentrop-Mussolini
Meeting

*March*
D III Repeatedly Tries to
Prevent Jewish Emigra-
tion from Southeast
Europe to Palestine

*March 9*
Ribbentrop Memorandum
to Mackensen

*March 10*
Filov Postpones Deporta-
tions from Old Bulgaria

*March 15*
Deportations from
Greece Begin

*March 15*
Ribbentrop's 2nd Memor-
andum to Mackensen

*March 20–21*
Deportations from
Thrace Begin

*March 22–29*
Deportations From
Macedonia Begin

*April 1*
Inland Replaces Abteilung
Deutschland

*April 4*
Ribbentrop Meets with
Hitler and Boris

*April 17*
Liquidation of Warsaw
Ghetto Begins

*April 17*
Ribbentrop Meets with
Hitler and Horthy

# Abbreviations

The following abbreviations are used in the reference notes.

| | |
|---|---|
| ADAP | *Akten zur Deutschen Aussenpolitik* |
| BDC | Berlin Document Center |
| DGFP | *Documents on German Foreign Policy* |
| IMT | *Trials of the Major War Criminals before the International Military Tribunal* |
| LGNF | *Landgericht* Nürnberg-Fürth |
| NSA | Nürnberg *Staatsarchiv* |
| PA | Politisches Archiv des Auswärtigen Amtes (Political Archives of the Foreign Office) |
| TWC | Trials of the War Criminals before the Nürnberg Military Tribunals |

# Notes

CHAPTER 1

1.  Andreas Hillgruber, "Die Endlösung und das deutsche Ostimperium als Kernstück des rassenideologischen Programms des Nationalsozialismus," *Vierteljahrshefte für Zeitgeschichte*, XX/2 (April 1972), 35; Martin Needler, "Hitler's Anti-Semitism: A Political Appraisal," *Public Opinion Quarterly*, XXIV (winter 1960), 668.

2.  George Mosse, *The Crisis of German Ideology* (New York, 1964), 292.

3.  Robert Koehl, "Feudal Aspects of National Socialism," *The American Political Science Review*, 54 (December 1960), 925-8.

4.  This phrase is borrowed from Karl Schleunes, *The Twisted Road to Auschwitz* (Urbana, 1970). For the evolution of Jewish policy in the prewar period, the author is especially indebted to both Schleunes and Uwe Dietrich Adam, *Judenpolitik im Dritten Reich* (Düsseldorf, 1972). An opposing interpretation, dating Hitler's decision to exterminate the Jews to 1924 (or even 1918), is found in Eberhard Jäckel, *Hitler's Weltanschauung* (Middletown, Connecticut, 1972), and Lucy Dawidowicz, *The War Against the Jews* (New York, 1975).

5.  Schleunes, *The Twisted Road to Auschwitz*, 80-1, 86, 88.

6.  Adam, *Judenpolitik im Dritten Reich*, 42-3.

7.  Helmut Genschel, *Die Verdrängung der Juden aus der Wirtschaft im Dritten Reich* (Göttingen, 1966), 63.

8.  Adam, *Judenpolitik im Dritten Reich*, 124, 148.

9.  Schleunes, *The Twisted Road to Auschwitz*, 258-9.

10. Ibid., 160, 164-5; Genschel, *Die Verdrängung der Juden aus der Wirtschaft im Dritten Reich*, 144, 146.

11. Adam, *Judenpolitik im Dritten Reich*, 181-2.

12. Genschel, *Die Verdrängung der Juden aus der Wirtschaft im Dritten Reich*, 145-6.

13. Both Heinz Höhne, *The Order of the Death's Head* (New York, 1969), 371, and Schleunes, *The Twisted Road to Auschwitz*, 178, emphasize the "rational" approach of the SD Jewish experts in comparison to the Party radicals. Schlomo Aronson, *Heydrich und die Anfänge des SD und Gestapo*. (Berlin, 1967), 275, 278, notes that this group also engaged in "pseudoscientific" and "absurd" research into mythical Jewish world organizations. What distinguished them was not their "rationality" but their early penchant for systematic final solutions on the one hand and their pragmatism on the other.

14. Quoted in Schleunes, *The Twisted Road to Auschwitz*, 204.

15. Ibid., 185–7; Hermann Graml, "Die Auswanderung der Juden aus Deutschland zwischen 1933 and 1939," *Gutachten des Instituts für Zeitgeschichte*, I (Munich, 1958), 79–80.

16. Höhne, *The Order of the Death's Head*, 389–91.

17. Eliahu Ben Elissar, *La Diplomatie du III<sup>e</sup> Reich et les Juifs 1933–1939* (Paris, 1969), 377–99.

18. *Trial of the War Criminals before the Nürnberg Military Tribunals* (Washington, 1949–54), XIII, 129–30.

19. Adam, *Judenpolitik im Dritten Reich*, 230–32.

20. Philip Friedmann, "The Lublin Reservation and the Madagascar Plan: Two Aspects of Nazi Jewish Policy During the Second World War," *YIVO Annual of Jewish Social Science*, VII (1953), 151–77.

21. Jüdische Historische Institut Warschau, *Faschismus—Getto—Massenmord* (Berlin, 1960), 37–8. This evaluation of Heydrich's *Endziel* is, needless to say, not universally shared. For arguments supporting this author's conclusions, see Adam, *Judenpolitik im Dritten Reich*, 248; and H.G. Adler, *Der Verwaltete Mensch* (Tübingen, 1974), xxvii, 107.

22. Adler, *Der Verwaltete Mensch*, 108–10, 126–35.

23. Gerald Reitlinger, *The Final Solution* (New York, 1961), 43–6; Friedmann, "The Lublin Reservation and the Madagascar Plan," 159–161; Adler, *Der Verwaltete Mensch*, 117–8.

24. A detailed account of the Madagascar Plan, in which the Foreign Office was much involved, will appear in chapter 4.

25. Raul Hilberg, *The Destruction of the European Jews* (Chicago, 1967), 83, 86; Adam, *Judenpolitik im Dritten Reich*, 304–5.

26. *Trials of the War Criminals before the Nürnberg Military Tribunals*, XIII, 169. Uwe Dietrich Adam denies the crucial significance of this document and argues that the irreversible decision to extend the killing process to the European Jews was not taken until the fall of 1941. *Judenpolitik im Dritten Reich*, 308–12. However, the testimony of both Adolf Eichmann and Rudolf Höss that they learned of this decision in the summer of 1941 confirms the importance of Göring's letter. Bernd Nellessen, *Der Prozess von Jerusalem* (Düsseldorf, 1964), 246; Rudolf Höss, *Commandant at Auschwitz* (Popular Library, New York, 1959), 173; *Faschismus—Getto—Massenmord*, 374; *Trial of the Major War Criminals before the International Military Tribunal* (Nürnberg, 1947–9) XI, 398.

27. For the euthanasia connection, see Reitlinger, *The Final Solution*, 123–36, and Dawidowicz, *The War Against the Jews*, 131–4.

28. Hilberg, *The Destruction of the European Jews*, 640, 4.

29. Schleunes and Adam in particular.

30. Hilberg, *The Destruction of the European Jews*, 33.

31. Ibid., 643.

32. Ibid., 770, 639, 18.

## CHAPTER 2

1. *Trial of the Major War Criminals before the International Military Tribunal* (Nürnberg, 1947–9), XVII, 107, XXXV, 523, and XL, 466. Hereafter cited as IMT.

2. An agency of the same name existed in the Weimar period, responsible for liaison to the political parties, until its dissolution in 1931 for reasons of economy. For a more detailed account of the subsequent organization, see the author's *"Referat Deutschland, Jewish policy, and the German Foreign Office, 1933–40," Yad Vashem Studies*, XII (1978), 25–54. The most comprehensive study of the Jewish question in international relations during the 1930s is Eliahu Ben Elissar, *La Diplomatie du III<sup>e</sup> Reich et les Juifs 1933–1939* (Paris, 1969).

3.   Politisches Archiv des Auswärtigen Amtes (hereafter cited as PA), Referat Deutschland 42/4, Bülow to Bülow-Schwante, March 23, 1933. T 120/8787/E612176-7.

4.   On Bülow's general reaction to the Nazi regime, see: Peter Krüger and Erich J.C. Hahn, "Der Loyalitätskonflikt des Staatssekretärs Bernhard Wilhelm von Bülow im Frühjahr 1933," *Vierteljahrshefte für Zeitgeschichte*, XX (1972), 376–410.

5.   PA, Referat Deutschland: 42/2, Bülow-Schwante note, March 24, 1933; 42/4, Bülow-Schwante draft and note to Dieckhoff, Köpke, and Gaus, April 19, 1933. T 120/8787/E612175, E612179-82.

6.   PA, Referat Deutschland 42/4, Bülow to Bülow-Schwante and circular initialed by Neurath and Bülow, April 30, 1933. T 120/8787/E612178 and E612192-6.

7.   Wounded in World War I, Bülow-Schwante had secured a Foreign Office post in Vienna, which he resigned in 1919 when discovered committing an indiscretion with an older woman of Austrian society. He rejoined the Foreign Office in 1933 on the urging of cousin Bernhard. As a member of the conservative veteran's organization, the *Stahlhelm*, he was taken into the SA in October of 1933 but barred from full Party membership until 1936. Schumburg received his doctorate in law from Göttingen University in 1923. He joined the Party on January 1, 1934, attracted Himmler's attention while accompanying the latter's trip to Rome in October 1936, and was immediately inducted into the SS as an *Untersturmführer* (Second Lieutenant). On Bülow-Schwante, see Paul Schwarz, *This Man Ribbentrop* (New York, 1943), 73–5; Berlin Document Center (hereafter cited as BDC), Party and SA files; Nürnberg Staatsarchiv (hereafter cited as NSA), Trials of the War Criminals before the Nürnberg Military Tribunal (hereafter cited as TWC), Case XI, Transcript, 9795 (testimony of Bülow-Schwante). On Schumburg, see BDC, Party and SS files.

8.   PA: Referat Deutschland 43/4, Bülow-Schwante circular (drafted by Schumburg), July 11, 1933, T 120/8789/E612445-64; Inland II A/B 39/1, circular on the Jewish question, February 28, 1934, T 120/8788/E612298-311.

9.   Ben Elissar, *La Diplomatie du III^e Reich et les Juifs 1933–1939*, 136–41.

10.   PA, Inland II A/B 34/2: London to Foreign Office, September 27; Bülow-Schwante memorandum, October 16; Neurath to London, October 30, 1934. T 120/K1505/K330158-60, K330148, K330156.

11.   David Yisraeli, "The Third Reich and the Transfer Agreement," *Journal of Contemporary History*, VI/2 (1971), 129–131; Ben Elissar, *La Diplomatie du III^e Reich et les Juifs*, 87–94.

12.   PA, Inland II A/B:39/1, circular on the Jewish question, February 28, 1934; 39/3, Bülow-Schwante to RMI, September 6, 1935. T 120/8788/E612298-311, E612402-3.

13.   PA: Inland II A/B 43/3, Hinrichs memorandum, January 9, and Schumburg note, February 17, 1937, T 120/7055/E524042-4, E524053; Büro des Chefs der AO, vol. 86, Bülow-Schwante memorandum, June 11, 1937, T 120/72/51637-8.

14.   PA, Inland II A/B 43/3, Clodius memorandum, June 11, 1937. T 120/7055/E524070-1.

15.   Ben Elissar, *La Diplomatie du III^e Reich et les Juifs*, 208, 216.

16.   Adam, *Judenpolitik im Dritten Reich*, 115–24, 148.

17.   PA, Inland II A/B 39/3, Röhrecke to Bülow, August 19, 1935. T 120/8788/E612366-7.

18.   PA, Inland II A/B 34/3, Röhrecke to Bülow, August 21, 1935. T 120/8788/E612387-92.

19.   PA, Inland II A/B 347/3, Personalien.

20.   For further details on this affair, see below, chapter 3, p. 25.

21.   PA: Inland II g 169, Frick to high Reich authorities, June 14, 1938, T120/K774/K205601-10; Inland II A/B 27/2, Order for Registration of Jewish Property, April 26, 1938, T 120/K1500/K325188-94.

22.  Genschel, *Die Verdrängung der Juden aus der Wirtschaft im Dritten Reich*, 142; Adam, *Judenpolitik im Dritten Reich*, 162-3.

23.  PA, Inland II A/B 27/2: Bülow-Schwante note, April 23, 1938; Schumburg to Weizsäcker, May 20, 1938. T 120/K1500/K325196-7/, K325235-6.

24.  PA, Inland II A/B 27/2: Weizsäcker to Brinkmann, May 31; Brinkmann to Göring and Foreign Office, June 14; and Göring to Funk, June 17, 1938. T120/K1500/K325267-70, K325288, K325300.

25.  PA, Inland II A/B 27/2: Schumburg to Foreign Minister, June 10; Hinrichs and Schumburg to Foreign Minister (initialed by Weizsäcker), June 30, 1938. T 120/K1500/K328094-5, K328098-100.

26.  Ben Elissar, *La Diplomatie du III<sup>e</sup> Reich et les Juifs*, 303–321; Helmut Heiber, "Die Ausweisung von Juden polnischer Staatsangehörigkeit im Oktober 1938," *Gutachten des Instituts für Zeitgeschichte*, II (Stuttgart, 1966), 90–3.

27.  Ben Elissar, *La Diplomatie du III<sup>e</sup> Reich et les Juifs*, 247, 253.

28.  *Documents on German Foreign Policy 1918–1945* (hereafter cited as DGFP), Series D, V (Washington, 1953), 900–903.

29.  PA, Inland II A/B 45/1, Weizsäcker memorandum, August 2, 1938. T 120/7051/E523520-1.

30.  PA, Inland II A/B 45/1, Schumburg draft, October 21, 1938. T 120/7051/E523554-6.

31.  DGFP, D, V, 905–12; PA, Inland II A/B 45/1: Woermann to Referat Deutschland, November 16; Woermann to London, December 2 and 7, 1938, T 120/7051/E523569, E523616, and E523577.

32.  Ben Elissar, *La Diplomatie du III<sup>e</sup> Reich et les Juifs*, 385–6.

33.  DGFP, D, V, 912–3, 920.

34.  Ibid., 921–2, 925.

35.  Ben Elissar, *La Diplomatie du III<sup>e</sup> Reich et les Juifs*, 389–90.

36.  PA, Inland II A/B 45/1: Rublee to Wohlthat, February 1, and Wohlthat to Rublee, February 2, 1939. T 120/7051/E523631-8.

37.  DGFP, D, V, 938–40.

38.  PA, Inland II g 177, Hinrichs to Ribbentrop, February 7, 1939. T 120/1512/372129.

39.  Ibid., marginalia; DGFP, D, V, 926–33; PA, Inland II g 177, Hinrichs to Heydrich, February 10, 1939, T 120/1512/372133.

40.  PA, Inland II A/B 45/1, Hinrichs to Lischka, March 14, 1939. T 120/7051/E523800-2.

41.  PA, Inland II A/B 56/3, Heinburg memorandum, October 13, with Schumburg note, October 17, 1939.

42.  PA, Inland II A/B 56/3: DNB report, October 22; Schumburg to Weizäcker, October 23, 1939.

43.  PA, Inland II A/B 56/3: DNB Rome, November 11, on report in *Corriere della Sera;* DNB Rome, December 1, on report in *Tevera*; and DNB Amsterdam, December 28, 1939, on report in *Daily Herald*.

44.  *Faschismus—Getto—Massenmord*, 51-4.

45.  PA: Unterstaatssekretär—Judenfrage, DNB Bern, February 16, 1940, on report in *Neue Züriche Zeitung*, T 120/1125/321643; Inland II A/B 42/2, excerpt from *Politiken* of Copenhagen, February 16, and Schumburg to Müller, February 20, 1940.

46.  PA, Inland II A/B 42/2: Weizsäcker to Referat Deutschland, February 16, Bielfeld and Neuwirth to Weizsäcker, February 17; and Schumburg to Weizsäcker, February 26, 1940.

47.  PA, Inland II A/B 42/2: Report of Jewish Aid Committee of General Government March 14; and Schumburg to Weizsäcker, March 21, 1940.

48.   PA, Inland II g 173: Schumburg to Weizsäcker, March 29; and draft note to RSHA, April 2, 1940. T 120/K774/K205691-3.

49.   PA, Inland II g 173: Göring to high Reich authorities, March 21, 1940; and Schumburg to Weizsäcker, April 2, 1940. T 120/K774/K205695-6.

## CHAPTER 3

1..   For a more detailed study of Luther's career, see the author's *"Unterstaatssekretär Martin Luther and the Ribbentrop Foreign Office," Journal of Contemporary History*, XII/2 (April 1977), 313–344. On Luther's early life: BDC, Luther's Party and SA files; Hans-Adolf Jacobsen, *Nationalsozialistische Aussenpolitik 1933–38* (Frankfurt/M., 1968), 279-81, 303-9; Paul Seabury, *The Wilhelmstrasse: A Study of German Diplomats under the Nazi Regime* (Berkeley, 1954), 73–4, 107-8.

2.   Landgericht Nürnberg-Fürth 2 Ks 3/53 (hereafter cited as LGNF), Hauptakten, XI, 1812. Rademacher testimony, 1968.

3.   On Luther's intra-Bureau intrigues, in addition to Jacobsen, see: Paul Kleist, *Zwischen Hitler und Stalin* (Bonn, 1959), 10–15.

4.   PA, Luther Handakten: vol. 23, Luther to Lorenz, September 29, 1942; vol. 22, Luther circular, June 29, 1938. T 120/2223/475435-8, 475428-9.

5.   PA, Luther Handakten, vol. 27/1: Luther to Ribbentrop, July 13, 1938 (T 120/2237/476238-42); draft order creating Referat Partei, September 25, 1938, and duplicate of November, 1938 (T 120/2237/476236-7); and Luther to Ribbentrop, November 2, 1938.

6.   On the embezzlement affair, in addition to Seabury, see: Erich Kordt, *Wahn und Wirklichkeit* (Stuttgart, 1948), 373.

7.   PA, Luther Handakten, vol. 39, Kriebel circular, May 14, 1940. T 120/1920/428241-2.

8.   PA, Luther Handakten, vol. 3, Luther to Dörnberg, February 23, 1940.

9.   PA, Luther Handakten, vol. 3, Luther memorandum, April 16, 1940.

10.   PA: Inland II A/B 347/3, Geschäftsplan, May 7, 1940; Luther Handakten, vol. 8, Schröder circular.

11.   For the details of Luther's expansionism in the Foreign Office, the reader is again referred to the author's *"Unterstaatsekretär Martin Luther and the Ribbentrop Foreign Office,"* 322–4.

12.   Siegfried Kasche to Croatia, Adolf Heinz Beckerle to Bulgaria, and Dietrich von Jagow to Hungary, which added to Manfred von Killinger in Rumania and Hans Ludin in Slovakia, brought the SA contingent to five.

13.   PA, Luther Handakten, vol. 7, Kieser to Rademacher, July 21, 1941.

14.   BDC, Walter Büttner Party and SS files; PA, Luther Handakten, vol. 27/1, List of June 20, 1938.

15.   LGNF 2 Ks 3/53, Hauptakten, XI, 1945 (Büttner testimony); Jacobsen, *NS-Aussenpolitik*, 280.

16.   PA, Luther Handakten, vol. 18, Luther to Jury, December 20, 1941. T 120/2211/474492-4.

17.   PA, Luther Handakten, vol. 10, 11, and 13, miscellaneous correspondence about Garben and Müller.

18.   Ulrich von Hassell, *The Von Hassell Diaries* (New York, 1947), 290; Kleist, *Zwischen Hitler und Stalin*, 12; NSA, TWC, Case XI, Transcript, 9761, Steengracht testimony; Ernst von Weizsäcker, *Memoirs of Ernst von Weizsäcker* (Chicago, 1951), 272; Walter Schellenberg, *The Labyrinth* (New York, 1956), 272.

19.   Schellenberg, *The Labyrinth*, 246.

20. Rudolf Rahn, *Ruheloses Leben* (Duesseldorf, 1949), 142.

21. Schellenberg, *The Labyrinth*, 246.

22 PA, Luther Handakten, vol. 10, Luther to Krümmer, August 31 and September 10, 1942. T 120/1136/324079-83.

23. PA, Luther Handakten vol. 4, Luther to Schröder, February 24, 1940.

24. PA, Luther Handakten, vol. 4, Luther to Weizsäcker, August 29, 1940, and Weizsäcker marginal note.

25. PA, Luther Handakten, vol. 27/2, Luther to Ribbentrop, May 6, 1941. T 120/2237/276206-7.

26. PA, Luther Handakten, vol. 9, Luther circular, April 28, 1942.

27. Reitlinger, *The Final Solution*, 74.

28. Urteil in dem Strafverfahren gegen Franz Rademacher. Das Schwurgericht bei dem Landgericht Nürnberg-Fürth, 85 Ks 4/50, p. 3–4. Hereafter cited as: 1st Rademacher Judgment.

29. LGNF 2 Ks 3/53, Beiakten, III, Part 1. Rademacher Foreign Office personnel file (NG-2447) and BDC party file (NG-2458).

30. Urteil in dem Strafverfahren gegen Franz Rademacher. Das Schwurgericht bei dem Landericht Bamberg, 2 Ks 3/53, p. 9. Hereafter cited as: 2nd Rademacher Judgment.

31. LGNF 2 Ks 3/53, Beiakten, III, Part 1, 12. Rademacher interrogation, September 23, 1947.

32. 1st Rademacher Judgment, 3.

33. LGNF 2 Ks 3/53, Beiakten, III, Part 1, 3. Rademacher interrogation, September 23, 1947.

34. Ibid.

35. Author's interview with Erster Staatsanwalt Dr. Klarmann, Landgericht Bamberg, May 10, 1973.

36. LGNF 2 Ks 3/53, Beiakten, III, Part 1, 4. Rademacher interrogation, September 23, 1947.

37. PA, Inland II A/B 55/2, Wurm to Rademacher, June 5, 1940. T 120/2029/444597.

38. PA, Inland II A/B 347/1, Library inventory, July 10, 1941.

39. LGNF 2 Ks 3/53, Beiakten, III, Part 1: NG-2879 (Rademacher to Personnel Division, August 1, 1940) and p. 37–8 (Rademacher interrogation, October 14, 1947).

40. PA, Inland II A/B 347/3, Rademacher to Jahn, January 31, 1941.

41. PA, Inland II A/B 350/3, Rademacher note, July 5, 1941.

42. BDC, Todenhöfer Party and SA files; PA: Luther Handakten, vol. 3, Luther to Gottfriedsen, August 15, 1940; Inland II A/B 350/3, Luther to Schröder, August 15, 1940.

43. Einstellungsverfügung in dem Ermittlungsverfahren 24 Js 3/69 (Z) Staatsanwalt Köln gegen Dr. Herbert Müller-Roschach, p. 3.

44. Ibid., 4.

45. PA, Inland II A/B 347/3: Heydrich to Luther, February 18; Rademacher memorandum, March 9; and Luther to Heydrich, March 23, 1942.

46. PA, Luther Handakten vol. 12, Weege to Luther, February 26, 1942.

47. PA, Luther Handakten, vol. 12, Weiler to Luther, June 15, 1942.

48. LGNF 2 Ks 3/53, Hauptakten, III, 347. Klingenfuss interrogation, February 4, 1949.

49. LGNF 2 Ks 3/53, Beiakten, III, Part 4, 3–5. Klingenfuss interrogation, November 3, 1947.

50. LGNF 2 Ks 3/53, Beiakten, III, Part 4, NG-3569. Klingenfuss affidavit, November 11, 1947.

51. LGNF 2 Ks 3/53, Hauptakten, I, 126. Report of Office of Chief of Counsel for War Crimes, July 26, 1948.

52. LGNF 2 Ks 3/53, Beiakten, III, Part 4, 6. Klingenfuss interrogation, November 3, 1947.

53. The most detailed vita of Hahn is found in: Anklage gegen Fritz-Gebhardt von Hahn und Adolf Heinz Beckerle, Js 2/63, Landgericht Frankfurt, pp. 22–39. A copy of this indictment is at the Landgericht Nürnberg-Fürth, listed as: Beiakte zur 2 Ks 3/53, IV, Parts 1 and 2. A shorter vita is contained in: Urteil in dem Strafverfahren gegen Fritz-Gebhardt von Hahn, Landgericht Frankfurt, Ks 2/67, pp. 2–9. A copy is at the Political Archives of the German Foreign Office in Bonn.

## CHAPTER 4

1. The evolution of the idea of Madagascar as a resettlement area for European Jews has been exhaustively treated by three generations of scholars: Eugene Hevesi, "Hitler's Plan for Madagascar," *Contemporary Jewish Record,* IV (1941), 381–95; Philip Friedmann. "The Lublin Reservation and the Madagascar Plan: Two Aspects of Nazi Jewish Policy During the Second World War," *YIVO Annual of Jewish Social Science,* VII (1953), 151–77; and Leni Yahil, "Madagascar—Phantom of a Solution for the Jewish Question," *Jews and Non-Jews in Eastern Europe 1918–1945,* ed. by Bela Vago and George L. Mosse (New York, 1974), 315–34.

2. PA, Inland II A/B 347/3, Rademacher memorandum, "Gedanken über die Arbeiten und Aufgaben des Ref. D III," June 3, 1940.

3. PA, Inland II g 177. T 120/1512/372108.

4. PA, Inland II g 177, Rademacher memorandum, "Bisherige Entwicklung des Madagaskar-Plans des Referats D III," August 30, 1940, T 120/1512/372050-2; NSA, Zz 431, Nr. 1, Rademacher affidavit, July 20, 1948. On Beamish, see Adler, *Der Verwaltete Mensch,* 69.

5. PA, Inland II A/B 55/2, Wurm to Rademacher, June 5, 1940; Article "Wohin mit den Juden?"; and Rademacher to Wurm, June 12, 1940. T 120/2029/444597-600.

6. PA, Inland II g 177, Rademacher memorandum, August 30, 1940, T 120/1512/372050-2; and *Akten zur Deutschen Aussenpolitik,* (hereafter cited as ADAP), Series D, X, 92–4 (Rademacher memorandum, "Die Judenfrage im Friedensvertrage," July 3, 1940).

7. Galeazzo Ciano, *The Ciano Diaries 1939–43* (Garden City, N.Y., 1947), 265–6; Paul Schmidt, *Hitler's Interpreter* (New York, 1951), 178.

8. PA, Inland II g 177, Heydrich to Ribbentrop, June 24, 1940. T 120/1512/372047.

9. Leni Yahil, "Madagascar—Phantom of a Solution for the Jewish Question," 321.

10. PA, Inland II g 177, Rademacher memorandum, August 30, 1940. T 120/1512/372050-2.

11. ADAP, D, X, 92.

12. PA, Inland II g 177, Rademacher memorandum, "Plan zur Lösung der Judenfrage," July 2, 1940. T 120/1512/372104.

13. ADAP, D, X, 94.

14. One example: PA Inland II g 184, Rademahcer to Copenhagen, July 22, 1940. T 120/2707/D531294.

15. PA, Inland II A/B 35/2, Wurm to Rademacher, August 3, 1940.

16. PA, Inland II A/B 35/2. Memorandum of Dr. Burgdörfer, July 17, 1940. T 120/3071/D612577-80.

17. PA, Inland II g 177, Memorandum of Dr. Schumacher. T 120/1512/372099-102.

18. PA, Inland II g 177, Excerpt from *Meyer's Lexicon.* T 120/1512/372096-7.

19.    PA, Inland II g 177, Rademacher memorandum, "Gedanken über die Grüdung einer intereuropäischen Bank für die Verwertung des Judenvermögens in Europa," August 12, 1940. T 120/1512/372106.

20.    PA, Inland II g 177, RSHA Madagaskar Projekt. T 120/1512/372056-71.

21.    PA, Inland II g 177, Marginal note by Rademacher, August 2, 1940. T 120/1512/372108.

22.    ADAP, D, X, 389.

23.    PA, Inland II g 177, Rademacher memorandum, August 30, 1940. T 120/1512/372050-2.

24.    Bernhard Lösener, "Als Rassereferent im Reichsministerium des Innern," *Vierteljahrshefte für Zeitgeschichte*, IX/3 (July, 1961), 296.

25.    PA, Inland II A/B 54/2, Note of Ref. Deutschland to Kult.

26.    PA, Inland II A/B 45/la: Woermann note, September 30, 1939; Müller to Foreign Office, October 17, 1939; Müller to Foreign Office, May 21, 1940; and Luther to D III, May 27, 1940.

27.    PA, Inland II A/B 45/la, Rademacher memorandum, July 10, 1940.

28.    PA, Inland II A/B 47/2 I.

29.    Numerous examples can be cited from the files of Inland II A/B 45/la and 45/2, as well as the refusal to permit the transit of Slovak Jews across Germany in Gesandtschaft Pressburg 332/2, Eichmann to Rademacher, May 5, 1941, T 120/K1646/K403725.

30.    PA, Inland II g 182, Schellenberg circular, May 20, 1941. T 120/K804/K205120-3.

31.    PA, Inland II A/B 45/la, Weintz (RF-SS) to D III, September 25, 1940.

33.    Krausnick cites Schellenberg's order of May 20, 1941, which contains the ominous phrase "in view of the doubtless imminent final solution of the Jewish question," as proof that Hitler had at this time decided on the Final Solution for all European Jews. Helmut Krausnick, "The Persecution of the Jews," *Anatomy of the SS State* (New York, 1965), 67. This ignores the fact that the phrase had first appeared in September, 1940, and that Schellenberg's circular did not create any new policy of preventing Jewish emigration from occupied territories, but rather merely affirmed a policy which had been consistently carried out since the spring of 1940. Thus neither the phraseology nor the policy was new. Hitler may indeed have decided on the Final Solution at this time, but there is nothing in Schellenberg's letter to prove this.

33.    PA, Inland II g 189, Welck to Foreign Office, October 28, 1940. T 120/K773/K204450.

34.    PA, Inland II g 189, Heydrich to Luther, October 29, 1940. T 120/K773/K204459-60.

35.    ADAP, D, XI (Bonn, 1964), 376. Todenhöfer to Luther, October 31, 1940.

36.    PA, Inland II g 189, anonymous report forwarded from Gaus to Luther, November 3, 1940. T 120/K773/K204453-4. For the earlier anonymous letter. *Referat Deutschland* 42/2, Schumburg to Müller, February 23, 1940.

37.    PA, Inland II g 189, Rademacher to Kramarz, November 9, 1940. T 120/K773/K204461.

38.    PA, Inland II g 189, Hencke to D III, November 19, 1940; and Grote to D III, November 20, 1940. T 120/K773/K204468-9, K204464.

39.    PA, Inland II g 189: Rademacher to Luther, November 21, 1940; and Rademacher draft. T 120/K773/K204446-7, K204474.

40.    PA, Inland II g 189, Sonnleithner to Luther, November 22, 1940. T 120/K773/K204473.

41.    PA, Inland II A/B 45/la: Hencke to Foreign Office, November 30, 1940; Grote to D III, December 12, 1940; OKH to Foreign Office, January 6, 1941; and military administration to OKH, December 18, 1940.

42.    PA, Inland II A/B 45/2, Rademacher to RSHA, January 15, 1941, and handwritten note.

43.    PA, Inland II A/B 45/2: OKH to Foreign Office, February 10 and 27; Welck to D III, February 14, and 21; Rademacher to RSHA, January 15, February 20 and 27, 1941.

44.    PA, Inland II A/B 45/2: Sipo-SDIV D 6 to Luther, February 28, 1941; Rademacher to RSHA, March 5 and 20, 1941; and Sipo-SD IV D 4 to Luther, March 22, 1941.

45.    PA, Inland II A/B 45/2, OKH to D III, May 13, 1941.

46.    PA, Inland II A/B 45/2: Welck to D III, June 4, 1941; Todenhöfer to Sipo-SD, June 11; Sipo-SD IV D 4 to D III, July 7, 1941.

47.    The Interior Ministry was as uninformed as the Foreign Office. PA, Inland II g 189, Rademacher to Luther, November 22, 1941. T 120/K773/K204446-7.

48.    PA, Inland II g 189, New York Times clippings. T 120/K773/K204607.

49.    PA, Inland II A/B 45/1a, Wülisch to D III, August 7, 1940.

50.    PA, Inland II A/B 45/2: Press clipping from Time; and anonymous letter, February 15, 1941.

51.    PA, Inland II g 169, Luther to RMI, May 16, 1940. T 120/K774/K205630.

52.    Martin Broszat, "Das deutsch-slowakische Verhältnis 1939/40 und sein Rückwirkung auf die slowakische Judenpolitik," Gutachten des Instituts für Zeitgeschichte (Munich, 1958), I, 223–5; Yeshayahu Jelinek, "Slovakia's Internal Policy and the Third Reich," Central European History, IV/3 (1971), 243–8; Yeshayahu Jelinek, "Storm-troopers in Slovakia: the Rodobranna and the Hlinka Guard," Journal of Contemporary History, VI/3 (1971), 108–9; Norman Rich, Hitler's War Aims, II, The Establishment of the New Order (New York, 1974), 55–63.

53.    PA, Luther Handakten, vol. 32, Killinger to Luther, August 1 and 6, 1940. T 120/4442/E086118 and E086197.

54.    PA, Luther Handakten, vol. 32: Adviser salary list, August 26, 1940; and Luther to Killinger, October 15, 1940. T 120/4442/E086118 and E086040-1.

55.    Hermann Graml, "Der deutsche Gesandte in der Slowakei," Gutachten des Instituts für Zeitgeschichte (Stuttgart, 1966), II, 340.

56.    Ibid.

57.    PA, Luther Handakten, vol. 2: Ribbentrop to OKW, August 3, 1940; and Führer Order, November 20, 1940, T 120/2143/468437-8, 468445; and Norman Rich, Hitler's War Aims, II, 200–205.

58.    BDC, Abetz SS-file.

59.    PA, Inland II g 189, Abetz to Foreign Minister, August 20, 1940. T 120/K773/K204577.

60.    PA, Inland II g 189, Luther and Rademacher to Personal Staff of RF-SS and to Hoppe, August 23, 1940. T 120/K773/K204577.

61.    PA, Inland II g 189, Rademacher note, August 31, 1940. T 120/K773/K204571.

62.    PA, Inland II g 189, Heydrich to Luther, September 20, 1940. T 120/K773/K204567-8.

63.    PA, Inland II g 189, Luther to Abetz, September 28, 1940. T 120/K773/K204565-6.

64.    PA, Inland II g 189, Schleier to Foreign Office, November 9, 1940. T 120/K773/K204561.

65.    PA, Inland II g 189, Luther to Abetz, November 16, 1940. T 120/K773/K204564.

66.    PA, Inland II g 189, Gaus to Rademacher, December 19, 1940. T 120/K773/K204548-9.

67.    PA, Inland II A/B 37/1: Schmid to Weizsäcker, February 27, 1941; Weizsäcker to Schmid, March 19, 1941. T 120/3069/D612057-8, D612061.

68.    PA, Inland II A/B 37/2, Rademacher note, February 15, 1940. T 120/3669/D612105-6.

69.    PA, Inland II A/B 37/2: Freytag note, February 27, 1941; Woermann memorandum, March 1, 1941. T 120/3069/D612107-110.

70.    PA, Inland II A/B 37/2: Rademacher to Luther, March 4; Luther memorandum, March 18, 1941. T 120/3069/D612111-2, D612063-4.

71.    PA: Inland II A/B 26/4, Luther to RSHA, June 16, 1941, T 120/K785/K208095; Inland II A/B 67/5, Todenhöfer to Prague, June, 1941.


CHAPTER 5


1.    LGNF 2 Ks 3/53, Hauptakten, II, 288–9. Affidavit of Dr. Emil Hoffmann.

2.    PA, Inland II g 202: Ludin to D II, August 7, 1941; and Killinger to D II, August 7, 1941. T 120/2251/478108, 478112.

3.    PA, Inland II g 202, Luther to Heydrich, August 8, 1941. T 120/2251/478113–5.

4.    LGNF 2 Ks 3/53, Beiakten, Ia, Part I, 142-4, Himmler-Ribbentrop Agreement, August 8, 1941; and PA, Inland II g 202, Heydrich to Luther, August 23, 1941, T 120/2251/478117-8.

5.    PA, Inland II g 431, Einsatzgruppen Reports, Nr. 1 + 2, T 120/465/226362-441; Martin Broszat, "Das dritte Reich und die rumänische Judenpolitik," *Gutachten des Instituts für Zeitgeschichte*, I, 146.

6.    PA, Inland II g 203, Killinger to D III, August 6, 1941. T 120/K773/K204987.

7.    ADAP, D, XIII, Part 1 (Göttingen, 1970), 264; PA, Inland II g 203, Killinger to D III, August 26, 1941, T 120/K773/K204962-3; M. Broszat, "Das dritte Reich und die rumänische Judenpolitik," 150.

8.    PA, Inland II g 203, Ritter to Luther, August 27, 1941. T 120/K773/K204965-6.

9.    PA, Inland II g 202, Tighina Agreement, August 30, 1941. T 120/6737/E510829-34.

10.    PA, Inland II g 202, Killinger to Luther, September 1, 1941. T 120/2251/478119-20.

11.    PA, Inland II g 202, Picot to Streckenbach, September 6 and 9, 1941; Picot note, September 16, 1941. T 120/2251/478124-6, 478128.

12.    *Trials of the War Criminals before the Nürnberg Military Tribunals*, XIII, 443.

13.    PA, Politische Abteilung IX 93, Hübner to Weizsäcker, September 5, 1941.

14.    PA, Inland II A/B 54/1, Montevideo to D III, September 2, 1941.

15.    PA, Inland II g 172: Rademacher to Luther, August 21, 1941; Luther note, August 22, 1941; Luther memorandum to Ribbentrop, August 22, 1941. T 120/K796/K210292-3, K210277-8.

16.    PA, Inland II g 172, Rademacher report, September 8, 1941. T 120/K796/K210287-8.

17.    PA, Inland II g 172, Büro RAM to Luther, August 31, 1941. T 120/K796/K210284.

18.    PA, Inland II A/B 42/3, Anonymous letter; Gaus to Rademacher, September 1, 1941; Picot to Sipo-SD IV, September 5, 1941; Eichmann to D II, November 5, 1941; Eichmann to D III, December 3, 1941.

19.    PA, Inland II g 172: Weizsäcker to Luther, September 15, 1941; Luther to Weizsäcker, September 19 and 22, 1941; Weizsäcker marginal note, September 24, 1941. T 120/K796/K210253, K210262-3.

20.    Norman Rich, *Hitler's War Aims*, II, 264–8, 282–5; PA, Inland II g 194, Weizsäcker to Abteilung Deutschland, November 22, 1941, T 120/K773/K205117; and ADAP, D, XIII, Part 2, 475–6.

21.    PA: Gesandtschaft Belgrad 62/6, Portiz note, May 7, 1941, T 120/K1597/K390686; Inland II A/B 65/4, Rademacher memorandum, May 22, 1941.

22.    PA, Inland II A/B 65/4, Benzler to Foreign Office, August 14, 1941.

23.    LGNF 2 Ks 3/53, Hauptakten, II, 254, Affidavit of Helmut Triska; and NG-3354, Rademacher statement written in Nürnberg, July 30,1948.

24. 2nd Rademacher Judgment, 43.
25. ADAP, D, XIII, Part 1, 378.
26. Ibid., 386.
27. 2nd Rademacher Judgment, 38.
28. LGNF 2 Ks 3/53, Hauptakten: II, 266 (Benzler affidavit, 1949); and XI, 1911 (Benzler testimony, 1968). The author is aware that his interpretation of Turner's behavior is not shared by other historians. For example, Norman Rich characterizes Turner as "a doctrinaire Nazi who . . . was anxious to inaugurate policies in line with Nazi party principles. . . ." *Hitler's War Aims*, II, 283-4. However, Benzler had no self-serving purpose in his testimony of both 1949 and 1968 in crediting Turner with the initiative to get the Serbian Jews out of danger, as Benzler was not on trial and Turner was dead. I have thus accepted Benzler's statements, particularly as they are reinforced by Rademacher's report that Turner urged upon him as well the deportation of the Serbian Jews to Rumania.
29. 2nd Rademacher Judgment, 44.
30. NG-3354, Rademacher statement written in Nuernberg, July 30, 1948.
31. PA, Inland II g 194, Luther to Belgrade, September 10, 1941. T 120/K773/K205193.
32. PA, Inland II g 194, Benzler to Foreign Office, September 12, 1941, and Luther marginalia. T 120/K773/K205189.
33. NG-3354, Rademacher statement written in Nürnberg, July 30, 1948.
34. PA, Inland II g 194, Rademacher marginalia, September 13, 1941, on Benzler letter of September 12, 1941. T 120/K773/K205189.
35. PA, Inland II g 194, Rademacher to Luther, September 13, 1941. T 120/K773/K205188.
36. PA, Inland II g 194, Luther to Belgrade, September 16, 1941. T 120/K773/K205187.
37. PA, Inland II g 194, Benzler to Ribbentrop, September 28, 1941. T 120/K773/K205184-5.
38. 2nd Rademacher Judgment, 50.
39. PA, Inland II g 194, Luther to Ribbentrop, October 2, 1941. T 120/K773/K205180-1.
40. PA, Inland II g 194, Büro RAM to Luther, October 3, 1941. T 120/K773/K205175.
41. PA, Inland II g 194, Luther to Belgrade, October 4, 8, and 15, 1941. T 120/K773/K205171, K205173-4.
42. LGNF Hauptakten, VIII, 1262. Rademacher interrogation, October, 1966.
43. ADAP, D, XIII, Part 2, 570-2.
44. The following account of Rademacher's Belgrade trip is based upon his own report, printed in: ADAP, D, XIII, Part 2, 570-2, and on the 2nd Rademacher Judgment, 53-8, unless otherwise indicated.
45. 2nd Rademacher Judgment, 41.
46. Ibid., 76.
47. Norbert Müller and Martin Zöller, "Okkupationsverbrechen der Faschistischen Wehrmacht gegenüber der serbischen Bevölkerung im Herbst 1941," *Zeitschrift für Militärgeschichte*, IX, 1970, 712.
48. Ibid., 714.
49. LGNF 2 Ks 3/53, Beiakten, II, Part 1-3, 96-7. Turner to Hildebrandt, October 17, 1941.
50. 2nd Rademacher Judgment, 71.
51. *The Von Hassell Diaries*, 224.
52. LGNF 2 Ks 3/53, Hauptakten, V, no page number, letter of Karl-Johann von Schönebeck, February 13, 1952.
53. LGNF 2 Ks 3/53 Hauptakten, X, 1792. Interrogation of Werner Picot, April, 1964.

54.   PA, Inland II g 194, Rademacher supplement, November 15, 1941, and Weizsäcker handwritten notation, November 19, 1941. T 120/K773/K205178.

55.   PA, Inland II g 194, Weizsäcker to Abteilung Deutschland, November 22, 1941. T 120/K773/K205177.

56.   PA, Inland II g 194, Luther to Weizsäcker, December 12, 1941. T 120/K773/K205163-4.

57.   PA, Gesandtschaft Belgrade 62/6: Benzler to Zagreb, October 29, 1941; Troll to Belgrade, November 3, 1941. T 120/K1597/K390752-3.

58.   ADAP, D, XIII, Part 2, 805.

59.   PA, Inland II g 177, Göring to Heydrich, July 31, 1941. T 120/1512/372045.

60.   Bernd Nellessen, Der Prozess von Jerusalem (Düsseldorf, 1964), 246.

61.   PA, Inland II A/B 47/1, Eichmann to D III, August 28, 1941.

62.   PA, Gesandtschaft Pressburg 312/5: Rademacher to Bratislava, October 4, 1941; and Ludin to D III, October 22, 1941. T 120/K1644/K403480–1.

63.   PA, Politische Abteilung III 245, Luther memorandum, October 13, 1941. T 120/3762/E040598–9.

64.   PA, Politische Abteilung III 245, Luther memorandum, October 17, 1941. T 120/3762/E040596-7.

65.   PA, Inland II A/B 59/3, Wurm to Rademacher, October 23, 1941.

66.   PA, Inland II g 174: Rademacher to Luther, October 27, 1941, and Luther marginalia; Rademacher to Weizsäcker, October 29, 1941. T 120/703/261459-60.

67.   PA, Inland II g 174: Killinger to Foreign Office, November 13, 1941; Kasche to Foreign Office, November 21, 1941. T 120/703/261455 and 261447.

68.   PA, Gesandtschaft Pressburg 312/5, memorandum to Ludin, December 2, 1941. T 120/K1655/K403488.

69.   PA, Inland II g 174, Ludin to D III, December 4, 1941. T 120/703/261445-6.

70.   ADAP, E, I (Göttingen, 1969), 198–9.

71.   LGNF 2 Ks 3/53, Hauptakten, V, 666 and 742.

72.   PA, Inland II A/B 46/1, Müller to D III, August 21, 1941.

73.   PA, Gesandtschaft Lissabon 171/9, D V to Lisbon, October 4, 1941. T 120/K1605/K391681.

74.   PA, Inland II A/B 46/2 I: Huene to D III, November 12, 1941; and Rademacher note, November 14, 1941.

75.   PA, Inland II g 196, Luther to Müller, November 5, 1941. T 120/K813/K205224-5.

76.   PA, Inland II g 189, Schleier to Foreign Office, October 30, 1941. T 120/4643/E209332.

77.   PA, Inland II g 189: Rademacher to Freytag, October 31, and Schleier to Foreign Office, November 4, 1941, T 120/4643/E209327-8; Weizsäcker to Ribbentrop, November 1, Bruns to Weizsäcker, November 2, and Luther to Abetz, November 5, 1941, T 120/4643/209329-31, E 209323-4; Rademacher hand-written note, November 13, 1941, T 120/K773/K205220.

78.   PA, Inland II g 172, Luther to Ribbentrop, November 3, 1941. T 120/K796/K210249.

79.   PA, Inland II g 172, Memoranda by Rödiger, November 14; Freytag, November 17; Davidsen, November 21; and Mohrat, November 25, 1941. T 120/K796/K210241-5.

80.   ADAP, E, I, 120.

81.   PA, Inland II g 174, Herbert Müller to Eichmann, January 22, 1942. T 120/703/261439-40.

82.   PA, Inland II g 172, Rademacher to RSHA, March 5, 1942. T 120/K796/K210236.

83.   PA, Inland II g 179, Lohse to Ostministerium, August 6, 1941. T 120/5117/E295676.

84. PA, Inland II g 179, Albrecht memorandum, November 19, 1941. T 120/5117/E295672/4.

85. PA, Inland II g 183, Memorandum on Popov reception, November 26, 1941. T 120/2330/486176-85.

86. PA, Inland II g 183, Rademacher draft for Luther memorandum, December 4, 1941. T 120/2330/486167-9.

87. PA, Inland II g 183, Albrecht memorandum, December 11, 1941. T 120/2330/486195-8.

88. ADAP, E, I, 132–3.

89. This phrase belongs to Dr. Robert W. M. Kempner. Interview, January 24, 1974.

90. PA, Inland II g 431, Müller to Ribbentrop, October 30, 1941. T 120/465/226349.

91. PA, Inland II g 431, Picot covering letter, November 15, 1941. T 120/465/226352.

92. PA, Inland II g 431, Report Nr. 1. T 120/465/226362-404.

93. PA, Inland II g 431, Report Nr. 2. T 120/465/226405-441.

94. PA, Inland II g 431, Report Nr. 3. T 120/465/226442-87.

95. PA, Inland II g 431, Report Nr. 5. T 120/465/226527-60.

96. PA, Inland II g 173: Richter and Killinger report, October 23, 1941; Jagow to D III, November 14, 1941; Rademacher to Jagow, November 19, 1941. T 120/K773/K205152-3, K205147-8.

97. PA, Inland II g 431, Heydrich to Ribbentrop, November 25, 1941. T 120/465/226561.

98. PA, Inland II g 431, Report Nr. 6. T 120/465/226562-601.

99. PA, Inland II g 431, Bruns to D II, December 8, 1941. T 120/465/226607.

100. PA, Inland II g 431, Luther to Ribbentrop, December 10, 1941. T 120/465/226602-6.

101. PA, Inland II g 431, Hahn report, December 10, 1941. T 120/465/226354-60.

102. PA, Inland II g 431, Circulation sheet. T 120/465/226608.

103. PA, Inland II g 431, Circulation sheet. T 120/465/226353.

104. PA, Inland II g 431, Picot to Weizsäcker, January 8, 1942, and Weizsäcker marginalia. T 120/465/226351.

105. PA, Inland II g 431, Heydrich to Ribbentrop, January 16, 1942. T 120/465/226656, 226696.

106. PA, Inland II g 431, Report Nr. 7. T 120/465/226657-94.

107. PA, Inland II g 431, Report Nr. 8 T 120/465/226697-719.

108. PA, Inland II g 431, Circulation sheets. T 120/465/226695, 226720.

109. PA, Inland II g 431: Müller to Ribbentrop, March 3, 1942; and Lohmann to D II, March 11, 1942. T 120/465/226721, 226743.

110. PA, Inland II g 431, Report Nr. 10. T 120/465/226722-42.

111. PA, Inland II g 431, Luther summary, March 14, 1942. T 120/465/226745-8.

112. PA, Inland II g 431, Heydrich to Ribbentrop, April 23, 1942. T 120/465/226749.

113. PA, Inland II g 431, Report Nr. 11. T 120/465/226750-75.

114. PA, Inland II g 431, Circulation sheet. T 120/465/226777.

115. LGNF 2 Ks 3/53, Hauptakten, X, 1641-3. NG-1944, Lösener affidavit.

116. PA, Inland II g 177, Heydrich to Luther, November 29, 1941, and Luther and Rademacher marginalia. T 120/1512/372043-4.

117. PA, Inland II g 177, Unsigned memorandum, "Wünschen und Ideen." T 120/1512/372043-4.

118. PA, Inland II g 177, Heydrich to Luther, January 8, 1942. T 120/1512/372039.

119. ADAP, E, I, 267-75.

120. Robert M. W. Kempner, *Das Dritte Reich im Kreuzverhör* (Munich, 1969), 188-9.

121. PA, Inland II g 177, Luther to Rintelen, August 21, 1942. T 120/1512/371996-2007.

122. Nellessen, *Der Prozess von Jerusalem*, 206.

123.   ADAP, E, I, 403.

124.   PA, Inland II g 177: Woermann to Rademacher, February 14, 1942. Rademacher to Luther, February 24, 1942; Luther handwritten notation, February 26, 1942. T 120/3910/E050132-3.

125.   PA, Inland II g 177, Luther to Rintelen, August 21, 1942. T 120/1512/371996-2007.

126.   PA, Inland II g 179: Leibbrandt to Foreign Office, January 22, 1942; and draft ordinance. T 120/5117/E295649-68.

127.   PA, Inland II g 179, Herbert Müller hand-written notation, January 27, 1942. T 120/5117/E295651.

128.   PA, Inland II g 179, Rödiger memorandum, January 27, 1942. T 120/5117/E295672/3.

129.   PA, Inland II g 179: Protocol of the conference of January 29, 1942; Herbert Müller report, January 30, 1942. T 120/5117/E295643–8, E295672/1.

130.   PA, Inland II g 177, Heydrich to Luther, January 26, 1942, and Luther marginalia, February 28, 1942. T 120/1512/372023.

131.   PA, Inland II g 177, Rademacher memorandum, March 7, 1942. T 120/1512/372020-1.

132.   LGNF 2 Ks 3/53, Hauptakten: II, 254 (Triska affidavit, 1949); II, 244 (Büttner affidavit, 1949); XI, 1947 (Kieser testimony, 1968).

133.   LGNF 2 Ks 3/53, Hauptakten, II, 207, 212, 220. Rademacher interrogation, 1948.

134.   LGNF 2 Ks 3/53, Hauptakten, III, 332. Rademacher written statement, 1949.

135.   LGNF 2 Ks 3/53, Hauptakten, II, 188. Rademacher interrogation, 1948.

136.   LGNF 2 Ks 3/53, Hauptakten: II, 241 (Schröder affidavit, 1949); II, 245 (Büttner affidavit, 1949); XI, 1890, 1892 (Gödde testimony, 1968); XI, 1946 (Büttner testimony, 1968).

137.   LGNF 2 Ks 3/53, Hauptakten, II, 241 (Schröder affidavit, 1949) and 244 (Büttner affidavit, 1949); and NSA, Zz 431, Nr. 3 (Schröder affidavit, 1948).

138.   LGNF 2 Ks 3/53: Hauptakten, IX, 1439 (Klingenfuss interrogation, 1967) and 1870 (Klingenfuss testimony, 1968); and Beitakten, III, Part 4, 6, (Klingenfuss affidavit, 1947).

139.   LGNF 2 Ks 3/53, Hauptakten: II, 241; and XI, 1968.

140.   Author's interview with Dr. Robert M. W. Kempner, January 24, 1974.

141.   LGNF 2 Ks 3/53: Hauptakten, XI, 1867 (Klingenfuss testimony, 1968); and Beiakten, III, Part 4, 8 (Klingenfuss interrogation, 1947).

142.   PA, Inland II A/B 347/3, Rademacher to Schröder, March 24, 1942.

143.   Einstellungsverfügung in dem Ermittlungsverfahren 24 Js 3/69 (Z) Staatsanwalt Köln gegen Dr. Herbert Müller-Roschach, 129–30. Hereafter cited as: Müller Investigation.

144.   Ibid., 131, 133.

145.   PA, Inland II A/B 42/2, D III to RSHA and Propaganda Ministry, initialed by Herbert Müller, November 25, 1941.

146.   PA, Inland II A/B 42/2, *New York Post* clipping of October 23, 1941, initialed by Herbert Müller, December 8, 1941.

147.   Müller Investigation, 150.

148.   PA, Inland II A/B 54/1, Eichmann to D III, November 19, 1941.

149.   Müller Investigation, 158.

150.   I am grateful to Professor Yehuda Bauer of the Hebrew University of Jerusalem for this information on *Relico.*

151.   PA, Inland II A/B 37/1, German Red Cross to Foreign Office, January 24, 1941; and Rödiger note. T 120/3069/D612079-81.

152.   PA, Inland II A/B 37/1, Müller to Rödiger, February 5, 1942; and Rademacher to German Red Cross, February 23, 1942. T 120/3069/D612082-4.

153.   Müller Investigation, 5 and 146.

154.   PA, Luther Handakten, vol. 10: Rademacher to Luther, November 21, 1942; and Luther to Müller, December 23. 1942.

CHAPTER 6

1.   Rich, Hitler's War Aims, II, 121–7; Seabury, *The Wilhelmstrase,* 114, 116.

2.   Rich, *Hitler's War Aims,* I, 219–20, and II, 343–7; Seabury, *The Wilhelmstrasse,* 116.

3.   PA, Inland II g 177, Luther to Rintelen, August 21, 1942. T 120/1512/371996-2007.

4.   Ibid., and PA, Gesandtschaft Pressburg 312/5: Luther to Ludin, February 16, and Ludin to Foreign Offie, February 20, 1942, T 120/K1644/K403503-4. The original D III file on the Slovak deportations did not survive. The texts of the various telegrams can be found in duplicate in the files of the state secretary and the Bratislava embassy. However, one has to rely on Luther's detailed report to Ribbentrop in August, 1942, to find out who initialed what.

5.   LGNF 2 Ks 3/53, Beiakten, II, 11–13, Part 1, 114 and 119. NG-3571.

6.   LGNF 2 Ks 3/53, Hauptakten, IX, 1475. Rademacher interrogation, April, 1967.

7.   PA, Inland II g 189: Eichmann to Rademacher, March 9; and Luther to Paris, March 11, 1942. T 120/702/261431-2.

8.   PA, Inland II g 189, Eichmann to Rademacher, March 11; Luther to Paris, March 13; and Schleier to D III, March 13 and 14, 1942. T 120/702/261427-30.

9.   ADAP, E, II (Göttingen, 1972), 97.

10.   PA, Inland II g 202: Ostministerium to Foreign Office, February 10; Luther to RAM, February 11; Sonnleithner to Luther, February 13, 1942. T 120/6737/E510850-2.

11.   PA, Inland II g 202: Bräutigam to Foreign Office, February 28, March 5 and 17, 1942, with enclosures. T 120/6737/E510821-7. See also: Martin Broszat, "Das dritte Reich und die rumänische Judenpolitik," *Gutachten des Instituts fur Zeitgeschichte,* I, 163-5.

12.   PA, Inland II g 202, Eichmann to Foreign Office, April 14, 1942. T 120/6737/E510813-5

13.   PA, Inland II g 202: Killinger to D III, March 23; Neubacher to D III, May 1; Killinger to D III, May 29, 1942. T 120/6737/E510804, E510809, E510798.

14.   PA, Inland II g 202, Triska handwritten note of May 16, 1942, T 120/6737/E510806; and LGNF 2 Ks 3/53, Hauptakten, II, 254, Triska affidavit January, 1949. Triska maintains that the Jews were shot by Rumanian units. Broszat assumes they were killed by a *Kommando* of the *Volksdeutschen Mittelstelle.* See Broszat, 165.

15.   PA, Inland II g 202, Bräutigam to Rademacher, May 19, 1942. T 120/6737/E510802.

16.   LGNF 2 Ks 3/53, Hauptakten: III, 309 (Rademacher written statement, April, 1949), and XI, 1836 (Rademacher testimony, 1968); 2nd Rademacher Judgment, 121–2; and NG-1871, Luther to Rademacher, May 27, 1942.

17.   Edmond Paris, *Genocide in Satellite Croatia,* 1941–45 (Chicago, 1961), 117–9; and Milan Markovic, "Staatskommission zur Feststellung der Verbrechen des Okkupators und seiner Helfershelfer," in LGNF 2 Ks 3/53, Beiakten, II Parts 1–3, 120–4. On participation of *Volksdeutsch* units: PA, Gesandtschaft Agram, Judenfrage, T 120/K1702/K406769-72.

18.   Milan Markovic, "Staatskommission zur Feststellung der Verbrechen des Okkupators und seiner Helfershelfer"; Robert M. W. Kempner, *Eichmann und Komplizen* (Zurich, 1961), 295–6; Reitlinger, *The Final Solution,* 362–4.

19.   Kurt Heinberg affidavit, NG-2570.

20.   PA, Politische Abteilung IV 348, Rademacher memorandum, May 23, 1942. T 120/2272/479629-32.

21.   PA: Gesandtschaft Pressburg 312/5, Ludin to Foreign Office, April 6, 1942, T 120/K1644/K403512; and Inland II g 177, Luther to Rintelen, August 21, 1942, T 120/1512/371996-2007.

22.   PA: Inland II g 177, Luther to Rintelen, August 21, 1942, T 120/1512/371996-2007; Büro Staatssekretär, Slowakei II, Luther to Ribbentrop, March 29, 1942, T 120/613/249540; Gesandtschaft Pressburg 312/5, Ludin to D III, April 6, 1942, T 120/K1644/K403512; and S. Fauck, "Das Deutsch-Slowakische Verhältnis 1941–43 und seine Rückwirkung auf die slowakische Judenpolitik," *Gutachten des Instituts für Zeitgeschichte,* II, 65–6.

23.  PA, Gesandtschaft Pressburg 312/5, Ludin to Foreign Office, April 1, 1942, T 120/K1644/K403510; and Livia Rothkirchen, "Vatican Policy and the 'Jewish Problem' in 'Independent' Slovakia 1939–45," *Yad Vashem Studies*, VI, 1967, 39–40.

24.  Yeshayahu Jelinek, "The 'Final Solution'—The Slovak Version," *East European Quarterly*, IV/4 (1971), 437–41.

25.  PA: Büro Staatssekretär, Slowakei II, Ludin to Luther, April 18, 1942, T 120/613/249566; Gesandtschaft Pressburg 312/5, Luther to Ludin, March 20 and April 11, Note verbal of May 1, and Slovak note to Pressburg embassy, June 23, 1942, T 120/K1644/K403506, K403531, K403545, and K403581.

26.  PA, Büro Staatssekretär, Slowakei II, Ludin to Foreign Office, June 26, 1942. T 120/613/249622.

27.  PA, Büro Staatssekretär, Slowakei II, Weizsäcker to Ludin, June 30, 1942. T 120/613/249624.

28.  PA, Inland II A/B 68/2, Protocol of June 30, 1942, T 120/5611/E402519; Hermann Graml, "Der Deutsche Gesandte in der Slowakei," *Gutachten des Instituts für Zeitgeschichte*, II, 342-3; S. Fauck, "Das Deutsch-Slowakische Verhältnis 1941–43 und seine Rückwirkung auf die slowakische Judenpolitik," *Gutachten*, II, 67; D. Ebert, "Statische Angeben über das Schicksal der Juden in Slowakei," *Gutachten*, II, 75.

29.  PA, Inland II A/B 68/2, Slovak General Consul to Foreign Office Representative in Prague, September 19, 1941.

30.  ADAP, E, I, 478–9.

31.  PA, Inland II g 175, Rademacher to RWM and RFM, March 7, 1942. T 120/K800/K210943.

32.  PA, Gesandtschaft Pressburg 312/5, Slovak note to German embassy, March 28, 1942. T 120/K1644/K403553-4.

33.  PA, Inland II A/B 68/2, Slovak general consul in Prague to Foreign Office representative, April 24, and May 6, 1942.

34.  PA, Inland II g 175, Draft of D III memorandum, May, 1942. T 120/2256/478584-8.

35.  PA, Inland II g 175: Summary of meeting of July 30, 1942, T 120/2256/478580-2; and Klingenfuss to RSHA, October 24, 1942.

36.  PA, Inland II g 175, Klingenfuss memorandum, July 23, 1942. T 120/2256/478573.

37.  PA, Inland II g 175, Note of Slovak embassy, September 22, 1942. T 120/2256/478564-5.

38.  PA, Inland II g 175, Klingenfuss memorandum, September 28; Hudeczek to D III, October 14; Klingenfuss to Luther, October 21; Klingenfuss to Hudeczek, October 29, 1942; RWM to Foreign Office, January 14, 1943. T 120/2256/478549, 478553-5, 478560-3.

39.  PA, Inland II g 175, Slovak note, January 8, 1943. T 120/2256/478551.

40.  PA, Inland II g 175, Luther to Weizsäcker, January 29, 1943. T 120/2256/478546-8.

41.  PA, Inland II g 175, Thadden note, July 26, 1944. T 120/K797/K201847.

42.  PA, Botschaft Paris 1125/1, Zeitschel to Sipo-SD and Dr. Best, May 5, 1942. T 120/3769/E042691-2.

43.  PA: Inland II g 172, Abetz to Foreign Office, May 15; Rademacher to Weizsäcker, May 15; and Woermann to D III, May 19, 1942, T 120/K796/K210227-31, K210234-5; and Politische Abteilung IV 348, Rademacher memorandum, May 23, 1942, T 120/2272/479629-32; ADAP, E, II, 394–5.

44.  LGNF 2 Ks 3/53, Hauptakten, IX, 1476. Rademacher interrogation, April, 1967.

45.  PA, Inland II g 189, Eichmann to Rademacher, June 22, 1942. T 120/702/261423-4.

46.  PA, Inland II g 189, Luther to Abetz, Bargen, and Bene, June 28, 1942. T 120/702/261422.

47.  *Das Dritte Reich und Seine Diener: Dokumente*, ed. by Leon Poliakov and Josef Wulf (Berlin, 1956), 122. Zeitschel to Paris, Sipo-SD, June 27, 1942.

48.  PA, Inland II g 187, Schleier to Foreign Office, September 11, 1942. T 120/5549/E387802–3.

49.  PA, Inland II g 189, Abetz to Luther, July 2, 1942. T 120/702/261415–6.

50.  PA, Inland II g 189, Luther to Abetz, July 10, 1942. T 120/702/261414.

51.  Pierre Laval, *Diary* (New York, 1948), 97–9.

52.  LGNF 2 Ks 3/53, Beiakten, II, 11–13, Part 1, 168. Dannecker to Knochen, July 6, 1942. (Weizsäcker Exhibit Nr. 465).

53.  PA, Inland II g 189, Bene to Foreign Office, July 3, 1942. T 120/702/261420–1.

54.  PA, Inland II A/B 61/4, Bargen to Foreign Office, July 9, 1942, and Luther note.

55.  LGNF 2 Ks 3/53, Hauptakten, XI, 1929. Bargen testimony, 1968.

56.  PA: Inland II g 189, Schleier to Foreign Office, September 11, 1942, T 120/5549/E387802–3; and Inland II g 196, Bene to Foreign Office, July 17, 1942, T 120/5403/E362475.

57.  PA, Inland II g 189, Luther to Eichmann, July 29, 1942. T 120/702/261411.

58.  PA, Inland II g 187, Abetz to Foreign Office, September 15, 1942. T 120/5549/E387804–5.

59.  PA: Inland II g 172, Paris to Belin, June 12, and Rumanian note, June 23, 1942, T 120/K796/K210204–5, K210200–1; Inland II g 200, Suhr to Rademacher, June 26, 1942, T 120/K816/K212593.

60.  PA, Inland II g 190, Bargen to Foreign Office, July 18, 1942. T 120/5787/E421262.

61.  PA, Inland II g 183, Weiler note, June 2, 1942. T 120/2330/ 486202.

62.  PA, Inland II g 189: Abetz to Luther, July 2; Bene to Luther, July 3, 1942. T 120/702/261415–6, 261420–1.

63.  PA, Inland II A/B 26/4, Eichmann to Rademacher, July 9, 1942. T 120/K785/K208127.

64.  PA: Inland II g 187, Abetz to Luther, July 15, 1942, T 120/5549/E387828–9; Inland II g 189, Luther to RSHA, July 29, 1942, T 120/702/261411.

65.  PA, Inland II g 183, Luther to Beckerle, June 19, 1942. T 120/2330/486203–5.

66.  PA, Inland II g 183, Beckerle to D III, July 6, 1942. T 120/2330/486208–9.

67.  PA, Inland II g 183: Klingenfuss draft to RSHA, July 14; Stahlburg note, July 29; and Klingenfuss note, August 3, 1942. T 120/2330/486212–4, 486210.

68.  PA, Inland II g 172, Luther to Killinger, June 22, 1942. T 120/K796/K210202–3.

69.  LGNF 2 Ks 3/53, Hauptakten, III, 436 (Klingenfuss interrogation, October, 1949); PA, Inland II g 172, Klingenfuss memorandum, July 21, 1942, T 120/K796/K210198–9.

70.  PA, Inland II g 172, Woemann memorandum, July 24, 1942. T 120/K796/K210196-7.

71.  PA, Inland II g 172, Gödde to Rademacher, July 27; Klingenfuss memorandum, August 4; and Luther note, August 9, 1942. T 120/K796/K210195, K210191–2.

72.  PA, Inland II g 200, Killinger to Luther, August 11, 1942. T 120/K816/K212606-7.

73.  PA, Inland II g 200, Luther to Eichmann, Paris, Brussels, Haag, and Prague, August 20, 1942. T 120/K816/K212608–10.

74.  PA, Inland II g 190: Klingenfuss note, August 3; and Luther to Bargen, August 14, 1942. T 120/5787/E421260–1.

75.  PA, Inland II g 187, Klingenfuss to Sonnleithner, August 18, 1942. T 120/5549/E387833.

76.  PA, Inland II g 187, Abetz to Luther, July 2; Luther to Ribbentrop, July 25; Sonnleithner to Klingenfuss, August 3; and Woermann to D III, August 16, 1942. T 120/5549/E387828–32, E387834–5.

77.  PA, Inland II g 209, Luther memorandum, August 11, 1942. T 120/5231/E310870–1.

78.  PA, Inland II g 209, Klingenfuss draft for Luther telegram to Jagow, August 17, 1942. T 120/5231/E310864–9.

242    Notes

79.    PA, Inland II g 177, Rintelen to Luther, August 28, 1942. T 120/1512/371973–4.

80.    PA, Inland II g 187, Abetz to Foreign Office, September 7 and 15; Luther to Rome, September 17, 1942. T 120/2257/478665 and 5548/E387804–5, and E387809–11.

81.    Inland II g 209, Klingenfuss to Suhr, August 28, 1942. T 120/5231/E310860.

82.    PA, Inland II g 187, Abetz to Foreign Office, September 16, 1942. T 120/5549/E387806–8.

83.    Inland II g 209, Hungarian note, September 17, 1942. T 120/5231/E310852–5.

84.    PA, Inland II g 187, Luther to Abetz, September 22, 1942. T 120/5549/E387795–6.

85.    PA, Inland II g 196: Bene to D III, September 17; Rademacher to Bene, September 25; Bene to D III, October 8, 1942. T 120/5403/E362417, E362432, E362425.

86.    PA, Inland II g 187: Luther to Ribbentrop, September 22, 1942; and Sonnleithner to Luther, October 3, 1942. T 120/5549/E387792–3, E387788.

87.    PA, Inland II g 209, Luther memorandum, October 6, 1942. T 120/5231/E310814–21.

88.    PA, Inland II g 207, Luther to Ankara, October 12, 1942. T 120/2241/476302–3.

89.    PA, Inland II g 192, Italian note, October 10, 1942; and Mackensen to Foreign Office, October 1, 1942. T 120/5602/E401592–6.

90.    PA, Inland II g 192, Luther to Ribbentrop, October 20, 1942. T 120/5602/E401489–91.

91.    PA, Inland II g 207, Kroll to Foreign Office, October 15; Luther to Paris and Haag, October 27 and November 4, 1942. T 120/2241/476304, 476306–8.

92.    PA, Inland II g 209: Jagow to Foreign Office, October 13; Klingenfuss to Smend, November 9; Klingenfuss to RSHA, December 3; Hungarian note, December 2, 1942. T 120/5231/E310804, E310784, E310770, E310734–41.

## CHAPTER 7

1.    Michael Ledeen, "The Evolution of Italian Fascist Anti-Semitism," *Jewish Social Studies*, XXXVII/1 (1975), 3–17; Renzo De Felice, *Storia degli ebrei italiani sotto il fascismo* (Turin, 1961), 465–7; Leon Poliakov and Jacques Sabille, *The Jews under Italian Occupation* (Paris, 1955); Meir Michaelis, "The Attitude of the Fascist Regime to the Jews in Italy," *Yad Vashem Studies*, IV (1960), 7–41; Gene Bernardini, "The Origins and Development of Racial Anti-Semitism in Fascist Italy," *Journal of Modern History*, 49/3 (September 1977), 431–53.

2.    On Hungary: Randolph L. Braham, "The Holocaust in Hungary: An Historical Interpretation of the Role of the Hungarian Radical Right," *Societas—A Review of Social History*, II/3 (summer 1972), 195–220, and "The Rightists, Horthy, and the Germans: Factors Underlying the Destruction of Hungarian Jewry," *Jews and Non-Jews in Eastern Europe*, ed. by Bela Vago and George Mosse (New York, 1974), 137–56; Martin Broszat, "Das deutsch-ungarische Verhältnis und die ungarische Judenpolitik in den Jahren 1938–41," *Gutachten des Instituts für Zeitgeschichte*, I, 183–200; Nathaniel Katzburg, "Hungarian Jewry in Modern Times: Political and Social Aspects," *Hungarian-Jewish Studies*, I, ed. by Randolph Braham (New York, 1966), 137–70; C.A. Macartney, "Hungarian Foreign Policy during the Inter-War Period, with Special Reference to the Jewish Question," *Jews and Non-Jews in Eastern Europe*, 125–136; and Bela Vago, "Germany and the Jewish Policy of the Kallay Government," *Hungarian-Jewish Studies*, II (New York, 1969), 183–210.

On Rumania: Martin Broszat, "Das dritte Reich und die rumänische Judenpolitik," *Gutachten des Instituts für Zeitgeschichte*, I, 102–182; Stephen Fischer-Galati, "Fascism, Communism, and the Jewish Question in Romania," *Jews and Non-Jews in Eastern Europe*, 157–75; Th. Lavi, "The

Background to the Rescue of Romanian Jewry During the Period of the Holocaust," Ibid., 177–186; and "Documents on the Struggle of Rumanian Jewry for Its Rights During the Second World War," *Yad Vashem Studies*, IV (1960), 261–315.
On Bulgaria: Frederick Chary, *The Bulgarian Jews and the Final Solution* (Pittsburgh, 1972); S. Fauck, "Das Deutsch-Bulgarische Verhältnis 1939–44 und seine Rückwirkung auf die Bulgarische Judenpolitik," *Gutachten des Instituts für Zeitgeschichte*, II, 49–59; and Nissan Oren, "The Bulgarian Exception: A Reassessment of the Salvation of the Jewish Community," *Yad Vashem Studies*, VII (1968), 83–106.

3.    Bela Vago and George Mosse, *Jews and Non-Jews in Eastern Europe* (New York, 1974), xiii-xvi.

4.    Ibid., xvi.

5.    Bela Vago, "The Attitude Toward the Jews as a Criterion of the Left-Right Concept," *Jews and Non-Jews in Eastern Europe*, 24–9.

6.    For a more detailed account of the so-called "Luther Revolt," see the author's "Unterstaatssekretär Martin Luther and the Ribbentrop Foreign Office." The following sources have been used in reconstructing these events: a) LGNF 2 Ks 3/53, Hauptakten: II, Rademacher interrogation of 1948, and affidavits of Walter Büttner, Walter Kieser, Friedrich Gaus (all 1948) and Gerhard Klopfer (1949); XI, testimony of Walter Kieser and Walther Gödde (1969). b) NSA: Zz 431, Nr. 10 and 11; TWC, Case XI, Transcript, 9761-7 (Steengracht testimony), and Steengracht Defense Books I (Prüfer affidavit) and II B (Bucholz and Möhrung affidavits). c) Schellenburg, *The Labyrinth*, 323-8; Seabury, *The Wilhelmstrasse*, 131-3; Kleist, *Zwischen Hitler und Stalin*, 13–14; Höhne, *The Order of the Death's Head*, 589–90.

7.    Gödde note in Büttner papers, quoted in: Höhne, *The Order of the Death's Head*, 590.

8.    NSA, TWC, Case XI, Steengracht Document Book I, Exhibit 6 (Prüfer affidavit).

9.    PA, Inland II g 192, Rademacher memorandum, January 10, 1942, and Luther marginalia. T 120/K810/K212130-4.

10.    PA: Inland II A/B 60/3, Walther to Foreign Office, May 19 and June 9, 1942, T 120/K786/K208197-200, K208203-4; Inland II g 189, Abetz to Foreign Office, July 4, 1942, T 120/702/261417.

11.    PA, Inland II g 194, Schnell to Foreign Office, July 18, 1942. T 120/2324/485793-4.

12.    PA, Inland II g 194, Luther to Ribbentrop, July 24, 1942. T 120/2324/485795-6.

13.    Ibid., with marginalia by Weizsäcker and Sonnleithner; and PA, Inland II g 194, Lohmann to Luther, August 8, 1942, T 120/2324/485798.

14.    PA, Inland II g 200, Eichmann to Luther, July 26, 1942. T 120/K816/K212604.

15.    PA, Inland II g 200, Drafts of Luther to Killinger and Müller, August 4, 1942. T 120/K816/K212602-3.

16.    2nd Rademacher Judgment, 139.

17.    PA, Inland II g 200, Luther marginalia on draft letter to Müller, August 8, 1942. T 120/K816/K212602.

18.    PA, Inland II g 200, Klingenfuss to Eichmann, August 11; and Killinger to Luther, August 12, 1942. T 120/K816/K212626-7, K212617.

19.    PA, Inland II g 200, Luther to Müller, August 17, 1942. T 120/K816/K212615-6.

20.    PA, Inland II g 200, Luther to Ribbentrop, August 15, 1942. T 120/K816/K212615-6.

21.    PA, Inland II g 200, Luther to Ribbentrop, August 17, 1942. T 120/K816/K212619-21.

22.    PA, Inland II g 200, Rintelen to Luther, August 19, 1942, with copy of report of Sipo-SD to Reichsführer-SS, July 26, 1942. T 120/K816/K212612-3.

23.    PA, Inland II g 200, Luther to Rintelen, August 19, 1942, T 120/K816/K212614; LGNF 2 Ks 3/53, Hauptakten, II, 285, Rintelen affidavit, 1949.

24.   PA, Inland II g 177, Luther to Ribbentrop, August 21, 1942, T 120/1512/371996-2007; LGNF 2 Ks 3/53, Hauptakten, XI, 1836, Rademacher testimony, 1968.

25.   PA, Inland II g 194: Troll to Foreign Office, July 30, 1942; and Kasche to Foreign Office, August 20, 1942. T 120/2324/485799, 485801.

26.   PA, Inland II g 194, Luther to Mackensen, August 22, 1942. T 120/2324/485802.

27.   Jacques Sabille, "Attitude of the Italians to Persecuted Jews in Croatia," *The Jews under Italian Occupation*, 138.

28.   PA, Inland II g 194, Mackensen to Foreign Office, August 25, 1942. T 120/2324/485807.

29.   LGNF 2 Ks 3/53, Hauptakten, II, 288–9. Hoffmann affidavit, February, 1949.

30.   Ibid., 201. Rademacher interrogation, 1948. Rademacher claimed that the motive behind this snub was to demonstrate to Lecca their disapproval of the "wild deportations" into the Ukraine in the spring of 1942 and the execution of the 28,000 Jews in *Volksdeutsche* villages in Transnistria, but this was a transparent attempt by Rademacher to show how indignant he had been about the few atrocities against the Jews that he allegedly became aware of. That the snub took place as Rademacher described is undoubted; the timing makes it probable that it was a piece of petty revenge concocted by Luther, who was unable to vent his frustrations against Richter and the RSHA.

31.   PA, Inland II g 177, Rintelen to Luther, August 28, 1942. T 120/1512/371973-4.

32.   PA, Inland II g 200, Killinger to Luther, August 28, 1942. T 120/K816/K212622-4.

33.   PA, Inland II g 200, Luther to Killinger, September 2; Killinger to Luther, September 7; and Luther note, September 12, 1942. T 120/K816/K212530, K212625.

34.   PA, Inland II g 187, Italian note, September 2, 1942. T 120/5549/E387822-3.

35.   PA, Inland II g 189, Abetz to Foreign Office, July 4, 1942. T 120/702/261417.

36.   PA, Inland II g 187, Luther to Abetz, September 7; Abetz to Foreign Office, September 12; Weizsäcker to Luther, September 12, 1942. T 120/5549/E387818-9, E387816-7, E387799.

37.   PA, Inland II g 194, Luther to Ribbentrop, September 10; and Rintelen to Luther, September 17, 1942. T 120/2324/485807, 485811.

38.   PA, Inland II g 194: Luther to Kasche and Mackensen, September 22; Kasche to Luther, September 23; Mackensen to Luther, September 24, 1942. T 120/2324/485816-7, 485819-20.

39.   PA, Inland II g 194, Kasche to Luther, September 19, 1942. T 120/2324/485818.

40.   PA, Inland II g 183: Beckerle report, July 21, 1942; Rademacher to Luther, August 17, 1942, with Luther marginalia; cancelled memorandum to Ribbentrop drafted by Rademacher, August 27, 1942. T 120/2330/486218-20.

41.   PA, Inland II g 183, Luther to Ribbentrop, September 11, 1942, with marginalia by Weizsäcker and Ribbentrop. T 120/2330/486223-6.

42.   IMT, X, 108.

43.   *Staatsmänner und Diplomaten bei Hitler*, ed. by Andreas Hillgruber, II (Frankfurt/M., 1970), 106–111.

44.   PA, Inland II g 200, Richter report forwarded to Foreign Office, November 26, 1942. T 120/K816/K212666-9.

45.   PA, Inland II g 208, Luther memorandum, September 24, 1942, T 120/5231/E310856. Hearsay evidence that Hitler violently criticized Ribbentrop on September 23, 1942, for lack of success in solving the Jewish question comes from Cecil von Renthe-Fink, the German ambassador to Copenhagen, who claimed that he heard the story from a member of Ribbentrop's staff. Leni Yahil, *The Rescue of Danish Jewry* (Philadelphia, 1969), 73.

46.   *Staatsmänner und Diplomaten bei Hitler*, II, 118–9; PA, Inland II g 194, Rintelen to Luther, September 25, 1942, T 120/2324/485822.

47. Fischer-Galati, "Fascism, Communism, and the Jewish Question," *Jews and Non-Jews in Eastern Europe*, 171; Broszat, "Das dritte Reich und die rumänische Judenpolitik," *Gutachten des Instituts für Zeitgeschichte*, I, 132.

48. Fischer-Galati, "Fascism, Communism, and the Jewish Question," 171; Th. Lavi, "The Background to the Rescue of Romanian Jewry During the Period of the Holocaust," *Jews and Non-Jews in Eastern Europe*, 185-6; Broszat, "Das dritte Reich und die rumänische Judenpolitik," 167.

49. PA, Inland II g 200, Killinger to Luther, August 28, 1942. T 120/K816/K212622-4.

50. PA, Inland II g 200: Richter through Killinger and Abteilung Deutschland to Eichmann, September 15, 1942; and Luther to Bucharest, September 29, 1942, T 120/K816/K212626-7; and *Dokumente über Methoden der Judenverfolgung* (Frankfurt/M., 1959), 75-6.

51. PA, Inland II g 200, Richter report forwarded to Foreign Office, October 5, 1942. T 120/K816/K212646-50.

52. PA, Inland II A/B 59/1: Killinger to Foreign Office, October 6; Klingenfuss to Luther and Krümmer, November 3, 1942.

53. PA, Inland II g 200, Richter report forwarded to Foreign Office, November 26, 1942. T 120/K816/K212666-9.

54. PA, Inland II g 200: Gödde to Klingenfuss, December 12; and Luther to Klingenfuss, December 14, 1942. T 120/K816/K212673-4.

55. PA, Inland II g 200, Rademacher draft memorandum, December 7, 1942. T 120/K816/K212671-2.

56. Martin Broszat, "Das deutsch-ungarische Verhältnis und die ungarische Judenpolitik in den Jahren 1938–41," 186–94.

57. Randolph Braham, "The Kamenets Podolsk and Delvidek Massacres: Prelude to the Holocaust in Hungary," *Yad Vashem Studies*, IX (1973), 134-56.

58. PA, Inland II g 208, OKW to Foreign Office, July 21, 1942. T 120/5231/E310845. For the entire Heszlenyi affair, see: Randolph Braham, "The Holocaust in Hungary: An Historical Interpretation of the Role of the Hungarian Right," *Societas—A Review of Social History*, II/3 (summer 1972), 197–8, 201–5.

59. Martin Broszat, "Das deutsch-ungarische Verhältnis und die ungarische Judenpolitik in den Jahren 1938–41," *Gutachten des Instituts für Zeigeschichte*, I, 196–7.

60. PA, Inland II g 208, OKW to Foreign Office, July 21, 1942. T 120/5231/E310845. On the ambivalence of Kallay toward Germany and the Jews in this period, see: Bela Vago, "Germany and the Jewish Policy of the Kallay Government," *Hungarian-Jewish Studies*, II, 185–91.

61. PA, Inland II g 208, Klingenfuss note, August 1, and Schliep marginalia, August 3, 1942. T 120/5231/E310848.

62. PA, Inland II g 208, Klingenfuss to Eichmann, August 5 and September 17, 1942. T 120/5231/E310846-7, E310843-4.

63. PA, Inland II g 208, Eichmann to Klingenfuss, September 25, 1942. T 120/5231/E310841-2.

64. Randolph Braham, "The Rightists, Horthy, and the Germans: Factors Underlying the Destruction of Hungarian Jewry," *Jews and Non-Jews in Eastern Europe*, 150.

65. PA, Inland II g 208: Rademacher to Klingenfuss, October 2; and Rademacher memorandum, October 3, 1942. T 120/5231/E310851, E310831-2.

66. PA, Inland II g 208, Luther to Ribbentrop, October 6, 1942. T 120/5231/E310814-21.

67. PA, Inland II g 208, Rintelen to Weizsäcker and Luther, October 11, 1942. T 120/5231/E310825-6.

68.   PA, Inland II g 208: Weizsäcker to Luther and Luther to Weizsäcker, October 12, 1942, T 120/5231/E310825-6.

69.   PA, Inland II g 208, Weizsäcker memorandum, October 14, 1942. T 120/5231/E310801.

70.   PA, Inland II g 208: Luther to Rintelen, October 13; Luther to Jagow, October 14, 1942. T 120/5231/E310808-12, E310805-7.

71.   PA, Inland II g 208, Jagow to Foreign Office, October 17, 1942. T 120/5231/E310792.

72.   PA, Inland II g 208: Jagow to Foreign Office, October 19; and two reports of October 23, 1942. T 120/5231/E310787-90.

73.   PA, Inland II g 208, Jagow to Foreign Office, October 27 and November 13, 1942. T 120/5231/E310785-6, E310781-2.

74.   PA, Inland II g 208: Luther memorandum, November 26; and Luther to Ribbentrop, December 3, 1942. T 120/5231/E310771, E310779-80.

75.   PA, Inland II A/B 68/2: Wisliceny report, October 8, and Ludin to Foreign Office, October 13, 1942. Randolph Braham gives the probable indentity of the Fay in question as Gedeon Fay-Halazy, a ministerial assistant secretary who had served under Kallay in the Foreign Office. "The Holocaust in Hungary: An Historical Interpretation of the Role of the Hungarian Right," 202–3.

76.   PA, Inland II g 208, Himmler to Ribbentrop, November 30, 1942. T 120/5231/E310765-7.

77.   PA, Inland II g 208, Sonnleithner to Luther, December 12; and Luther to Jagow, December 14, 1942. T 120/5231/E310762-4.

78.   *The Destruction of Hungarian Jewry*, ed. by Randolph Braham (New York, 1963), 187.

79.   PA, Inland II g 208, Luther memorandum, December 14, 1942; and Hungarian note, December 2, 1942. T 120/5231/E310743-4, E310734–41.

80.   PA, Inland II, g 208, Luther to Ribbentrop, January 16, 1942. T 120/5231/E310750.

81.   PA, Inland II g 208, Jagow to Foreign Office, February 18, 1942. T 120/5231/E310724.

82.   Frederick Chary, *The Bulgarian Jews and the Final Solution*, 37–54; S. Fauck, "Das Deutsch-Bulgarische Verhältnis 1939–44 und seine Rückwirkung auf die Bulgarische Judenpolitik," *Gutachten des Instituts für Zeitgeschichte*, II, 48–51.

83.   Hahn Judgment, 107.

84.   PA, Inland II g 183, Klingenfuss to Luther, October 9, 1942. T 120/2330/486236.

85.   PA, Inland II g 183, Luther to Beckerle, October 15, 1942. T 120/2330/486234-5.

86.   PA, Inland II g 183: Beckerle to Foreign Office, November 2 and 16; Bulgarian note, November 12, 1942. T 120/2330/486237, 486261-3.

87.   PA, Inland II g 183, Klingenfuss to Eichmann, November 23, 1942. T 120/2330/486240.

88.   PA, Inland II g 183, Eichmann to Luther, December 10, 1942. T 120/2330/486270-1.

89.   PA, Inland II g 183, Klingenfuss draft to Heinrich Müller, December 11, 1942. T 120/2330/486265.

90.   PA, Inland II g 183: Hahn to Wallenberg, January 2; note by Wallenberg, January 5, 1942; and Hahn note. T 120/2330/486266-8.

91.   PA, Inland II g, 194, Mackensen to Foreign Office, October 8, 1942. T 120/2324/485824.

92.   Jacques Sabille, "Attitude of the Italians to the Persecuted Jews in Croatia," *Jews Under Italian Occupation*, 138–9.

93. PA, Inland II g 194, Kasche to Foreign Office, October 16, 1942. T 120/2324/485837-9.

94. PA, Inland II g 194, Luther to Mackensen, October 20, 1942. T 120/2324/485840-1.

95. PA, Inland II g 190, Suhr to Rademacher, July 11, 1942. T 120/5787/E421270-2.

96. PA, Inland II g 190, Klingenfuss to Altenburg, July 16, 1942. T 120/5787/E421265.

97. PA, Inland II g 190, Altenburg to Foreign Office, July 27, 1942. T 120/5787/E421258-9. Altenburg had put himself into a dangerous position. First, he had not notified the Foreign Office of his negotiations with Ghigi. Then when asked his opinion on the introduction of marking in the German zone, he openly opposed it. This lends support to the allegation of Robert Kempner that according to Angelo Giuseppe Roncalli, the wartime Papal Nuncio in Istanbul (and later Pope John XXIII), Altenburg worked behind the scenes to encourage and strengthen Italian resistance to German Jewish policy. *Eichmann und Komplizen,* 308; and author's interview with Kempner, January 24, 1974.

98. PA, Inland II g 190, Suhr to Rademacher, August 18, 1942. T 120/5787/E421254-5.

99. PA, Inland II g 190: Bismarck to Foreign Office, August 19; Luther to Altenburg, September 15, 1942. T 120/5787/E421250-3.

100. PA, Inland II g 177, handwritten note, T 120/1512/371949; and *Judenverfolgung in Italien, den italienisch bezetzten Gebieten und in Nordafrika,* ed. by United Restitution Organization (Frankfurt/M., 1962), 93 (excerpt from protocol of Mussolini-Himmler meeting).

101. LGNF 2 Ks 3/53, Hauptakten: II, 199 (Rademacher interrogation, 1948); XI, 1939 (Rademacher testimony, 1968).

102. PA, Inland II g 192, Luther to Ribbentrop, October 22, 1942. T 120/5602/E410599-608.

103. PA, Inland II g 194: Kasche to Foreign Office, October 20; Luther to Mackensen, October 24, 1942. T 120/2324/485845-7.

104. Sabille, "Attitude of the Italians to the Persecuted Jews in Croatia," 141.

105. PA, Inland II g 194, Mackensen to Foreign Office, October 28, 1942. T 120/2324/485848-9.

106. PA, Inland II g 194, Kasche to Foreign Office, November 9 and 10, 1942. T 120/K810/K212084 and 2324/485862-3.

107. PA, Inland II g 194, Kasche to Foreign Office, November 20, 1942. T 120/2324/48581.

108. PA, Inland II g 194: Kasche to Foreign Office, December 4; and Klingenfuss to Rome, December 15, 1942 (copy of Kasche report of December 9). T 120/2324/485872-3, 485877.

109. PA, Inland II g 194, Bismarck to Foreign Office, December 19, 1942. T 120/2324/485879.

110. Sabille, "Attitude of the Italians to the Persecuted Jews in Croatia," 146.

111. Hilberg, *The Destruction of the European Jews,* 457; PA, Inland II g 194, Kasche and Helm to Foreign Office and RSHA, March 4, 1943. T 120/2324/485882.

112. PA, Inland II g 190: Luther to Altenburg, October 23; Altenburg to Luther, October 25; Luther to Altenburg, October 28; and Altenburg to Luther, November 7, 1942. T 120/5787/E421244, E421246-8.

113. PA, Inland II g 190: Luther to Rome, December 5; Mackensen to Foreign Office, December 10, 1942. T 120/5787/E421241-3.

114. PA, Inland II g 190: Luther to Altenburg, December 15; Altenburg to Luther, December 19, 1942; Altenburg to Luther, January 10, 1943. T 120/5787/E421236-8.

115. PA, Inland II g 190, Altenburg to Foreign Office, January 13, 1942. T 120/5787/E421235.

116. PA, Inland II g 177, Rademacher compilation of proposals for measures against Mischlinge, June 11, 1942. T 120/1512/372010-12. Hilberg, *The Destruction of the European*

*Jews*, 268-77, and Adler, *Der Verwaltete Mensch*, 278-322, have very complete accounts of this problem.

117.    ADAP, E, II, 490 (Rademacher memorandum, March 7, 1942); and PA, Inland II g 177, Rademacher compilation, June 11, 1942, T 120/1512/372010-12.

118.    PA, Inland II g 177: Rademacher compilation, June 11; and Rademacher through Luther, Gaus, and Woermann, to Weizsäcker, June 11, 1942. T 120/1512/37009-12.

119.    PA, Inland II g 177, Suhr to Rademacher, August 12, 1942. T 120/1512/371957.

120.    PA, Inland II g 177, Rademacher and Klingenfuss to Luther, Woermann, Gaus, and Weizsäcker, September 7, 1942. T 120/1512/371953-6.

121.    *Trials of the War Criminals before the Nuernberg Military Tribunals*, XIII, 254.

122.    PA, Inland II g 177, Luther to Chief of Sipo-SD, October 2, 1942. T 120/1512/ 371951.

123.    PA, Inland II g 177, Suhr to Rademacher, October 16, 1942, and Klingenfuss note. T 120/1512/371950.

124.    PA, Inland II g 177, Minutes of conference of October 27, 1942. T 120/1512/ 371943-7.

125.    PA, Inland II g 177, Luther to Weizsäcker, Woermann, and Gaus, December 7, 1942. T 120/1512/371940-1.

126.    PA, Inland II g 196, Bene to Foreign Office, August 13 and 25, 1942, and March 26, 1943. T 120/5403/E362441, E362433-4, E362399-402.

127.    PA, Inland II g 182, Bargen to Foreign Office, September 24, 1942. T 120/5311/ E337845.

128.    PA, Inland II g 182, Bargen to Foreign Office, November 11 and 25, 1942. T 120/K804/K211050 and 5311/E337844.

129.    PA, Inland II g 182, Luther to Bargen, December 4, 1942. T 120/5311/E337841-3.

130.    1st Rademacher Judgment, 140.

131.    PA, Inland II g 182, Bargen to D III, January 5, 1943. T 120/K804/K211043.

132.    PA, Inland II g 182, Luther to Bargen and Rademacher to RSHA, January 25, 1943. T 120/K804/K211042.

133.    1st Rademacher Judgment, 140.

## CHAPTER 8

1.    LGNF 2 Ks 3/53, Beiakten, III, Part 4, 6. Klingenfuss interrogation, October, 1947.

2.    LGNF 2 Ks 3/53, Hauptakten, IX, 1441. Klingenfuss interrogation, February, 1967.

3.    LGNF 2 Ks 3/53, Hauptakten, VIII, 1185. Klingenfuss to Prof. Gülich, May 17, 1958.

4.    LGNF 2 Ks 3/53, Hauptakten, III, 438. Klingenfuss interrogation, October, 1949.

5.    LGNF 2 Ks 3/53, Hauptakten, VIII, 1185. Klingenfuss to Gülich, May 17, 1958.

6.    LGNF 2 Ks 3/53: Sonderheft Auslieferungssache Klingenfuss 3c Js 1321-24/49, 5 (Klingenfuss interrogation, October, 1947); Hauptakten, IX, 1440 (Klingefuss interrogation, February, 1967).

7.    LGNF 2 Ks 3/53, Beiakten, III, Part 4, 5-7. Klingenfuss interrogation, October, 1947.

8.    Ibid., 8; and LGNF 2 Ks 3/53, Hauptakten, II, 241 (Schröder affidavit, January, 1949).

9.    PA, Inland II A/B 347/3, Rademacher to Luther, June 15, 1942.

10.    PA, Luther Handakten, vol. 13, Luther note, January 6, 1943; and Hahn Judgment, 165 and 174.

11.   LGNF 2 Ks 3/53, Hauptakten, II, 271 (Kieser affidavit, February, 1949) and 245 (Büttner affidavit, February, 1949); XI, 1895 (Gödde testimony, 1968); Beiakten, III, Part 1, 67 (Rademacher interrogation, December, 1947).

12.   LGNF 2 Ks 3/53, Beiakten, III, Part 1: 7, 17, 49, 61. Rademacher interrogations, 1947.

13.   LGNF 2 Ks 3/53, Hauptakten, II, 198 and 216. Rademacher interrogation, 1948.

14.   LGNF 2 Ks 3/53, Hauptakten, II, 246. Büttner affidavit, February, 1949.

15.   LGNF 2 Ks 3/53, Hauptakten, II, 256. Ashton affidavit, January, 1949.

16.   LGNF 2 Ks 3/53, Hauptakten, II, 241. Schröder affidavit, January, 1949.

17.   LGNF 2 Ks 3/53, Hauptakten: II, 271 (Kieser affidavit, February, 1949); II, 244 (Büttner affidavit, February, 1949).

18.   LGNF 2 Ks 3/53, Hauptakten, II, 269a (Hahn affidavit, February, 1949); II, 262 (Pausch interrogation, February, 1949); IX, 1586 (Pausch interrogation, June, 1967); XI, 1857 (Pausch testimony, 1968).

19.   PA, Inland II A/B 59/4, Rademacher to Wurm, March 27, 1943.

20.   LGNF 2 Ks 3/53, Hauptakten, XI, 1869. Klingenfuss testimony, 1968.

21.   PA, Inland II g 169a, Thadden memorandum, May 15, 1943. T 120/K781/K209619.

22.   Hilberg, *Destruction of the European Jews,* 233, 253–4.

23.   Hahn Judgment, 60–1.

24.   Ibid., 164.

25.   PA, Inland II A/B 347/3, Hahn to Personnel Division, December 18, 1942.

26.   PA, Inland II A/B 72/5: Press Division to D III, December 19, 1942; Tass Release; and Hahn notation.

27.   PA, Inland II g 169a, Rödiger to D III, December 29, 1942.

28.   PA, Inland II g 169a: Hahn memorandum, December 30, 1942; Rademacher memorandum, January 14, 1942. T 120/5782/E420973–4.

29.   LGNF 2 Ks 3/53, Hauptakten, IX, 1423. Hahn interrogation, September, 1962.

30.   Ibid., 1415.

31.   Ibid., 1424–5.

32.   LGNF 2 Ks 3/53: Hauptakten, II, 262 (Pausch interrogation, February, 1949); Beiakten, IV, Parts 1 and 2, 471 (Pausch interrogation, November, 1964).

33.   LGNF 2 Ks 3/53, Hauptakten, IX, 1416. Hahn interrogation, 1962.

34.   PA, Inland II A/B 42/3, Hahn to Bohle. March 4, 1943.

35.   PA, Inland II g 186: Blücher to Foreign Office, January 29; and Luther (drafted by Hahn) to Helsinki, February 4, 1943. T 120/K807/ K211599-601.

36.   LGNF 2 Ks 3/53, Hauptakten, IX, 1593–4. Pausch interrogation, 1967.

37.   PA, Inland II A/B 347/3, Note, March 13, 1943.

38.   LGNF 2 Ks 3/53, Beiakten, IV, Parts 1 and 2, 492 (Thadden interrogation); Hahn Judgment, 7.

39.   PA, Inland II g 192: Ribbentrop to Luther, January 13; Mackensen to Foreign Office, January 16; and Bismarck to Foreign Office, January 27, 1943. T 120/5602/E401568-70, E401561, E401558.

40.   PA, Inland II g 204: Luther to Bern, December 28, 1942; and Bern to Foreign Office, January 4, 1943. T 120/K818/K212976-8.

41.   PA, Inland II g 203a, Klingenfuss to Eichmann, January 22, 1943. T 120/K817/K212913.

42.   PA: Inland II g 176, Hahn to Chief Sipo-SD, February 8, 1943, T 120/K798/K210820-1; Inland II g 177, Kaltenbrunner to Foreign Office, March 5, 1943, T 120/1512/E372211-19.

43.   PA, Inland II A/B 72/3, Schleier to Foreign Office, January 27 and March 1, 1943.

44.   PA, Inland II g 206: Moltke to Foreign Office, February 24, 1943, T 120/K820/ K213058–9; Bergmann to Madrid, February 27, 1943, T 120/5793/E421637; Woermann note and Spanish note, March 22, 1943, T 120/K820/K213075–6.

45.   PA, Inland II A/B 67/4, Woermann note, March 20, and Rademacher marginalia, March 23, 1943.

46.   PA: Inland II g 184, Best to Foreign Office, February 18, 1943, T 120/2591/D524818; Inland II A/B 63/4, Pausch to Eichmann, March 23, 1943.

47.   PA, Inland II g 207, Luther to Paris, January 28, 1943. T 120/2241/476317.

48.   PA, Inland II A/B 70/3, Achenbach (Paris) to Foreign Office, February 12, 1943.

49.   PA, Inland II A/B 70/3: Hahn note, February 17; and Papen to Foreign Office, February 23, 1943.

50.   PA, Inland II A/B 70/3: Hahn note, February 17; Melchers memorandum, February 19; and Woemann memorandum, February 23, 1943.

51.   PA, Inland II A/B 70/3: Thadden note, July 2, and Melchers marginalia; Thadden note, September 22, 1943.

52.   PA, Inland II A/B 69/1: Gerlach to Swedish Consul, Prague, December 30, 1942; Swedish note in Berlin, January 22, 1943.

53.   PA, Inland II A/B 69/1: Swedish note, February 4, and Rademacher marginalia, February 5; Rademacher to Eichmann, Prague, Stockholm, February 5; and Hahn note, February 16, 1943.

54.   PA, Inland II A/B 69/1: Gerlach to Foreign Office, February 23; and Hahn marginalia on Woermann instructions, February 27, 1943.

55.   PA, Inland II A/B 69/1: Eichmann to Hahn, March 1; Pol VI to Hahn, March 6; Rademacher to Stockholm, March 12, 1943.

56.   PA, Inland II A/B 69/1: Swedish memorandum, March 8; and Pausch to Eichmann, March 12, 1943.

57.   PA, Inland II A/B 69/1: Pausch to Gerlach, March 16; Rademacher to Weizsäcker, March 25, 1943.

58.   PA, Inland II A/B 69/1, Pausch to Wagner, April 5, 1943.

59.   PA, Inland II A/B 69/1, Hahn memorandum, April 16, 1943.

60.   PA, Inland II A/B 69/1, Thadden note, October 18, 1943; and Hahn Judgment, 94.

61.   On German occupation during Renthe-Fink's tenure, see: Norman Rich, *Hitler's War Aims*, II, 106–111. The most comprehensive study of German Jewish policy in Denmark is Leni Yahil, *The Rescue of Danish Jewry*.

62.   ADAP, E, I, 185–6.

63.   PA, Inland II g 184, Renthe-Fink to Foreign Office, January 20, 1942. T 120/2707/ D531393–6.

64.   PA, Inland II g 184: Clausen to Grundherr, August 19; Rademacher to Gödde, and Luther note, September 2, 1942. T 120/2591/D524882–7.

65.   PA, Inland II g 184: Klingenfuss draft, September 12, T 120/2591/D524878–81; and Rademacher to Luther, September 18, 1942, T 120/2707/ D531444.

66.   PA, Inland II g 184, Luther to Renthe-Fink, October 8, 1942. T 120/2591/D524853–4.

67.   PA, Inland II g 184, Klingenfuss note, December 23, 1942. T 120/2591/D524843.

68.   PA, Inland II g 184, Best to Foreign Office, January 13, 1943. T 120/2591/D524836–8.

69.   PA, Inland II g 184, Luther to Ribbentrop, January 28, 1943, and Ribbentrop marginal note. T 120/2591/D524827–9.

70.   The author's interpretation of Luther's attitude toward the Jewish question in Denmark differs in perspective from that of Leni Yahil in *The Rescue of Danish Jewry*. She relies on Cecil von

Renthe-Fink's estimate of his own role in this matter, in which he claims to have continually frustrated and sabotaged the efforts of the extremists in the Foreign Office, that is Luther and Rademacher, to force the issue. Yahil credits Renthe-Fink's clever reports, subtlely portraying the difficulties contrary to German interests that would arise in Denmark if the Jewish question were pushed too hard, with having a significant effect upon German policy.

Undoubtedly from Renthe-Fink's perspective, Luther and Rademacher were extremists on the Jewish question in Denmark. However, an evaluation of Luther's behavior in Denmark not just from Renthe-Fink's viewpoint but in comparison to his actions elsewhere in Europe does not sustain the thesis of the clever ambassador thwarting the activist undersecretary. When Luther was intent upon an activist policy, the tactics employed by Renthe-Fink were clearly inadequate to stop him and even had the opposite effect of inflaming him further, as occurred in Serbia and Belgium. Luther simply did not behave with the same ferocity in Denmark as elsewhere.

The documents show that Luther asked Heydrich at the Wannsee Conference to postpone deportations in Denmark, that he approved Rademacher's and Grundherr's recommendation of September 18, 1942, for "mild" pressure that did not even go so far as directly approaching the Danish government, that he did not act upon Ribbentrop's authorization of September 24, 1942, to deport the Danish Jews, and that he endorsed Best's moderate proposals in January 1943. Unless one assumes that Renthe-Fink (and later Best) could lead Luther around by the nose where Weizsäcker, Benzler, Bargen, and others had all failed, one must conclude that this consistently cautious policy was Luther's own.

The fact that Luther accepted Renthe-Fink's evaluation of the situation does not prove that he was manipulated by the ambassador, only that Luther had concluded that the deportation of a small number of Danish Jews was not worth the political difficulties it would cause, an assessment that future events proved correct. Luther had many other sources of information in Denmark, including the attaché Gustav Meissner (a former member of Luther's Party Advisory Office in the Ribbentrop Bureau) and Rademacher, who frequently visited there as part of his duties as the Foreign Office expert on nationalist movements abroad (in this case, Clausen's Danish Nazis). Thus Renthe-Fink's reports did not "fool" or thwart Luther, but constituted an accurate evaluation of the situation which Luther accepted because they were confirmed by his other sources of information. Luther, not Ribbentrop or Renthe-Fink, determined the pace of Foreign Office Jewish policy in Denmark during this period. If the pace was slow, it was because of Luther, not in spite of him.

71. PA, Inland II g 190, Luther to Altenburg, January 7, 1943. T 120/5787/E421237.

72. PA, Inland II A/B 64/3, Luther to Altenburg, January 23, 1943.

73. LGNF 2 Ks 3/53, Hauptakten, X, 1754. Klingenfuss to Bamberg Staatsanwaltschaft, March 16, 1968.

74. PA, Inland II g 190, Günther to Foreign Office, January 25, 1943. T 120/5787/E421230-1.

75. PA, Inland II g 190: Luther to Athens, January 25; Altenburg to Foreign Office, January 26; Rademacher to Bratislava, February 5, 1943. T 120/5787/E421227-9. The Rademacher telegram to Bratislava of February 5, 1943, was drafted by Hahn on January 29 and must have been communicated by telephone to Bratislava immediately, for Wisliceny received his travelling papers in Bratislava on February 2, 1943. Hahn Judgment, 229.

76. PA, Inland II g 190, Bergmann (drafted by Hahn) to Rome, February 5, 1943. T 120/5787/E421224-6.

77. PA, Inland II g 190, Mackensen to Foreign Office, March 2, 1943. T 120/5787/E421223.

78. PA, Inland II g 190, Mackensen to Foreign Office, March 13, 1943. T 120/5787/E421218.

79. PA, Inland II g 190, Bergmann (drafted by Rademacher and Pausch) to Ribbentrop, March 19, 1943. T 120/5787/E421177-9, E421215-7.

80. PA, Inland II g 183, Beckerle to Foreign Office, January 22, 1943. T 120/2330/486278-80.

81.    PA, Inland II g 183, Dannecker reports, February 8 and 16, 1943. T 120/2330/486288–9, 486293–4.

82.    PA, Inland II g 183: Beckerle to Foreign Office, February 16; and Hahn to Eichmann, February 18, 1943. T 120/2330/486291-2.

83.    PA, Inland II g 183, Dannecker report, February 23, 1943. T 120/2330/486297-9.

84.    PA, Inland II g 192a: Beckerle to Foreign Office, February 23; and Hahn to Eichmann, March 4, 1943. T 120/5784/E421079–90 and T 120/K782/K207369.

85.    Hahn Judgment, 132–7. Also: Aleksandar Matkovski, "The Destruction of Macedonian Jewry in 1943," Yad Vashem Studies, III (1959), 96.

86.    For a detailed analyses of the complicated political situation in Bulgaria which led to the decision to postpone deportations, see: Chary, The Bulgarian Jews and the Final Solution 1940–1944, 90–100; and Oren, "The Bulgarian Exception," 96–8. The German view of events is found in three reports, PA: Inland II g 183, Pausch memorandum, April 3, 1943, T 120/2330/486304–7, and Hoffman report, April 5, 1943, T 120/2330/ 486316–21; and Inland II A/B 62/3, Beckerle to Foreign Office, March 26, 1942, T 120/5778/E420913–4.

87.    PA, Inland II g 183, Hoffmann report, April 5, 1943. T 120/2330/ 486316-21.

88.    PA, Büro des Staatssekretärs, Bulgarien, vol. 5, Ribbentrop to Beckerle, April 4, 1943. T 120/267/173890-1.

89.    PA, Inland II g 183, Dannecker report, February 8, 1943. T 120/2330/486288-9.

90.    PA, Inland II g 183, Witte report, March 18, 1943. T 120/K783/ K207597-611.

91.    PA, Inland II g 192, Bismarck to Foreign Office, February 4, 1943. T 120/5602/E401546.

92.    PA, Inland II g 192, Schleier to Foreign Office, January 23, 1943. T 120/5602/E401554-5.

93.    Leon Poliakov, "The Jews under Italian Occupation in France," The Jews under Italian Occupation, 22–3.

94.    PA, Inland II g 192, Schleier to Foreign office, January 23, 1943. T 120/5602/E491554-5.

95.    PA, Inland II g 192, Schleier to Foreign Office, January 13 and 23, 143. T 120/5602/E401574, E401554-5.

96.    PA, Inland II g 187: Luther to Paris, January 26; and Schleier to Foreign Office, January 30, 1943. T 120/5549/E387766-7, E387753.

97.    PA, Inland II g 192, Luther to Rome, January 31, 1943. T 120/5602/E401549-51.

98.    PA: Inland II g 192, Bismarck to Foreign Office, February 4, 1943, T 120/5602/E401544-5; and Inland II g 187, Mackensen to Foreign Office, February 12, 1943, February 12, 1943, T 120/5549/E387748.

99.    PA, Inland II g 187: Hahn to Paris, February 19; and Hahn to Rome, February 19, 1943. T 120/5549/E387738, E387740-2.

100.    PA, Inland II g 192, Himmler to Ribbentrop, January 29, 1943. T 120/5602/401508-12.

101.    PA, Inland II g 192: Sonnleithner to D III, February 23; and Büro RAM to Bergmann, February 24, 1943. T 120/5602/E401522-3.

102.    PA, Inland II g 192, Bergmann to Ribbentrop, February 24, 1943. T 120/5602/E401514.

103.    PA, Inland II g 192, Hahn to Eichmann, February 25, 1943. T 120/5602/E401514.

104.    PA, Inland II g 192, Bergmann (drafted by Rademacher and Hahn) to Sonnleithner, February 25, 1943. T 120/2257/478652-7.

105.    PA, Inland II g 189, Bergmann to Sonnleithner, February 26, 1943. T 120/K789/K209361.

106.    PA, Inland II g 189, Ribbentrop to Rome, March 9, 1943, T 120/K789/K208965-70;

*Judenverfolgung in Italien, den italienisch besetzten Gebieten und in Nordafrika*, 155–6 (Protocol of Ribbentrop-Mussolini conference, February 25, 1943).

107.	PA, Inland II g 192, Schleier to Foreign Office, March 1 and 4, 1943. T 120/5602/E401496 and K810/K212256–8.

108.	PA, Inland II g 189, Ribbentrop to Mackensen, March 9, 1943. T 120/K789/K208965–70.

109.	PA, Inland II g 189, Mackensen to Ribbentrop, March 12, 1943. T 120/K789/K208961–4.

110.	PA, Inland II g 189, Ribbentrop to Mackensen, March 13, 1943. T 120/K789/K208956–60.

111.	PA, Inland II g 189, Mackensen to Ribbentrop, March 18, 1943. T 120/K789/K208953-5.

112.	PA, Inland II g 189, Mackensen to Ribbentrop, March 20, 1943. T 120/K789/K208936–9.

113.	Poliakov, "The Jews under the Italian Occupation in France." 34–5.

114.	Ibid., 37.

115.	Zanvel Diamant, "Jewish Refugees on the French Riviera," *YIVO Annual of Jewish Social Sciences*, VII, 274.

116.	Sabille, "Attitude of the Italians to the Persecuted Jews in Croatia," 147-8.

117.	PA, Inland II g 200, Killinger to Foreign Office, December 12, 1942. T 120/K 816/K212680-1.

118.	PA, Inland II g 200, Luther to Bucharest, January 8, 1943, T 120/K816/K212682-3; 2nd Rademacher Judgment, 146.

119.	PA, Inland II g 200: OKW to Foreign Office, January 15, with two intelligence reports enclosed; Hahn to Bucharest, January 23; Richter and Killinger to Foreign Office, March 2, 1943. T 120/K816/K212700-6, K212712.

120.	PA, Inland II g 197a: Transocean reports, February 3; Beckerle to Foreign Office, February 4, 1943. T 120/K782/K207309-10, K207315.

121.	PA, Inland II g 1972: Hahn note and two telegrams to Sofia, February 13, 1943. T 120/7716/E548811 and K782/K207320-1, K207311-3.

122.	PA, Inland II g 1972, Beckerle to Foreign Office, February 16 and 27, 1943. T 120/5784/E421079-81.

123.	PA, Inland II g 197a, UP report, March 2, 1943. T 120/K782/K207360.

124.	LGNF 2 Ks 3/53, Hauptakten, IX, 1958. Pausch interrogation, 1967.

125.	PA, Inland II g 197a: Hahn to Sofia, March 3, 1943, T 120/K782/K297363; and Beckerle to Foreign Office, March 5, 1943, T 120/7716/E548805.

126.	PA: Inland II g 197a, Eichmann to Hahn, March 3, 1943, T 120/K782/K297363; Inland II g 174a, DNB-report, March 4, 1943, T 120/7716/E548805.

127.	PA, Inland II g 197a, Bergmann (initialed by Rademacher and Hahn) to Rome, Budapest, Sofia, Bucharest, Bratislava, and Zagreb, March 6, 1943. T 120/5784/E421977-8.

128.	PA, Inland II g 197a, DNB-report, March 8, 1943. T 120/7716/E548807.

129.	PA, Inland II g 197a, Rademacher to Budapest and Bucharest, March 9, 1943. T 120/5784/E421073-4.

130.	PA, Inland II g 197a: Günther to Hahn, March 10; Killinger to Foreign Office, March 10, 1943. T 120/7716/E548808 and K782/K207350-1.

131.	PA, Inland II g 197a, Pausch (sent under Rademacher's name) to Budapest and Bucharest, March 12, 1943. T 120/7716/E548809 and 5784/E421067-8.

132.	PA, Inland II g 197a: Killinger to Foreign Office, March 13; Beckerle to Foreign Office, March 13, 1943. T 120/K782/K207341 and 5784/E421075-6.

133.	PA: Inland II g 200, Rademacher to Bucharest, March 18, 1943, T 120/K816/

K212721; Inland II g 183, Rademacher to Sofia, March 15, 1943, T 120/K787/K208488; Inland II g 197a, Rademacher to Budapest, March 16, 1943, T 120/5784/E421072.

134.　PA: Inland II g 197a, Killinger to Foreign Office, March 24, and Beckerle to Foreign Office, March 16, 1943, T 120/7716/E548802-4; Inland II g 182, Beckerle to Foreign Office, March 16, 1943, T 120/K787/K208490.

135.　PA, Inland II g 197a, Werkmeister (Budapest) to Foreign Office, no date. T 120/K782/K207338-9.

136.　Hahn Judgment, 165.

137.　IMT, XXXV, 428.

138.　PA, Inland II g 208: Jagow to Foreign Office, March 1; Bergmann (drafted by Rademacher) to Ribbentrop, March 5; Bergmann to Bormann, March 9, 1943. T 120/5231/E310718-21, E310707-10.

## CHAPTER 9

1.　LGNF 2 Ks 3/53, Hauptakten: IX, 1409, 1412 (Picot interrogation, 1962); X, 1793 (Picot interrogation, 1968).

2.　LGNF 2 Ks 3/53, Hauptakten, II, 219. Rademacher interrogation, 1948.

3.　LGNF 2 Ks 3/53, Hauptakten, VIII, 1185. Klingenfuss to Gülich, May 17, 1958.

4.　Hannah Arendt, *Eichmann in Jerusalem* (New York, 1963), 25, 49.

5.　Ibid., 54.

6.　LGNF 2 Ks 3/53, Hauptakten, II, 272 (Kieser affidavit, 1949). On the Luther-Heydrich animosty, see also: NSA, Zz 431, Nr. 10; and Schellenberg, *The Labyrinth*, 246.

## APPENDIX I

1.　NSA, TWC, Case XI, Transcript, 9766 (Steengracht testimony); S. Payne Best, *The Venlo Incident* (London, 1950), 126; Rahn *Ruheloses Leben,* 142; Schellenberg, *The Labyrinth,* 328; Kempner, *Eichmann und Komplizen,* 278.

2.　Seabury, *The Wilhelmstrasse,* 196.

3.　*Trials of the War Criminals,* XIV, 498, 950, 965.

4.　2nd Rademacher Judgment, 11.

5.　Author's interview with Dr. Robert M. W. Kempner, January 24, 1974.

6.　LGNF 2 Ks 3/53, Beiakten, III, Part 1. Rademacher interrogations.

7.　LGNF Ks 3/53, Hauptakten, VIII, 1250. Excerpt from a letter from Kempner to the Oberstaatsanwalt in Bamberg, October 10, 1956.

8.　The Belgrade notes are part of NG 3354. The other notes are in the Nürnberg Staatsarchiv as Zz 431, Nr 10 and 11. The Belgrade account flatly denied his responsiblity for the shootings. His account of the Luther revolt, on the other hand, is in accord with the accounts of most other witnesses. It was not until he was later on trial before a German court that Rademacher embellished and distorted his version of the affair to enhance his own image as a central figure in the conspiracy.

9.　LGNF 2 Ks 3/53, Hauptaken, III, 349; Beiakten, III, Part 4, 1-12, and Sonderheft Auslieferungssache Klingenfuss 3 c Js 1321-24/49, 38-43. Klingenfuss interrogations.

10.　LGNF 2 Ks 3/53, Hauptakten, I, 1-134.

11.　Ibid., III, 395.

12.　Ibid., IV, 509, 516, 527.

13. Ibid., II 411; IV, 588-90.

14. 1st Rademacher Judgment, 24.

15. Ibid., 22–41.

16. Ibid., 78–80.

17. Ibid., 85–94.

18. Ibid., 102–114.

19. Ibid., 97–8.

20. Ibid., 127.

21. Ibid., 137.

22. Ibid., 143–4.

23. Ibid., 147–51.

24. LGNF 2 Ks 3/53, Hauptakten, VII, 1029–30.

25. Ibid., 1060–5.

26. Der 1. Strafsenat des Bundesgerichtshofs, 1 StR 709/52 in der Strafsache gegen Franz Rademacher, 1–2.

27. Ibid., 13–17.

28. Ibid., 19–24.

29. Ibid., 2.

30. Landgericht Berlin, (506) 3 P KMs 13.58 (181.57): Strafsache gegen 1) Robert Hans Kremer, 2) Kurt Paul Willi Gunkel, 8–12.

31. LGNF 2 Ks 3/53, Beiakten, Sonderheft Auslieferungssache Klingenfuss 3c Js 1321–24/49, 58–9.

32. LGNF 2 Ks 3/53, Hauptakten, VIII, 1184–8.

33. Ibid., 1172–82.

34. Ibid., 1198–1201.

35. Hahn Judgment, 8.

36. Ibid., 9.

37. LGNF 2 Ks 3/53, Beiakten, IV, Part 3, 20–22 (Anklage gegen Horst Wagner, Landgericht Essen, 29 Ks 4/67); Hauptakten, VIII, 1297.

38. LGNF 2 Ks 3/53, Hauptakten, IX, 1416–24. Hahn interrogation, September, 1962.

39. LGNF 2 Ks 3/53, Beiakten, IV, Parts 1 and 2, 15–16. Anklage gegen Hahn and Beckerle.

40. Hahn Judgment, 1.

41. 2nd Rademacher Judgment, 12.

42. NS-Verbrecher der Spionage für Israel Beschuldigt/Verhaftete Deutsche Sollen Syrische Waffenlieferungen an Algerische Rebellen Verraten Haben," *Frankfurter Allgemeine Zeitung,* No. 67, March 20, 1966.

43. LGNF 2 Ks 3/53, Hauptakten, XI, 1811. Rademacher testimony, 1968.

44. LGNF 2 Ks 3/53, Hauptakten, VIII, 1283. Rademacher to Foreign Office, September 21, 1966.

45. LGNF 2 Ks 3/53, Hauptakten, IX, 1461, 1494.

46. Ibid., X, 1680.

47. LGNF 2 Ks 3/53, Hauptakten, IX, 1440. Klingenfuss interrogation, 1967.

48. LGNF 2 Ks 3/53, Hauptakten, IX, 1448–9. Amrhein letter, March 6, 1967.

49. 2nd Rademacher Judgment, 98–103.

50. Ibid., 187–9.

51. LGNF 2 Ks 3/53, Hauptakten, XI, 1868–70. Klingenfuss testimony, 1968.
52. 2nd Rademacher Judgment, 191–200.
53. Ibid., 201–4.
54. Ibid., 118–20.
55. Ibid., 125–7, 130–1.
56. Ibid., 150–5.
57. Ibid., 163–5.
58. Ibid., 172–86.
59. Ibid., 224–8.
60. Hahn Judgment, 175–7.
61. Ibid., 185.
62. Ibid., 179–81.
63. Ibid., 196–8.
64. Ibid., 203.
65. Ibid., 204–8.
66. Ibid., 218–221.
67. Ibid., 223–9.
68. Ibid., 230, 240.
69. Ibid., 252.
70. Ibid., 246–8.
71. Müller Investigation, 5–7.
72. Ibid., 1–3, 6.
73. Ibid., 158.
74. Ibid., 125–6.
75. Ibid., 150, 143.
76. Ibid., 166–71.
77. Ibid.
78. Ibid., 176, 178.
79. Bundesgerichtshof: Urteil 1 StR 107/69 in der Strafsache gegen Franz Rademacher, 15–17.
80. Ibid., 18–20.
81. Ibid., 20–3.
82. Ibid., 24.
83. LGNF 2 Ks 3/53, Hauptakten, XIII, 2310; and Verfügung.

# Bibliography

## A. UNPUBLISHED SOURCES

*I. Political Archives*

A major source of unpublished material essential to this book was the Political Archives of the German Foreign Office in Bonn. When *Abteilung Deutschland* was dissolved in 1943, its functions were dispersed among other branches of the Foreign Office. So were its files. The files of D III pertaining to the Jewish question are found under *Inland* II *Geheim* and *Inland* II A/B. The files of *Inland*, particularly those of *Inland* II *Geheim*, were found in great disorder after the war and were not reorganized before microfilming. Upon their return to the German Foreign Office in 1958, these files were finally reorganized in a sensible fashion. In the Archives they must be ordered through a special *Inland Repertorium*, not through George Kent's *A Catalog of Files and Microfilms of the German Foreign Ministry Archives* (4 vols., Stanford, 1962–72), the catalog used for the vast bulk of the Foreign Office files of that period. All footnote references to *Inland* files have been made to the *Paket* number as listed in the *Inland Repertorium*.

The office papers or *Handakten* of Martin Luther have also been of inestimable value. Other *Aktengruppen* that contain certain documents relevant to the Jewish question in the war period are: *Büro Staatssekretär, Büro Unterstaatssekretär,* various sections of the *Politische Abteilung,* and various European embassies.

Most of the Archives material cited in this book have been microfilmed. Some in fact have been microfilmed as many as three times. Where possible I have always given one microfilm reference (serial and frame numbers) in each footnote. Where no microfilm reference has been made, then the item was either not filmed or was filmed with an electric-counter system so that the frame number was not stamped on the original document. A large number of the Archives documents cited in this study were selected as evidence for the American Military Tribunals in Nürnberg in 1948 and were cataloged by NG number. Though many historical studies refer to these documents by their NG number

257

only, I have not attempted to give this identification in addition to the archive and microfilm references in the footnotes. It should also be noted that all the Foreign Office materials related to the Jewish question in Hungary may be found in facsimile in Randolph Braham's *The Destruction of the Hungarian Jews: A Documentary Account.*

## II. Court Records

Court records comprised the second major source of unpublished material for this book. These in turn are of two sorts: first, a collection of official judgments; and second, the complete files, some 35 volumes, of the entire Rademacher proceedings, located in the archives of the *Staatsanwaltschaft* of the State Court of Nürnberg-Fürth.

A. Judgments:

*Bundesgerichtshof:*
Urteil 1 StR 709/52 in der Strafsache gegen Franz Rademacher (copy at the Landgericht Nürnberg-Fürth).
Urteil 1 StR 107/69 in der Strafsache gegen Franz Rademacher (copy at the Landgericht Bamberg).

*Landgericht Bamberg:*
Urteil in dem Strafverfahren gegen Franz Rademacher 2 Ks 3/53.

*Landgericht Berlin:*
Strafsache gegen 1) Robert Kremer und 2) Kurt Gunkel (506) 3 P KMs 13.58 (181.57) (copy at the Landgericht Bamberg).

*Landgericht Frankfurt:*
Urteil in dem Strafverfahren gegen Fritz-Gebhardt von Hahn Ks 2/67 (copy at the Politisches Archiv des Auswärtigen Amtes, cited as ZB 8/80/02/69).

*Landgericht Nürnberg-Fürth:*
Urteil in dem Strafverfahren gegen Franz Rademacher 85 Ks 4/50 (copy at the Institut für Zeitgeschichte).

B. Rademacher Proceedings: 2 Ks 3/53 Landgericht Nürnberg-Fürth.

*Hauptakten:*
I-XIII.

*Beiakten:*
[including: Sonderheft Auslieferungssache Klingenfuss 3c 1321–24/49; Anklage gegen von Hahn und Beckerle Js 2/63 Frankfurt; Anklage gegen Horst Wagner 29 Ks 4/67 Essen; Einstellungsverfügung in dem Ermittlungsverfahren 24 Js 3/69 (Z) StA Köln gegen Dr. Herbert Müller-Roschach; various interrogations and affidavits.]

III. *Nürnberg Staatsarchiv*
Zz 431 (Rademacher file).

Trials of the War Criminals before the Nürnberg Military Tribunals, Case XI: Transcript and Steengracht Document Books, I and IIa.

IV. *Berlin Document Center*
Personnel files of NSDAP, SA, and SS.

## B. PUBLISHED DOCUMENTS

*Akten zur Deutschen Aussenpolitik, 1918–1945.* Series D, vol. X-XIII. Baden-Baden, Frankfurt, Bonn, and Göttingen, 1951–70. Series E, vol. I-II. Göttingen, 1969–72.

Braham, Randolph B., ed. *The Destruction of the Hungarian Jews: A Documentary Account.* 2 vols. New York, 1963.

*Documents on German Foreign Policy 1918–1945.* Series D, V. Washington, 1953.

Hill, Leonidas, ed. *Die Weizsäcker-Papiere, 1933–1950.* Berlin, 1974.

Hillgruber, Andreas, ed. *Staatsmänner und Diplomaten bei Hitler.* 2 vols. Frankfurt/M., 1967–70.

Jüdische Historische Institut Warschau. *Faschimus—Getto—Massenmord. Dokumentation über Ausrottung und Widerstand der Juden in Polen während des zweiten Weltkrieges.* Berlin, 1960.

Krausnick, Helmut, ed. "Denkschrift Himmlers über die Behandlung der fremdvölkischen im Osten (Mai 1940)." *Vierteljahrshefte für Zeitgechichte,* V/2 (April 1957), 194–8.

*Nazi Conspiracy and Agression.* 8 vols. Washington, 1946.

Poliakov, Leon, and Josef Wulf, ed. *Das Dritte Reich und die Juden: Dokumente un Aufsätze.* Berlin, 1955.

———. *Das Dritte Reich und seine Diener: Dokumente.* Berlin, 1956.

*Trials of the Major War Criminals before the International Military Tribunal.* 42 vols. Nürnberg, 1947–9.

*Trials of the War Criminals before the Nürnberg Military Tribunals.* 14 vols. Washington, 1949–53.

United Restitution Organization. *Documente über Methoden der Judenverfolgung im Ausland.* Frankfurt/M., 1959.

———. *Dokumentsammlung über die Judenverfolgung in Rumänien.* 4 vols. Frankfurt/M., 1959–60.

———. *Judenverfolgung in Italien, den italienisch besetzten Gebieten und in Nordafrika.* Frankfurt/M., 1962.

## C. BOOKS AND ARTICLES

Abetz, Otto. *Das Offene Problem: Ein Rückblick auf zwei Jahrzehnte deutscher Frankreichpolitik.* Köln, 1951.

Adam, Uwe Dietrich. *Judenpolitik im Dritten Reich*. Düsseldorf, 1972.

Adler, H. G. *Der Verwaltete Mensch: Studien zur Deportation der Juden aus Deutschland*. Tübingen, 1974.

Arendt, Hannah. *Eichmann in Jerusalem*. Revised Edition. New York, 1965.

———. *The Origins of Totalitarianism*. Second Edition. Cleveland, 1958.

Arndt, I. "Entziehung und Verbringung jüdischen Vermögens (Ausland und Deutschland)." *Gutachten des Instituts für Zeitgeschichte*, II, 95–125. Stuttgart, 1966.

Aronson, Shlomo. *Heydrich und die Anfänge des SD und der Gestapo (1931–1935)*. Berlin, 1967.

Bahrdt, Hans Paul. "Soziologische Reflexionen über die gesellschaftlichen Voraussetzungen des Antisemitismus in Deutschland." *Entscheidungsjahr 1932: Zur Endphase der Weimarer Republik,* ed. by Werner Mosse. Tübingen, 1965.

Bein, A. "Modern Anti-Semitism and its Effect on the Jewish Question." *Yad Vashem Studies*, III (1959), 7–17.

Ben Elissar, Eliahu. *La Diplomatie du III^e Reich et les Juifs*. Paris, 1969.

Bernardini, Gene. "The Origins and Development of Racial Anti-Semitism in Fascist Italy." *Journal of Modern History*, 49/3 (September 1977), 431–53.

Binion, Rudolph. "Hitler's Concept of Lebensraum: The Psychological Basis." *The History of Childhood Quarterly*, I/2 (1973), 187–258.

Bracher, Karl Dietrich. *The German Dictatorship*. New York, 1970.

Bracher, Karl Dietrich, and Wolfgang Sauer, Gerhard Schulz. *Die nationalsozialistische Machtergreifung. Studien zur Errichtung des totalitären Herrschaftssystems in Deutschland 1933/34*. Köln, 1960.

Braham, Randolph L. "The Holocaust in Hungary: An Historical Interpretation of the Role of the Hungarian Radical Right." *Societas—A Review of Social History*, II/3 (summer 1972), 195–220.

———. "The Kamenets Podolsk and Delvidek Massacres: Prelude to the Holocaust in Hungary." *Yad Vashem Studies*, IX (1973), 133–156.

———. "The Rightists, Horthy, and the Germans: Factors Underlying the Destruction of Hungarian Jewry." *Jews and Non-Jews in Eastern Europe 1918–1945*, ed. by Bela Vago and George Mosse. New York and Jerusalem, 1974.

Broszat, Martin. "Das deutsch-slowakische Verhältnis 1939/40 und seine Rückwirkung auf die slowakische Judenpolitik." *Gutachten des Instituts für Zeitgeschichte*, I, 221–9. Munich, 1958.

———. "Das deutsch-ungarische Verhältnis und die ungarische Judenpolitik in der Jahren 1938–41." *Gutachten des Instituts für Zeitgeschichte*, I, 183–200. Munich, 1958.

———. "Das dritte Reich und die rumänische Judenpolitik." *Gutachten des Instituts für Zeitgeschichte*, I, 102–83. Munich, 1958.

———. "Soziale Motivation und Führerbindung im Nationalsozialismus." *Vierteljahrshefte für Zeitgeschichte*, XVIII (1970), 392–409.

Browning, Christopher. "Referat Deutschland, Jewish Policy and the German Foreign Office 1933–40." *Yad Vashem Studies*, XII (1978), 25–54.

———. "Unterstaatssekretär Martin Luther and the Ribbentrop Foreign Office." *Journal of Contemporary History*, XII/2 (1977), 313–344.

Bullock, Alan. *Hitler: A Study in Tyranny*. Revised Edition. New York, 1962.

Chary, Frederick B. *The Bulgarian Jews and the Final Solution, 1940–1944*. Pittsburg, 1972.

Cianfarra, Camille. *The Vatican and the War*. New York, 1944.

Ciano, Galeazzo. *The Ciano Diaries 1939–43*. New York, 1947.

Dawidowicz, Lucy. *The War Against the Jews 1933–1945*. New York, 1975.

De Felice, Renzo. *Storia degli ebrei italiani setto il fascismo*. Turin, 1961.

Diamant, Zanvel. "Jewish Refugees on the French Riviera." *YIVO Annual of Jewish Social Sciences*, VII (1953), 264–280.

Ebert, D. "Statistische Angaben über das Schicksal der Juden in der Slowakei," *Gutachten des Instituts für Zeitgeschichte*, II, 73–8. Stuttgart, 1966.

Ebner, Josef. "Historische Betrachtungen zur Hitlerära in Rumänien." *Zeitschrift für die Geschichte der Juden*, I (1964), 43–54.

Ettinger, Shmuel. "Jews and Non-Jews in Eastern and Central Europe Between the Wars: An Outline." *Jews and Non-Jews in Eastern Europe 1918–1945*, ed. by Bela Vago and George Mosse. New York and Jerusalem, 1974.

Fauck, S. "Das deutsch-bulgarische Verhältnis 1939–44 und seine Rückwirkung auf die bulgarische Judenpolitik." *Gutachten des Instituts für Zeitgeschichte*, II, 46–59. Stuttgart, 1966.

———. "Das deutsch-slowakische Verhältnis 1941–43 und seine Rückwirkung auf die slowakische Judenpolitik." *Gutachten des Instituts für Zeitgeschichte*, II, 61–73. Stuttgart, 1966.

———. "Judenverfolgung in Nizza 1942/3." *Gutachten des Instituts für Zeitgeschichte*, II, 43–6. Stuttgart, 1966.

Fischer-Galati, Stephen. "Fascism, Communism, and the Jewish Question in Romania." *Jews and Non-Jews in Eastern Europe 1918–1945*, ed. by Bela Vago and George Mosse. New York and Jerusalem, 1974.

Friedmann, Philip. "The Lublin Reservation and the Madagascar Plan: Two Aspects of Nazi Jewish Policy During the Second World War." *YIVO Annual of Jewish Social Science*, VII (1953), 151-77.

Genschel, Helmut. *Die Verdrängung der Juden aus der Wirtschaft im Dritten Reich*. Göttingen, 1966.

Graml, Hermann. "Die Auswanderung der Juden aus Deutschland zwischen 1933 und 1939." *Gutachten des Instituts für Zeitgeschichte*, I, 79–85. Munich, 1958.

――――. "Die Behandlung von Juden fremder Staatsangehörgikeit in Deutschland," *Gutachten des Instituts für Zeitgeschichte*, I, 85–7. Munich, 1958.

――――. "Der deutsche Gesandte in der Slowakei." *Gutachten des Instituts für Zeitgeschichte*, II, 337–43. Stuttgart, 1966.

Hassell, Ulrich von. *The Von Hassell Diaries 1938–1944*. Garden City, N.Y., 1947.

Heiber, Helmut. "Die Ausweisung von Juden polnischner Staatsangehörigkeit in Oktober 1938." *Gutachten des Instituts für Zeitgeschichte*, II, 90–93. Stuttgart, 1966.

――――. "Die deutsche *Beeinflussung* der Rassenpolitik des faschistischen Italien bis 1943." *Gutachten des Instituts fü Zeitgeschichte*, II, 80–92. Stuttgart, 1966.

Henkys, Reinhard. *Die nationalsozialistischen Gewaltverbrechen*. Stuttgart, 1964.

Hevesi, Eugene. "Hitler's Plan for Madagascar." *Contemporary Jewish Record*, V (1941), 381–95.

Hilberg, Raul. *The Destruction of the European Jews*. Chicago, 1961.

Hill, Leonidas. "The Vatican Embassy of Ernst von Weizsäcker 1943–1945." *Journal of Modern History*. 39/2 (June 1967), 138–59.

――――. "The Wilhelmstrasse in the Nazi Era." *Political Science Quarterly*, LXXXII/4 (December 1967), 546–70.

Hillgruber, Andreas. "Die Endlösung und das deutsche Ostimperium als Kernstück des rassenideologischen Programms des Nationalsozialismus." *Vierteljahrshefte für Zeitgeschichte*, XX/2 (April 1972), 133–53.

――――. *Hitlers Strategie: Politik und Kriegsführung 1940–1941*. Frankfurt/M., 1965.

*Hitler's Ten-Year War on the Jews*, ed. by Boris Shub. New York, 1943.

Höhne, Heinz. *The Order of the Death's Head*. New York, 1969.

Hory, Ladislas, and Martin Broszat. *Der kroatische Ustasche-Staat 1941–1945*. Stuttgart, 1964.

Höss, Rudolf. *Commandant at Auschwitz*. New York (Popular Library), 1959.

Jäckel, Eberhard. *Hitler's Weltanschauung*. Middletown, Conn., 1972.

Jacobsen, Hans-Adolf. *Nationalsozialistische Aussenpolitik 1933–38*. Frankfurt/M., 1968.

Jelinek, Yeshayahu. "The 'Final Solution'—The Slovak Version." *Eastern European Quarterly*, IV/4 (1971), 431-41.

――――. "Slovakia's Internal Policy and the Third Reich." *Central Euronean History*, IV/3 (1971), 242–70.

――――. "Storm-troopers in Slovakia: The Rodobranna and the Hlinka Guard." *Journal of Contemporary History*, VI/3 (1971), 97–120.

————. "The Vatican, the Catholic Church, the Catholics, and the Persecution of Jews during World War II: The Case of Slovakia." *Jews and Non-Jews in Eastern Europe 1918–1945,* ed. by Bela Vago and George Mosse. New York and Jerusalem, 1974.

Kallay, Miklos. *Hungarian Premier.* New York, 1954.

Katzburg, Nathanial. "Hungarian Jewry in Modern Times: Political and Social Aspects." *Hungarian-Jewish Studies,* I, ed. by Randolph L. Braham. New York, 1966.

Kempner, Robert M. W. *Das Dritte Reich im Kreuzverhör.* Munich, 1969.

————. *Eichmann und Komplizen.* Zurich, 1961.

————. *SS im Kreuzverhör.* Munich, 1964.

Kersten, Felix. *The Kersten Memoirs 1940–45.* New York, 1957.

Koehl, Robert. "The Character of the SS." *Journal of Modern History,* 34 (1962), 275–83.

————. "Feudal Aspects of National Socialism." *The American Political Science Review,* 54 (1960), 921–33.

————. Toward an SS typology: Social Engineers." *American Journal of Economics and Sociology,* XVIII/2 (January 1959), 113–26.

Kordt, Erich. *Wahn und Wirklichkeit: Die Aussenpolitik des Dritten Reiches.* Stuttgart, 1948.

Krausnick, Helmut. "The Persecution of the Jews." *Anatomy of the SS State,* 3–124. New York, 1965.

Laval, Pierre. *The Diary of Pierre Laval.* New York, 1948.

Lavi, Th. "The Background to the Rescue of Romanian Jewry During the Period of the Holocaust." *Jews and Non-Jews in Eastern Europe 1918–1945,* ed. by Bela Vago and George Mosse. New York and Jerusalem, 1974.

————. "Documents on the Struggle of Rumanian Jewry for Its Rights during the Second World War," *Yad Vashem Studies,* IV (1960), 261–315.

Ledeen, Michael. "The Evolution of Italian Fascist Anti-Semitism." *Jewish Social Studies,* XXXVII/1, (1975), 3–17.

Levin, Nora. *The Holocaust: The Destruction of European Jewry 1933–45.* New York, 1968.

Lösener, Bernhard. "Als Rassereferent im Reichsministerium des Innern." *Vierteljahrshefte für Zeitgeschichte,* IX/3 (July 1961), 264–313.

Löwenthal, Zdenko, ed. *The Crimes of the Fascist Occupants and their Collaborators against Jews in Yugoslavia.* Belgrade, 1957.

Macartney, C. A. "Hungarian Foreign Policy during the Inter-War Period, with Special Reference to the Jewish Question." *Jews and Non-Jews in Eastern Europe 1918–1945,* ed. by Bela Vago and George Mosse. New York and Jerusalem, 1974.

Matkovski, Aleksandar. "The Destruction of the Macedonian Jewry in 1943." *Yad Vashem Studies,* III (1959), 203–58.

Michaelis, Meir. "The Attitude of the Fascist Regime to the Jews in Italy." *Yad Vashem Studies,* IV (1960), 7–41.

Milgram, Stanley. "The Perils of Obedience." *Harper's Magazine,* 247/1483 (December 1973), 62–80.

Mosse, George. *The Crisis of German Ideology.* New York, 1964.

———. "Die Deutsche Rechte und die Juden." *Entscheidungsjahr 1932: Zur Endphase Weimarer Republik,* ed. by Werner Mosse. Tübingen, 1965.

———. *Germans and Jews.* New York, 1970.

Müller, Norbert, and Martin Zöller. "Okkupationsverbrechen der Faschistischen Wehrmacht gegenüber der serbischen Bevölkerung im Herbst 1941." *Zeitschrift für Militärgeschichte,* IX (1970), 704–15.

Münz, Max. "Die Verantwortlichkeit für die Judenverfolgung im Ausland während der nationalsozialistischen Herrschaft." Doctoral dissertation, University of Frankfurt/M., 1958.

Needler, Martin. "Hitler's Anti-Semitism: A Political Appraisal." *Public Opinion Quarterly,* 24 (winter 1960), 665–9.

Nellessen, Bernd. *Der Prozess von Jerusalem.* Düsseldorf, 1964.

Oren, Nissan. "The Bulgarian Exception: A Reassessment of the Salvation of the Jewish Community." *Yad Vashem Studies,* VII (1968), 83–106.

Paris, Edmond. *Genocide in Satellite Croatia, 1941–1945.* Chicago, 1961.

Payne-Best, S. *The Venlo Incident.* London, 1950.

Pendorf, Robert. *Mörder und Ermordete.* Hamburg, 1961.

Peterson, E. N. "The Bureaucracy and the Nazi Party." *Review of Politics,* 28 (1966), 172–92.

———. *The Limits of Hitler's Power.* Princeton, 1969.

Poliakov, Leon. *Harvest of Hate.* London, 1956.

———. "The Jews under Italian Occupation in France." *The Jews under Italian Occupation,* ed. by Leon Poliakov and Jacques Sabille. Paris, 1955.

Rahn, Rudolf. *Ruheloses Leben: Aufzeichnungen und Erinnerungen.* Düsseldorf, 1949.

Reitlinger, Gerald. *The Final Solution: The Attempt to Exterminate the Jews of Europe 1939–1945.* New York, 1961.

———. *The SS: Alibi of a Nation 1922–1945.* New York, 1957.

Ribbentrop, Joachim von. *Zwischen London und Moskau: Erinnerungen und letzte Aufzeichnungen.* Leoni am Starnberger See, 1953.

Rich, Norman. *Hitler's War Aims,* vol. I, *Ideology, the Nazi State, and the Course of Expansion,* and vol. II, *The Establishment of the New Order.* New York, 1973–74.

Robinson, Jacob. *And the Crooked Shall Be Made Straight. The Eichmann Trial, the Jewish Catastrophe, and Hannah Arendt's Narrative.* New York, 1965.

Rothkirchen, Livia. "Vatican Policy and the 'Jewish Problem' in 'Independent' Slovakia 1939–45." *Yad Vashem Studies*, VI (1967), 27–53.

Sabille, Jacques. "Attitude of the Italians to the Jews in Occupied Greece." *The Jews under Italian Occupation,* ed. by Leon Poliakov and Jacques Sabille. Paris, 1955.

———. "Attitude of the Italians to the Persecuted Jews in Croatia." *The Jews under Italian Occupation*, ed. by Leon Poliakov and Jacques Sabille. Paris, 1955.

Schechtman, Joseph B. "The Transnistria Reservation." *YIVO Annual of Jewish Social Studies,* VII (1953), 178–196.

Schellenberg, Walter. *The Labyrinth: Memoirs of Walter Schellenberg.* New York, 1956.

———. *Memoiren.* Köln, 1959.

Schleunes, Karl. *The Twisted Road to Auschwitz.* Urbana, Illinois, 1970.

Schmidt, Paul. *Hitler's Interpreter.* New York, 1951.

Schwarz, Paul. *This Man Ribbentrop.* New York, 1943.

Seabury, Paul. *The Wilhelmstrasse: A Study of German Diplomats under the Nazi Regime.* Berkeley, 1954.

Stockhorst, Erich. *Fünftausend Köpfe: Wer War Was im Dritten Reich.* Bruchsal, 1967.

Teich, Meier. "Die Grosse Tragödie des Bessarabischen Judentums." *Zeitschrift für die Geschichte der Juden*, III (1966), 233–42.

Tenenbaum, Joseph. "The Crucial Year 1938." *Yad Vashem Studies,* II (1958), 49–77.

Vago, Bela. "The Attitude toward the Jews as a Criterion of the Left-Right Concept." *Jews and Non-Jews in Eastern Europe, 1918-1945,* ed. by Bela Vago and George Mosse. New York and Jerusalem, 1974.

———. "Germany and the Jewish Policy of the Kallay Government." *Hungarian-Jewish Studies,* II, ed. by Randolph L. Braham. New York, 1969.

Waite, Robert. "Adolf Hitler's Anti-Semitism: A Study in History and Psychoanalysis." *The Psychoanalytic Interpretation of History*, ed. by Benjamin Wolman. New York, 1971.

Weizsäcker, Ernst von. *Memoirs of Ernst von Weizsäcker.* Chicago, 1951.

Yahil, Leni. "Madagascar—Phantom of a Solution for the Jewish Question." *Jews and Non-Jews in Eastern Europe 1918-1945,* ed. by Bela Vago and George Mosse. New York and Jerusalem, 1974.

———. *The Rescue of Danish Jewry.* Philadelphia, 1969.

Yisraeli, David. "The Third Reich and the Transfer Agreement." *Journal of Contemporary History,* VI/2 (1971), 129–48.

# Index

Abetz, Otto, 41, 45, 49, 66, 70, 88–9, 99–103, 105–6, 114, 122
Abteilung Deutschland, 30–1, 36, 44, 48, 50, 57, 72, 79, 81, 86, 120–1, 145, 148–9, 152–3, 171, 174–5, 180, 183, 194, 202; character of, 26–7, 29, 82, 84, 112, 181; creation of, 21, 25; dissolved, 114, 150, 187; jurisdiction of, 23, 25–6
Adviser for Jewish Affairs, in Bulgaria, 133-4, 203; in Greece, 161, 203; in Rumania, 52–3, 89, 125; in Slovakia, 48, 50, 52-3, 91, 131
Adviser system, in Croatia, 89; in Rumania, 52-3; in Slovakia, 48, 50, 89
Albrecht, Erich, 67, 69, 71, 80, 117, 124
Albrecht, Archduke of Hungary, 132
Altenburg, Günther, 89, 136-7, 140-1, 161, 203
Ambrosio (Italian general), 169
American Jews, 39, 50-1, 54, 70, 72, 99-100
Anschluss, 5, 17
Anti-Jewish League, 30
Anti-Semitic Action (*Antisemitische Aktion*), 30, 41
Anti-Semitism, of Bülow, 12; in eastern Europe, 4, 110-111, 125-6; of Foreign Office old guard, 11, 13; of Hitler, 1-3, 183; in Italy, 110; of Luther, 28; of Rademacher, 30, 42, 178-9
Antonescu, Ion, 53-4, 92, 110, 115-6, 125-9, 170
Antonescu, Mihai, 53, 93, 116, 118, 121, 124, 126-7
Arabs, 14, 122, 171
Arendt, Hannah, 182-3
Argentina, 189, 193, 195

Armistice Commission at Wiesbaden, 44-6
Army, German, 6, 8-9, 31, 47, 53, 69, 72, 83-5, 91-3, 136, 140, 180, 204; in Serbia, 57-62, 64-5, 94. *See also* OKH, OKW, military administration
Arrow Cross, 31, 111
Aryanization, 4–6, 16, 53, 71, 122, 138
Aschenauer, Rudolph, 197
Ashton, Georg, 150
Auschwitz, 9, 91, 192, 200–1, 205
Auslandsinstitut, 32
Auslandsorganisation, 25, 28, 32, 54
Austria, Eichmann in, 5, 76
Austrian Jews, 100, 164; deported 7, 19, 21, 47
Avarna (Italian general), 167–8

Bardossy, Laszlo, 127-8
Bargen, Werner von, 88, 101; 104, 145-6, 191, 200
Bastianini, Giuseppe, 169
Beamish, H. H., 37
Beckerle, Adolph Heinz, 89, 103, 133-4, 162-4, 171-3, 193, 199
Belev, Alexander, 163
Belgium, 8, 44, 47, 79, 88, 102, 104, 141, 145-6, 161, 185, 198; deportations of Jews from, 79, 100-2, 145-6, 161, 192, 200-1, 205-6
Belgrade, massacres at, 60-4, 76, 191-2, 197
Belzec, 126
Bene, Otto, 88-9, 101-2, 106, 144-5, 148, 190, 199
Benzler, Felix, 56-65, 89, 146
Bergen Belsen, 158
Berger, Gottlob, 132

*267*